Security Technologies for the World Wide Web

For quite a long time, computer security was a rather narrow field of study that was populated mainly by theoretical computer scientists, electrical engineers, and applied mathematicians. With the proliferation of open systems in general, and the Internet and the World Wide Web (WWW) in particular, this situation has changed fundamentally. Today, computer and network practitioners are equally interested in computer security, since they require technologies and solutions that can be used to secure applications related to electronic commerce (e-commerce). Against this background, the field of computer security has become very broad and includes many topics of interest. The aim of this series is to publish state-of-the-art, high standard technical books on topics related to computer security. Further information about the series can be found on the WWW by the following URL:

http://www.esecurity.ch/serieseditor.html

Also, if you'd like to contribute to the series and write a book about a topic related to computer security, feel free to contact either the Commissioning Editor or the Series Editor at Artech House.

Recent Titles in the Artech House
Computer Security Series

Rolf Oppliger, Series Editor

For a complete listing of the *Artech House Computing Library,* turn to the back of this book.

Security Technologies for the World Wide Web

Rolf Oppliger

Artech House
Boston • London

Library of Congress Cataloging-in-Publication Data
Oppliger, Rolf.
   Security technologies for the World Wide Web / Rolf Oppliger.
      p. cm. — (Artech House computing library)
   Includes bibliographical references and index.
   ISBN 1-58053-045-1 (alk. paper)
      1. Computer security. 2. World Wide Web (Informational retrieval sytems)—
   Security measure. I. Title. II. Series.

QA76.9A25 068   1999   99-045835
005.8 21—dc21   CIP

British Library Cataloguing in Publication Data
Oppliger, Rolf
   Security technologies for the World Wide Web. — (Artech
   House computing library)
   1. World Wide Web (Information retrieval system)—Security
   measures
   1. Title
   005.8

   ISBN 1-58053-045-1

Cover design by Lynda Fishbourne

International Standard Book Number: 1-58053-045-1
Cataloging-In-Publication: 99-045835

10 9 8 7 6 5 4 3

To my wife, Isabelle

Contents

Preface

Necessity is the mother of invention,
and computer networks are the mother of modern cryptography.

— Ronald L. Rivest[1]

During the last couple of years, I have been working on security issues related to TCP/IP-based networks. The results of this work are summarized in *Authentication Systems for Secure Networks* and *Internet and Intranet Security* [1,2]. The two books overview and fully discuss the technologies that can be used in networks based on the transport control protocol (TCP) and the Internet protocol (IP) to provide access control and communication security services. They are mainly written for computer scientists, electrical engineers, and network practitioners with a solid background in computer and communication security.

More recently, I was asked whether the two books could also be used to educate professional Webmasters in security matters. Unfortunately, I realized that while the books cover the technologies used to secure applications for the World Wide Web (WWW), they are written in a language that is somehow inappropriate for professional Webmasters. Note that these folks are generally familiar with network operating system issues and communication protocols, but they are neither security

---

[1]In: "Cryptography as Duct Tape," a short note written to the Senate Commerce and Judiciary Committees in opposition to mandatory key recovery proposals on June 12, 1997.

experts nor cryptographic specialists. They may not even be interested in architectural details and design considerations for cryptographic technologies and protocols that are not widely deployed.

Having in mind the professional Webmaster who must be educated in security matters within a relatively short period of time, I decided to write a book that serves as a corresponding security primer. While writing this book, I realized that it could also be used by common Web users and application developers. The resulting book, *Security Technologies for the World Wide Web*, overviews and briefly discusses the major topics that are relevant for Web security. Note that the term "WWW security" means different things to different people:

- For Webmasters, it's confidence that their sites won't be hacked and vandalized or used as a gateway to break into their local area networks (LANs);

- For Web users, it's rather the ability to browse securely through the Web, knowing that no one is looking into their communications;

- Finally, for the proponents of electronic commerce applications, it's the ability to conduct commercial and financial transactions in a safe and secure way.

According to [3], Web security refers to "a set of procedures, practices, and technologies for protecting web servers, web users, and their surrounding organizations." In this book, we mainly focus on the technologies that can be used to provide security services for the WWW. Some of the technologies are covered in detail, whereas others are briefly introduced and left for further study. The reader of this book will get a sufficiently complete overview of the major topics that are relevant for the WWW and the security thereof. As such, the book is intended for anyone who is concerned about security on the Web, is in charge of security for a network, or manages an organization that uses the WWW. It can be used for lectures, courses, and tutorials. It can also be used for self-study or serve as a handy reference for Web professionals. Further information can also be found in other books on WWW security. I particularly recommend [3 – 5]. There is also a frequently asked questions (FAQ) document available on the Web that is maintained and periodically updated by Lincoln D. Stein, who's the author of [5].[2]

While it is not intended that this book be read linearly from front to back, the material has been arranged so that doing so has some merit. In particular, *Security*

---

[2]Another FAQ document that discusses the use of cryptography for Web applications is available from RSA Data Security, Inc. at URL http://www.rsa.com/html/webmasterfaq.html.

Technologies for the World Wide Web has been organized in fifteen chapters that are summarized as follows:

- In Chapter 1, we introduce the Internet, the WWW, vulnerabilities, threats, and countermeasures, as well as a generic model that is used to discuss the various aspects of security.

- In Chapter 2, we elaborate on some existing user authentication and authorization schemes specified for the hypertext transfer protocol (HTTP).

- In Chapter 3, we address the implications of proxy servers and firewalls for Web-based applications.

- In Chapter 4, we introduce cryptographic techniques that are employed by many security technologies for the WWW.

- In Chapter 5, we overview and briefly discuss the cryptographic security protocols that have been proposed and partly implemented for the Internet and the WWW.

- In Chapter 6, we focus on two transport layer security protocols, namely the secure sockets layer (SSL) and transport layer security (TLS) protocols.

- In Chapter 7, we overview and briefly discuss some electronic payment systems used in e-commerce applications for the Internet and the WWW.

- In Chapter 8, we address the problem of how to manage public key and attribute certificates in a corporate environment.

- In Chapter 9, we focus on potential risks related to executable (or active) content.

- In Chapter 10, we address common gateway interface (CGI) and application programming interface (API) scripts as well as their security implications for Web servers.

- In Chapter 11, we elaborate on mobile code and agent-based systems, as well as their security implications.

- In Chapter 12, we overview and discuss technologies used for copyright protection in the digital world of the WWW.

- In Chapter 13, we address the increasingly important field of privacy protection and anonymity services for the WWW.

- In Chapter 14, we address censorship on the Internet and the WWW.

- In Chapter 15, we draw some conclusions and predict future developments in the field.

The book also includes a glossary that defines major terms, as well as a list of abbreviations and acronyms. References are included at the end of each chapter. At the end of the book, an "About the Author" page is appended to tell you a little bit about me. Also, there is an index that will help you find particular terms.

Some authors make a clear distinction between client-side security, server-side security, and document security, and structure their books accordingly [5]. This book does not follow this approach but uses a more functional organization instead. More precisely, the various chapters outlined above address zero, one, or even more than one of the above-mentioned classes of security issues. The following table summarizes the relationship between the classes of security and the fifteen chapters of the book (an X in the line indicates that the class of security is addressed in the corresponding chapter):

Chapters	1	2	3	4	5	6	7	8	9	10	11	12	13	14	15
Client-side security	X	X	X	X	X	X		X	X		X		X	X	
Server-side security	X	X	X	X	X	X		X		X	X		X		
Document security	X			X	X	X						X			

There has been a long tradition in the computer and network security literature to provide various kinds of checklists. This book breaks with this tradition, mainly because security is more than checking off items on checklists. The single most important thing in security is to understand the underlying concepts and technological approaches. If you understand them, it is a simple exercise to formulate and implement your own checklist(s).

While time brings new technologies and outdates current technologies, I have attempted to focus primarily on the conceptual approaches to provide security services for the WWW. The Web is changing so rapidly that any book is out of date by the time it hits the shelves in the bookstores. By the time you read this book, several of my comments will probably have moved from the future to the present, and from the present to the past, resulting in inevitable anachronisms.

Due to the nature of this book, it is also necessary to mention company, product, and service names. It is, however, important to note that the presence or absence of a specific name neither implies any criticism or endorsement, nor does it imply that the corresponding company, product, or service is necessarily the best available. For a more comprehensive products overview, I particularly recommend the *Computer Security Products Buyers Guide* that's compiled and published annually by the Computer Security Institute (CSI) based in San Francisco, California.[3]

Whenever possible, I add some uniform resource locators (URLs) as footnotes to the text. The URLs point to corresponding information pages provided on the Web. While care has been taken to ensure that the URLs are valid now, due to the dynamic nature of the Web, these URLs as well as their contents may not remain valid forever. Similarly, I use screen shots to illustrate some graphical user interfaces (GUIs). Most of these screen shots are taken from Netscape Navigator (version 4.05) and Microsoft Internet Explorer (version 4.0). However, most software vendors, including Netscape Communications and Microsoft, tend to update and modify their GUIs periodically. Therefore, chances are that the GUI you currently use looks (slightly or completely) different than the one replicated in this book.

Finally, I would like to take the opportunity to invite you as a reader of this book to let me know your opinion and thoughts. If you have something to correct or add, please let me know. If I haven't expressed myself clearly please let me know, too. I appreciate and sincerely welcome any comment or suggestion, in order to update the book periodically. The best way to reach me is to send an electronic mail (e-mail) message to `rolf.oppliger@acm.org` or `oppliger@computer.org`. You can also visit my homepage and drop a message there. The page can be found on the Web by following the URL `http://www.ifi.unizh.ch/~oppliger`. In addition, I have also established a homepage for this book. The page is located at URL `http://www.ifi.unizh.ch/~oppliger/wwwsec.html`.

REFERENCES

[1] R. Oppliger, *Authentication Systems for Secure Networks*, Artech House, Norwood, MA, 1996.

[2] R. Oppliger, *Internet and Intranet Security*, Artech House, Norwood, MA, 1998.

[3] S. Garfinkel, and E.H. Spafford, *Web Security & Commerce*, O'Reilly & Associates, Sebastopol, CA, 1996.

[4] A.D. Rubin, D. Geer, and M.J. Ranum, *Web Security Sourcebook*, John Wiley & Sons, Inc., New York, NY, 1997.

[5] L.D. Stein, *Web Security: A Step-by-Step Reference*, Addison-Wesley, Reading, MA, 1998.

---

[3] `http://www.gocsi.com`

Trademark Information

Many screen shots in this book are copyright 1999 Microsoft Corporation or Netscape Communications Corporation. All rights reserved. These pages may not be reprinted or copied without the express written permission of Microsoft or Netscape Communications.

Microsoft Corporation and Netscape Communications Corporation have not authorized, sponsored, endorsed, or approved this publication and are not responsible for its content. Microsoft and the Microsoft Corporate Logos are trademarks and trade names of Microsoft Corporation. Similarly, Netscape and the Netscape Communications Corporate Logos are trademarks and trade names of Netscape Communications Corporation. All other product names and/or logos are trademarks of their respective owners.

Acknowledgments

One of the more pleasurable tasks of being an author is to thank all the people who have contributed to and been involved in the conception, research, writing, and production of a book. Once again, my warmest thanks are due to Kurt Bauknecht from the University of Zürich, Switzerland, for his ongoing interest, encouragement, and support. The book has gained a lot from discussions with and information provided by Andres Albanese, Bruno Berger, Daniel Bleichenbacher, Domenico Ferrari, Marcel Frauenknecht, Christian Graber, Daniel Graf, Andreas Greulich, Bruno Gschwend, Dieter Hogrefe, Hansjürg Mey, Günther Pernul, Marc Studer, and Peter Trachsel (in alphabetical order). As well, René Bach, Fritz Hohl, and my brother, Hans Oppliger, have done a great job in proofreading parts of the manuscript, and providing me with corrections and useful comments, suggestions, and pointers for further material. I'd also like to thank Artech House for publishing the book, Julie Lancashire, Paul Santoro, Judi Stone, Susanna Taggart, Michael Webb, Viki Williams, and Jon Workman (again in alphabetical order) for making the publishing process most convenient to me, Lynda Fishbourne for designing the book cover, and David Chadwick for reviewing the entire manuscript. It has been a pleasure to work with all of them. Finally, my deepest thanks are reserved for my wife, Isabelle. Once again, she has tolerated the long writing hours into the night, the scattered papers and manuscripts, the numerous business trips, and many other inconveniences while I completed this book. Without her love and support, this book would not have been possible.

Chapter 1

Introduction

This book assumes that the reader is familiar with the fundamentals of computer networks and distributed systems in general, and TCP/IP networking in particular. Refer to [1 – 4] for a comprehensive introduction, or Chapter 2 of [5] for a corresponding summary. In this chapter, we overview the scope of this book. In particular, we introduce the Internet and the World Wide Web (WWW) in Sections 1.1 and 1.2, distinguish between vulnerabilities, threats, and countermeasures in Section 1.3, and introduce a generic model used to discuss the various aspects of security in Section 1.4.

1.1 INTERNET

The emerging use of TCP/IP networking has led to a global system of interconnected hosts and networks that is commonly referred to as the *Internet*.[1] The Internet was created initially to help foster communications among government-sponsored

---

[1] Note the definite article and the capital letter "I" in the term "the Internet." More generally, the term "internet" is used to refer to any TCP/IP-based internetwork, whereas the term "intranet" is used to refer to a TCP/IP-based corporate or enterprise network.

1

researchers and grew steadily to include educational institutions, commercial organizations, and government agencies. As such, the Internet has experienced a triumphant advance during the last decade. Today, the Internet is the world's largest computer network and has been doubling in size each year since 1988. With this phenomenal rate of growth, it's size is increasing faster than any other network ever created, including the public switched telephone network (PSTN). Early in 1998, more than 2 million Web servers and more than 30 million computer systems were connected to the Internet [6]. Consequently, the Internet is commonly seen as the basis and first incarnation of an information superhighway, or national information infrastructure (NII) as, for example, promoted by the U.S. government.

But in spite of its exacting role, the initial, research-oriented Internet and its TCP/IP communications protocol suite were designed for a more benign environment than now exists. It could, perhaps, best be described as a collegial environment, where the users mutually trusted each other and were interested in a free and open exchange of information. In this environment, the people on the Internet were the people who actually built the Internet. Later on, when the Internet became more useful and reliable, these people were joined by others with different ethical interests and behaviors. With fewer common goals and more people, the Internet steadily twisted away from its original intent.

Today, the Internet environment is much less collegial and trustworthy. It contains all the dangerous situations, nasty people, and risks that one can find in society as a whole. Along with the well-intentioned and honest users of the Internet, there are also people who intentionally try to break into computer systems connected to it. Consequently, the Internet is plagued with the kind of delinquents who enjoy the electronic equivalent of writing on other people's walls with spray paint, tearing off mailboxes, or hanging around in the streets annoying the neighborhood. In this environment, the openness of the Internet has turned out to be a double-edged sword. Since its very beginning, but especially since its opening in the 1990s and its ongoing commercialization, the Internet has become a popular target to attack. The number of security breaches has in fact escalated more than in proportion to the growth of the Internet as a whole.[2]

Security problems on the Internet receive public attention, and the media carry stories of high-profile malicious attacks via the Internet against government, business, and academic sites. Perhaps the first and still most significant incident was the Internet Worm, launched by Robert T. Morris, Jr. on November 2, 1988 [7,8]. The

---

[2]There are many statistics that illustrate this point. For example, refer to the publications of the Computer Security Institute (CSI) at http://www.gocsi.com or the reports and articles published by the CERT Coordination Center (CERT/CC) at http://www.cert.org.

Internet Worm flooded thousands of hosts connected to the Internet and woke up the Internet community accordingly. It gained a lot of publicity and led to increased awareness of security issues on the Internet. In fact, the computer emergency response team (CERT[3]) that is operated by the Software Engineering Institute at Carnegie Mellon University was created in the aftermath of the Internet Worm, and other CERTs have been founded in various countries around the world.[4] Today, the CERT at Carnegie Mellon University serves as the CERT coordination center (CERT/CC) for the Internet community.

Since the Internet Worm incident, reports of network-based attacks, such as password sniffing, IP spoofing, sequence number guessing, session hijacking, flooding, and other denial-of-service attacks, as well as exploitations of well-known bugs and design limitations, have grown dramatically [9 – 11]. In addition, the use and wide deployment of executable content, such as provided by Java applets and ActiveX controls, has provided new possibilities to attack hosts or entire sites.[5]

Many Internet breaches are publicized and attract the attention of the Internet community, while numerous incidents go unnoticed. For example, early in 1994, thousands of passwords were captured by sniffer programs that had been remotely installed on compromised hosts on various university networks connected to the Internet. At the end of the same year, sequence number guessing attacks were successfully launched by Kevin Mitnick against several computing centers, including Tsutomu Shimomura's San Diego Center for Supercomputing [12]. This story actually shocked the world when it became *New York Times* headline news on January 23, 1995. In 1996, several forms of denial-of-service attacks were launched, such as e-mail bombing and TCP SYN flooding [13]. Also late in 1996, Dan Farmer conducted a security survey of approximately 2,200 computing systems on the Internet.[6] What he found was indeed surprising: almost two-thirds of the more interesting Internet or Web sites had serious security problems that could have been exploited by determined attackers. More recently, several Web sites of large companies and federal offices have been vandalized, and Webjacking has become a popular activity for casual Internet hackers.[7]

---

[3]http://www.cert.org

[4]Many of these CERTs are member organizations of the Forum of Incident Response and Security Teams (FIRST).

[5]Contact the WWW homepage of DigiCrime at URL http://www.digicrime.com to convince yourself that executable content is in fact dangerous. Problems related to executable content are also addressed in Chapter 9 of this book.

[6]http://www.trouble.org/survey/

[7]Note, however, that the real losses caused by these Webjacking activities are comparably small, since the Web pages that are vandalized are often located outside the firewall (for easy

In spite of the fact that unscrupulous people make press headlines with various types of attacks, the vulnerabilities they exploit are usually well known. For example, security experts warned against passwords transmitted in cleartext at the very beginning of (inter)networking, and Robert T. Morris, Jr. described sequence number guessing attacks for BSD UNIX version 4.2 when he was with AT&T Bell Laboratories in 1985 [14,15]. Some of the problems related to Internet security are a result of inherent vulnerabilities in the TCP/IP protocols and services, while others are a result of host configuration and access controls that are poorly implemented or too complex to administer. Additionally, the role and importance of system administration is often shortchanged in job descriptions, resulting in many administrators being, at best, part-time and poorly prepared. This is further aggravated by the tremendous growth of the Internet.

Today, individuals, commercial organizations, and government agencies depend on the Internet for communication and research, and thus have much more to lose if their sites are compromised. In fact, virtually everyone on the Internet is vulnerable, and the Internet's security problems are the center of attention, generating much fear throughout the computer and communications industries. Concerns about security problems have already begun to chill the overheated expectations about the Internet's readiness for full commercial activity, possibly delaying or preventing it from becoming a mass medium for the NII or the global information infrastructure (GII). Several studies have independently shown that many individuals and companies are abstaining from joining the Internet simply because of security concerns. At the same time, analysts are warning companies about the dangers of not being connected to the Internet. In this conflicting situation, almost everyone agrees that the Internet needs more and better security. In a workshop held by the Internet Architecture Board (IAB) in 1994, scaling and security were nominated as the two most important problem areas for the Internet architecture as a whole [16]. This has not changed so far and is not likely to change in the near future [17].

1.2   WWW

The WWW is a virtual network that is overlaid on the Internet. It comprises all clients[8] and servers that communicate with one another using the *Hypertext Transfer*

---

access for the casual Web user).

[8]In WWW parlance, HTTP clients are often called *browsers*. In this book, we are going to use the terms "HTTP client," "client," "browser," and "Web browser" synonymously. Note, however, that most browsers provide client support for other application protocols in addition to HTTP, such as Telnet, FTP, and Gopher.

Protocol (HTTP). HTTP, in turn, is a simple client/server application protocol that is layered on top of a reliable transport service, such as provided by the Transport Control Protocol (TCP). The protocol defines how WWW resources[9] are requested and transmitted across the Internet as American Standard Code for Information Interchange (ASCII) encoded messages. In addition to the HTTP specifications mentioned below, there are many books that overview or at least summarize the major features of HTTP. Among these books, I particularly recommend Chapter 4 of [18].

HTTP and the WWW were conceived by Tim Berners-Lee and his colleagues at the European Laboratory for Particle Physics (CERN[10]) located in Geneva, Switzerland. It was envisioned as a way of publishing physics papers on the Internet without requiring that physicists go through the laborious process of downloading a file and printing it out. As such, HTTP and the WWW have been in use since 1989. Note, however, that the first version of HTTP, referred to as HTTP/0.9 (version 0.9), was only a very simple protocol for raw data transfer across the Internet.

HTTP is a request/response protocol. What this basically means is that the client sends an HTTP request message to the server, and the server sends back a corresponding HTTP response message. There are no multiple-step handshakes in the beginning as with other TCP/IP application protocols, such as Telnet or the file transfer protocol (FTP). In the case of HTTP/0.9, the browser would establish a TCP connection to the appropriate port of the origin server and send a request message like

```
GET /index.html
```

to the server. The server, in turn, would respond with the contents of the requested resource (the file `/index.html` in the example given above). There were no request headers, no request methods other than GET, and the response had to be a file written in a special language, namely *hypertext markup language* (HTML). All current servers are capable of understanding and handling HTTP/0.9 requests, but the protocol is so simple that it is not very useful anymore.

Originally developed on NeXT computers, the WWW didn't really take off until a team of researchers at the National Center for Supercomputer Application (NCSA) of the University of Illinois wrote Mosaic, a browser for the X Window system. This browser soon became the standard against which all others were compared. Marc

---

[9]Examples of WWW resources include text and HTML files, GIF, and JPEG image files, or any other file that stores digitally encoded data in some specific format.

[10]The acronym is derived from the French name of the research laboratory.

Andreessen, who was the head of the original Mosaic development team went on to cofound a start-up company called Mosaic Communications. The company first created a new browser called Mozilla.[11] Afterwards, the company was renamed *Netscape Communications* and the corresponding browser was renamed Netscape Navigator.

In the meantime, several browsers and servers had extended HTTP from version 0.9 with new features, such as request headers and additional request methods, as well as a message format that conforms to the *multipurpose Internet mail extensions* (MIME) specification originally proposed for Internet-based electronic messaging. The resulting HTTP/1.0 (version 1.0) specification was officially released in early 1996 as RFC 1945 [19]. Nevertheless, HTTP/1.0 does not sufficiently take into consideration the effects of hierarchical proxies, caching, the need for persistent connections, and virtual hosting. In addition, the proliferation of incompletely implemented applications calling themselves "compliant to HTTP/1.0" required a protocol version change in order for two communicating applications to determine each other's capabilities. Consequently, an updated version of the HTTP specification was officially released in January 1997 as RFC 2068 [20]. This specification of HTTP/1.1 (version 1.1) has in the meantime entered the Internet Standards Track. The basic operation of HTTP/1.1 remains the same as for HTTP/1.0, and the protocol ensures that browsers and servers of different versions can still interoperate correctly. More precisely, if the browser understands version 1.1, it uses HTTP/1.1 on the request line instead of HTTP/1.0. When the server sees this version number, it can make use of HTTP/1.1 features. If, however, an HTTP/1.1 server sees a lower version number, it adjusts its responses to use that protocol version instead.

Knowing how the internals of the WWW work is essential for Webmasters and useful for casual Web users. In short, information is displayed on the Web as a series of pages (i.e., written in HTML). The pages are usually stored on dedicated computers called Web servers. In practice, the term Web server is used interchangeably to refer to the computer on which the Web pages reside, and the program on the computer that receives HTTP requests messages and transmits resources in corresponding response messages. Besides transmitting resources, a Web server can also run a program in response to an incoming HTTP request. Originally, these programs were invoked using the *common gateway interface* (CGI). Although CGI makes it simple to have a Web server perform a specific operation, such as a database lookup, it is not efficient because it requires that a separate program be started for each incoming HTTP request. A more efficient technique is to have the Web server

---

[11]Note that sometimes browsers are still called Mozilla.

itself perform the specific operation. A variety of application programming interfaces (APIs), such as the Microsoft Internet Server API (ISAPI) or the Netscape Server API (NSAPI) are now available to support this function.

If a browser wants to retrieve a HTML document named `index.html` from the root directory of a Web server's document tree, it establishes a TCP connection and sends a corresponding HTTP request message to the server. In essence, the HTTP request message includes the following information:

- A request method that indicates the purpose of the request;

- A reference that indicates the resource to which the method should be applied;

- A number indicating the protocol version;

- A MIME-like message containing request modifiers, client information, and possibly some body content.

In theory, a resource reference may be given in one of the following three forms:

- A uniform resource identifier (URI);

- A uniform resource locator (URL);

- A uniform resource name (URN).

In practice, however, URLs are most commonly used. Refer to RFC 1738 [21] and RFC 1808 [22] for definitive information on URL syntax and semantics. As an example, consider the following HTTP request message:

```
GET /index.html HTTP/1.0
Connection: Keep-Alive
User-Agent: Mozilla/4.05 [en] <WinNT; U>
Host: x.y.z
Accept: image/gif, image/jpeg, ...
Accept-Language: en
Accept-Charset: iso-8859-1,*,utf-8
```

In this example, the browser located at host `x.y.z` wants to retrieve the HTML document `index.html` that is located in the root directory of the Web server's document tree. There are several request headers that provide additional information about the client to the server. For example, the User-Agent header indicates that the user runs the English version of the Netscape Navigator version 4.05 on a Windows NT platform. Similarly, the browser indicates the MIME types it's able to receive (including image/gif and image/jpeg), the language it prefers (en standing for English), as well as the character sets it's able to understand. Finally, the HTTP request message header is always finished up with an empty line.

In response to such a request message, the Web server sends back an HTTP response message that consists of a status line, including the message's protocol version and a success or error code, followed by a MIME-like message containing some server information, entity metainformation, and possibly some body content. Consequently, an HTTP response message (to the above-mentioned message requesting my homepage at http://www.ifi.unizh.ch/~oppliger/index.html) may look as follows:

```
HTTP/1.1 200 OK
Date: Mon, 21 Sep 1998 09:05:13 GMT
Server: Apache/1.2.5
Last-Modified: Tue, 05 May 1998 06:28:06 GMT
ETag: "136e70-16f-354eb176"
Connection: close
Content-Type: text/html

<HTML>
<META HTTP-EQUIV="Refresh" CONTENT="1; URL=index_main.html">
   <HEAD>
      <TITLE>Rolf Oppliger</TITLE>
   </HEAD>
   <BODY BGCOLOR="000000" TEXT="FFFFFF">
   <FONT FACE="helvetica" "arial">
      <CENTER>
         <P>
         <HR>
         <H1>Welcome to the Home Page of Rolf Oppliger</H1>
         <HR>
      </CENTER>
   </BODY>
</HTML>
```

Obviously, the first line of the HTTP response message includes a status code. In this case, the status code 200 means that the request is in order (OK). The HTTP response headers that follow give information either about the server or the returned resource. For example, the Server response header gives the server version, whereas the Last-Modified header indicates the last modification date o the requested resource (the file `index.html`). In either case, a Content-Type heade is required to inform the browser about the type of the provided resource. Iɪ the example given above, the content type is `text/html`, which indicates a text document written in HTML. Finally, the HTTP response message may include the requested resource.

In practice, it is often more convenient to send a HEAD request instead of ꜱᴛ. A HEAD request makes the server behave exactly as if it waꞌ handling a GET, but it doesn't bother to send the actual resource. This makes iꞋ ᵐuch easier to see the response header, and means that the user doesn't have tꞋ wait to download the entire resource. For example, if you want to see ᵗhat response headers the Web server running at `www.ifi.unizh.ch` sends back for `/~oppliger/index.html`, you can use the following command in a Telnet session to the port where the Web server is running (typically port number 80):

```
HEAD /~oppliger/index.html HTTP/1.0
```

In this case, the server's HTTP response message would look as follows (note that the actual HTML document is not included in the HTTP response message):

```
HTTP/1.1 200 OK
Date: Mon, 21 Sep 1998 09:00:07 GMT
Server: Apache/1.2.5
Last-Modified: Tue, 05 May 1998 06:28:06 GMT
ETag: "136e70-16f-354eb176"
Connection: close
Content-Type: text/html
```

In addition to GET and HEAD, there are many other methods specified in the HTTP/1.1 specification, such as POST, PUT, DELETE, OPTIONS, and TRACE. In addition, the HTTP/1.1 specification defines a total of 46 headers that are divided into four categories: general headers, request headers, response headers, and entity headers. Refer to the protocol specification or [18] for a more comprehensive overview of the syntax and semantics of these HTTP headers.

As mentioned previously, HTTP communication usually takes place over TCP connections. The default port is 80, but other ports may be used, as well. This does not preclude HTTP from being implemented on top of any other TCP/IP protocol, or on even any other communications protocol stack. HTTP only presumes a reliable transport layer; any protocol that provides such guarantees can be used to carry HTTP data traffic. In HTTP/1.0, most implementations used a new TCP connection for each HTTP request and response exchange. In HTTP/1.1, however, a connection may be used for one or more HTTP request and response message exchanges, although connections may be closed for a variety of reasons. The resulting persistent connections help reduce HTTP latency.

In the simplest case, a browser directly requests a Web server, and the Web server directly responds to the browser. A more complicated situation occurs when one or more intermediates are present in the request and response chain. The most important examples of intermediates are proxy servers and firewalls, as further addressed in Chapter 3 of this book.

1.3   VULNERABILITIES, THREATS, AND COUNTERMEASURES

In general, a *vulnerability* refers to a weakness that can be exploited by an intruder to violate a system or the information it contains. In a computer network or distributed system, passwords transmitted in cleartext often represent the major vulnerability. The passwords are exposed to eavesdropping and corresponding sniffing attacks. Similarly, the ability of a network host to boot with a network address that has originally been assigned to another host refers to another vulnerability that can be used to spoof that particular host and to masquerade accordingly. Unfortunately, the power of Web technology in general and HTTP in particular also makes the WWW vulnerable to a number of serious attacks.

A *threat* refers to a circumstance, condition, or event with the potential to either violate the security of a system or to cause harm to system resources. Computer networks and distributed systems are susceptible to a wide variety of threats that may be mounted either by intruders[12] or legitimate users. As a matter of fact, legitimate users are more powerful adversaries, since they possess internal information that is not usually available to intruders.

Finally, a *countermeasure* is a feature or function that either reduces or eliminates one (or several) system vulnerability(ies) or counters one (or several) threats. For example, the use of strong authentication techniques reduces the vulnerability of passwords transmitted in the clear and counters the threat of password sniffing and replay attacks. Similarly, the use of cryptographic authentication at the network

---

[12]The term *hacker* is often used to describe computer vandals that break into computer systems. These vandals call themselves hackers, and that is how they got the name, but in my opinion, they don't deserve it. In this book, we use the terms *intruder* and *attacker* instead.

layer effectively eliminates attacks based on machines spoofing other machines' IP addresses and counters IP spoofing attacks.

In essence, this book is about countermeasures that can be used and deployed to secure the WWW. Note, however, that security in general and WWW security in particular are vague terms that may mean various things to different people. Security is a property that is not provable by nature. The very best we can show is resistance against a certain set of attacks we know and with which we are familiar. There is nothing in the world that can protect us against new types of attack. For example, timing attacks, differential fault analysis (DFA), and differential power analysis (DPA) are the latest tools in the never-ending competition between cryptographers and cryptanalysists.

In this book, we are not going to formally define the term "security." Instead, we focus on techniques and mechanisms that are available today and that can be used to provide WWW security in terms of access control and communication security services. The assumption is that if a WWW application is able to provide these security services, there are at least some obstacles to overcome in order to successfully attack the application. If the security services are well designed and properly implemented, the resulting obstacles are far too big to be overcome by occasional intruders. Before we delve into the technical details, we want to briefly introduce a generic security model that puts into perspective the various aspects of security.

1.4   GENERIC SECURITY MODEL

Discussing security in computer networks and distributed systems is difficult, mainly because the term "security" is hard to define and even harder to quantify. Security is a subjective feeling that is received differently by different people. What somebody considers to be secure may be considered by somebody else to be completely insecure. An example to illustrate this point is an airplane flight: while many people consider flying to be secure, there are also people who refuse to fly mainly for security and safety reasons.

To satisfy a customer of the security and safety properties of a particular product or service is a difficult (marketing) task. How do you, for example, persuade a potential buyer about the security and safety properties of a specific car? A somehow unsatisfactory solution for a car dealer is to invite a potential buyer for a ride and to steer the car straight into the next tree. If the buyer remains uninjured, chances are that he or she is convinced about the security and safety properties of the car model. Unfortunately, the car itself will be damaged and the dealer will have to give the buyer another one. Consequently, marketing professionals have come up with better solutions, such as tests conducted by independent consumer societies. The good marketing approach is aimed at increasing the reputation of a product or service in terms of security and safety. For example, in the car industry, Volvo has managed to steadily achieve this kind of reputation. Many people buy a Volvo car simply because they want to increase their security and safety when driving on the road. Unfortunately, a similar appreciation of security and safety properties has not yet been developed within the information technology (IT) industry.

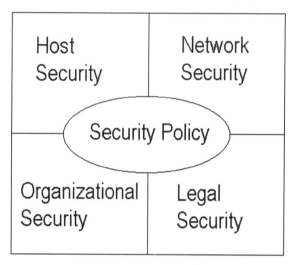

Figure 1.1   A generic security model for computer networks and distributed systems.

In general, there are many aspects involved in securing a networked or distributed system. First and foremost, there must be a security policy that formalizes the proper and improper uses of a (networked or distributed) system, the possible threats against the system, and countermeasures to protect assets from these threats. Most importantly, the security policy is to specify the goals that should be achieved. For example, a possible goal for a corporate intranet would be that any access from external sites requires strong authentication of the requesting user at a security gateway. This goal can be achieved, for example, by using a one-time password or challenge-response system. If another goal were the transparent encryption of the data traffic between internal and external sites, the use of Internet or transport layer security protocols would be another possibility to implement the security policy. After having specified a security policy, there are several aspects related to host, network, organizational, and legal security that must be addressed. The situation is comparable with politics and the military: politics may declare war, but the military must conduct it. Similarly, the security policy must specify the goals, but host and network security techniques and mechanisms must meet these goals. For example, the hosts must run a secure (network) operating system to protect internal resources against outside attacks. Similarly, the hosts must communicate over links that are considerably secure. Either the links are physically secure or they are secured through other means, such as cryptographic algorithms and protocols. Additionally, organizational security controls must be defined and put in place to enforce the technical (host and network) security techniques and mechanisms. If organizational security controls do not exist, everybody will try to do everything, effectively circumventing any security policy. Finally, legal security controls must ensure that if somebody misbehaves or maliciously attacks a system within the computer network or distributed system, he or she can be prosecuted and punished accordingly.

Following this line of argumentation, a generic security model for computer networks and distributed systems may take into account the following five aspects:

- Security policy;
- Host security;
- Network security;
- Organizational security;
- Legal security.

These aspects are illustrated in Figure 1.1 and further addressed in the remaining part of this chapter. Whereas the rest of this book focuses exclusively on network security, the other aspects of security are equally important and should also be considered with care. It is simply not possible to achieve WWW security if these aspects are not adequately addressed.

1.4.1 Security Policy

As mentioned before, a security policy must specify the goals that should be achieved with regard to the security of a networked or distributed system. In fact, if a security policy is not specified, it is useless to talk about security. Typical statements found in a security policy include phrases such as "any access from the Internet to intranet resources must be strongly authenticated and properly authorized at the security gateway," or "any classified data must be properly encrypted for transmission." The security policy should be specified by management, without taking into account the technical implementation and enforcement. In fact, the security policy should be driven by requirements rather than technical considerations.

1.4.2 Host Security

Host security has traditionally addressed questions, such as

- How to securely authenticate users;
- How to effectively control access to system resources;
- How to securely store and process data within the system;
- How to do the audit trail.

These and similar questions have all been studied within the computer security community for quite a long time. A special field of study in this area is the evaluation and certification of IT systems and products. For example, based on the Bell-LaPadula and Biba access control models, the National Computer Security Center (NCSC) of the U.S. National Security Agency (NSA) developed the *Trusted Computer Security Evaluation Criteria* (TCSEC), also known as "Orange Book," in the late 1980s [23]. In Europe, similar developments in Germany, France, the United Kingdom, and the Netherlands led to the *Information Technology Security Evaluation Criteria* (ITSEC) [24]. Europe, the United States, and Canada are working together to come up with *Common Criteria* (CC). In December 1997, version 2 of the CC was officially released and proposed to the ISO for international standardization [25].[13]

Note, however, that except for some government-sponsored programs, the idea of evaluating and certifying IT systems and products never really took off in the commercial world. One problem that has remained unsolved in the past is the extension of security evaluation and certification criteria to networked and distributed environments. Except for some interpretations of the TCSEC, namely the *Trusted Network Interpretation* (TNI) [26], there is hardly any work that has been done in this particular area. Many operating systems that actually provide support for networking are being evaluated and certified in standalone mode only. The most prominent example is the TCSEC C2 certificate that has been granted to the Windows NT operating system. It is assumed that security evaluation and certification

---

[13]Further information regarding the CC project can be found on the WWW by following the URL http://scrc.ncsl.nist.gov/nistpubs/cc/

criteria will be refined for being applicable for networked and distributed systems, as soon as the idea proves to be of commercial value.

1.4.3 Network Security

Network security addresses questions such as how to efficiently control access to computer networks and distributed systems, and how to securely transmit data between them. In network security parlance, one clearly distinguishes between a security service and a security mechanism:

- A *security service* is a quality of a system present to satisfy a security policy;

- A *security mechanism* is a concrete mechanism or procedure used to actually implement such a quality (one or several security services).

Consequently, a security service identifies what is needed, whereas a security mechanism describes how to achieve it. For example, the security architecture for the open systems interconnection (OSI) reference model enumerates the following five classes of *security services* [27,28]:

1. Authentication services;
2. Data confidentiality services;
3. Data integrity services;
4. Access control services;
5. Non-repudiation services.

Network users and applications must be able to selectively make use of services that conform to their security requirements. These requirements are individual by nature, and may vary from user to user or application to application. There are also some security services that are not enumerated in the OSI security architecture, such as anonymity services as further addressed in Chapter 13 of this book.

In addition to the security services mentioned above, the OSI security architecture also enumerates a couple of security mechanisms that can be used to implement the security services. In particular, the following eight *specific security mechanisms* are enumerated in the OSI security architecture:

1. Encipherment;
2. Digital signature mechanisms;
3. Access control mechanisms;

4. Data integrity mechanisms;

5. Authentication exchange mechanism;

6. Traffic padding mechanism;

7. Routing control mechanism;

8. Notarization mechanism.

Complementary to these specific security mechanisms, the OSI security architecture also enumerates the following five *pervasive security mechanisms*:

1. Trusted functionality;

2. Security labels;

3. Event detection;

4. Security audit trail;

5. Security recovery.

The OSI security architecture is extensively covered in the literature. In particular, Chapter 3 of [5] is dedicated entirely to the OSI security architecture. From a more practical point of view, it is appropriate to distinguish between access control and communication security services:

- *Access control services* are used to logically separate (inter)networks and to essentially control access to corporate networks which are also called intranets in the case of TCP/IP-based networks;

- *Communication security services* are used to protect communications within and between these networks. According to the OSI security architecture, communication security services include authentication, data confidentiality and integrity, as well as non-repudiation services.

The predominant technology to provide access control services for corporate networks and intranets is the firewall technology as further addressed in Part II of [5] and Chapter 3 of this book. With regard to communication security services, many cryptographic protocols have been proposed for the various network layers of both the OSI reference model and the Internet model. These protocols are addressed in Part III of [5] and Chapter 5 (or Chapter 6 in the case of the SSL and TLS protocols) of this book.

1.4.4 Organizational Security

Any technical solution for host and network security must be backed up with organizational security controls. In fact, organizational security is required where technical host and network security mechanisms alone do not or only insufficiently work. There is a quotation from Richard H. Baker that elaborates on the problem regarding technical versus organizational security [29]:

> "Security continues to be and probably will always be a people problem. If you overlook that, you're in trouble."

According to this quotation, it is dangerous to depend on technical (host and network) security mechanisms alone. If people are not convinced about the need for the security mechanisms that are put in place, they will always try to circumvent them. In one of his later books, Baker has even been more succinct in this point [30]:

> "The real challenges are human, not technical. Oldtimers will recognize a once-popular saying that the most important part of an automobile is the nut that holds the steering wheel. That's still true, even though a modern steering wheel may also contain an air bag and any number of controls and antitheft devices."

Our personal experience is in line with this quotation. In fact, human behavior is still the most important factor with regard to security and safety. Human behavior can be influenced by education and organizational security controls. Education is very important. If people understand the security controls they must rely on, they will make use of them instead of always trying to circumvent them. Additionally, organizational security controls must be put in place to make illegitimate procedures more difficult. Organizational security controls include directions and instructions that are released to define legitimate human behavior.

An analogy that may help better understand security in computer networks and distributed systems is the existing highway system, and the way we try to achieve safety and security on it.[14] In particular, we use and deploy several technical and organizational measures to achieve safe and secure traffic:

- On the technical side, we try to build highways in a way that minimizes the risks of careless drivers being able to cause serious accidents. We also require drivers to have a license and cars to have passed a vehicle inspection test.

---

[14]Similar things could also be said for the airway system.

- On the organizational side, we have educational programs, traffic laws, and police to enforce these laws.

Using this analogy, it is obvious that we can learn several things from the way we handle security and safety in the real world.

1.4.5 Legal Security

Finally, it is possible that host or network security techniques or mechanisms will fail and not provide sufficient protection against more sophisticated attacks. Similarly, it is possible that organizational security controls won't be able to back up technical deficiencies. In this case, it is important to have the possibility to legally prosecute the attacker(s). Consequently, legal security is a major topic with regard to computer networks and distributed systems. Again, there is an analogy to better illustrate this point: We are all familiar with the postal delivery service. We send letters in envelopes in order to protect the confidentiality of the contents. In addition, we trust the employees of the postal delivery service not to open the envelopes and to respect the privacy of the post accordingly. However, if we recognized that a letter was opened during its delivery, we would have cause to suspect the employee(s) of the postal delivery service of not respecting the privacy of the post, and a case could even be brought to court. One can reasonably expect that similar legal security controls will be put in place in computer networks and distributed systems, and that the need for non-repudiation services will be the major driving force for this development to happen.

REFERENCES

[1] S. Carl-Mitchell, and J.S. Quaterman, *Practical Internetworking with TCP/IP and UNIX*, Addison-Wesley, Reading, MA, 1993.

[2] D. Comer, *Internetworking with TCP/IP: Principles, Protocols, and Architecture*, 3rd Edition, Prentice-Hall, Englewood Cliffs, NJ, 1995.

[3] A.S. Tanenbaum, *Computer Networks*, 3rd Edition, Prentice-Hall, Englewood Cliffs, NJ, 1996.

[4] F. Wilder, *A Guide to the TCP/IP Protocol Suite*, 2nd Edition, Artech House, Norwood, MA, 1998.

[5] R. Oppliger, *Internet and Intranet Security*, Artech House, Norwood, MA, 1998.

[6] R.H. Zakon, "Hobbes' Internet Timeline," Request for Comments 2235, (FYI 32), November 1997.

[7] E.H. Spafford, "The Internet Worm: Crisis and Aftermath," *Communications of the ACM*, Vol. 32, 1989, pp. 678 – 688.

[8] J.A. Rochlis, and M.W. Eichin, "With Microscope and Tweezers: The Worm from MIT's Perspective," *Communications of the ACM*, Vol. 32, 1989, pp. 689 – 703.

[9] P.J. Denning, *Computers under Attack: Intruders, Worms, and Viruses*, ACM Press/Addison-Wesley, New York, NY, 1990.

[10] P.G. Neumann, *Computer-Related Risks*, ACM Press/Addison-Wesley, New York, NY, 1995.

[11] J.D. Howard, *An Analysis Of Security Incidents On The Internet 1989 – 1995*, Ph.D. Thesis, Carnegie Mellon University, April 1997.

[12] T. Shimomura with J. Markoff, *Takedown*, Hyperion, New York, NY, 1996.

[13] C.L. Schuba, I.V. Krsul, M.G. Kuhn, E.H. Spafford, A. Sundaram, and D. Zamboni, "Analysis of a Denial of Service Attack on TCP," *Proceedings of IEEE Symposium on Security and Privacy*, 1997, pp. 208 – 223.

[14] R.T. Morris, "A weakness in the 4.2BSD UNIX TCP/IP Software," Computer Science Technical Report No. 117, AT&T Bell Laboratories, Murray Hill, NJ, February 1985.

[15] S.M. Bellovin, "Security Problems in the TCP/IP Protocol Suite," *ACM Computer Communication Review*, Vol. 19, No. 2, 1989, pp. 32 – 48.

[16] R. Braden, D. Clark, S. Crocker, and C. Huitema, "Report of the IAB Workshop on Security in the Internet Architecture (February 8 – 10, 1994)," Request for Comments 1636, June 1994.

[17] S. Bellovin, "Report of the IAB Security Architecture Workshop," Request for Comments 2316, April 1998.

[18] A. Luotonen, *Web Proxy Servers*, Prentice Hall PTR, Upper Saddle River, NJ, 1998.

[19] T. Berners-Lee, R. Fielding, and H. Frystyk, "Hypertext Transfer Protocol - HTTP/1.0," Request for Comments 1945, May 1996.

[20] R. Fielding, J. Gettys, J. Mogul, H. Frystyk, and T. Berners-Lee, "Hypertext Transfer Protocol - HTTP/1.1," Request for Comments 2068, January 1997.

[21] T. Berners-Lee, L. Masinter, and M. McCahill, "Uniform Resource Locators (URL)," Request for Comments 1738, December 1994.

[22] R. Fielding, "Relative Uniform Resource Locators (URL)," Request for Comments 1808, June 1995.

[23] U.S. Department of Defense, *Trusted Computer System Evaluation Criteria*, Standard DoD 5200.28-STD, Fort George G. Meade, MD, 1985.

[24] Commission of the European Communities, *Information Technology Security Evaluation Criteria*, Version 1.2, Directorate General XIII, 1991.

[25] Common Criteria Implementation Board (CCIB), *The Common Criteria for Information Technology Security Evaluation*, Version 2, 1997.

[26] U.S. Department of Defense, *Trusted Network Interpretation of the Trusted Computer System Evaluation Criteria*, Fort George G. Meade, MD, 1987.

[27] ISO/IEC 7498-2, Information Processing Systems — Open Systems Interconnection Reference Model — Part 2: Security Architecture, 1989.

[28] ITU X.800, Security Architecture for Open Systems Interconnection for CCITT Applications, 1991.

[29] R.H. Baker, *Computer Security Handbook*, McGraw-Hill, New York, NY, 1991.

[30] R.H. Baker, *Network Security: How to Plan for It and Achieve It*, McGraw-Hill, New York, NY, 1995.

Chapter 2

HTTP User Authentication and Authorization

In this chapter, we elaborate on HTTP user authentication and authorization schemes. In particular, we introduce the topic in Section 2.1, and address HTTP basic authentication (specified for HTTP/1.0), HTTP digest authentication (specified for HTTP/1.1), and certificate-based authentication in Sections 2.2 to 2.4. Finally, we address authorization and access control in Section 2.5, and draw conclusions in Section 2.6.

2.1 INTRODUCTION

In general, organizations run Web servers to make resources publicly available and accessible to arbitrary users. In this situation, the Web servers are typically configured to accept requests from anonymous users, and there is no need for user authentication and authorization accordingly. Sometimes, however, organizations also run Web servers whose resources must not be available and accessible to everybody. For example, access to a Web server may be restricted to the employees of an organization, or certain resources may only be accessible to customers who have paid a subscription fee or have signed nondisclosure agreements. In all of these situations, there may be need for proper access control.

In general, there are several techniques that may be employed to control access to resources on Web servers [1]:

- Restricting access by using hidden URLs (URLs that are kept secret);
- Restricting access to a particular group of computers based on those computers' address information (e.g., IP addresses);
- Restricting access to a particular group of users based on their identity information and corresponding credentials.

Obviously, the easiest way to restrict access is by storing the resources, such as HTML files and CGI scripts, in hidden locations on the HTTP server. This refers to the technique of restricting access by using URLs that are kept secret and hidden. Hidden URLs are about as secure as a key underneath a door mat. Nobody can access the resources unless they know what URLs to use. But anybody who knows a hidden URL has full access to the resource it refers to. Furthermore, this information is transitive. You might tell a friend of yours about a specific URL, and he might tell a friend of his, and so on, until finally the URL gets posted to a mailing list or newsgroup, or it may even end up in a link in another HTML document. At this point, the URL may get registered by so-called Web "spiders" — automated programs that sweep through all the pages on a Web server, adding keywords from each page to a central database. Lycos[1] and AltaVista[2] are two well-known and heavily used HTML index servers of this kind. If a Web spider follows the HTML link, it will add the formerly hidden URL, along with identifying index entries, to its database. Thereafter, someone searching for the resource might be able to find it through the index service. In general, hidden URLs should only be used if its compromise and the loss of the resource's confidentiality does not pose a serious problem. Aviel D. Rubin, Daniel Geer, and Marcus J. Ranum have put this in other words [2]:

"As everyone in the data security business is fond of saying, 'Obscurity is not security.' If you want to protect data, you will have to do better than naming it /tmp/nobody_would_guess_this_URL.html; you will need to provide a security mechanism."

As of this writing, most Web servers allow their administrators to restrict access to a particular group of computers based on those computers' address information. The address information can be specified by the computers' IP addresses or DNS hostnames. In fact, restricting access to specific IP addresses or a range of IP addresses is relatively simple and works well for an organization that wishes to restrict

---

[1] http://www.lycos.com
[2] http://www.altavista.com

access to people on its intranet. For example, you might consider restricting access to an intranet Web server to the range of IP addresses that has been assigned to your organization. Instead of specifying computers by IP addresses, most Web servers also allow their administrators to restrict access on the basis of DNS hostnames. This has the advantage that IP addresses can be changed without having to change the Web server's configuration files, as well (as long as the DNS hostnames remain unchanged). The disadvantage of restricting access based on DNS hostnames is that the DNS itself can be attacked and misused. Either way, it is important to note that host-based addressing is not foolproof. In fact, IP spoofing can be used to transmit IP packets that appear to come from a different computer than the one actually used. This is more of a risk for CGI scripts than for HTML documents. Also note that a firewall system can also be used to restrict access to a particular group of computers based on those computers' address information.

Finally, restricting access to a particular group of users based on their identity information and corresponding credentials is one of the most effective ways of controlling access. For example, if the users of a Web server are widely dispersed (eventually using temporarily assigned IP addresses), or the administrator needs to be able to control access on an individual basis, it is necessary to implement user-specific authentication and authorization schemes. In short, the process of verifying the identity of a requesting user is called *user authentication*, whereas the process of granting the privileges to access particular resources is called *user authorization*. In the simplest case, each user is given a username and a password. The username identifies the person who wishes to access the HTTP server, and the password authenticates the person. To increase security, more sophisticated user authentication schemes may be used.

In general, setting up HTTP user authentication and authorization takes two steps:

- First, a file containing the user authentication information is created;
- Second, the Web server is told what resources to protect and which users to allow access (after proper authentication).

The format of the file containing the user authentication information is generally similar to a standard UNIX password file, with the username and password entries being separated with a colon. An administrator cannot just type in the usernames and passwords because the passwords should be stored in encrypted form. There are programs and administration tools that can be used to create a user file and to add or modify user entries accordingly. For example, the `htpasswd` program is a C program that is supplied in the support directory of many Web server software packages.

In the following two sections, we address two user authentication schemes that have been proposed for HTTP: basic authentication and digest authentication. They both implement a password-based protection scheme for HTTP. Issues related to the configuration of the corresponding Web server software are addressed in a later section.

2.2   HTTP BASIC AUTHENTICATION

Part of the HTTP/1.0 specification is the *HTTP basic authentication* scheme that provides password-based protection for resources stored in specific branches of a Web server's document tree [3]. The HTTP basic authentication scheme is currently supported by most browser and Web server software packages (including, for example, Netscape Navigator and Microsoft Internet Explorer).

In short, if a browser requests a resource that is protected with HTTP basic authentication, the Web server requires the browser to provide some authentication information (typically a username and a corresponding password). Therefore, the client either remembers this information from a previous session, or prompts the user to type in the corresponding information. In either case, the browser forwards the information to the Web server in the clear. For example, let's assume that a browser requests the resource /~oppliger/Protected_Area/ (which refers to a directory listing) located within the document tree of the Web server running at www.ifi.unizh.ch. Let's further assume that the entire directory Protected_Area is password-protected. In this situation, the browser does not yet know that the requested resource is password-protected and sends out a normal-looking HTTP request message to the Web server. Remember from Chapter 1 that such a message may look as follows:

```
GET /~oppliger/Protected_Area/ HTTP/1.0
Connection: Keep-Alive
User-Agent: Mozilla/4.05 [en] <WinNT; U>
Host: x.y.z
Accept: image/gif, image/jpeg, ...
Accept-Language: en
Accept-Charset: iso-8859-1,*,utf-8
```

After having received this HTTP request message, the Web server recognizes that the requested resource is located in a password-protected branch of the server's document tree. As further explained in Section 2.5, the server recognizes that the branch is password-protected because it contains a specific file (named .htaccess in the case of the Apache server software). Instead of directly returning the requested resource, the Web server generates an HTTP response message that may look as follows:

```
HTTP/1.0 401 Unauthorized
Date: ...
Server: ...
...
WWW-Authenticate: Basic realm="Rolf Oppliger's Protected Area"
```

Obviously, the HTTP response message starts with a 401 status code, indicating that the browser has requested a resource for which it needs proper authentication and authorization. In addition, the server may also return Date, Server, and possibly some other HTTP response headers. Finally, the server returns a WWW-Authenticate response header that specifies the use of the HTTP Basic Authentication scheme (indicated with the keyword Basic) for a specific realm (indicated with the realm name Rolf Oppliger's Protected Area).

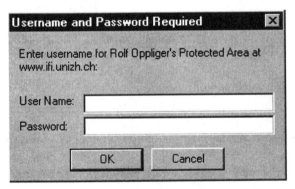

Figure 2.1   The Netscape Navigator 4.05 "Username and Password Required" prompt. © 1999 Netscape Communications Corporation.

After having received the HTTP response message, the browser uses the realm name to prompt the user to enter his or her username and proper password for this particular realm. Figures 2.1 and 2.2 illustrate the corresponding Netscape Navigator 4.05 "Username and Password Required" and Microsoft Internet Explorer 4.0 "Enter Network Password" prompts. If the user obeyed and properly entered his or her username and password, the browser would send a second HTTP request message to the Web server. This time, the HTTP request message may look as follows (the headers not relevant for the discussion are omitted entirely):

```
GET /~oppliger/Protected_Area/ HTTP/1.0
...
Authorization: Basic ...
```

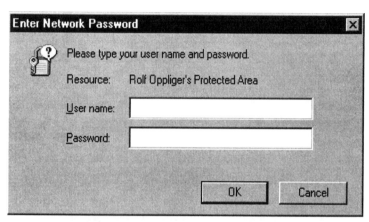

Figure 2.2   The Microsoft Internet Explorer 4.0 "Enter Network Password" prompt. © 1999 Microsoft Corporation.

This time, the HTTP request message includes an Authorization header that refers to the HTTP basic authentication scheme (again indicated with the keyword `Basic`) and holds the user's authentication information (indicated with three dots). In short, the authentication information includes the username and password (separated with a colon) in Base64-encoded form. The encoding of the authentication information in the HTTP basic authentication scheme is illustrated in Figure 2.3.

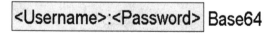

Figure 2.3   The encoding of the authentication information in the HTTP basic authentication scheme.

In spite of the fact that the authentication information is Base64-encoded, there is nothing that protects it against passive eavesdropping. Anyone who intercepts the HTTP request message that is sent from the browser to the Web server can obtain the corresponding authentication information, decode the username and password, and (mis)use this information illegitimately to access protected resources within the document tree of the Web server. To make things worse, also take into account that HTTP is stateless, and that the browser must reauthenticate itself to the server each time it accesses a protected resource (not just the first time it enters a password-protected branch of the directory tree). In order to make that transparent to the user, browsers usually remember the username and password used to access a resource and retransmit them automatically whenever the user wants to access another resource in the same branch of the directory tree. This is convenient but also causes many password transmissions that are transparent and "invisible" to the user. Consequently, the HTTP basic authentication scheme is considered weak. The situation is comparable to the lack of strong authentication mechanisms in many other TCP/IP application protocols, such as Telnet and FTP.

2.3 HTTP DIGEST AUTHENTICATION

Part of the HTTP/1.1 specification is an improved and better user authentication and authorization scheme called *HTTP digest authentication* [4]. More precisely, the specification of the HTTP digest authentication scheme is given in a companion RFC that has also been submitted to the Internet Standards Track [5]. It has been proposed that HTTP digest authentication be included in the HTTP/1.1 specification (or a later HTTP specification) at some later point in time.[3]

Like the HTTP basic authentication scheme, the HTTP digest authentication scheme is based on a simple challenge-response mechanism to verify that the user knows a specific password that represents a shared secret. However, unlike HTTP basic authentication, this verification is done without actually sending the password in the clear (which we have seen to be the major vulnerability of the HTTP basic authentication scheme).

In short, a Web server using the HTTP digest authentication scheme challenges the browser with a nonce (a random number or a longer value that contains information about the current transaction). The browser, in turn, must return a valid response that contains a hash value of the following components:

- The username;

---

[3]More recently, an Internet Draft entitled "HTTP Authentication: Basic and Digest Access Authentication" has been written to replace [5] in the future. Look out for a file named `draft-ietf-http-authentication-*.txt` in an Internet Draft archive. As of this writing, the latest document is `draft-ietf-http-authentication-03.txt` which was published on September 2, 1998.

- The password;
- The nonce;
- The HTTP method;
- The URL of the requested resource.

An optional header may also allow the server to specify the algorithm that must be used to create the hash value. By default the MD5 algorithm is used [6]. As further explained in Chapter 4, an MD5 hash value is 128 bits long. As such, it can be represented in 32 ASCII printable characters that each represent a hexadecimal number.

The HTTP digest authentication scheme begins in much the same way as the HTTP basic authentication scheme. If a server receives a request for an access-protected resource, and an acceptable Authorization header is not sent together with the HTTP request message, the server returns an HTTP response message that may look as follows:

```
HTTP/1.1 401 Authorization Required
Date: ...
Server: ...
...
WWW-Authenticate: Digest ...
```

Aside from the fact that the response header now specifies HTTP/1.1, the main difference is that the WWW-Authenticate header now suggests the use of the HTTP digest authentication scheme (indicated with the keyword Digest). In addition, the server also provides further information in the WWW-Authenticate header (indicated with three dots). In particular, the server provides a realm name and a nonce. Again, the realm name is rendered for the user so he or she knows which username and password to provide. The nonce is a server-specified data string that may be uniquely generated each time a 401 response message is compiled. It is recommended that the nonce be Base64-encoded or a hexadecimal number.[4] The contents of the nonce are implementation dependent. A recommended nonce would be computed as follows:

$$h(IP_C, " : ", TS, " : ", K_S)$$

---

[4]Specifically, since the string is passed in the header lines as a quoted string, the double-quote character is not allowed.

Again, a notation to express and better understand such expressions is introduced in Chapter 4. In the meantime, it is sufficient to know that h is used to refer to a one-way hash function, such as MD5, IP_C is the IP address of the client (or browser) making the request, TS is a server-generated timestamp, and K_S is a secret key that is known exclusively to the Web server. In addition, the use of a comma implies concatenation.

With a nonce of the above-mentioned form, the server can limit the reuse of a nonce to the IP address to which it was issued (because of IP_C) and limit the time of the nonce's validity (because of TS). Also, the secret key K_S is used to make it computationally infeasible for an attacker to generate nonces. In either case, an implementation may choose not to accept a previously used nonce to protect against replay attacks.

Optionally, the WWW-Authenticate header may also provide a comma-separated list of URLs (domain), a string of data specified by the server that should be returned by the client unchanged (opaque), a string indicating a pair of algorithms used to produce the hash value (algorithm), and a flag, indicating that the previous request from the client was rejected because the nonce value was stale (stale). Refer to [5] for a more comprehensive overview and description of these optional parameters.

In response to the HTTP response message, the client prompts the user to enter his or her username and password. This is similar to the user prompts in the HTTP Basic Authentication scheme (if it were implemented, it would look similar or identical to Figures 2.1 and 2.2). If the user entered the requested information, the browser would compute a digest value and return it to the Web server in an HTTP request message that may look as follows:

```
GET /~oppliger/Protected_Area/ HTTP/1.1
...
Authorization: Digest ...
```

This time the Authorization header contains the digest response of the client. The keyword Digest implies the use of the HTTP Digest Authentication scheme, whereas the three dots indicate a response value that contains the username, the realm string, the nonce, the requested URL, and the correct response to the server's challenge (represented by the nonce). To compute the response value, the client concatenates the following three components:

- The hash value of a colon-separated list that comprises the unquoted username, realm string, and password;

- The nonce and a colon;
- The hash value of the method and the requested URL (again separated with a colon).

Finally, the concatenated value is hashed once more and quoted to form the actual digest response value. Optionally, the Authorization header may also contain a digest of the entity body and some of the associated entity headers (`digest`), the algorithm (`algorithm`), and the opaque value (`opaque`). Again, refer to [5] for a more comprehensive overview and description of these optional parameters.

The following example is taken from [5]. It is assumed that an access-protected resource `http://www.nowhere.org/dir/index.html` is being requested from a Web server. Both client and server know that the username for this resource is "Mufasa," and that the corresponding password is "CircleOfLife." The first time the client requests the resource, no Authorization header is sent, so the Web server responds with the following message:

```
HTTP/1.1 401 Unauthorized
WWW-Authenticate: Digest realm="testrealm@host.com",
                         nonce="dcd98b7102dd2f0e8b11d0f600bfb0c093",
                         opaque="5ccc069c403ebaf9f0171e9517f40e41"
```

The important thing to notice is that the Web server challenges the browser with a nonce (`dcd98b7102dd2f0e8b11d0f600bfb0c093` in this example). In response to this message, the client prompts the user to enter his or her username and password (for the realm `testrealm@host.com`) and computes the digest response value according to the forumla given above (`e966c932a9242554e42c8ee200cec7f6` in this example). Afterwards, the client provides a new HTTP request message that includes the following Authorization header:

```
Authorization: Digest    username="Mufasa",
                         realm="testrealm@host.com",
                         nonce="dcd98b7102dd2f0e8b11d0f600bfb0c093",
                         uri="/dir/index.html",
                         response="e966c932a9242554e42c8ee200cec7f6",
                         opaque="5ccc069c403ebaf9f0171e9517f40e41"
```

Upon receiving the Authorization header, the server can check the validity of the digest response value. In particular, it can look up the password that corresponds to the submitted username, recompute the digest response value for this password, and compare the result to the digest response value that was originally provided by the client. If the values match, the client is authenticated.

Note that the Web server does not need to know the user password in the clear. As long as the first hash value mentioned above (the hash value of a colon-separated list that comprises the unquoted username, realm string, and password) is available, the digest response value can be recomputed and the client-provided Authorization header can be verified by the server accordingly. Also note that a client may remember the username, password, and nonce values, so that future requests within the specified domain may include the appropriate Authorization header. The server may choose to accept old Authorization headers, even though the nonces that are included might not be fresh. Alternatively, the server could return a 401 response with a new nonce value, causing the client to retry the request. By specifying the `stale` value as true, the server hints to the client that the request should be retried with the new nonce, without prompting the user for a new username and password.

In the following chapter, we address the implications of proxy servers and firewalls for Web applications. As with HTTP basic authentication, the use of proxy servers must be completely transparent in HTTP digest authentication. That is, the proxy servers must forward the WWW-Authenticate, Authentication-info, and Authorization headers as they are. If a proxy server wanted to authenticate a client before a request is forwarded to a Web server, it would have to use appropriate Proxy-Authenticate and Proxy-Authorization headers. In fact, the HTTP digest authentication scheme may be used for authenticating users to proxies, proxies to proxies, and proxies to end servers by use of the Proxy-Authenticate and Proxy-Authorization headers as specified for HTTP/1.1 [4].

In addition, there is a potential difficulty in using HTTP authentication schemes (either HTTP basic or digest authentication) together with caching mechanisms implemented by most proxy servers. Note that one goal of a proxy server is to cache resources that have been downloaded once to serve requests that are issued by multiple clients. Consequently, if a resource has been downloaded by an authenticated client, the resource may end up in a proxy server cache, from where it may be redistributed to multiple (not authenticated) clients. To protect against this redistribution, HTTP/1.1 specifies that when a proxy server has received an HTTP request message containing an Authorization header and a response message from relaying that request, it must not return that response message as a reply to any other request, unless one of the following two cache-control directives was sent in the corresponding original HTTP response message:

- If the original HTTP response message includes the `must-revalidate` cache-control directive, the proxy server can cache the resource and use it to serve further requests for the same resource. Each time the resource is requested, the proxy server has to first reauthenticate the client (using the HTTP request headers from the new request to allow the origin Web server to authenticate the client);

- Alternatively, if the original HTTP response includes the `public` cache-control directive, the proxy server can cache the resource and use it to serve further requests for the same resource (without client reauthentication).

The strength of HTTP digest authentication is that passwords are not transmitted in the clear. Provided that the user has picked a good (and randomly chosen) password, it is computationally infeasible for an attacker to derive the password from the hash value of the response. For further protection, the user's password should not be stored in plaintext on the server side, where it could be stolen by someone with access to the server. Only the hashed value should be stored in a user file of the server (remember from our previous discussions that the server only needs a hash value to recompute the digest response value). This is similar to the way that UNIX and Windows NT store passwords. As a final precaution, the requested URL is also part of the hashed response value. If the response is intercepted by an eavesdropper who attempts to play it back to gain access to the server, he or she will be able to get access only to that single URL. He or she will be unable to generate new responses to gain access to documents that are found in other branches of the server's directory tree. Servers can further protect themselves against replay attacks by adding a timestamp to the nonce so that responses automatically expire after a short period of time.

Nevertheless, the HTTP digest authentication scheme also suffers from known limitations. For example, both the HTTP basic and digest authentication schemes are vulnerable to the "man-in-the-middle" attack from a hostile or compromised server. The reason for that is the lack of server-side authentication. According to its specification, the HTTP digest authentication scheme is intended as a replacement for the HTTP basic authentication scheme and nothing more. It is still a password-based system, and as such it suffers from all the problems of a password-based system on either side of the communication. For example, digest authentication requires that the authenticating party (usually the server) store some data derived from the username and password in a user file associated with a given realm. The security implications of this are that if this file is compromised, then an attacker gains immediate access to documents on the server using this realm. On the other hand, a brute force attack would be necessary to obtain a user's password. This is why the realm is part of the hashed data stored in the password file. It means that if one digest authentication password file is compromised, it does not automatically compromise others with the same username and password (though it does expose them to brute force attack). This is somewhat similar to the UNIX salt mechanism. There are two important security consequences of this:

- First, the user password file must be protected as if it contained unencrypted passwords.

- Second, the realm name should be unique among all realms that any single user is likely to use. In particular, a realm name should include the name of the host doing the authentication (contrary to the example given previously in this chapter).

Furthermore, no provision is made in the specification of the HTTP digest authentication scheme for the initial arrangement between the user and server to establish the user password. Consequently, the HTTP digest authentication scheme is not intended to be a complete answer to the need for security on the WWW. Note that this scheme does not provide data confidentiality and integrity services either. The intent is simply to create an authentication and authorization scheme that avoids the major vulnerability of the HTTP basic authentication scheme (the plaintext transmission of the password). As such, HTTP digest authentication is far superior to HTTP Basic Authentication.

As of this writing, several Web server software packages support Digest Authentication, including, for example, the Apache 1.2 server (if compiled with the `mod_digest` module supplied with the standard Apache software distribution). Unfortunately, none of the commercial browsers, including Netscape Navigator and Microsoft Internet Explorer, have been modified to make use of HTTP Digest Authentication. The major reason for this astonishing fact is that those browsers typically implement the SSL or TLS protocol as discussed in Chapter 6. If the browser and server are communicating with HTTP on top of SSL or TLS (using HTTPS), the problem of password sniffing automatically goes away. The encrypted channel is set up before any HTTP header passes across the network, so the username and password are part of the encrypted SSL data stream and cannot be sniffed accordingly.

2.4 CERTIFICATE-BASED AUTHENTICATION

As mentioned before, we learn about the secure sockets layer (SSL) and transport layer security (TLS) protocols that are used to secure communications between browsers and HTTP servers in Chapter 6. Using HTTP on top of SSL or TLS makes user authentication and authorization simple and straightforward (server-side authentication is mandatory in SSL and TLS, whereas client-side authentication is optional). In short, Web servers authenticate themselves using site certificates, whereas individual users authenticate themselves using personal certificates. The use of site and personal certificates is addressed later in this book.

In addition to superior security, there is another advantage related to the use of (site and personal) certificates. As further explained in Chapter 4, a certificate generally binds a public key to an identity. This identity can, in turn, be used to control access to system resources. For example, if a certificate states that Rolf Oppliger (the entry in the CN field of an X.509v3 certificate) is a staff member of the BFI (the entry in the OU field of the corresponding certificate), then a group-based access control can be implemented without having to manage user identities. This simplifies the configuration management of a Web server considerably. The use of certificates to implement group-based access controls is taken up again in Chapter 8, when we address a distributed certificate management system (DCMS) for corporate environments.

2.5 AUTHORIZATION AND ACCESS CONTROL

Based on the HTTP authentication and authorization schemes explained in the previous sections, Web server software packages generally provide support for user-based and group-based access controls. For example, the Apache server allows an administrator to define authorized users, give them passwords, and place them in groups similar to the UNIX and Window NT operating systems. The syntax that is used to specify access control rules heavily depends on the Web server software being used. Refer to your software manual for a description of the syntax you must use. In the explanations that follow, we refer to the Apache Web server software that is widely deployed today [7].

Earlier in this chapter, we said that a program called htpasswd can be used to create a user file, and to add or modify entries in this file. To create a new user file and add the username "Rolf" with the password "testentry" to the file /usr/local/etc/httpd/users, you may run the following command (after having properly installed the htpasswd program somewhere on your command execution path):

```
htpasswd -c /usr/local/etc/httpd/users Rolf
```

The -c argument tells the htpasswd program to create a new user file (located at /usr/local/etc/httpd/users in this example). Running the command, you will be prompted to enter a password for the user Rolf, and to confirm it by entering it again. Other users can be added to the existing file in the same way, except that the -c argument is not needed anymore. As well, the same command can also be used to modify the password of an existing user. Refer to [1] for a simple Perl-based user management tool.

After having added a couple of users, the user file (located at /usr/local/etc/httpd/users) may look as follows:

```
Isabelle:Lo6WOzxvNGXd2
Rolf:xaDZLGMern9kU
Hans:unqQqFnHGh7Xs
Caroline:OZnnGFJG1TP6s
Marianne:YfJ3k4tgrVO4c
Kaethe:j5RiAU5K9iuaM
```

In each entry, the first field refers to the username, and the second field refers to the encrypted password (the two fields being separated with a colon). Since the UNIX password encryption routine is typically used for encryption, each password is encoded as 13 printable characters. Note that in spite of the fact that two users (Caroline and Kaethe in the example given above) have chosen the same password, the corresponding encrypted passwords are different. This is due to the salt mechanism that's being used in the UNIX password encryption routine. In short, a 2-character plaintext prefix in the encrypted password is used as a parameter for the actual encryption and decryption routine. The aim is to make dictionary attacks more difficult.[5]

To get the server to use the usernames and passwords that are stored in the user file, a corresponding realm must be configured. In short, a realm is a part of a Web server's document tree that is to be restricted to some or all of the users itemized in the user file. This is typically done on a per-directory basis, with a directory (and all of its subdirectories) being protected (Apache 1.2 and later versions also let you protect individual files). The directives to create the protected area of a realm can be placed in a .htaccess file in the directory concerned, or in a <Directory> section of the Web server's access configuration file access.conf. To

---

[5]Note that an attacker can encrypt each entry of a dictionary and compare arbitrary encrypted passwords against this dictionary. Any match reveals a valid password. If, however, the password encryption and decryption routines additionally depend on a random parameter, such as a 2-character plaintext prefix in the case of a UNIX password, the attacker has to encrypt the entire dictionary for each password he wants to break. Consequently, dictionary attacks are still possible but they only apply for one particular password.

allow a directory to be restricted within a `.htaccess` file, the `access.conf` file must allow user authentication and authorization to be set up in a `.htaccess` file. This is controlled by the `AuthConfig` override. In particular, the `access.conf` file must include `AllowOverride AuthConfig` to allow user authentication and authorization in `.htaccess` files. In the explanations that follow, we assume the `AuthConfig` override is included in the Web server's access configuration file.

To restrict a directory to any user listed in the user file just created, you must create a `.htaccess` file that may look as follows:

```
AuthName "Rolf Oppliger's Protected Area"
AuthType Basic
AuthUserFile /usr/local/etc/httpd/users

require valid-user
```

The first directive, `AuthName`, specifies a realm name for the protected directory. The name is used by the browser to prompt the user to enter his or her username and password (as illustrated in Figure 2.1 and Figure 2.2 for Netscape Navigator and Microsoft Internet Explorer). In this example, the realm name is `Rolf Oppliger's Protected Area`. Once a user has entered a valid username and password (one that is contained in the corresponding user file), any other resources within the same realm can be accessed with the same username and password. As discussed previously in this chapter, the browser simply retransmits the username and password without prompting the user to enter authentication information again. The second directive, `AuthType`, tells the Web server what scheme to use for user authentication (`Basic` or `Digest`). The third directive, `AuthUserFile`, informs the Web server about the actual location of the user file created with the `htpasswd` program. Finally, a fourth directive, `AuthGroupFile`, may be used to inform the server about the location of a group file. This directive is not used in the example given above.

So far, the directives tell the server where to find the user and group files and what authentication scheme to use. The final stage is to tell the server which usernames from the user file are valid for particular access methods. This is done with the `require` directive. In the example given above, the argument `valid-user` tells the server that any username and password in the user file can be used to access the realm. However, the realm could also be configured to allow only certain users in. For example, the line

```
require user Isabelle Rolf
```

would only allow the users Isabelle and Rolf to access the realm (after proper authentication). If user Bob (or any other user) wanted to access the same realm — even with a correct password — access would be denied. This is useful to restrict different areas (realms) of your server to different people defined within the same user file. A user authorized to access different realms, must still remember only a single password.

If you want to grant access to a particular realm only to specific users defined in the user file, you can list them in the `require` directive (as shown on the previous page). However, you then have to include user information into your .htaccess files. This may not be convenient if there are many users. Fortunately, there is a way around this, using a group file. This operates in a similar way to UNIX groups: any particular user can be a member of any number of groups. A group file consists of lines giving a group name followed by a space-separated list of users in that group. For example, two groups, `staff` and `admin`, are defined as follows:

```
staff:Isabelle Rolf
admin:Alice Bob Carol
```

Remember from the explanations given above that the `AuthGroupFile` directive is used to inform the Web server about the actual location of the group file. You then use the `require` directive to restrict users to one or more particular groups. For example, you can create a group called `staff` containing users who are allowed to access internal resources. To restrict access to just users in the `staff` group, you would require the following entry in the appropriate .htaccess file:

```
require group staff
```

Again, multiple groups can be listed, possibly together with `require user` directives. In this case, any user in any of the listed groups, or any user listed explicitly, can access the resources in the realm. For example, the entry

```
require group staff admin
require user adminuser
```

would allow any user in group `staff` or group `admin`, or the user `adminuser`, to access the resources after having entered a valid password.

Using the `htpasswd` program to create a list of users in a user file, and maintaining a list of groups in a corresponding group file is a relatively easy task. However, if the number of users becomes large, the server has a lot of processing to do in finding a user's authentication information. This processing must be done for every request to access the protected realm (even though the user only enters his or her password once, the server has to reauthenticate on every request). This can be slow with a lot of users, and adds to the Web server load. Much faster access is possible using so-called DBM format files. DBM format files are a simple and relatively standard method of storing information for quick retrieval. Each item of information stored in a DBM file consists of two parts: a key and a corresponding value. If you know the key, you can access and retrieve the corresponding value very quickly. The DBM file maintains an index of the keys, each of which points to where the value is stored within the file, and the index is usually arranged such that values are accessed with the minimum number of file system accesses even for very large numbers of keys. In practice, on many systems, a DBM file is actually stored in two files on the disk. If, for example, a DBM file called users is created, it will actually be stored in files called users.pag and users.dir. Some newer versions of DBM only create one file. Provided the key is known in advance DBM format files are a very efficient way of accessing information associated with that key. For user authentication, the key is the username, and the value stores their (encrypted) password. Looking up usernames and their passwords in a DBM file is more efficient than using a plaintext file when more than a few users are involved. This is particularly important for Web servers sites with lots of users (say, over 10,000), or where there are lots of accesses to authenticated pages.

In addition to DBM format files, user and group lists can also be stored in other database formats. It is even possible to have an arbitrary external program check whether the given username and password are valid (this could be used to write an interface to check against any other database or authentication service). Modules are also available to check against the system password file, or to use a Kerberos authentication system.

In the exemplary .htaccess file given above, the require directive is not put inside a <Limit> section. In general, a <Limit> section is established between the <Limit> and </Limit> directives. It can be used to establish an access control policy for the directory. The format is <Limit X Y ...>, where each of the parameters is one of the HTTP access methods GET, POST, PUT, or DELETE. Clients that try to use one of the listed methods are restricted according to the rules listed within the section. If no method is listed, the restrictions apply to all methods. In most Web servers and .htaccess files, the require directive may be used inside a <Limit> section. The following example illustrates this point:

```
AuthName "Rolf Oppliger's Protected Area"
```

```
AuthType Basic
AuthUserFile /...

<Limit>
   require valid-user
</Limit>
```

In this example, the restrictions apply to all HTTP methods. To limit access to the POST method, the following sequence is used:

```
AuthName "Rolf Oppliger's Protected Area"
AuthType Basic
AuthUserFile /...

<Limit POST>
   require group staff
</Limit>
```

Now only members of the group staff will be allowed to POST. Other users (also unauthenticated ones) can still use other methods, such as GET. This could be used to allow a CGI program to be accessed by anyone, but only authorized users can post information to it.

2.6 CONCLUSIONS

As of this writing, most Web server software packages can be used to authenticate and authorize users that request resources, and to control access to these resources accordingly. For example, it is always possible to use hidden URLs or to restrict access to a particular group of computers based on those computers' address information (IP addresses or DNS hostnames). In addition, it is also possible to employ one of the HTTP user authentication and authorization schemes that are described in this chapter: HTTP basic authentication (specified for HTTP/1.0) and HTTP digest authentication (specified for HTTP/1.1). Unfortunately, HTTP digest authentication is rarely implemented in browser software. This is because HTTP digest authentication is always less secure than a full-fledged cryptographic security protocol, such as SSL or TLS. Consequently, most browsers implement SSL or TLS and leave beside HTTP digest authentication. As introduced in this chapter and further addressed in Chapter 6, SSL and TLS employ certificate-based authentication mechanisms.

In addition to proper HTTP user authentication and authorization, it may be equally important to protect the confidentiality, integrity, and authenticity of data in transmission, as well as to provide non-repudiation services for communicating peers. These issues are addressed in subsequent chapters of this book.

REFERENCES

[1] S. Garfinkel, and E.H. Spafford, *Web Security & Commerce*, O'Reilly & Associates, Sebastopol, CA, 1996.

[2] A.D. Rubin, D. Geer, and M.J. Ranum, *Web Security Sourcebook*, John Wiley & Sons, Inc., New York, NY, 1997.

[3] T. Berners-Lee, R. Fielding, and H. Frystyk, "Hypertext Transfer Protocol - HTTP/1.0," Request for Comments 1945, May 1996.

[4] R. Fielding, J. Gettys, J. Mogul, H. Frystyk, and T. Berners-Lee, "Hypertext Transfer Protocol - HTTP/1.1," Request for Comments 2068, January 1997.

[5] J. Franks, P. Hallam-Baker, J. Hostetler, P. Leach, A. Luotonen, E. Sink, and L. Stewart, "An Extension to HTTP: Digest Access Authentication," Request for Comments 2069, January 1997.

[6] R.L. Rivest, and S. Dusse, "The MD5 Message-Digest Algorithm," Request for Comments 1321, April 1992.

[7] B. Laurie, and P. Lauried, *Apache: The Definitive Guide*, O'Reilly & Associates, Sebastopol, CA, 1997.

Chapter 3

Proxy Servers and Firewalls

In this chapter, we address the implications of proxy servers and firewalls for Web-based applications. After a brief introduction in Section 3.1, we address packet filtering and stateful inspection in Section 3.2, circuit-level gateways in Section 3.3, as well as application-level gateways and proxy servers in Section 3.4. In Section 3.5, we overview and discuss some firewall configurations. In Section 3.6, we elaborate on possibilities to configure a browser to make use of proxy servers, whereas in Section 3.7, we conclude with a discussion of the firewall technology as a whole. Note that the focus of this chapter is on getting out of a firewall from a corporate intranet. This is the usual situation one faces when dealing with firewalls. For mobile users and remote workers, however, the situation is completely different and their primary focus is on getting through a firewall from the Internet. This leads to reverse proxies and the need for strong authentication mechanisms. The use of reverse proxies is further addressed in Chapter 6. Also note that parts of this chapter are taken from [1]. Refer to part two of [1] for a more comprehensive overview and discussion of the firewall technology.

41

3.1 INTRODUCTION

While Internet connectivity offers enormous benefits in terms of increased availability and access to information, Internet connectivity is not always a good thing, especially for sites with low levels of security. As we discussed in Chapter 1, the Internet suffers from glaring security problems that, if ignored, could have disastrous impacts for unprepared sites. Inherent problems with TCP/IP protocols and services, the complexity of host and site configuration, vulnerabilities introduced in the software development process, as well as a wide variety of other factors all contribute to making unprepared Web sites open for intruder activities and other security-related threats. For example, host systems and access controls are usually difficult to configure and test for correctness. As a result, they are often accidentally misconfigured, and this may result in intruders gaining unauthorized and illegitimate access to system resources. To make things worse, some vendors still ship their systems with access controls configured for maximum (i.e., least secure access), which can result in unauthorized and illegitimate access if left as is. Furthermore, a number of security incidents have occurred that are due in part to vulnerabilities discovered by intruders. Since many UNIX systems have their network code derived from BSD UNIX that is publicly available in source code, intruders have been able to study the code for bugs and error conditions that may be exploited to gain unauthorized and illegitimate access. The bugs exist in part because of the complexity of the software, and the inability to test it under all circumstances and in all environments. Sometimes the bugs are discovered and corrected; other times, however, little can be done except to rewrite the entire code, which is usually the option of last resort.

As a consequence, host security is hard to achieve and does not scale well in the sense that as the number of hosts increases, the ability to ensure that security is at a high level for each host decreases. Given the fact that secure management of a single system is already a demanding task, managing many such systems can easily result in mistakes and omissions. A contributing factor is that the role of system administration is often undervalued and performed in a rush. As a result, some systems will be less secure than others, and these systems will be the ones that ultimately break the security of either a Web site or an entire intranet environment.

As already mentioned in the introduction, this book does not address host and site security. There was an Internet Engineering Task Force (IETF) Site Security Handbook (SSH) Working Group (WG) chartered within the User Services Area. The IETF SSH WG revised and updated the site security handbook that was originally published in 1991 [2] in a document referenced as RFC 2196 and FYI 8 [3].

In addition, the WG has also produced [4].

In days of old, brick walls were built between buildings in apartment complexes so that if a fire broke out, it would not spread from one building to another. Quite naturally, these walls were called "firewalls." Today, when a private network is connected to a public network, its users are usually enabled to reach and communicate with the outside world. At the same time, however, the outside world can also reach and interact with the private network. In this dangerous situation, an intermediate system can be plugged between the private network and the public network to establish a controlled link, and to erect a security wall or perimeter. The aim of this intermediate system is to protect the private network from network-based attacks that may originate from the outside world, and to provide a single choke point where security and audit may be imposed. Note that all traffic in and out of the private network can be enforced to pass through this checkpoint. Also note that this checkpoint provides a good place to collect information about system and network use and misuse. In fact, the intermediate system may record all events that occur between the private network and the outside world.

Quite naturally, these intermediate systems are called *firewall systems*, or *firewalls* in short.[1] A firewall represents a blockade between a privately owned and protected intranet (that is assumed to be secure and trusted) and another network, typically a publicly owned network or an internet (that is assumed to be nonsecure and untrusted). The purpose of the firewall is to prevent unwanted and unauthorized communications into or out of the protected network.

In addition to the physical firewall analogy mentioned above, there are other analogies that may help to better understand and motivate for the use of firewalls:

- Passports are generally checked at the border of a country;

- Apartments are usually locked at the entrance and not necessarily at each door within each unit;

- Similarly, offices don't usually have a door to the outside world;

- And yet, a bank still has a vault to store money and valuable goods.

Other analogies include the toll booth on a bridge, the ticket booth at a movie theatre, and the checkout line at the supermarket. These analogies and the first three analogies itemized above illustrate that it sometimes makes a lot of sense to

---

[1]In other literature, Internet firewalls are sometimes referred to as "secure Internet gateways" or "security gateways." We are not going to use these alternative terms in this book.

aggregate security functions at a single point. As well, the bank analogy illustrates that additional security precautions may be required under certain circumstances. Note that a firewall is conceptually similar to locking the doors of a house or employing a doorperson. The objective is to ensure that only properly authenticated and authorized people are able to physically enter the house. Unfortunately, this protection is not foolproof and can be defeated with enough effort. The basic idea is to make the effort too hard for the average burglar, so that he or she will eventually go away and find another target. However, just in case the burglar does not go away and somehow manages to enter the house, we lock up our valuable goods in a safe. According to this analogy, the use of a firewall may not always be sufficient, especially in the high-security environments we typically live in these days.

In their famous book on firewalls and Internet security, William R. Cheswick and Steven M. Bellovin define a firewall (system) as a collection of components placed between two networks that collectively have the following properties [5]:

- All traffic from inside to outside, and vice versa, must pass through the firewall;

- Only authorized traffic, as defined by the local security policy, will be allowed to pass;

- The firewall itself is immune to penetration.

These properties are design goals. A failure in one aspect does not necessarily mean that the collection is not a firewall, but simply that it is not a good one. Consequently, there are different grades of security that a firewall can achieve. Note that there must be a (local) security policy for the firewall to enforce.

Another way to define a firewall was created by the Swiss Federal Strategy Unit for Information Technology (FSUIT) as part of its network security policy (NSP). According to this policy, a system is considered a firewall if it is able to fulfill the following requirements:

- Users who wish to establish (inbound or outbound[2]) connections must be strongly authenticated;

---

[2]In this book, the terms "inbound" and "outbound" are used to refer to connections or IP packets from the point of view of the protected network, which is typically an intranet. Consequently, an outbound connection is a connection initiated from a client on an internal machine to a server running on an external machine. Note that while the connection as a whole is outbound, it includes both outbound IP packets (those from the internal client to the external server) and inbound IP packets (those from the external server to the internal client). Similarly, an inbound connection is one that is initiated from a client on an external machine to a server on an internal

- Data and data streams that are allowed to pass through the firewall must be associated with previously authenticated and authorized users.

Again, it is a policy decision whether data is allowed to pass through the firewall or not. So this definition also leads to the necessity of an explicit firewall policy. Later in this chapter, we distinguish between packet filters and application gateways. It is interesting to note at this point that the second definition explicitly requires the use of application gateways. Since application gateways operate at a higher layer in a communications protocol stack, they typically have access to more information than simple packet filters, and can therefore be programmed to operate more intelligently and to be more secure. Some vendors, for marketing reasons perhaps, blur the distinction between a packet filter and a firewall to the extent that they call any packet-filtering device a firewall. For the sake of clarity, however, we make a clear distinction between packet filters (operating at the network or Internet layer) and firewalls (operating at some higher layer) in this book. This distinction is emphasized by the second definition given above. The definition can be applied not only to TCP/IP-based firewalls, but to modem pools with serial line interfaces and remote access servers that provide support for strong user authentication and authorization, as well.

From a more pragmatic point of view, a firewall refers to a collection of hardware, software, policy, and the operational procedures (that implement the policy) that is placed between a private network, typically a corporate intranet, and an external network, typically the Internet. As such, the firewall implements parts of a network security policy by forcing all data traffic to be directed or routed to the firewall, where it can be examined and evaluated accordingly. In essence, a firewall seeks to prevent unwanted and unauthorized communications into or out of a corporate intranet, and to allow an organization to enforce a network security policy on data traffic flowing between its intranet and the Internet. Typically, a firewall also requires its users to strongly authenticate themselves before any further action is deployed. The second definition given above makes this requirement mandatory for a firewall system to provide. In this case, strong authentication mechanisms are used to replace password-based and address-based authentication mechanisms.

The general reasoning behind firewall usage is that without a firewall, a site is more exposed to inherently insecure host operating systems, TCP/IP protocols and

---

machine. Following this terminology, the inbound interface for an IP packet refers to the physical network interface on a router that the packet actually appeared on, while the outbound interface refers to the physical network interface the packet will go out on if it isn't denied by the application of a specific packet filter rule.

services, as well as probes and attacks from the Internet. In an environment without a firewall, network security is totally a function of each host, and all hosts must, in a sense, cooperate to achieve a uniformly high level of security. The larger the network, the less manageable it usually is to maintain all hosts at the same level of security. As mistakes and lapses in security become more common, break-ins occur not only as a result of complex attacks, but also because of simple errors in configuration files and inadequately chosen passwords. Assuming that software is buggy, we conclude that most host systems have bugs, vulnerabilities, and security holes that may eventually be exploited by intruders. Contrary to conventional hosts, firewalls are designed to run less software, and hence potentially have fewer bugs, vulnerabilities, and security holes. In addition, firewalls generally have advanced logging and monitoring facilities and can be professionally administered. With firewall usage, only a few hosts are exposed to direct attacks from the Internet.

Later in this chapter, we discuss the advantages and disadvantages of firewall technology as a whole. Probably the main disadvantage is that a firewall can't protect a site or corporate intranet against insider attacks. For that matter, internal firewalls may be used to control access between different administration and security domains, or to protect sensitive parts of a corporate intranet. Internal firewalls are sometimes called *intranet firewalls*. From a purely technical point of view, there is nothing that distinguishes an intranet firewall from an Internet firewall except for the policy it enforces. Consequently, we are not going to differentiate between intranet and Internet firewalls in the rest of this book.

There are many books that cover firewall technology. As a matter of fact, most books that have addressed Internet and intranet security in the past are actually books on firewalls [5 – 7], or put much emphasis on firewall technology [8]. There are also some scientific papers and reports available that address specific topics related to firewalls [9,10]. The design of a former firewall configuration at AT&T is described in [5,11], and the design of the DEC Screening External Access Link (SEAL) firewall configuration is addressed in [12].[3] Meanwhile, the US National Institute of Standards and Technology (NIST) has also started activities related to the Internet and security-related problems. In particular, it has made publicly available a document that provides a basic overview of firewall components and the general reasoning behind firewall usage [13]. In Europe, the German Information Security Agency (GISA) has expanded its IT Baseline Protection Manual with a section that covers firewall technology [14]. Finally, there is a Ph.D. thesis written by Christoph L. Schuba [15]. According to this thesis, *firewall technology* refers to

---

[3]The DEC SEAL firewall was marketed by DEC in the early 1990s.

a set of mechanisms that can enforce a network security policy on communication traffic entering or leaving a domain, whereas a *firewall system* (or firewall) is an instantiation of the firewall technology. The thesis also proposes a reference model for firewall technology that focuses on functionality provided by firewall systems to enforce network domain security policies.

In the sections that follow, we focus on technologies that are used to build and configure firewalls. In particular, we address packet filtering and stateful inspection, circuit-level gateways, as well as application-level gateways and proxy servers.

3.2 PACKET FILTERING AND STATEFUL INSPECTION

In general, a *router* is an internetworking device that runs a custom operating system to transfer packets between two or more physically separated network segments.[4] It operates at the network layer in the OSI reference model, or the Internet layer in the Internet model, respectively. As such, it routes IP packets by consulting tables that indicate the best path the packet should take to reach its final destination. More precisely, a router receives an IP packet on one network interface and forwards it on another network interface, possibly in the direction of the destination IP address. If the router knows on what interface to forward the packet, it does so. Otherwise, if it is not able to route the packet, it usually returns the packet using an Internet control management protocol (ICMP) destination unreachable message to its source IP address.

Because every IP packet contains a source and destination IP address, packets bound for a particular host or network segment can be selectively filtered by a packet filtering device. Also, transport layer protocols, such as TCP or UDP, generally add source and destination port numbers to each message as part of their header information. These port numbers indicate which processes on each side of the communication will finally receive the message encapsulated within the IP packet. This information can also be used to make some more intelligent packet filtering decisions.

A *packet filter* is a multiported internetworking device that applies a set of rules to each incoming IP packet in order to decide whether it will be forwarded or dropped. IP packets are filtered based on information usually found in packet headers, such as

---

[4]In spite of the fact that most routers in use today are able to route multiple protocols, we mainly focus on IP routing in this book. This is because IP is by far the most dominant network layer protocol used within the Internet and the WWW.

- Protocol numbers;

- Source and destination IP addresses;

- Source and destination port numbers;

- TCP connection flags;

- Other options.

Routers that support packet filtering (and are able to screen and selectively filter IP packets accordingly) are sometimes also referred to as *screening routers*. Many commercial router products provide the capability to screen IP packets and to filter them in accordance with a set of packet filter rules. These router products are actually screening routers. For example, Cisco routers use a fairly simple syntax to define packet filter rules. Each network interface on a Cisco router is assigned an access group, which is basically an integer number referencing the interface. Packet filtering commands for that interface are then expressed in access lists[5] that are associated with access groups. The router, in turn, matches each IP packet routed to a particular network interface against the access lists associated with the access group of that particular network interface.

Note that a screening router is always a packet filter, whereas the opposite is not always true. A packet filter may not be able to route IP packets, so a packet filter is not necessarily a screening router. Also note that packet filters are stateless, meaning that each IP packet is examined isolated from what has happened in the past, forcing the filter to make a decision to permit or deny each packet based upon the packet filter rules. This behavior is sometimes also referred to as *static packet filtering*, meaning that the packet filter rules are static and context-insensitive.

There are some practical problems related to the use of static packet filtering. For example, consider an FTP session initiated by a client running on an internal machine (a machine located inside the packet filtering device). The FTP session basically consists of two TCP connections:

- An outbound control connection initiated by the client;

- An inbound data connection initiated by the server.

---

[5]More precisely, Cisco routers provide support for two types of access lists: standard access lists and extended access lists. Refer to the corresponding product documentation for more information on this topic.

The outbound connection is initiated by the client from a random port to the FTP server control port 21, whereas the inbound connection is initiated by the FTP server data port 20 to a specific port on the client side. More precisely, the client informs the server about the port number it should use to connect to for the inbound connection by using an FTP PORT command (the port number being an argument for that command). To open the data connection, the server establishes a TCP connection to that particular port. Consequently, the packet filtering device will see an inbound TCP segment trying to establish an inbound connection. Most packet filters are configured to discard these kinds of TCP segments and drop the corresponding IP packets accordingly.

From the packet filter's point of view, the problem of FTP exists because the data connection is inbound, meaning that it is established from an external server to an internal client. The problem is trivially solvable if both connections (the FTP control connection and the FTP data connection) are established outbound. Following this line of argumentation, *passive mode FTP* has been proposed as a preliminary solution in a corresponding RFC [16]. In passive mode FTP, instead of sending out an FTP PORT command, the client waits for the server to specify a particular port number and establishes an outbound TCP connection to that particular port. As a result, any packet filter sitting between the client and the server experiences two outbound TCP connections (instead of one outbound and one inbound connection, as in the case of normal mode FTP). In general, the network security policy that drives the packet filtering device allows outbound connections to be established at will and tolerates passive mode FTP accordingly.

In summary, passive mode FTP represents a viable solution for intelligently filtering FTP traffic. It is, however, not a general solution and other application protocols may come up with different problems that can't be addressed with passive mode. A more general solution to the problem was developed and proposed by the firewall market leader, CheckPoint Software Technologies Ltd.,[6] for its FireWall-1 product. In this solution, a technology called *stateful inspection* was suggested to introduce some state into the packet filtering process. Consequently, the resulting packet filter rules are dynamic and context-sensitive, the first attribute also being reflected in the term *dynamic packet filtering* that is sometimes used as a synonym for stateful inspection.

In short, stateful inspection (or dynamic packet filtering) looks at the same header information as static packet filtering does, but can also peek into the payload data where the transport and application layer data usually appear. More

---

[6]http://www.checkpoint.com

importantly, stateful inspection maintains state information about past IP packets. It compares the first packet in a TCP connection to the packet filter rules, and if the packet is permitted, state information is added to an internal database. Think of this state information as representing an internal virtual circuit in the firewall on top of the transport layer association. This information permits subsequent packets in that association to pass quickly through the firewall. If the rules for a specific type of service require examining application data, then part of each packet must still be examined. For example, a dynamic packet filtering device (e.g., a FireWall-1 product) can react to seeing an FTP PORT command by creating a dynamic rule permitting a TCP connection back from the FTP server to that particular port number on the client side. Logging, or authentication as required by the rules, generally occurs at the application layer. Although the opportunity for better logging is present, stateful inspection firewalls typically only log the source and destination IP addresses and port numbers, similar to logging with a packet filter or screening router. Today, several router vendors, including Cisco, are exploiting adding stateful inspection to their products.

In spite of the fact that you can introduce state information to improve the capabilities of a packet filtering device, the problem remains that there is no such thing as an association between a data stream and a previously authenticated and authorized user (as required, for example, in our second definition for a firewall system). To make things worse, there is no such thing as a user on the Internet layer where packet filtering occurs. Consequently, true firewalls must operate above the Internet layer, typically at the transport or application layer.

In general networking terminology, an *application gateway* or *gateway* refers to an internetworking device that connects one network to another for a specific application. Therefore, the gateway must understand and implement the corresponding application protocol. In the client/server model, a gateway refers to an intermediate process running between the client that requests a particular service and the server that provides the service. In this model, the gateway functions as a server from the client's point of view, and as a client from the server's point of view. In general, a gateway either works at the application layer or at the transport layer:

- If the gateway works at the application layer, it is usually called an *application-level gateway*, or *proxy server* in short.

- If the gateway works at the transport layer, it is usually called a *circuit-level gateway*.

Most gateways used in firewall configurations work at the application layer and actually represent application-level gateways or proxy servers. In either case, the application gateway runs on a firewall host and performs a specific function as a proxy on the user's behalf. If the application gateway is an application-level gateway, then the function is application-specific. Otherwise, the function is not application-specific and the application gateway is actually a circuit-level gateway. In the following two sections, we address circuit-level gateway and application-level gateways or proxy servers in more depth.

3.3   CIRCUIT-LEVEL GATEWAYS

The idea of a *circuit-level gateway* is fundamentally different from packet filtering (either static or dynamic packet filtering). In essence, a circuit-level gateway takes a TCP connection request from a client, authenticates and authorizes the client, and establishes a second TCP connection to the origin server on the client's behalf. After having successfully established this second TCP connection, the circuit-level gateway simply relays data forth and back between the two connections. In particular, it does not interfere with the data stream. This differentiates a circuit-level gateway from an application-level gateway or proxy server that is able to actually understand the application protocol employed by the two endpoints of the connection.

The single circuit-level gateway that is actually in widespread use is *SOCKS*.[7] SOCKS follows a customized client approach, meaning that it requires customizations and modifications to client software, but no change is usually required to user procedures. More precisely, SOCKS requires modifications either to the client software or the TCP/IP stack to accommodate the interception at the firewall between the client and the server:

- A client that has been modified to handle SOCKS interactions is commonly referred to as a socksified client. Following this terminology, Netscape Navigator and Microsoft Internet Explorer are socksified HTTP clients, as they accommodate interactions with a SOCKS server. A socksified client issues SOCKS calls that are transparent to the users.

- Socksified TCP/IP stacks are also available, which may obviate the need for client software modifications.

---

[7]http://www.socks.nec.com

In either case, the SOCKS server resides at the firewall and interacts with the socksified clients or TCP/IP stacks. There are no further changes required for the servers that reside on the Internet or intranet.

Table 3.1
Socket Calls and SOCKS Counterparts

SOCKS Call	Socket Call
Rconnect	connect
Rbind	bind
Rlisten	listen
Rselect	select
Rgetsockname	getsockname
Raccept	accept

SOCKS and the SOCKS protocol for communications between a socksified client and a SOCKS server were originally developed by David and Michelle Koblas in 1992 [17]. Today, there are also several SOCKS software packages publicly and freely available on the Internet.[8] They typically consist of two components: a SOCKS server or daemon called socksd, and a SOCKS library that can be used to replace regular Socket calls in the client software. More precisely, you recompile and link the client software with a few preprocessor directives to intercept and replace the regular TCP/IP networking Socket calls with their SOCKS counterparts, as summarized in Table 3.1.

The design goal of SOCKS was to provide a general framework for TCP/IP applications to securely use the services of a firewall. Complying with these design goals, SOCKS is independent of any supported TCP/IP application protocol. When a socksified client requires access to an Internet server, it must first open a TCP connection to the appropriate port on the SOCKS server residing on the firewall system. The SOCKS server is conventionally located on TCP port 1,080. If the TCP connection is established, the client sends a connection relay request to the SOCKS server. This request includes the following information:

• Desired destination address;

• Desired destination port;

• Authentication information.

---

[8] ftp://ftp.nec.com/pub/socks or ftp://ftp.cup.hp.com/dist/socks/socks.tar.gz

The SOCKS server evaluates the information in the connection relay request. During this evaluation, it may perform various functions, such as authentication, authorization, message security-level negotiation, and so on. The SOCKS server either accepts the request and establishes a corresponding connection to the Internet application server, or rejects the request. The evaluation depends on the configuration data of the SOCKS server. In either case, the SOCKS server sends a reply back to the client. Among other things, the reply includes information indicating whether the request was successful. Once the requested connection is established, the SOCKS server simply relays data between the client and server.

There are currently two versions of SOCKS available: SOCKS version 4 and SOCKS version 5. SOCKS V4 has been widely used in firewall systems. However, as SOCKS evolves from version 4 to version 5, the application scope of SOCKS has also been extended. Firewall is just one, a traditional one, of the SOCKS V5 applications. Today, work on SOCKS V5 is mainly driven by the NEC Corporation.[9] Also, the SOCKS V5 protocol is being standardized by the IETF Authenticated Firewall Traversal (AFT) WG and specified in [18].

As compared to SOCKS V4, the current version 5 of SOCKS provides some additional functionality:

- SOCKS V5 supports a handshake between the client and the SOCKS server for authentication method negotiation. The first message is sent by the client to the SOCKS server. It declares the authentication methods the client is currently able to support. The second message is sent from the SOCKS server back to the client. It selects a particular authentication method according to the SOCKS server's security policy. If none of the methods declared by the client meets the security requirements of the SOCKS server, communications are dropped.

- After the authentication method has been negotiated, the client and SOCKS server start the authentication process using the chosen method. Two authentication methods are specified in corresponding RFCs: password-based authentication [19] and Kerberos V5 GSS-API authentication [20]. Kerberos and the generic security service application programming interface (GSS-API) are further addressed in [21]. The approach for use of GSS-API in SOCKS V5 is to authenticate the client and server by successfully establishing a security context. This context can then be used to protect messages that are subsequently exchanged. Prior to use of GSS-API primitives, the client and server should be locally authenticated and have established default GSS-API credentials.

---

[9]SOCKS5 and SOCKS5Toolkit are registered trademarks of NEC Corporation.

- Depending on the underlying authentication methods implemented via GSS-API, a client can negotiate with the SOCKS server about the security of subsequent messages. In the case of Kerberos V5, either integrity and/or confidentiality services are provided for the rest of messages, including the client's proxy request, the SOCKS server's replies, and all application data. Note that this feature is well suited for use by reverse proxy servers, since it supports data encryption between clients (on the Internet) and the SOCKS server.

- One of the connection requests in SOCKS V5 is for a UDP association that results in a virtual proxy circuit for traversing UDP-based application data. The approach is conceptually similar to stateful inspection, as it occurs on the Internet layer. As a result, the SOCKS V5 library can be used to socksify both TCP- and UDP-based applications, while the SOCKS V4 library can only be used to socksify TCP-based applications.

Due to their fundamental differences, the SOCKS V5 protocol specification does not require any provision for supporting the SOCKS V4 protocol. However, it is a simple matter of implementation to enable SOCKS V5 servers to communicate with V5 and V4 clients and servers. For example, the NEC Corporation has made publicly available a SOCKS V5 reference implementation for both UNIX and Windows NT that supports the SOCKS V4 protocol as well. Also, the implementation supports the two authentication methods mentioned above, and has a built-in address resolution proxy that enables clients to be fully operational without having DNS support. A client can pass the DNS name, instead of the resolved IP address, to the SOCKS server and the server will resolve the address on the client's behalf.

Finally, note that the only difference between a circuit-level gateway and a simple port forwarding mechanism is that with a circuit-level gateway, the client is aware of the intermediate system, whereas in the case of a port forwarding mechanism, the client may be completely oblivious of the existence of the intermediary. Also, a circuit-level gateway is generic, and any TCP connection can be handled by the same gateway (if enabled in its configuration). Contrary to that, a port forwarding mechanism is usually specific to a specific service, meaning that all qualifying TCP segments are forwarded to a specific port of the destination server.

3.4   APPLICATION-LEVEL GATEWAYS AND PROXY SERVERS

An *application-level gateway* or *proxy server* is conceptually similar to a circuit-level gateway.[10] The main difference is that the former understands the application protocol being relayed, whereas the second is generic and not application-specific. Consequently, a specific application-level gateway or proxy server is implemented for each application protocol a firewall must support. In the rest of this chapter, we use the terms application-level gateway and proxy server synonymously and interchangeably.

Typically, when a client contacts an application-level gateway using one of the TCP/IP application protocols, such as Telnet, FTP, or HTTP, the gateway asks for some valid user authentication and authorization information. In the easiest case, this information simply consists of a username and a corresponding password. However, if the proxy server is accessible from the Internet, it is strongly recommended to use some strong authentication mechanisms, such as provided by one-time passwords (e.g., SecurID) or challenge-response systems (e.g., S/Key and OPIE). If the proxy server accepts the user authentication and authorization information, it either connects to a preconfigured remote system, such as an SMTP or LDAP server, or asks the user to enter the name of a remote system to be accessed on the user's behalf, such as an FTP or Web server. In the second case, it is up to the user to respond accordingly and to provide the name of a remote system. The proxy server, in turn, contacts the remote system and establishes a secondary TCP connection to that system. After having established the secondary TCP connection, the proxy server fully controls the data stream that is being relayed between the two connections. In particular, the proxy server can scan the data stream for specific protocol commands or data contents, as well as enforce specific restrictions on inbound and outbound data traffic. For example, the former DEC SEAL firewall could be configured so that outbound FTP traffic was restricted to authorized users and to a limited bandwidth. The intent here was to prevent theft of valuable programs or data. While of limited utility against insiders who could easily copy the desired files on removable storage media, the technique is useful and effective against intruders who lack physical access.

In order to properly authenticate a user, an application-level gateway or proxy server must have access to some identification and authentication information. In

---

[10]The term "proxy server" was also chosen to better reflect the fact that it acts on behalf of the client. Note, however, that the client must always know that it is using a SOCKS server, whereas it does not have to know that it is using a proxy server. This point is further addressed when we talk about transparent proxying later in this chapter.

principle, this information can be either locally stored or remotely archived and made available through a security server. Obviously, the second approach is preferable, since it makes it possible to aggregate security management functions for several firewall systems and network access servers (NAS) at a single point. Typically, a standardized protocol is used to retrieve the information required to authenticate and authorize users from a security server. There are two competing proposals for such a protocol:

- Livingston Enterprises, Inc. has developed a protocol named remote authentication dial-in user service (RADIUS) [22]. In short, the RADIUS protocol can be used to carry authentication, authorization, and configuration information between an NAS that desires to authenticate its users and a shared authentication or security server. Livingston Enterprises, Inc. has also made publicly and freely available RADIUS security server software. A companion protocol that can be used to carry accounting information between a NAS and a shared authentication or security server is specified in [23].

- Cisco has developed a similar family of protocols for the terminal access controller access control system (TACACS) [24], extended TACACS (XTACACS), and TACACS+. Refer to the Cisco manuals for the corresponding TACACS, XTACACS, and TACACS+ commands.

Both protocols (RADIUS and the protocol family for the TACACS derivates) are widely supported by commercial firewall systems and network access servers today. They are not further addressed in this book.

In general, the entire process of contacting an application-level gateway before connecting to the origin server can be made transparent. In this context, the term "transparent proxying" is usually used in two different meanings:

- The more traditional meaning of transparent proxying is that a user will not see or experience any difference in whether his or her requests are made directly to the origin server(s) or through a proxy server. The mechanism to implement transparent proxying is to provide users with modified client software that is able to establish the required connections on the users' behaves. We have said that SOCKS is using this approach.

- In addition, a new meaning of transparent proxying has recently been introduced. In this case, transparent proxying means that the client software must not be aware of the proxy servers that may be running on intermediate systems.

Note that traditional client software usually is aware that it's talking to proxy servers, since their use is typically configured in the client software (the client software has to make the distinction between direct requests and requests made through a proxy server). In transparent proxying, however, the access router is configured to redirect any request for an origin server located on the Internet to the proxy server. This allows the proxy server to intercept all HTTP requests that are targeted at some origin server on the Internet.

The second notion of transparent proxying leaves both the user and the client completely unaware of the existence of an intermediate proxy server. As of this writing, a steadily increasing number of firewall vendors offer application-level gateways with corresponding proxy servers that provide support for transparent proxying in the second meaning mentioned above.

3.5 FIREWALL CONFIGURATIONS

The Internet community uses the term *bastion host* to refer to a computer system that is part of a firewall configuration and hosts one or several application gateways. The term "bastion" comes from the heavily fortified projections on the exteriors of castles in medieval times. A bastion host should be configured to be particularly secure, since it is exposed to direct attacks from the Internet. Typically, a bastion host is located in a secure environment by residing on a secure operating system. In this case, the secure operating system must protect the firewall code and files from outside attacks. More often than not, the firewall code is the only application that is permitted to execute on the bastion host. Absence of other applications reduces the possibility of unauthorized attempts to penetrate the firewall. In spite of the fact that most bastion hosts run a modified and downstripped version of the UNIX operating system, there is increasing demand for Windows NT-based firewalls. Also, there are some firewalls that come along with a special and highly secure operating system. One example of this kind is the Sidewinder firewall developed and marketed by the Secure Computing Corporation.[11]

In general, a firewall system consists of (static or dynamic) packet filters and application gateways (either circuit-level gateways or application-level gateways). There are many possibilities to combine these components in firewall configurations, and two exemplary configurations are overviewed and discussed next. The two configurations — screened subnet firewalls and dual-homed firewalls — are most

---

[11]http://www.securecomputing.com

commonly used in practice today. Refer to [7] for a more comprehensive treatment of possible firewall configurations and for some practical advice.

3.5.1   Screened Subnet Firewalls

Figure 3.1 illustrates the architecture of a *screened subnet firewall* configuration. In short, a screened subnet firewall consists of two screening routers used to create an outer network segment that is also called a screened subnet or demilitarized zone (DMZ).[12] The DMZ may host application gateways running on one or more bastion hosts, as well as some additional servers that require carefully controlled Internet access (i.e., public HTTP servers). In addition to the outer network segment, there may be also an inner network segment that is separated from the outer network segment with a screening router. Internal servers may be running on machines connected to the inner network segment.

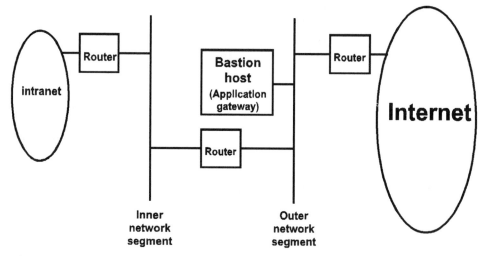

Figure 3.1   The architecture of a screened subnet firewall configuration.

Note that the two screening routers provide redundancy in that an attacker would have to subvert both routers in order to reach internal machines. Also note that the bastion host and the additional servers on the DMZ could be set up to be the only systems seen from the Internet; no other system name would be known or used in a DNS database that is made accessible to the outside world.

---

[12]The DMZ is named after the strip of no-man's-land between North and South Korea.

A screened subnet firewall configuration can be made more flexible by permitting certain services to pass around the bastion host and the corresponding application gateways. As an alternative to passing services directly between the intranet and Internet, you can also locate the systems that need these services directly on the screened subnet. We already mentioned that the DMZ may house servers that require carefully controlled Internet access in addition to the bastion host.

3.5.2   Dual-Homed Firewalls

In TCP/IP parlance, the term *multihomed host* is used to refer to a host with multiple network interfaces. Usually, each network interface is connected to a separate network segment and the multihomed host can either route or forward IP packets between those network segments. If, however, IP routing and IP forwarding are disabled on the multihomed host, it provides isolation between the network segments and may be used in a firewall configuration accordingly. To disable IP routing is usually a relatively simple and straightforward task. It basically means to turn off any program that might be advertising the host as a router. To disable IP forwarding is considerably more difficult, and may require modifying the operating system kernel. Fortunately, a number of UNIX vendors now provide supported parameters for turning off IP forwarding.

A *dual-homed host* is a special example of a multihomed host, namely one that has two network interfaces. Again, IP routing and IP forwarding are disabled to provide isolation between the two network segments the dual-homed host interconnects. A *dual-homed firewall* configuration is built around and makes use of a dual-homed host (bastion host).

Figure 3.2 illustrates the architecture of a dual-homed firewall configuration. In its simplest form, it consists of a dual-homed host with two network interfaces that serves as bastion host. IP forwarding and routing capabilities are disabled so that IP packets can no longer be routed between the two network segments. The application gateways are running on the bastion host. In addition, a screening router is typically placed between the bastion host and the Internet. In this configuration, the bastion host's external network interface is connected to an outer network segment that hosts a screening router, and this router, in turn, is connected to the Internet. The aim of the screening router is to ensure that any IP packet arriving from the Internet is correctly addressed to the bastion host. If a packet arrives with another destination IP address, it must be discarded. Note that the outer network segment between the bastion host and the external screening router can also host specialized systems, such as information or network access servers. Also note that some firewall configurations have a second screening router placed between the bastion host and the intranet. In this case, the bastion host's internal network interface is connected to an inner network segment that hosts another screening router. This router, in turn, is connected to the intranet (as illustrated in Figure 3.2). Note that the bastion host of a dual-homed firewall configuration can also be replicated for efficiency reasons. The resulting configuration is sometimes also called a *parallel dual-homed firewall*. It may consist of several bastion hosts that are all connected to both the inner and outer network segments. In this case, the various proxy and SOCKS servers may run on different hosts.

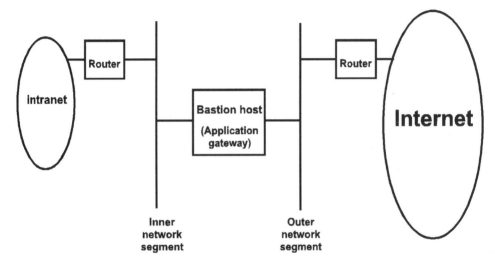

Figure 3.2   The architecture of a dual-homed firewall configuration.

In summary, the dual-homed firewall is a simple but secure configuration. As such, it is used and widely deployed within the Internet community. Unfortunately, there are also some practical problems related to the fact that until recently no proxy servers exist for nonstandardized TCP/IP application protocols, such as Lotus Notes, SQLnet, and some proprietary SAP protocols. In this case, the dual-homed firewall configuration turns out to be rather inflexible, and this inflexibility could turn out to be disadvantageous for some Web sites. Contrary to this, the screened subnet firewall configuration is more flexible but also less secure than the dual-homed firewall. Note that the application gateways can always be circumvented in this configuration. Consequently, where throughput and flexibility are important or required, a screened subnet firewall configuration may be the preferable choice.

3.6   CONFIGURING THE BROWSER

First of all, it is important to note that most parts of a firewall configuration are transparent and "invisible" to the Web user and his or her browser. For example, packet filters and screening routers operate on the IP packets originated or received by particular hosts without having the corresponding users be able to influence the packet filtering behavior. Similarly, a user doesn't have to care whether a firewall is configured as dual-homed or screened subnet. In fact, the browser configuration is the same in both cases.

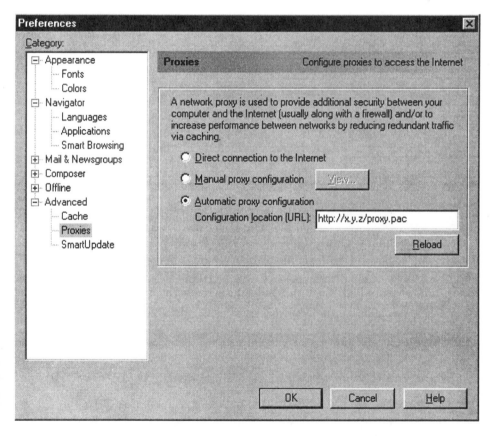

Figure 3.3   Configuring the use of proxies in Netscape Navigator. © 1999 Netscape Communications Corporation.

The only thing a Web user sitting behind a firewall system must do is configure his or her browser to properly interact with the proxy servers that may be running on the bastion host. The corresponding configuration steps are browser-specific and are overviewed next.

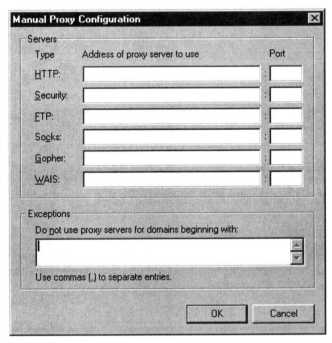

Figure 3.4   Manual Proxy Configuration menu of Netscape Navigator. © 1999 Netscape Communications Corporation.

3.6.1   Netscape Navigator

A user of Netscape Navigator can configure the use of proxy servers (proxies) in the Category Advanced > Proxies tab of the Edit > Preferences ... menu. As illustrated in Figure 3.3, the user can choose to have a direct connection to the Internet, manually configure proxies, or make use of automatic proxy configuration:

- A user not sitting behind a firewall generally has a direct connection to the Internet. In this case, the user has to select the radiobox shown at the top of Figure 3.3 (labeled "Direct connection to the Internet").

- A user sitting behind a firewall who wants (or has to) manually configure the proxies selects the radiobox shown in the middle of Figure 3.3 (labeled "Manual proxy configuration"). In this case, the user can press the View... button to get to the corresponding Manual Proxy Configuration menu illustrated in Figure 3.4. In this situation, the user can configure proxy servers for HTTP, HTTPS,[13] FTP, SOCKS, Gopher, and WAIS. For each of these application protocols, the user can specify an IP address or DNS name and a corresponding port number for a proxy server. In general, the only entry that is required is for HTTP. At the bottom of the Manual Proxy Configuration menu, the user can also specify a comma-separated list of exceptions (domains or domain name beginnings that do not use proxy servers at all). Finally, by pressing the OK button, the user can activate his or her settings.

- A user sitting behind a firewall who wants to make use of automatic proxy configuration selects the radiobox shown at the bottom of Figure 3.3 (labeled "Automatic proxy configuration"). In this case, the user has to indicate a URL that points to a proxy auto-config (PAC) file that is typically named `proxy.pac`. In Figure 3.3, `http://x.y.z/proxy.pac` is specified for the configuration location, meaning that the corresponding PAC file `proxy.pac` can be retrieved from host `http://x.y.z` (in general, it is up to the firewall administrator to inform users about the current location of the PAC file). In short, the PAC file is written in JavaScript and must define the following function:

```
function FindProxyForURL(url, host)
{
    ...
    ...
    return ...
}
```

There are two arguments for a `FindProxyForURL` function call: `url` specifies the full URL being accessed, and `host` specifies the hostname extracted from the URL (this is only for convenience, since it is the same string as between `://` and the first `:` or `/` after that). The `FindProxyForURL` function returns a string describing the configuration. If the return string is null, no proxies should

---

[13]Unfortunately, the terms "SSL" or "HTTPS" (standing for HTTP with SSL support) are not used in the manual proxy configuration menu. Instead, the more general term "Security" is used.

be used. The string can contain any number of the following building blocks, separated by a semicolon:

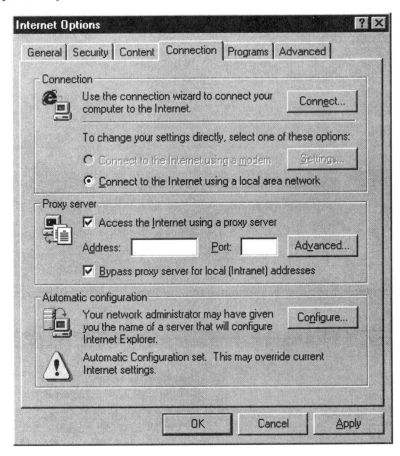

Figure 3.5   The Connection tab in the Internet Options menu of Microsoft Internet Explorer. © 1999 Microsoft Corporation.

– `DIRECT` — In this case, connections should be made directly, without using any proxies;

– `PROXY host:port` — In this case, the specified proxy server should be used;

– `SOCKS host:port` — In this case, the specified SOCKS server should be used.

If there are multiple semicolon-separated settings returned by the `FindProxyForURL` function, the left-most setting will be used, until the Netscape Navigator fails to establish a connection to the proxy. In this case, the next value will be used. As usual, the user must press the Reload button to actually activate the desired setting.

In a corporate environment, it is common that the network administrator provides a PAC file that can be used by all Web users. The proxy autoconfiguration support of Netscape Navigator is further explained in Appendix A of [25].

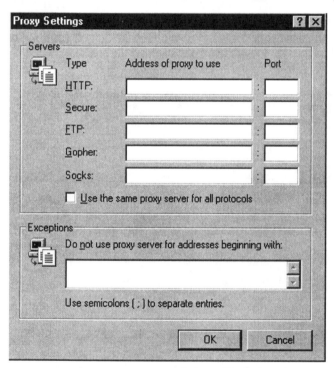

Figure 3.6 The Proxy Settings menu for Microsoft Internet Explorer. © 1999 Microsoft Corporation.

3.6.2 Microsoft Internet Explorer

Similarly, a user of Microsoft Internet Explorer can configure his or her browser in the Proxy server and Automatic configuration sections of the Connection tab in the View > Internet Options... menu. This tab is illustrated in Figure 3.5. In short, manual proxy configuration can be established using the Proxy server section, whereas automatic proxy configuration can be established using the Automatic configuration section (the Proxy server and Automatic configuration sections refer to the rectangles of the same names in Figure 3.5).

If you access the Internet using a proxy server, you must check the appropriate box in the Proxy server section. Doing so gives you the option to indicate the address (IP address or DNS name) and port number of a corresponding proxy server.

If you want to use more proxy servers for services other than HTTP, you can press the Advanced... button. In this case, you enter the Proxy Settings menu that is illustrated in Figure 3.6. Similar to the corresponding menu of Netscape Navigator, the user of the Internet Explorer can configure his or her browser to support HTTP, HTTPS,[14] FTP, Gopher, and SOCKS.

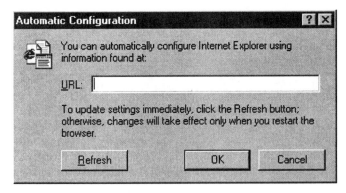

Figure 3.7   The Automatic Configuration dialog box of Microsoft Internet Explorer. © 1999 Microsoft Corporation.

Also similar to Netscape Navigator, it is possible to specify an exceptions list (using semicolons to separate the entries as mentioned in Figure 3.6). Contrary to Netscape Navigator, however, the current version of Internet Explorer does not provide support for WAIS proxy servers (proxies). It is possible to use a checkbox to indicate that the same proxy server should be used for all above-mentioned protocols.

If you want to use the automatic proxy configuration option, you must press the Configure... button in the Automatic Configuration section. Doing so opens an Automatic Configuration dialog box as illustrated in Figure 3.7. In this dialog

---

[14]Similar to Netscape Navigator, the term "Secure" is used instead of SSL or HTTPS.

box, you enter a URL for a PAC file. The syntax of the PAC file is identical to the one used by Netscape Navigator.

3.7 CONCLUSIONS

Depending on its basic components and configuration, several grades of firewall security can usually be obtained. For example, there is no security by allowing unrestricted access between a corporate intranet and the Internet. Next, packet filters can be added to obtain a certain level of data traffic interception, and stateful inspection technologies may help to make more intelligent decisions whether to forward particular IP packets. Also, the firewall can include both packet filters and application gateways. A variety of circuit-level and application-level gateways can be added along with different strengths of the corresponding authentication mechanisms. Similarly, the firewall can also reside on a secure operating system,[15] thereby improving the underlying security for the firewall code and files. Finally, the firewall can provide support for Internet layer security protocols, such as the IP security protocol (IPSP), and Internet key management protocol (IKMP) that we describe and further discuss in Chapter 5. This facility can be used to build secure tunnels between firewall-protected sites and to build virtual private networks (VPNs) accordingly. And last but not least, a company can also deny any access to and from the Internet, thereby ensuring isolation and complete security from the outside world. Although this is seemingly a theoretical option in these euphoric times for Internet access, it is still the only prudent approach to follow for certain highly secure environments.

Firewall systems are a fact of life on the Internet today. If properly implemented and deployed, they provide effective access control services for corporate intranets. Consequently, more and more network managers are setting up firewalls as their first line of defense against outside attacks. Nevertheless, the firewall technology has remained an emotional topic within the Internet community. Let's briefly summarize their main concerns:

- Firewall advocates consider firewalls as important additional safeguards, because they aggregate security functions in a single point, simplifying installation, configuration, and management. Also, many companies use Web sites as corporate ambassadors to the Internet, and locate the sites on a server that is a

---

[15]In this context, a secure operating system refers to an operating system that is hardened and minimized, meaning that anything not urgently required for the firewall's functionality is stripped off.

part of their firewall. They use them to store public information about corporate products and services, files to download, bug fixes, and so forth. From a U.S. manufacturer's and vendor's point of view, the firewall technology is interesting mainly because it doesn't use cryptographic techniques and can therefore be freely exported. In addition, the technology's use is not restricted to the TCP/IP protocols or the Internet, and very similar techniques can be used in any packet switched data network, such as X.25 or ATM networks.

- Firewall detractors are usually concerned about the difficulty of using firewalls, requiring multiple logins and other out-of-band mechanisms, as well as their interference with the usability and vitality of the Internet as a whole. They claim that firewalls foster a false sense of security, leading to lax security within the firewall perimeter.

At minimum, firewall advocates and detractors both agree that firewalls are a powerful tool for network security, but that they aren't by any means a panacea or a magic bullet for all network and Internet-related security problems. Consequently, they should not be regarded as a substitute for careful security management within a corporate intranet. Also, a firewall is useful only if it handles all traffic to and from the Internet. This is not always the case, since many sites permit dial-in access to modems that are located at various points throughout the site. This is a potential backdoor and could negate all the protection provided by the firewall. A much better method for handling modems is to concentrate them into a modem pool. In essence, a modem pool consists of several modems connected to a terminal server. A dial-in user connects to the terminal server and then connects from there to other internal hosts. Some terminal servers provide security features that can restrict connections to specific hosts, or require users to strongly authenticate themselves. Obviously, RADIUS, TACACS, and TACACS+ can again be used to secure communications between the terminal server and a centralized security server. Sometimes, authorized users also wish to have a dial-out capability. These users, however, need to recognize the vulnerabilities they may be creating if they are careless with modem access. A dial-out capability may easily become a dial-in capability if proper precautions are not taken. In general, dial-in and dial-out capabilities should be considered in the design of a firewall and incorporated into it. Forcing outside users to go through the strong authentication of the firewall should be reflected in the firewall policy.

In summary, firewall systems provide basic access control services for corporate intranets. But firewalls are not going to solve all security problems. A pair of historical analogies can help us better understand the role of firewall technology for the current Internet [26]:

- Our Stone Age predecessors lived in caves, each inhabited by a family whose members knew each other quite well. They could use this knowledge to identify and authenticate one another. Someone wanting to enter the cave would have to be introduced by a family member trusted by the others. History of human society has shown that this security model is too simple to work on a large scale. As families grew in size and started to interact with one another, it was no longer possible for all family members to know all other members of the community, or even to reliably remember all persons who had ever been introduced to them.

- In the Middle Ages, our predecessors lived in castles and villages surrounded by town walls. The inhabitants were acquainted with each other, but this web of knowledge was not trusted. Instead, identification and authentication, as well as authorization and access control, were centralized at a front gate. Anyone who wanted to enter the castle or village had to pass the front gate and was thoroughly checked there. Those who managed to pass the gate were implicitly trusted by all inhabitants. But human history has shown that this security model doesn't work either. For one thing, town walls don't protect against malicious insider attacks; for another, town walls and front gates don't scale easily (since they are so massively static). Many remnants of medieval town walls bear witness to this lack of scalability.

Using the above analogies, the Internet has just entered the Middle Ages. The simple security model of the Stone Age still works for single hosts and local area networks. But it no longer works for wide area networks in general and the Internet in particular. As a first — and let's hope intermediate — step, firewalls have been erected at the Internet gateways. Because they are capable of selectively dropping IP datagrams, firewalls also restrict the connectivity of the Internet as a whole. The Internet's firewalls are thus comparable to the town walls and front gates of the Middle Ages. Screening routers correspond to general-purpose gates, while application gateways correspond to more specialized gates.

We don't see town walls anymore. Instead, countries issue passports to their citizens to use worldwide for identification and authentication. It is possible and very likely that the Internet will experience similar developments. Trusted third parties (TTPs) could issue locally or globally accepted certificates for Internet principals, and these certificates could then be used to provide security services such as authentication, data confidentiality and integrity, access control, and non-repudiation services. This approach is further addressed in the remaining parts of this book.

REFERENCES

[1] R. Oppliger, *Internet and Intranet Security*, Artech House, Norwood, MA, 1998.

[2] P. Holbrook, and J. Reynolds, "Site Security Handbook," Request for Comments 1244, July 1991.

[3] B. Fraser, "Site Security Handbook," Request for Comments 2196 (obsoletes RFC 1244), For Your Information 8, September 1997.

[4] E. Guttman, L. Leong, and G. Malkin, "Users' Security Handbook," Request for Comments 2504, For Your Information 34, February 1999.

[5] W.R. Cheswick, and S.M. Bellovin, *Firewalls and Internet Security: Repelling the Wily Hacker*, Addison-Wesley, Reading, MA, 1994 (the second edition of this book is on its way and will probably be available early in 2000).

[6] K. Siyan, and C. Hare, *Internet Firewalls and Network Security*, New Riders Publishing, Indianapolis, IN, 1995.

[7] D.B. Chapman, and E.D. Zwicky, *Internet Security Firewalls*, O'Reilly & Associates, Sebastopol, CA, 1995.

[8] S. Garfinkel, and G. Spafford, *Practical UNIX and Internet Security*, 2nd Edition, O'Reilly & Associates, Sebastopol, CA, 1996.

[9] F. Avolio, and M. Ranum, "A Network Perimeter With Secure Internet Access," *Proceedings of the Internet Society Symposium on Network and Distributed System Security*, February 1994, pp. 109 – 119.

[10] W.R. Cheswick, and S.M. Bellovin, "Network Firewalls," *IEEE Communications Magazine*, September 1994, pp. 50 – 57.

[11] B. Cheswick, "The Design of a Secure Internet Gateway," *Proceedings of USENIX Summer Conference*, June 1990, pp. 233 – 237.

[12] M. Ranum, "A Network Firewall," *Proceedings of World Conference on System Administration and Security*, July 1992, pp. 153 – 163.

[13] J.P. Wack, and L.J. Carnahan, *Keeping Your Site Comfortably Secure: An Introduction to Internet Firewalls*, NIST, Draft Version, October 1994.

[14] German Information Security Agency (GISA), *IT Baseline Protection Manual*, 1996.

[15] C.L. Schuba, *On The Modeling, Design, and Implementation of Firewall Technology*, Ph.D. Thesis, Purdue University, December 1997.

[16] S.M. Bellovin, "Firewall-friendly FTP," Request for Comments 1579, February 1994.

[17] D. Koblas, and M.R. Koblas, "SOCKS," *Proceedings of USENIX UNIX Security III Symposium*, September 1992, pp. 77 – 82.

[18] M. Leech, M. Ganis, Y. Lee, R. Kuris, D. Koblas, and L. Jones, "SOCKS Protocol Version 5," Request for Comments 1928, March 1996.

[19] M. Leech, "Username/Password Authentication for SOCKS V5," Request for Comments 1929, March 1996.

[20] P. McMahon, "GSS-API Authentication Method for SOCKS Version 5," Request for Comments 1961, June 1996.

[21] R. Oppliger, *Authentication Systems for Secure Networks*, Artech House, Norwood, MA, 1996.

[22] C. Rigney, A. Rubens, W. Simpson, and S. Willens, "Remote Authentication Dial-In User Service (RADIUS)," Request for Comments 2138 (obsoletes RFC 2058), April 1997.

[23] C. Rigney, "RADIUS Accounting," Request for Comments 2139 (obsoletes RFC 2059), April 1997.

[24] C. Finseth, "An Access Control Protocol, Sometimes Called TACACS," Request for Comments 1492, July 1993.

[25] A. Luotonen, *Web Proxy Servers*, Prentice Hall PTR, Upper Saddle River, NJ, 1998.

[26] R. Oppliger, "Internet Kiosk: Internet Security Enters the Middle Ages," *IEEE Computer*, Vol. 28, October 1995, pp. 100 – 101.

Chapter 4

Cryptographic Techniques

As you probably know (and have already heard plenty of times), the foundation of communication security is cryptography, a special field of applied mathematics. Everything boils down to mathematics, and mathematics of the cryptographic techniques and systems you use provide an upper bound for the security of your overall communication system. What this basically means is that using strong cryptography is actually a necessary but not sufficient condition to provide communication security. Using cryptography and cryptographic techniques allows communicating parties to verify each others' identities without meeting in person, and it enables confidential data to be transmitted from location to location across potentially unsecure networks, such as the Internet, without risk of interception or tampering. The quote from Ronald L. Rivest that opened the preface of this book illustrates the importance of cyrptography for network security.

In this chapter, we introduce cryptographic techniques that are employed by many security technologies for the WWW (as well as for other networking infrastructures). In particular, we focus on cryptographic algorithms and protocols in Section 4.1, address one-way hash functions, secret key cryptography, and public key cryptography in Sections 4.2 to 4.4, discuss some legal issues that surround the use of cryptography in Section 4.5, and introduce a notation that can be used to describe cryptographic protocols in Section 4.6. Note, however, that this chapter is far too short to give a comprehensive overview about all topics that are relevant for cryptography. For this purpose, you must read one (or several) of the many books on cryptography that are available at your local bookstore. Among these books, I particularly recommend [1 – 3].

4.1   INTRODUCTION

According to [3], the term *cryptography* refers to the study of mathematical techniques related to aspects of information security such as confidentiality, data integrity, entity authentication, and data origin authentication. It is commonly agreed that cryptography is a major enabling technology for network security, and that cryptographic algorithms and protocols are the essential building blocks for secure computer networks and distributed systems:

- A *cryptographic algorithm* is an algorithm defined by a sequence of steps precisely specifying the actions required to achieve a specific security objective;

- A *cryptographic protocol* is a distributed algorithm defined by a sequence of steps precisely specifying the actions required of two or more entities to achieve a specific security objective.

Cryptographic algorithms and protocols are being studied both in theory and practice. The aim is to design and come up with algorithms and protocols that are both secure and practical. Note, however, that there are at least two basic approaches to discussing the security of cryptographic algorithms and protocols:

- On the one hand, *computational security* measures the computational effort required to break a specific cryptographic algorithm or protocol. An algorithm or protocol is said to be computationally secure if the best method for breaking it requires at least n operations, where n is some specified, usually very large number. The problem is that no known practical algorithm or protocol can be proven to be secure under this strong definition. In practice, an algorithm or protocol is called computationally secure if the best known method of breaking it requires an unreasonably large amount of computational resources (e.g., CPU time or memory). Another approach is to provide evidence of computational security by reducing the security of an algorithm or protocol to some well-studied problem that is thought to be difficult. For example, it may be possible to prove that an algorithm or protocol is secure if a given integer cannot be factored or if a discrete logarithm cannot be computed. Algorithms and protocols of this type are sometimes called provably secure, but it must be understood that this approach only provides a proof of security relative to the difficulty of solving another problem, not an absolute proof of security.

- On the other hand, *unconditional security* measures the security of a cryptographic algorithm or protocol when there is no bound placed on the amount of computation for an adversary. Consequently, an algorithm or protocol is called unconditionally secure if it cannot be broken, even with infinite computational resources at hand.

The computational security of a cryptographic algorithm or protocol can be studied from the point of view of computational complexity, whereas the unconditional security cannot be studied from this point of view (since computational resources are allowed to be infinite). The appropriate framework in which unconditional security must be studied is probability theory and the application thereof in communication or information theory.

Obviously, unconditional security is preferable from a security point of view, since it protects against a potentially powerful adversary. Unfortunately, unconditional security is very hard and expensive to achieve in some cases, and impossible in other cases. For example, theory shows that unconditionally secure encryption systems use very long keys, making them unsuitable for most practical applications. Similarly, there is no such thing as an unconditionally secure public key cryptosystem. The best we can achieve is provable security, in the sense that the problem of breaking the public key cryptosystem is arguably at least as difficult as solving a complex mathematical problem. Consequently, one is satisfied with computational security given some reasonable assumptions about the computational power of potential adversaries. But keep in mind that the security a computationally secure cryptographic algorithm or protocol provides is, for the most part, based on the perceived difficulty of a specific mathematical problem, such as the factorization problem or the discrete logarithm problem in the case of public key cryptography. Confidence in the security of such systems may be high because the problems are public and many minds have attempted to attack them. However, the vulnerability remains that a new insight or computing technology may defeat this type of cryptography. There are at least two developments that provide some evidence for this intrinsic vulnerability:

- In 1994, Peter W. Shor from the AT&T Bell Laboratories conceived randomized polynomial-time algorithms for computing discrete logarithms and factoring integers on a quantum computer, a computational device based on quantum mechanical principles [4]. Presently it is not known how to actually build a quantum computer, nor if this is even possible.

- In the same year, Len M. Adleman[1] demonstrated the feasibility of using tools from molecular biology to solve an instance of the directed Hamiltonian path problem, which is known to be hard[2] [5]. The problem instance was encoded in molecules of DNA, and the steps of the computation were performed with standard protocols and enzymes. Adleman notes that while the currently available fastest supercomputers can execute approximately 10^{12} operations per second, it is plausible for a DNA computer to execute 10^{20} or even more operations per second. Moreover, such a DNA computer would be far more energy-efficient than existing supercomputers. Similar to the quantum computer, it is not clear at present whether it is feasible to actually build a DNA computer with such performance characteristics. Further information on DNA computing can be found in [6].

Should either quantum computers or DNA computers ever become practical, they would have a significant impact on cryptography. In fact, most cryptographic algorithms and protocols that are computationally secure today would be rendered worthless. This would have a tremendous impact on most applications that are currently used in electronic commerce.

Cryptographic algorithms and protocols are used to establish secured channels (both in terms of authenticity and integrity, as well as confidentiality). Note the subtle difference between a physically secure channel and a secured channel. Certain channels are assumed to be secure, including trusted couriers and personal contacts between communicating parties, whereas other channels may be secured by physical or cryptographic techniques. Physical security may be established through physical means, such as dedicated communication links with corresponding access controls put in place, or the use of *quantum cryptography*. Contrary to conventional cryptography, the security of quantum cryptography does not rely upon any complexity-theoretic or probability-theoretic assumptions, but is based on the Heisenberg uncertainty principle of quantum physics [7]. As such, quantum cryptography is immune to advances in computing power and human cleverness. In the future, quantum cryptography may provide a physical alternative to unconditionally secure cryptographic algorithms and protocols. In the meantime, however, conventional and

---

[1]Len M. Adleman is a coinventor of the Rivest, Shamir, and Adleman (RSA) cryptosystem.

[2]According to theoretical computer science, the directed Hamiltonian path problem is NP-complete.

computationally secure cryptographic algorithms and protocols are much easier to use and deploy. Consequently, we are not going to delve into the details of quantum cryptography in this book.

In the three sections that follow we address the major building blocks that are used in cryptographic algorithms and protocols: one-way hash functions, secret key cryptography, and public key cryptography. Again, refer to the books mentioned at the beginning of this chapter for a more comprehensive overview and discussion of these and some other building blocks.

4.2   ONE-WAY HASH FUNCTIONS

Mainly because of their efficiency, one-way hash functions are of central importance in cryptographic algorithms and protocols. Informally speaking, a *one-way function* is easy to compute, but hard to invert. More formally speaking, a function $f : X \longrightarrow Y$ is one-way[3] if

- $f(x)$ is easy to compute for all $x \in X$;

- But it is computationally infeasible when given $y \in f(X) = Y$ to find an $x \in X$ such that $f(x) = y$.

This definition is still not precise in a mathematically strong sense, because it doesn't resolve what the terms "easy" and "computationally infeasible" actually mean. Nevertheless, we want to use this definition in this book. It is important to note that the existence of one-way functions is still an unproven assumption and that, until today, no function has been shown to be one-way. Obviously, a sufficiently large domain prohibiting an exhaustive search is a necessary but not sufficient condition for a function to be one-way.

In general, it is not required that a one-way function be invertible, and distinct input values may be mapped to the same output. A one-way function $h : X \longrightarrow Y$ for which $\mid Y \mid \ll \mid X \mid$ is called a *one-way hash function*. If, in addition to the conditions for a one-way hash function, it is also computationally infeasible to find distinct input values $x_1, x_2 \in X$ such that $h(x_1) = h(x_2)$, then h is called a *collision-resistant* one-way hash function. We will see that collision resistance is important, for example, to thwart theft of a digital signature from one message for attachment to another.

---

[3] An alternative term for "one-way" is "preimage-resistant."

Most collision-resistant one-way hash functions in use today are iterative. In short, a one-way hash function is iterative if data is hashed by iterating a basic compression function on subsequent blocks of data. The basic idea is illustrated in Figure 4.1. A message x is decomposed into n blocks of data $x_1, \ldots, x_n$. A basic compression function f is then applied to each block and the result of the compression function of the previous block. This continues until the result of the last compression step is interpreted as output $h(x)$. Examples of iterative one-way hash functions include MD2 [8], MD4 [9], MD5 [10], and SHA-1 [11]. MD2, MD4, and MD5 all produce 128-bit hash values, whereas SHA-1 produces 160-bit hash values. RIPEMD is another example of an iterative one-way hash function. It was developed as part of a European research project and is basically a variation of MD4. RIPEMD-160 is a strengthened version of RIPEMD producing another 160-bit hash value [12].

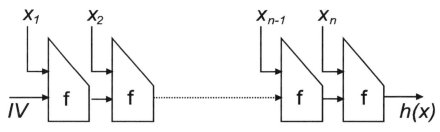

Figure 4.1   An iterative one-way hash function.

As of this writing, MD5 and SHA-1 are by far the most widely used and deployed one-way hash functions. MD5 takes as input a string of arbitrary length and produces as output a 128-bit hash value. In theory, we would need 2^{128} (in the worst case), or 2^{127} (in the average case) trials before finding a collision, and hence a new message that results in the same MD5 hash value. Even if each trial only lasted a nanosecond, this would still require some billions of billions of centuries in computing time. However, recent results in cryptographic research show that it is possible to take advantage of the particularities of the one-way hash function algorithm to speed up the search process. According to Paul van Oorschot and Michael Wiener, you can actually build a machine able to find messages that hash to an arbitrary value [13]. What this means is that cryptanalysis is catching up and that a 128-bit hash value may soon be insufficient. In addition, Hans Dobbertin has shown that MD5 is vulnerable to specific collision search attacks [14]. Taking this into account, SHA-1 and RIPEMD-160 appear to be a cryptographically stronger one-way hash function than MD5. In any case, implementors and users of one-way hash functions should be aware of possible cryptanalytic developments regarding any of these functions, and the eventual need to replace them.

4.3 SECRET KEY CRYPTOGRAPHY

Secret key cryptography refers to traditional cryptography. In this kind of cryptography, a secret key is established and shared between communicating peers, and the key is used to encrypt and decrypt messages on either side. Because of its symmetry, secret key cryptography is often referred to as *symmetric cryptography*.

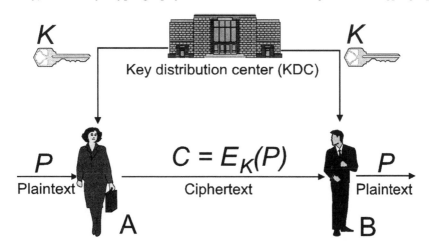

Figure 4.2 A secret key cryptosystem.

The use of a secret key cryptosystem is overviewed in Figure 4.2. Let's assume that A(lice) on the left side wants to send a confidential message to B(ob) on the right side. A therefore shares a secret key K with B. This key may be preconfigured manually or distributed by a key distribution center (KDC). Note that during its distribution, K must be secured in terms of confidentiality, integrity, and authenticity. This is usually done by having the KDC encrypt K with secret keys that it shares with A and B, respectively. A encrypts a plaintext message P by applying an encryption function E and the key K, and sends the resulting ciphertext $C = E_K(P)$ to B. On the other side, B decrypts C by applying the decryption function D and the key K. B therefore computes $D_K(C) = D_K(E_K(P)) = P$, and recovers the plaintext P accordingly.

Secret key cryptography has been in use for many years in a variety of forms. Examples of secret key cryptosystems that in widespread use are the data encryption standard (DES) [15], two-key and three-key triple-DES, the international data encryption algorithm (IDEA) [16], Blowfish [17], SAFER (K-64 or K-128) [18], CAST, RC2, RC4,[4] RC5, and RC6, as well as the upcoming advanced encryption standard (AES) that is being standardized by the U.S. National Institute of Standards and Technology (NIST) to replace DES in the future.

4.4 PUBLIC KEY CRYPTOGRAPHY

The idea of using one-way functions, which can only be inverted if a certain secret (a so-called "trapdoor") is known, has led to the invention of *public key cryptography* or *asymmetric cryptography* [19]. Today, public key cryptography is a battlefield for mathematicians and theoretical computer scientists. We are not going to delve into the mathematical details; instead, we address public key cryptography from a more practical point of view. From this point of view, a public key cryptosystem is a cryptosystem in which a user has a pair of mathematically related keys:

- A *public key* that can be published without doing any harm to the system's overall security;

- A *private key* that is assumed to never leave the possession of its owner.

For both the public and the private key, it is computationally infeasible for an outsider to derive one from the other. The use of a public key cryptosystem is overviewed in Figure 4.3. A(lice) and B(ob) each have a public key pair (k_A, k_A^{-1}) and (k_B, k_B^{-1}). The private keys k_A^{-1} and k_B^{-1} are kept secret, whereas the public keys k_A and k_B are publicly available in certified form (e.g., digitally signed by a certification authority as addressed further below).

If A wants to protect the confidentiality of a plaintext message P, she uses the public key of B, which is k_B, encrypts P with this key, and sends the resulting ciphertext $C = E_{k_B}(P)$ to B (the term $E_{k_B}(P)$ is abbreviated with $E_B(P)$ in Figure 4.3). On the other side, B uses his private key k_B^{-1} to successfully decrypt $P = D_{k_B^{-1}}(C) = D_{k_B^{-1}}(E_{k_B}(P))$ (the terms $D_{k_B^{-1}}(C)$ and $D_{k_B^{-1}}(E_{k_B}(P))$ are abbreviated with $D_B(C)$ and $D_B(E_B(P))$ in Figure 4.3).

A public key cryptosystem cannot only be used to protect the confidentiality of a message, but to protect its authenticity and integrity as well. If A wanted to

---

[4]Both the RC2 and the RC4 encryption algorithms were originally protected by trade secrets of RSA Data Security, Inc. However, the algorithms were disassembled, reverse-engineered, and anonymously posted to the Usenet in 1994 (RC4) and 1996 (RC2).

protect the authenticity and integrity of a message M, she would compute a digital signature S for M. Digital signatures provide an electronic analog of handwritten signatures for electronic documents, and — similar to handwritten signatures — digital signatures must not be forgeable, recipients must be able to verify them, and the signers must not be able to repudiate them later. However, a major difference between a handwritten signature and a digital signature is that the digital signature can't be constant, but must be a function of the entire document on which it appears. If this were not the case, a digital signature, due to its electronic nature, could be copied and attached to arbitrary documents.

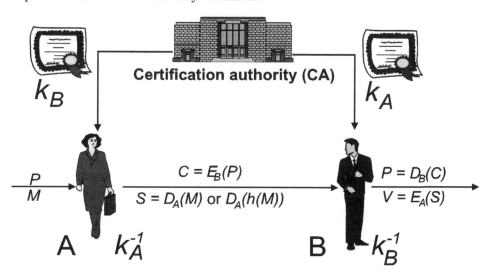

Figure 4.3   A public key cryptosystem.

Arbitrated digital signature schemes are based on secret key cryptography. In such a scheme, a TTP validates the signature and forwards it on the signer's behalf. True digital signature schemes, however, should come along without TTPs taking an active role. They usually require the use of public key cryptography: signed messages are sent directly from signers to recipients. In essence, a *digital signature scheme* consists of

- A key-generation algorithm that randomly selects a public key pair;

- A signature algorithm that takes as input a message and a private key, and that generates as output a digital signature for the message;

- A signature verification algorithm that takes as input a digital signature and a public key, and that generates as output a message and an information bit according to whether the signature is valid for the message.

A comprehensive overview and discussion of public key-based digital signature schemes is given in [20].

According to the OSI security architecture, a digital signature refers to data appended to, or a cryptographic transformation of, a data unit that allows a recipient of the data unit to prove the source and integrity of the data unit and protect against forgery (e.g., by the recipient). Consequently, there are two classes of digital signatures:

- A *digital signature giving message recovery* refers to the situation in which a cryptographic transformation is applied to a data unit. In this case, the data is automatically recovered if the recipient verifies the signature.

- In contrast, a *digital signature with appendix* refers to the situation in which some cryptographically protected data is appended to the data unit. In fact, the data represents a digital signature and can be decoupled from the data unit that it signs.

In the case of digital signatures with appendix, the bandwidth limitation of public key cryptography is unimportant due to the use of one-way hash functions as auxiliaries. Again referring to Figure 4.3, A can use her private key k_A^{-1} to compute a digital signature $S = D_A(M)$ or $S = D_A(h(M))$ for message M. In the second case, h refers to a collision-resistant, one-way hash function that is applied to M prior to generating the digital signature. Anybody who knows the public key of A can verify the digital signature by decrypting it with k_A, and comparing the result with another hash value that is recomputed for the same message with the same one-way hash function.

The most widely used public key cryptosystem is RSA, invented by Ronald L. Rivest, Adi Shamir, and Len M. Adleman at the Massachusetts Institute of Technology (MIT) in 1977 [21]. The RSA cryptosystem gets its security from the difficulty and intractability of the integer factorization problem. What this means is that it is fairly simple to multiply two large prime numbers, but difficult to compute the prime factors of a large number. One of the nice properties of RSA is that the same algorithm can be used for both message encryption and digital signature generation and verification. This is not the case for most other public key cryptosystems. For example, the ElGamal cryptosystem uses different algorithms for message encryption and digital signature generation and verification [22,23]. Like the Diffie-Hellman key exchange algorithm, the ElGamal cryptosystem gets its security from the intractability of the discrete logarithm problem in a cyclic group, such as the multiplicative group of a finite field. What this basically means is that, in general, the inverse operation of the exponentiation function is the logarithm function. There are efficient algorithms for computing logarithms in many groups; however, one does not know a polynomial-time algorithm for computing discrete logarithms in cyclic groups. For example, for a very large prime number p and two smaller numbers y and a, it is computationally intractable to find an x that satisfies the equation $y = a^x \bmod p$. The digital signature standard (DSS) proposed by NIST refers to an optimized modification of the ElGamal cryptosystem that can be used only for digital signature generation and verification [24].

The use of public key cryptography simplifies the problem of key management considerably. Note that in Figure 4.3, instead of providing A and B with a unique session key that is protected in terms of confidentiality, integrity, and authenticity, the KDC (which is now being called a "certification authority") has to provide A and B with the public key of the communicating peer. This key is public in nature and must not be protected in terms of confidentiality. Nevertheless, the use of public key cryptography usually requires an authentication framework that binds public keys to user identities. A *public key certificate* is a certified proof of such binding vouched for by a TTP or a *certification authority* (CA). The use of CAs alleviates the responsibility of individual users to verify directly the correctness of public keys. An analogy can be used to better illustrate this point [25]: In various states, the Department of Motor Vehicles (DMV) regulates the issuance of driver's licenses and ensures that an individual presents correct personal information when applying for a license. Similarly, CAs are used to confirm the identities of their subscribers and issue digital certificates. A variety of certificates are used for different purposes:

- Public key certificates used to authenticate Web servers are called *site certificates*;

- Public key certificates used to authenticate individual Web users are called *personal certificates*;

- Public key certificates used to authenticate software publishers are called *software publisher certificates* (a software publisher may be either an individual programmer or a commercial software company);

- Finally, there are also public key certificates that hold a CA's own public key in certified form. These certificates are called *certification authority certificates*, or *CA certificates* in short.

The ITU-T Recommendation X.509 specifies both a commonly used format for public key certificates, as well as a certificate distribution scheme [26]. It was first published in 1988 as part of the X.500 directory recommendations. The X.509 version 1 (X.509v1) format was extended in 1993 to incorporate two new fields to support directory access control, resulting in the X.509 version 2 (X.509v2) format. Additionally and as a result of attempting to deploy certificates within the global Internet, X.509v2 was revised to allow for additional extension fields. The resulting X.509 version 3 (X.509v3) specification was officially released in June 1996. Meanwhile, the ITU-T Recommendation X.509 has also been approved by the ISO/IEC JTC1 [27].

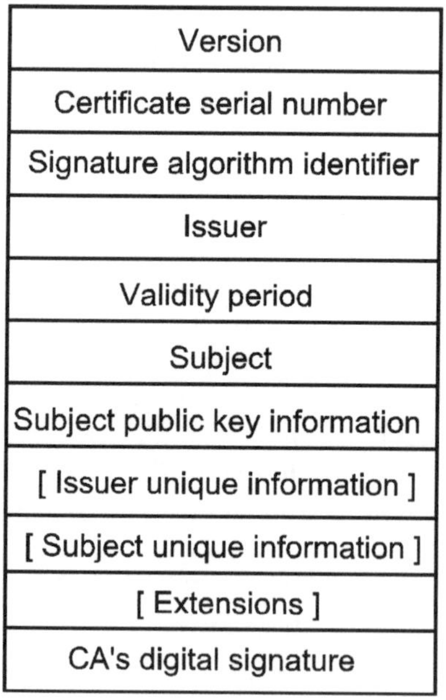

Version
Certificate serial number
Signature algorithm identifier
Issuer
Validity period
Subject
Subject public key information
[Issuer unique information]
[Subject unique information]
[Extensions]
CA's digital signature

Figure 4.4   The format of an X.509v3 public key certificate.

The format of an X.509v3 certificate is specified in a notation called abstract syntax notation one (ASN.1). One can apply the distinguished encoding rules (DER) to a certificate specified in ASN.1 format to produce a series of bytes suitable for transmission in computer networks. A detailed discussion of ASN.1 and its system of encoding rules (including DER) is beyond the scope of this book. Further information can be found in Chapter 7 and Appendix A of [25] or [28].

The format of an X.509v3 public key certificate is illustrated in Figure 4.4. It consists of the following fields (the fields in square brackets are optional):

- *Version:* Number that specifies to which version of the ITU-T Recommendation X.509 the encoded certificate actually conforms. The current legal values are 1, 2, and 3 (referring to the X.509 versions 1, 2, and 3).

- *Certificate Serial Number:* Serial number for the certificate assigned by the issuing CA. This number should be unique within all certificates issued by the CA.

- *Signature Algorithm Identifier:* Identifying name for the algorithm used for the digital signature of the certificate (e.g., RSA or DSA).

- *Issuer:* Identifying name for the CA that issued and digitally signed the certificate.

- *Validity Period:* Pair of dates that determines a time period in which the certificate is valid (unless it is explicitly revoked). More precisely, the pair consists of a start date, the date on which the certificate becomes valid, and an end date, the date after which the certificate ceases to be valid. Obviously, the certificate is not valid before the start date or after the end date. However, a CA may elect to maintain status information for a longer period of time.

- *Subject:* Identifying name for the user for whom the certificate has been issued. For example, the subject field may include the user name and address. For obvious reasons, a CA may issue more than one certificate with the same subject name for the same entity.

- *Subject Public Key Information:* Information that is being certified. This field typically includes the user's public key and the algorithm(s) for which the key is intended to be used.

- [*Issuer Unique Identifier*]: Optional field that allows the reuse of issuer names over time.

- [*Subject Unique Identifier*]: Optional field that allows the reuse of subject names over time.

- [*Extensions*]: Optional extension fields (as addressed below).

- *Certification Authroity's Digital Signature:* Digital signature for the entire certificate. The signature is computed for all other fields of the certificate.

The X.509v3 extensions provide a way to associate additional information for subjects, public keys, and managing certificates. As such, X.509v3 extension fields enable communities and organizations to define their own extensions and encode information specific to their needs in certificates. As further addressed in [25], an extension field has three parts: extension type, extension value, and criticality indicator.

- The *extension type* is a globally unique identifier that references the syntax and semantics of the extension value;

- The *extension value* contains the actual value of an extension field, which is described by the extension type.

- Finally, the *criticality indicator* is a flag that instructs a certificate-using application whether it is safe to ignore an extension field if it does not recognize the extension type. When processing a certificate, an application can safely ignore a noncritical extension field (an extension field with a nonset, criticality indicator flag) if it does not recognize the extension type. On the other hand, it should always reject a certificate that contains a critical extension field it does not recognize.

ITU and ISO/IEC have developed and published a set of standard extension fields. As already mentioned above, a CA is a TTP that creates, assigns, and distributes public key certificates. More precisely, the CA accepts certificate applications from entities, authenticates applications, issues certificates, and maintains status information about these certificates. In theory, it is sufficient to have one or a few CAs provide these services. In practice, however, it is more likely that certificates will be issued by several organizations for different purposes. For example, a company may issue certificates to its employees, a university may issue certificates to its students, and a city or state may issue certificates to its citizens. Following this line of argumentation, there will probably be more than one CA issuing certificates, and a user will probably possess more than one certificate (just as he or she carries more than one proof of identity today, such as a credit card and a driver's license).

The large-scale deployment of public key cryptography will require the coexistence of multiple CAs. These CAs will mutually certify their public keys, resulting in a connected graph of (mutually certifying) CAs. There are various graph structures and corresponding trust models such as that in [25], but the simplest and most notable is a certification hierarchy representing a tree with a single root CA. In a more general setting, a *public key infrastructure* (PKI) refers to an infrastructure that is used to issue and revoke public keys and public key certificates. As such, a PKI comprises a set of agreed-upon standards, CAs, structures between multiple CAs, methods to discover and validate certification paths, operational and management protocols, interoperable tools, and supporting legislation. A PKI structure between multiple CAs generally provides one or more certification paths between a subscriber and a certificate-using application. A *certification path* (or *certification chain*) refers to a sequence of one or more connected nodes between the subscriber and a root CA. The root CA, in turn, is a CA that the certificate-using application trusts and has securely imported and stored its public key certificate.

The criteria to issue (and revoke) certificates may also vary with different CAs. Some CAs may issue a certificate based on the name and address. Others may require proof of date of birth, fingerprints, and so on. Finally, some institutions, such as courts, may accept only notarized certificates. The actual rules on how certificates are issued (and revoked) are specified in a so-called *certificate practice statement* (CPS). A CPS clearly states a CA's policies and practices with regard to issuance and maintenance of public key certificates. Furthermore, a CPS may also contain information about the liabilities of a CA toward systems relying on its certificates, and the obligations of its subscribers toward the CA.

There are many companies that provide CA products and services. Examples include VeriSign, Entrust, and GTE CyberTrust in the United States and Canada, Baltimore Technologies in Europe, and Swisskey in Switzerland. Also, many software packages, such as Netscape Navigator and Microsoft Internet Explorer, are being distributed with a set of preconfigured CAs that the users accept and trust by default if they don't explicitly disable them. This problem is addressed in Chapter 6 when we talk about the SSL and TLS protocols that make heavy use of public key certificates for client and server authentication. In addition, problems related to managing certificates are also discussed in Chapter 8.

4.5 LEGAL ISSUES

There are some legal issues to keep in mind when using cryptographic techniques. In particular, there are patent claims, regulations for the import, export, and use of cryptographic techniques, as well as legislations for electronic and digital signatures.

4.5.1   Patent Claims

Patents applied to computer programs are called software patents. In the U.S. computer industry, software patents are a subject of ongoing controversy. Some of the earliest and most important software patents granted by the U.S. Patent and Trademark Office were in the field of cryptography. These software patents go back to the late 1960s and early 1970s. Although computer algorithms were widely thought to be unpatentable at the time, cryptography patents were granted because they were written as patents on encryption devices built in hardware. Indeed, most early encryption devices were built in hardware because general-purpose computers at the time simply could not execute the encryption algorithms fast enough in software. For example, IBM obtained several patents in the early 1970s on its Lucifer algorithm, which went on to become the DES [15]. Today, many secret key cryptosystems are also covered by patent claims. For example, DES is patented but royalty-free, whereas IDEA is patented and royalty-free for non commercial use, but requires a license for commercial use. Later in the 1970s, all of the pioneers in the field of public key cryptography filed for and obtained patents on their work. Consequently, the field of public key cryptography is largely governed by a couple of software patents. Fortunately, most of them have expired or are about to expire fairly soon.

Outside the United States, the patent situation is quite different. For example, patent law in Europe and Japan differs from U.S. patent law in one very important aspect. In the United States, an inventor has a grace period of one year between the first public disclosure of an invention and the last day on which a patent application can be filed. In Europe and Japan, there is no grace period. Any public disclosure instantly forfeits all patent rights. Because the inventions contained in the original patents related to public key cryptography were publicly disclosed before patent applications were actually filed, these algorithms were never patentable in Europe and Japan. As a consequence of the lack of patent claims, public key cryptography has been more widely adapted in European countries and Japan.

Under U.S. patent law, patent infringement is not a criminal offense, and the penalties and damages are the jurisdiction of the civil courts. It is the responsibility of the user of a particular cryptographic algorithm or technique to make sure that correct licenses have been obtained from the corresponding patent holders. If these licenses do not exist, the patent holders can sue the user in court. Therefore, most products that make use of cryptographic techniques come along with the licenses required to use them. With regard to the Internet standards process, for example, a written statement from the patent holder is required that a license will be made available to applicants under reasonable terms and conditions prior to approving a protocol specification for the Internet standards track.

4.5.2 Regulations

There are different regulations for the import, export, and use of cryptographic techniques. For example, the United States has been regulating the export of cryptographic systems and technical data regarding them for quite a long time. These regulations go far beyond the Wassenaar Arrangement on export controls for conventional arms and dual-use goods and technologies.[5] In the United States, certain cryptographic systems and technical data regarding them are considered to be defense articles and subject to federal government export controls accordingly. If a U.S. company wants to sell cryptographic systems and technical data to other countries, it therefore must have export approval. Exports are licensed by the Office of Export Administration of the Department of Commerce (DoC).

Unfortunately, the laws that drive these export controls are not too clear, and their interpretation changes over time. Sometimes vendors get so discouraged that they leave encryption out of their products altogether. Sometimes they generate products that, when sold overseas, have encryption mechanisms seriously weakened or removed. It is usually possible to get export approval for encryption if the key lengths are shortened. So, sometimes vendors intentionally use short keys or cryptosystems with varying key lengths. Probably the most widely deployed example of this kind is browser software (e.g., Netscape Navigator and Microsoft Internet Explorer) that comes in two versions: the U.S. domestic version that uses strong encryption with 128-bit RC4 session keys, and the international version of the same product that uses encryption with only 40-bit RC4 session keys. Due to some recent

---

[5]The Wassenaar Arrangement is a treaty originally negotiated in July 1996 and signed by 31 countries to restrict the export of dual-use goods and technologies to specific countries considered to be dangerous. The countries that have signed the Wassenaar Arrangement include the former Coordinating Committee for Multilateral Export Controls (COCOM) member and cooperating countries, as well as some new countries such as Russia. The COCOM was an international munitions control organization that also restricted the export of cryptography as a dual-use technology. It was formally dissolved in March 1994. More recently, the Wassenaar Arrangement was updated. The participating states of the Wassenaar Arrangement are: Argentina, Australia, Austria, Belgium, Bulgaria, Canada, Czech Republic, Denmark, Finland, France, Germany, Greece, Hungary, Ireland, Italy, Japan, Luxembourg, Netherlands, New Zealand, Norway, Poland, Portugal, Republic of Korea, Romania, Russian Federation, Slovak Republic, Spain, Sweden, Switzerland, Turkey, Ukraine, United Kingdom, and the United States. Further information on the Wassenaar Arrangement can be found on the Web by following the URL http://www.wassenaar.org

cryptanalytical attacks against 40-bit and 56-bit keys, it seems that a lower bound for a key length that protects against a brute-force attacks is 80 bits [29].

In addition to export regulations, there are also countries that regulate either the import or the use of cryptographic systems and technical data regarding them [30,31]. For example, India and South Korea regulate the import, whereas Russia regulates the use of cryptography.[6] Many countries have just begun to study the impact of publicly available cryptographic systems on the possibilities of intelligence gathering and legal interception. Among other institutions and organizations, this topic is also being studied by the Senior Officials Group on Information Security (SOG-IS) in Europe and the Working Party on Information Security and Privacy of the Organization for Economic Cooperation and Development (OECD).

4.5.3   Electronic and Digital Signature Legislation

A majority of states have enacted or are considering electronic or digital signature legislation in an effort to facilitate electronic commerce applications. According to [32], state legislation can be broken down into the following three models:

- *Limited legislative model:* This term refers to digital signature legislation that is very narrow in scope, covering only such things as government communications, certificates of birth and death, medical records, and voter registration. This type of legislation represents an incremental approach. Many states that have enacted it are considering other legislation models, as well.

- *Comprehensive legislative model:* This term refers to an all-encompassing regulatory approach that pertains to all communications, and provides for much, although not necessarily all, of the following: regulates CAs, prescribes duties of CAs and subscribers, sets forth warranty, liability and limitation of liability provisions, is technology-specific, sets forth the legal effects of digital signatures and electronic message and presumptions in adjudicating disputes, establishes a state agency as a CA and establishes repositories and prescribes their liability. The most well-known comprehensive legislations are the Utah Digital Signature Act in the U.S. and the SigG/SigV (Signaturgesetz and Signaturverordnung) in Germany.

- *Minimalist legislative model:* This term refers to legislation that pertains to all communications, is technology-neutral, and basically does little more than give

---

[6]Until recently, France regulated the use of cryptography.

legal effect to electronic signatures and electronic records. The Massachusetts Electronic Records and Signature Act, the last draft of which was published in November 1997, is an example of such a limited legislation.

It remains to be seen what model best suits the specific requirements of electronic commerce and corresponding applications.

4.6 NOTATION

In general, a *protocol* specifies the format and relative timing of information exchanged between communicating parties. As we have seen before, a *cryptographic protocol* is a protocol that makes use of cryptographic techniques. The following notation is used in this book to describe cryptographic protocols:

- Capital letters, such as A, B, C, ..., are used to refer to principals, whereas the same letters put in italics are used to refer to the corresponding principal identifiers. Note that many publications on cryptography and cryptographic protocols use names, such as Alice and Bob, to refer to principals (we have referred to Alice and Bob in previous sections of this chapter, as well). This is a convenient way of making things unambiguous with relatively few words, since the pronoun "she" can be used for Alice, and "he" can be used for Bob. However, the advantages and disadvantages of this naming scheme are controversial, and we are not going to use it in the rest of this book either.

- K is used to refer to a secret key. A secret key is basically a key of a secret key cryptosystem.

- The pair (k, k^{-1}) is used to refer to a public key pair, whereas k is used to refer to the public key and k^{-1} is used to refer to the corresponding private key.

  In either case, key subscripts are used to indicate principals. In general, capital letter subscripts are used for long-term keys, and small letter subscripts are used for short-term keys. For example, K_A is used to refer to A's long-term secret key, whereas k_b is used to refer to B's short-term public key.

- The term $\{M\}K$ is used to refer to a message M that is encrypted with the secret key K. Since the same key K is used for decryption, $\{\{M\}K\}K$ equals M. If K is used to compute and verify a message authentication code (MAC) for message M, then the term $\langle M \rangle K$ is used to refer to $\{h(M)\}K$, with h being a collision-resistant, one-way hash function.

- Similarly, the term $\{M\}k$ is used to refer to a message M that is encrypted with the public key k. The message can only be decrypted with the corresponding private key k^{-1}. If a public key cryptosystem is used to digitally sign messages, the private key is used for signing, and the corresponding public key is used for verifying signatures. Referring to the terminology of the OSI security architecture, the term $\{M\}k^{-1}$ is used to refer to a digital signature giving message recovery, and $\langle M \rangle k^{-1}$ is used to refer to a digital signature with appendix. Note that in the second case, $\langle M \rangle k^{-1}$ in fact abbreviates $M, \{h(M)\}k^{-1}$, with h being again a collision-resistant, one-way hash function.

- The term $X \ll Y \gg$ is used to refer to a certificate that has been issued by X for Y's public key. Note that $X \ll Y \gg$, in principle, implies that X has certified the binding of Y's long-term public key k_Y with Y's identity.

- T is used to refer to a *timestamp*. Timestamp subscripts are used to imply a temporal ordering.

- N is used to refer to a *nonce*. A nonce is a quantity that any given user of a cryptographic protocol is supposed to use only once. Various forms of nonce are a timestamp, a sequence number, or a large and unpredictable random number. In our notation, we use small letters in nonce subscripts to indicate particular principals. Small letters are used mainly because of the short-term nature of nonces. For example, N_a refers to a nonce that has been chosen by principal A.

- Finally, M, N is used to refer to the concatenation of the two message strings M and N.

In the protocol descriptions that follow, the term

$i \colon A \longrightarrow B \colon M$

is used to refer to step i, in which principal A is assumed to transmit a message M to principal B. Note that the notation of $\longrightarrow$ must be interpreted with care. The messages are sent in environments, where error, corruption, loss, and delay may occur. There is nothing in the environment to guarantee that messages are really made in numerical order by the principals indicated, received in numerical order or at all by the principals indicated, or received solely by the principals indicated.

REFERENCES

[1] D. Stinson, *Cryptography Theory and Practice*, CRC Press, Boca Raton, FL, 1995.

[2] B. Schneier, *Applied Cryptography: Protocols, Algorithms, and Source Code in C*, 2nd Edition, John Wiley & Sons, New York, NY, 1996.

[3] A. Menezes, P. van Oorschot, and S. Vanstone, *Handbook of Applied Cryptography*, CRC Press, Boca Raton, FL, 1996.

[4] P.W. Shor, "Algorithms for Quantum Computation: Discrete Logarithms and Factoring," *Proceedings of IEEE 35th Annual Symposium on Foundations of Computer Science*, 1994, pp. 124 – 134.

[5] L.M. Adleman, "Molecular Computation of Solutions to Combinatorial Problems," *Science*, 1994, pp. 1021 – 1024.

[6] G. Păun, G. Rozenberg, and A. Salomaa, *DNA Computing: New Computing Paradigms*, Springer-Verlag, New York, NY, 1998.

[7] C.H. Bennett, G. Brassard, and A.K. Ekert, "Quantum Cryptography," *Scientific American*, October 1992, pp. 50 – 57.

[8] B. Kaliski, "The MD2 Message-Digest Algorithm," Request for Comments 1319, April 1992.

[9] R.L. Rivest, "The MD4 Message-Digest Algorithm," Request for Comments 1320, April 1992.

[10] R.L. Rivest, and S. Dusse, "The MD5 Message-Digest Algorithm," Request for Comments 1321, April 1992.

[11] U.S. National Institute of Standards and Technology (NIST), "Secure Hash Standard (SHS)," FIPS PUB 180-1, April 1995.

[12] H. Dobbertin, A. Bosselaers, and B. Preneel, "RIPEMD-160: A strengthened version of RIPEMD," *Proceedings of Fast Software Encryption Workshop*, 1996, pp. 71 – 82.

[13] P. van Oorschot, and M. Wiener, "Parallel Collision Search with Applications to Hash Functions and Discrete Logarithms," *Proceedings of ACM Conference on Computer and Communications Security*, November 1994.

[14] H. Dobbertin, "The Status of MD5 After a Recent Attack," *RSA Laboratories' CryptoBytes*, Vol. 2, 1996, No. 2.

[15] U.S. National Institute of Standards and Technology (NIST), "Data Encryption Standard," FIPS PUB 46, January 1977.

[16] X. Lai, *On the Design and Security of Block Ciphers*, Ph.D. Thesis, ETH No. 9752, ETH Zürich, Switzerland, 1992.

[17] B. Schneier, "Description of a New Variable-Length Key, 64-Bit Block Cipher (Blowfish)," *Proceedings of Fast Software Encryption Workshop*, 1994, pp. 191 – 204.

[18] J.L. Massey, "SAFER K-64: A Byte-Oriented Block Ciphering Algorithm," *Proceedings of Fast Software Encryption Workshop*, 1994, pp. 1 – 17.

[19] W. Diffie, and M.E. Hellman, "New Directions in Cryptography," *IEEE Transactions on Information Theory*, IT-22(6), 1976, pp. 644 – 654.

[20] B. Pfitzmann, *Digital Signature Schemes*, Springer-Verlag, Berlin, Germany, 1996.

[21] R.L. Rivest, A. Shamir, and L. Adleman, "A Method for Obtaining Digital Signatures and Public-Key Cryptosystems," *Communications of the ACM*, 21(2), February 1978, pp. 120 – 126.

[22] T. ElGamal, *Cryptography and Logarithms Over Finite Fields*, Ph.D. Thesis, Stanford University, 1984.

[23] T. ElGamal, "A Public Key Cryptosystem and a Signature Scheme Based on Discrete Logarithm," *IEEE Transactions on Information Theory*, IT-31(4), 1985, pp. 469 – 472.

[24] U.S. National Institute of Standards and Technology (NIST), *Digital Signature Standard (DSS)*, FIPS PUB 186, May 1994.

[25] J. Feghhi, J. Feghhi, and P. Williams, *Digital Certificates: Applied Internet Security*, Addison-Wesley Longman, Reading, MA, 1999.

[26] ITU-T X.509, *The Directory — Authentication Framework*, November 1987.

[27] ISO/IEC 9594-8, *Information Technology — Open Systems Interconnection — The Directory — Part 8: Authentication Framework*, 1990.

[28] B. Kaliski, *A Layman's Guide to a Subset of ASN.1, BER, and DER*, Technical Note, RSA Data Security, Inc., Redwood City, CA, November 1993.

[29] M. Blaze, W. Diffie, R.L. Rivest, B. Schneier, T. Shimomura, E. Thompson, and M. Wiener, "Minimal Key Lengths for Symmetric Ciphers to Provide Adequate Commercial Security," Business Software Alliance, January 1996.

[30] L.J. Hoffman, *Building in Big Brother: The Cryptographic Policy Debate*, Springer-Verlag, New York, NY, 1995.

[31] S.A. Baker, and P.R. Hurst, *The Limits of Trust: Cryptography, Governments, and Electronic Commerce*, Kluwer Law International, Cambridge, MA, 1998.

[32] C.L. McCuen, "Digital/Electronic Signature State Legislative Models," GTE CyberTrust Solutions Inc., November 1997.

Chapter 5

Internet Security Protocols

In this chapter, we overview and briefly discuss some cryptographic security protocols that have been proposed, specified, and partly implemented for the Internet and the WWW. In particular, we introduce the topic in Section 5.1, address security protocols for the network access, Internet, transport, and application layers in Sections 5.2 to 5.5, and draw some conclusions in Section 5.6. Due to the nature of this chapter, it includes quite an extensive list of references. Further information on the protocols can also be found in [1] as well as [2,3].

5.1 INTRODUCTION

There is a strong consensus that providing security services in computer networks and distributed systems requires the use of cryptographic techniques, and that these techniques must be integrated into communication protocols accordingly. This is also true for the Internet and the WWW. Consequently, many cryptographic security protocols have been proposed, specified, and partly implemented for the Internet and the WWW in the recent past.

In the case of TCP/IP-based networks, cryptographic security protocols can operate at any layer of the corresponding communications protocol suite. Consequently, there are proposals for providing security services at the network access,

Internet, transport, and application layers. There are even some proposals to provide security services above the application layer. For the purpose of this book, however, these proposals are discussed together with proposals to provide security services at the application layer.

In general, it is difficult to say what layer is best suited to address the security requirements of specific applications and application protocols. The answer to this question heavily depends on the application. Instead of answering this question, we follow a more pragmatic approach and overview and briefly discuss the most important security protocols proposed in the past and that are used in practice. The advantages and disadvantages of the various protocol proposals are further addressed in the concluding remarks of this chapter.

5.2 NETWORK ACCESS LAYER SECURITY PROTOCOLS

In the TCP/IP communications protocol suite, the network access layer handles issues related to local area networking. Protocols that operate at this layer include Ethernet (IEEE 802.3), token bus (IEEE 802.4), token ring (IEEE 802.5), fiber distributed data interchange (FDDI), as well as protocols for dial-up networking, such as the serial line IP (SLIP) [4] and the point-to-point protocol (PPP) [5]. For all practical purposes, Ethernet is most widely deployed for local area networking and PPP is most often used for dial-up networking.

Figure 5.1   Graphical illustration of the problem facing a conference attendee who is traveling aboard and wants to connect his laptop to his home corporate intranet.

In the late 1980s, the IEEE started to address issues related to LAN and metropolitan area network (MAN) security. In particular, the IEEE 802.10 working group was formed in May 1988 to address LAN and MAN security. Meanwhile,

IEEE 802.10 specified several *standards for interoperable LAN/MAN security* (SILS) that are compatible with existing IEEE 802 and OSI standard specifications [6,7]. Unfortunately, SILS has not been particularly successful and there are hardly any products that implement the SILS specifications. Consequently, we do not address the work of IEEE 802.10 and SILS. Instead, we elaborate on some recent work that has been done to secure dial-up networking using PPP with security enhancements in this section.

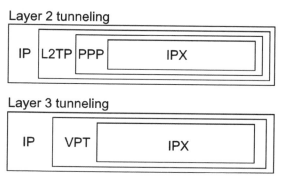

Figure 5.2   The layer 2 tunneling and layer 3 tunneling encapsulation schemes.

First, let's consider the problem facing a European conference attendee traveling in the United States who wants to connect his laptop to his home corporate intranet (for example, to read e-mail messages or download a PowerPoint presentation for the conference). This situation is illustrated in Figure 5.1. There are several solutions to this problem:

- An obvious solution is to use the PSTN or integrated services digital network (ISDN) to connect to a modem pool, or any other remote access server (RAS) located on the corporate intranet, and to set up a PPP connection accordingly. The major advantage of this solution is simplicity, whereas the disadvantages are related to security and costs. The problem with security is that dial-in access is relatively insecure and easily hacked, and — even more importantly — that the data traffic between the laptop and the intranet server goes unencrypted and unprotected. The problem with costs is that the user is charged the fees for a long distance call (or the company is charged the fees in the case of a modem pool with free charging or dial-back facilities).

- A more sophisticated solution is to use a *virtual private network* (VPN) tunnel. The most widely used method of creating VPN tunnels is by encapsulating network layer protocols, such as IP, IPX, or AppleTalk, inside PPP and then encapsulating the entire package inside a tunneling protocol, which is typically IP but could also be ATM or Frame Relay. This approach is commonly referred to as "layer 2 tunneling" since the passenger is a layer 2 protocol, such as PPP. Alternatively, network layer protocols can also be encapsulated directly into a tunneling protocol, such as 3Com's Virtual Tunneling Protocol (VTP). Consequently, this approach is referred to as "layer 3 tunneling" since the passenger is a layer 3 protocol. Figure 5.2 illustrates the layer 2 tunneling and layer 3 tunneling encapsulation schemes (for IPX encapsulated in IP). The major advantages of VPN tunnels are that data traffic is encapsulated in IP packets that can be routed over the public Internet, and that cryptographic techniques can be employed to secure the data traffic.

Figure 5.3   Layer 2 forwarding/tunneling from the Internet service provider's point of presence to the RAS on the corporate intranet.

Figure 5.3 illustrates the layer 2 forwarding/tunneling solution to the conference attendee problem mentioned above. In this solution, the connection is tunneled from the Internet service provider's *point of presence* (POP) to the RAS that is located on the corporate intranet. Note that a POP is sometimes also referred to as a *network access server* (NAS), a *front-end processor* (FEP), or a *dial-in server*. Whenever needed, we use the term POP in this book.

In the following subsections we further elaborate on the second approach. In particular, we briefly overview and partly discuss the various layer 2 forwarding/tunneling protocols that have been proposed in the past (layer 3 tunneling is further addressed in the following section). Today, there is strong consensus that the layer 2 tunneling protocol (L2TP) as proposed by an Internet Engineering Task Force (IETF) working group of the same name is actually the way to go.

5.2.1 Layer 2 Forwarding Protocol

Historically, the first proposal for a layer 2 forwarding/tunneling protocol was Cisco Systems' *Layer 2 Forwarding* (L2F) protocol as specified in RFC 2341 [8]. Since the L2F protocol is only of historical value, we are not going to delve into the technical details of the corresponding protocol specification in this book.

5.2.2 Point-to-Point Tunneling Protocol

The *Point-to-Point Tunneling Protocol* (PPTP) is the result of joint efforts of Microsoft Corporation and a set of networking products and NAS vendors, including Ascend Communications, 3Com/Primary Access, ECI Telematics, and U.S. Robotics. These companies originally constituted the PPTP Forum, whose resulting PPTP specification was made publicly available and submitted to the IETF in 1996.

Similar to the L2F protocol, PPTP was designed to solve the problem of creating and maintaining VPN tunnels over public TCP/IP-based networks using PPP [9,10]. As illustrated in Figures 5.1 and 5.3, a typical deployment of PPTP starts with a remote or mobile client, such as a laptop computer, that must be interconnected to a RAS located on a corporate intranet by using an ISP's POP (or NAS). As such, PPTP can be used to encapsulate PPP frames into IP packets for transmission over the Internet or any other publicly accessible TCP/IP-based network. In addition, it can also be used for private LAN-to-LAN interconnection. Thus, a remote system on network X can tunnel PPP data traffic to a gateway machine or RAS on network Y and appear to be sitting, with an internal IP address, on network Y. More specifically, a PPTP client can connect to a PPTP server in two ways:

- Either by using an ISP's POP that supports inbound PPP connections (if the client does not directly support PPTP);

- Or by using PPTP directly (if the client supports PPTP).

In the first case, the client establishes a first PPP connection to the ISP's POP and a second connection to the PPTP server that is located on the corporate intranet. This second connection actually uses PPTP and a sophisticated encapsulation scheme to tunnel PPP frames through the Internet (or any other TCP/IP-based network that interconnects the ISP's POP and the PPTP server). More precisely, network or Internet layer protocol data units (e.g., IP packets, IPX packets, or NetBEUI messages) are first framed using PPP. The resulting PPP frames are then encapsulated using a generic routing encapsulation (GRE) header [11] as well as an IP header that is used to route the frame through the Internet. Finally, the resulting IP packets are framed with still another media-specific header before they are forwarded to the interface connected to the Internet.

In the second case, the situation is comparably simple. The client first establishes a PPP connection to the ISP's POP and then uses PPTP to send encapsulated PPP frames to the PPTP server. Again, each PPP frame carries a network or Internet layer protocol data unit.

In either case, there is a TCP-based control session that is established in conjunction with the encapsulated data channel. The PPTP control session messages are used to query status and to convey signaling information between the client and the PPTP server. The control channel is initiated by the client to the server on TCP port 1723. In most cases, this is a bidirectional communication channel where the client can send messages to the server and vice versa.

PPTP does not specify specific algorithms for authentication and encryption, but provides a framework for negotiating particular algorithms. This negotiation is not specific to PPTP, and relies upon existing PPP option negotiations contained within the PPP compression protocol (CCP) [12], the challenge handshake authentication protocol (CHAP) [13], and some other PPP extensions and enhancements [14,15]. PPP sessions can negotiate compression algorithms as well as authentication and encryption algorithms.

Although PPTP has been submitted to the IETF for standardization,[1] it is currently available only for networks served by Windows NT 4.0 server or Linux systems. Currently, Microsoft's PPTP implementation (MS-PPTP) is the most widely used protocol to provide VPN dial-up connectivity at all. It is part of the Windows NT server software distribution and is also used extensively in commercial VPN products, such as Aventail[2] and Freegate.[3] The Microsoft PPTP server can only run under Windows NT, whereas client software is also available for Windows 95 and Windows 98 (and probably all future releases of the Windows operating systems). Configuration issues are further addressed in Chapter 6 of [10].

MS-PPTP authentication and encryption are addressed next. Afterward, we briefly summarize the results of a security analysis that has been performed for Microsoft's implementation of PPTP.

---

[1] `draft-ietf-pppext-pptp-*.txt`
[2] `http://www.aventail.com`
[3] `http://www.freegate.com`

MS-PPTP Authentication

Microsoft's implementation of PPTP (MS-PPTP) currently supports three authentication options:

- *Clear Password:* The client authenticates to the server by sending it a password in the clear;

- *Hashed Password:* The client authenticates to the server by sending it a hash of the password;

- *Challenge-Response:* The client and the server authenticate each other using MS-CHAP, which is Microsoft's version of the commonly used CHAP.

For obvious reasons, the clear password authentication option (clear password) is susceptible to password sniffing and is not secure. With regard to the hashed password authentication option (hashed password), Microsoft's implementation of PPTP for Windows NT actually uses two one-way hash functions: the Lan Manager hash function[4] and the Windows NT hash function.[5]

The Lan Manager hash function is based on the DES algorithm. It basically works as follows:

- First, the password is turned into a 14-character string, either by truncating longer passwords or padding shorter passwords with zeros;

- Second, all lowercase characters are converted to uppercase (numbers and non-alphanumeric characters remain unaffected);

- Third, the 14-byte string is split into two 7-byte strings, and a fixed constant is DES-encrypted using each 7-byte string as a key. Consequently, this step yields two 8-byte encrypted strings.

- Finally, the two resulting 8-byte encrypted strings are concatenated to create a single 16-byte hash value.

Contrary to that, the Windows NT hash function is based on the MD4 one-way hash function. It basically works as follows:

---

[4]The Lan Manager hash function was originally developed by Microsoft for IBM's OS/2 operating system, and was later integrated into Windows for Workgroups and optionally in Windows 3.1.

[5]The Windows NT hash function was developed by Microsoft specifically for Windows NT. It is specified in an Internet draft named `draft-ietf-pppext-mschap-*.txt`

- First, the password (up to 14 characters long and case-sensitive) is converted to Unicode;

- Second, the password is hashed using the MD4 one-way hash function, yielding a 16-byte hash value.

For obvious reasons, dictionary attacks are easy against the Lan Manager hash function.[6] The Windows NT hash function is an improvement over the Lan Manager hash function, because case sensitivity provides more entropy for the passwords, passwords can be longer than 14 characters, and hashing the entire password together instead of in small sections is better. However, neither of the two hash functions provides support for a salt mechanism, such as employed, for example, by the UNIX operating system.[7] Consequently, two people with the same password will always have the same Lan Manager and Windows NT hash values; so comparing a file of hashed passwords with a precomputed dictionary of hashed password candidates is still a fruitful attack. Also note that both hash values are always sent together. Therefore, it is possible to brute-force the password using the weaker hash function (the Lan Manager hash function), and then test various lower-case alternatives to actually find the other hash value (the Windows NT hash). In fact, Peter Mudge from L0pht Heavy Industries has written a program called L0phtcrack that automates the process of recovering passwords from their corresponding hash values.[8]

When using MS-CHAP, the challenge-response option of MS-PPTP authentication [16], the client first requests a login challenge, and the server sends back an

---

[6]Note that all characters are converted to uppercase, making the number of possible passwords smaller. Also, there is no salt mechanism (as addressed in the following footnote), causing two users with the same password to always have the same hashed password. Finally, the two 7-byte halves of the password are hashed independently, enabling the two halves to be attacked with brute-force independently.

[7]In many operating systems, user passwords are stored in one-way encrypted form. The one-way function that is used for this transformation is publicly known, so anybody could generate a codebook with password candidates transformed with this one-way function. In order to make it more difficult to generate such a codebook, the UNIX operating system uses a salt mechanism. The basic idea is to use a random number (which is also called "salt" or "salt value") as a parameter for the one-way function, and to store the salt as cleartext in the password file (together with the one-way encrypted password). When the operating system wants to check the user-supplied password, it has to feed the one-way function with the appropriate salt value (the one it reads from the password file). As a consequence, an attacker can only launch a dictionary attack against a specific salt value, and a dictionary attack against the entire set of users is no longer possible (or at least more difficult).

[8]http://www.l0pht.com/l0phtcrack/

8-byte random challenge. The client then calculates the Lan Manager hash value, adds five zero-bytes to actually create a 21-byte string, and partitions the string into three 7-byte keys. Each key is then used to encrypt the challenge with the DES algorithm, resulting in a 24-byte encrypted string. This string is sent to the server as a response. In addition, the client does the same with the Windows NT hash functions. The server, in turn, looks up one of the two hash values in its local database, encrypts the challenge with the corresponding hash value, and compares it with the encrypted hash value it has received. If they match, the authentication succeeds. Note that the server could make the comparison on the Lan Manager or Windows NT hash. In either case, the result would be the same. Which hash value the server uses actually depends on a flag set in the client's response message. If the flag is set, the server tests against the Windows NT hash value; if the flag is not set, the server tests against the Lan Manager hash value.

In either case, MS-CHAP must be used in order for subsequent PPTP packets to be encrypted. With either of the other two authentication options (clear or hashed password), no encryption is available in MS-PPTP.

MS-PPTP Encryption

In addition to the various PPTP authentication options, the *Microsoft Point-to-Point Encryption* (MPPE) protocol makes it also possible to encrypt PPTP packets [17]. In short, the MPPE protocol assumes the existence of a secret key shared by both ends of the connection, and uses the RC4 stream cipher with either a 40-bit key (in the international version), or a 128-bit key (in the U.S. domestic version). The method for negotiating the use of MPPE is through an option in the PPP CCP. After these negotiations, the PPP session begins passing payload packets of encrypted data (there is no message authentication or data integrity service provided for the packets).

According to the MPPE protocol specification, a 40-bit RC4 key is determined by first generating a deterministic 64-bit key from the Lan Manager hash value of the user's password using SHA-1, and then setting the high-order 24 bits of the key to the hexadecimal value 0xD1269E.[9] Similarly, a 128-bit RC4 key is determined by first concatenating the Windows NT hash value of the user's password and a 64-bit random nonce created by the server during the execution of the MS-CHAP, and then generating a deterministic 128-bit key again using SHA-1. In either case, the

---

[9]The MPPE protocol specification includes a flag for calculating the 40-bit RC4 key based on the Windows NT hash instead of the Lan Manager hash, but this feature was not implemented in the first version of MPPE.

resulting key is used to initialize the RC4 stream cipher in the usual manner, and then to encrypt data bytes. After every 256 packets a new RC4 key — 64 bits long for 40-bit encryption and 128 bits long for 128-bit encryption — is generated by hashing the previous key and the original key with SHA-1. Again, if the required key is 40 bits, the high-order 24 bits of the key are set to the hexadecimal value mentioned above.

A 40-bit version of MPPE is bundled with PPTP into Windows 95 and Windows NT 4.0 Dial-Up Networking. A 128-bit version is available for U.S. and Canadian citizens only.

Security Analysis

In 1998, Bruce Schneier from Counterpane Systems[10] and Peter Mudge from L0pht Heavy Industries[11] cryptanalyzed Microsoft's implementation of PPTP [18]. In summary, they found Microsoft's authentication protocol (MS-CHAP) to be weak and easily susceptible to dictionary attacks. Because both the Lan Manager and the Windows NT hash values are transmitted (even in a Windows NT-only environment), it is possible to attack the weaker hash function, which is basically the Lan Manager hash. Note that the last 8 bytes of the Lan Manager hash value is a constant if the password is seven characters or less (this is true despite the random challenge). Therefore, the last 8 bytes of the client's reply will be the server's challenge encrypted with that constant. Furthermore, it is also possible to effectively attack MS-CHAP itself [18].

An additional problem with MS-CHAP is that only the client is authenticated. Consequently, an attacker who hijacks a connection can trivially masquerade as the server. If encryption is enabled, the attacker will not be able to send and receive messages (unless he or she also breaks the encryption), but by reusing an old challenge value he or she can obtain two sessions encrypted with the same key. This can be further explored by the attacker.

With regard to the MPPE protocol, the security of the key is no greater than the security of the password. In either case, the overall security of the encryption is not 40 bits or 128 bits, but the number of bits of entropy in the password.[12] To make

---

[10]http://www.counterpane.com

[11]http://www.10pht.com

[12]In information theory, the entropy of a random variable X measures the amount of information provided by an observation of X. Equivalently, it is also the uncertainty about the outcome before an observation of X. Entropy is particularly useful for approximating the average number of bits required to encode the elements of X. For example, the English language has about 1.3 bits of entropy per character, and case variations, numbers, and nonalphanumeric characters increase this

things worse, the 40-bit RC4 encryption suffers from even more serious weaknesses. Because there is no salt mechanism,[13] an attacker can precompute a dictionary of ciphertext PPP headers, and then quickly look up a given ciphertext in this dictionary. Moreover, the same 40-bit RC4 key is generated every time a user initializes PPTP. Since RC4 is an output feedback (OFB) mode stream cipher, it is possible to break the encryption from the ciphertext from two sessions. Unfortunately, the same key is used in both the forward and backward direction, guaranteeing that the same keystream is used to encrypt two different plaintexts. As mentioned above, the 128-bit RC4 encryption uses a 64-bit nonce in the key generation process, making precomputated dictionary attacks impractical. Nevertheless, brute-force attacks against the password are still much more efficient than brute-force attacks against the keyspace. The use of the nonce also means that two sessions using the same password will have two different 128-bit RC4 keys, although the same key will be used to encrypt the plaintext in both directions. Remember that RC4 is an OFB mode stream cipher, and that MPPE does not provide authentication and integrity of the ciphertext stream. Consequently, an attacker can undetectably flip arbitrary bits in the ciphertext stream and compromise the integrity of the data stream accordingly. This attack does not require the attacker to know the secret key or the client's password (of course, higher level protocols might detect or prevent these sorts of attacks).

In addition to the attacks mentioned above, Schneier and Mudge have also shown how an attacker can either spoof resynchronization requests or forge MPPE packets with incorrect coherency counts. If this is done continuously just prior to the 256th packet exchange, where the session key would normally be updated, an attacker can succeed in forcing the encrypted communications channel to never rekey. In addition, they have described a number of other attacks against the Microsoft implementation of PPTP, such as passive monitoring of PPTP servers, spoofing PPP negotiation parameters, and numerous denial-of-service attacks against PPTP servers.

In June 1998, Microsoft posted a preliminary answer to Schneier's and Mudge's security analysis of MS-PPTP to the Internet. In its answer, Microsoft argued that for reasons of legacy compatibility, Microsoft had continued to support both the Lan Manager and the Windows NT hash function in its PPTP implementation, and that future releases of PPTP software would provide administrators with the ability to configure a PPTP server so that it would only accept the cryptographically

---

value significantly.

[13]The rationale behind the salt mechanism is explained in footnote 8.

stronger Windows NT hash function. With regard to the problem of having the session key(s) derived from the password's hash, Microsoft recommends the use of 128-bit encryption and that administrators enforce the use of strong passwords on their networks. Obviously, this answer does not satisfy the security-minded reader of this book. Also, the first part of the answer does not help people outside the U.S. and Canada.

More recently, Microsoft released an upgarde to its PPTP software. In Microsoft's PPTP implementation version 2, several improvements were made. For example, MS-PPTP v2 uses a unique key in each direction making certain cryptanalytical attacks more difficult (the keys for each direction are still derived from the same value, the user's password Windows NT hash value, but differently depending on the direction). Furthermore, the Lan Manager hash value of the user's password is no longer sent along with the stonger Windows NT hash value (to prevent password cracking programs from first breaking the Lan Manager hash and then using that information to break the Windows NT hash). Unfortunately (and due to the lack of a salt mechanism for password hashing), Microsoft's PPTP implementation version 2 is still vulnerable to offline password-guessing attacks, such as employed by the L0phtcrack program. Furthermore, version rollback attacks are possible to invoke the cryptanalytically weaker MS-CHAP version 1 and to attack the user's Lan Manager hash value accordingly. Refer to [19] for a comprehensive security analysis of MS-PPTP v2.

5.2.3   Layer 2 Tunneling Protocol

In June 1996, Microsoft and Cisco proposed and submitted a combination of Microsoft's PPTP implementation with Cisco's L2F protocol to the IETF PPP Extensions (PPPEXT) WG[14] to propose. The proposal was named *Layer 2 Tunneling Protocol* (L2TP). This collaborative protocol proposal was particularly good news, as it means that there would be just one industry-wide IETF specification for a VPN dial-up protocol, and very likely that the L2TP would consist of the best elements of the L2F protocol and the PPTP. Refer to the URL indicated in footnote 14 to get some updated information about L2TP.

In summary, layer 2 forwarding/tunneling protocols, such as the L2F protocol, the PPTP, and the L2TP, provide some means for virtual private networking. It is, however, important to note that if a protocol's (or protocol implementation's) cryptography is weak or inherently flawed, then the resulting security is no better than the security of a protocol that doesn't use cryptography at all. In fact, the

---

[14]http://www.ietf.org/html.charters/pppext-charter.html

resulting security may even be worse (since the claimed use of crytography may seduce people into transmitting sensitive data they would not transmit under normal circumstances). Note, however, that the fact that weak or inherently flawed cryptography can make the overall security worse is true for any protocol, not just the layer 2 forwarding/tunneling protocols we have addressed so far.

5.3   INTERNET LAYER SECURITY PROTOCOLS

A couple of years ago, the IETF chartered the *IP Security* (IPsec) WG to develop and standardize an *IP security protocol* (IPSP) and a corresponding *Internet key management protocol* (IKMP). In August 1995, a series of Request for Comment (RFC) documents was published that specified a first version of IPSP [20 – 24]. In fact, the Internet Engineering Steering Group (IESG) approved this protocol specification to enter the Internet standards track as a Proposed Standard. Since then, the participants of the IETF IPsec WG have been working hard to further refine the IP security architecture, and to finish up the IPSP and IKMP specifications accordingly [25,26]. More recently, revised versions of the corresponding documents were published as updated RFC documents [27 – 36]. In addition, an informal RFC provides a valuable roadmap for the various documents [37].

This section overviews and briefly discusses the results of the IETF IPsec WG that have been produced so far. In particular, it addresses the IP security architecture and the corresponding suite of IPsec protocols (including IPSP and IKMP), as well as implementations thereof.

The idea of providing security services at the network or Internet layer is not new, and several protocols had been proposed before the IETF IPsec WG even started to meet. Examples include:

- The security protocol 3 (SP3) developed by the NSA and NIST [38];

- The network layer security protocol (NLSP) mainly developed by the International Organization for Standardization (ISO) and specified in ISO/IEC 11577 [39];

- The *integrated NLSP* (I-NLSP) developed and proposed by the NIST;

- A protocol named SwIPe developed and prototyped by John Ioannidis and Matt Blaze [40].

All these protocols are more alike than they are different. In fact, they all use encapsulation as their enabling technique. What this basically means is that authenticated and encrypted network layer packets are contained within other packets. More precisely, outgoing plaintext packets are authenticated and encrypted and enclosed in outer network layer headers that are used to route the packets through the (inter)network. At the peer systems, the incoming packets are decapsulated, meaning that the outer network layer headers are stripped off and the inner packets are authenticated and decrypted, and forwarded to their final destination. As further explained below, the IPSP also makes use of IP encapsulation in one of its modes (tunnel mode). Note that IP encapsulation requires no changes to the existing Internet routing infrastructure. Since authenticated and encrypted IP packets have an unencrypted, normal-looking outer IP header, they can be routed as usual and processed at their final destination.

5.3.1   IP Security Architecture

The IETF IPsec WG has the charter to design an IP security architecture and a corresponding suite of IPsec protocols that can be used to provide cryptographically-based security for IPv4 and IPv6. Consequently, the IP security architecture is common for both IPv4 and IPv6. The main difference is that the suite of IPsec protocols has to be retrofitted into IPv4 implementations, whereas it must be present in all IPv6 implementations right from the beginning.

As mentioned above, the suite of IPsec protocols consists of two main protocols, namely the IPSP and IKMP. The IPSP, in turn, consists of two (sub)protocols, namely the authentication header (AH) and the encapsulating security payload (ESP) protocols. Similarly, the IKMP has evolved from two major protocol proposals, namely the Internet security association and key management protocol (ISAKMP) and the OAKLEY key determination protocol. These protocols are introduced and discussed in the following subsections.

The concept of a *security association* (SA) is fundamental to the IP security architecture. The IPSP makes use of SAs and a major function of the IKMP is the establishment and maintenance of these SAs. In short, an SA is a simplex "connection" or "relationship" that affords security services to the traffic carried by it. Security services are afforded to an SA by the use of AH, or ESP, but not both. If both AH and ESP protection is applied to a data stream, then two SAs must be established and maintained. Similarly, to secure bidirectional communications between two hosts or security gateways, two SAs (one in each direction) are required. The term SA bundle is applied to a sequence of SAs through which traffic must be processed to satisfy a specific security policy.

The IPsec architecture allows the user or system administrator to control the granularity at which a security service is offered. In the first series of RFCs, three approaches (of how to feed SAs with cryptographic keys) were distinguished:

- Host-oriented keying has all users on one host share the same session key for use on traffic destined for all users on another host;

- User-oriented keying lets each user on one host have one or more unique session keys for the traffic destined for another host (such session keys are not shared with other users);

- Session-unique keying has a single session key being assigned to a given IP address, upper-layer protocol, and port number triple (in this case, a user's FTP session may use a different key than the same user's Telnet session).

From a security point of view, user-oriented and session-unique keying are superior and therefore preferred. This is due to the fact that in many cases, a single computer system will have at least two suspicious users that do not mutually trust each other. When host-oriented keying is used and mutually suspicious users exist, it is sometimes possible for a user to determine the host-oriented key via well-known cryptanalytical attacks, such as chosen plaintext attacks. Once this user has improperly obtained the key in use, he or she can either read another user's encrypted traffic or forge traffic from this user. When user-oriented or session-unique keying is used, certain kinds of attack from one user onto another user's data traffic are simply not possible. Unfortunately, the distinction between the three keying approaches is no longer used in the current protocol specifications of the IETF IPsec WG.

An IPsec implementation operates in a host or security gateway (a router or a firewall system implementing the suite of IPsec protocols) environment, affording protection to IP data traffic. The protection offered is based on requirements defined by a security policy database (SPD) established and maintained by a user or system administrator (or by an application operating within constraints established by either of the above). In general, IP packets are selected for one of the three processing modes based on IP and transport layer header information matched against entries in the SPD. Each packet is either afforded IPsec security services, discarded, or allowed to bypass IPsec security services entirely.

Each SA is uniquely identified by a security parameters index (SPI), an IP destination address, and a security protocol identifier (AH or ESP). In addition to the SPD, there is a security association database (SAD) in each IPsec module. Each SA has an entry in the SAD defining the security parameters associated with that SA. In general, the IPSP protocols, AH and ESP, are largely independent of the associated SA and key management techniques, although the techniques involved do affect some of the security services offered by the protocols. The IP security architecture mandates support for both manual and automated SA and cryptographic key management as provided by the IKMP.

5.3.2   IP Security Protocol

According to the terminology introduced in the OSI security architecture (ISO/IEC 7498-2), the IPSP provides support for data origin authentication, connectionless data integrity (including protection against replay attacks), data confidentiality, access control, as well as limited traffic flow confidentiality services. These security services are provided at the Internet layer, offering protection for IP and/or upper layer protocols. As mentioned previously, the security services are provided by the use of two IPSP (sub)protocols, namely the AH and ESP. Each of these protocols supports two modes of use; transport mode and tunnel mode.

- In *transport mode*, the protocol provides protection primarily for upper layer protocols;

- In *tunnel mode*, the protocol is applied to entire tunneled IP packets (using IP encapsulation as enabling technique).

In general, a transport mode SA is established and maintained between two hosts. In IPv4, a transport mode security protocol header appears immediately after the IP header and any options, and before any higher layer protocols (e.g., TCP or UDP). In IPv6, a transport mode security protocol header appears after the base IP header and extensions, but may appear before or after destination options, and before higher layer protocols. Contrary to that, a tunnel mode SA is always applied to an IP tunnel. Whenever either end of an SA is a security gateway, the SA must be tunnel mode (note that for the case where traffic is destined for a security gateway, e.g., SNMP commands, the security gateway is acting as a host and transport mode is also allowed). For a tunnel mode SA, there is an outer IP header that specifies the IPsec processing destination, and an inner IP header that specifies the ultimate destination for the IP packet. In this case, the tunnel mode security protocol header appears after the outer IP header, and before the inner IP header.

Authentication Header

The IPSP AH protocol provides data origin authentication and connectionless data integrity for IP packets (hereafter referred to as just "authentication"). The precision of the authentication is a function of the granularity of the SA with which AH is employed. Depending on which cryptographic algorithm is used and how keying is performed, the AH may also provide non-repudiation of origin services. Finally, the AH may offer an antireplay service at the discretion of the receiver, to help counter specific denial-of-service attacks.

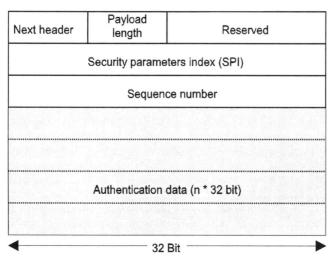

Figure 5.4   The authentication header (AH) format.

The Internet Assigned Numbers Authority (IANA) has assigned the protocol number 51 for the AH, so the header immediately preceding the AH must include 51 in its protocol or next header field. As specified in RFC 2402 [28] and illustrated in Figure 5.4, the AH header consists of an 8-bit Next Header field, an 8-bit Payload Length field, a 16-bit field that is reserved for future use, a 32-bit SPI field, a 32-bit Sequence Number field, and a variable-length $n*32$-bit Authentication Data field. The authentication data is computed by using an authentication algorithm and a cryptographic key specified in the corresponding SA. The sender computes the data prior to sending the IP packet, and the receiver verifies it upon reception. Several algorithms for authentication data computation and verification have been proposed in the past [41]. In particular, RFC 2403 [29] suggests the use of the HMAC construction with MD5 and RFC 2404 [30] suggests the use of the same construction with SHA-1. The HMAC construction is fully explained in [3]. In short, the HMAC construction takes as input the message M and the authentication key K, and produces as output the following expression:

$$HMAC_K(M) = h(K \oplus opad, h(K \oplus ipad, M))$$

This expression looks more complicated than it actually is. To compute $HMAC_K(M)$, the key K and an inner pad value $ipad$ ($ipad$ refers to the byte 0x36 repeated several times) are first added modulo 2. The result is then concatenated with the message M and hashed with the one-way hash function h (which can be either MD5 or SHA-1). Similarly, the result is then concatenated with the sum of K and an outer pad value $opad$ ($opad$ refers to the byte 0x5C repeated several times) modulo 2. Finally, this result is hashed with the appropriate one-way hash function h (MD5 or SHA-1). To make things more complicated, the resulting authentication data may be truncated to 96 bits. Depending on the one-way hash function in use, the resulting HMAC constructions are called HMAC-MD5-96 (in the case of MD5) and HMAC-SHA-1-96 (in the case of SHA-1).

As the AH protocol does not provide data confidentiality services, implementations thereof may be widely deployed, even in countries where controls on encryption would preclude deployment of technology that potentially offered data confidentiality services. Consequently, AH is an appropriate protocol to employ when confidentiality is not required.

Encapsulating Security Payload

As its name suggests, the IPSP ESP protocol uses IP encapsulation to provide data confidentiality, and partial traffic flow confidentiality (in tunnel mode and with the invocation of padding data to hide the size of an IP packet). Similar to the AH, the ESP protocol may also provide authentication (referring to data origin authentication and connectionless data integrity services). Note, however, that the scope of the authentication offered by the ESP is narrower than for the AH (i.e., the IP header(s) below the ESP header is not protected). If only the upper layer protocols need to be authenticated, then ESP authentication is an appropriate choice and is more space efficient than use of an AH encapsulating an ESP.

The IANA has assigned the protocol number 50 for the ESP, so the header immediately preceding the ESP must include 50 in its protocol or next header field. The ESP format is specified in RFC 2406 [32] and illustrated in Figure 5.5. It consists of a 32-bit SPI field and a 32-bit Sequence Number field that are not encrypted. The following fields are encrypted. They include a variable-length

Payload Data field, a variable-length Padding field, an 8-bit Pad Length field, and an 8-bit Next Header field. Additionally, the ESP may also include a variable-length $n*32$-bit Authentication Data field. The precise format of the ESP payload data depends on the particular encryption algorithm and transformation in use. The default algorithm suggested in RFC 2405 [31] is DES in cipher block chaining (CBC) mode with an explicit initialization vector (IV). But DES-CBC is just a default algorithm that may be replaced by other algorithms at will. For example, RFC 1851 specifies the experimental use of 3DES. Unfortunately, export, import, and use of specific encryption algorithms may be regulated in some countries. The algorithms for computing the authentication data are the same as the ones suggested for the AH.

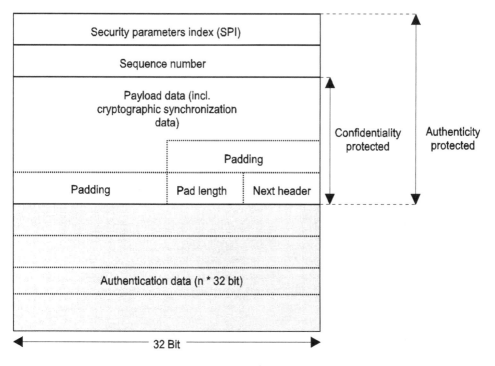

Figure 5.5 The encapsulating security payload (ESP) format.

Note that both AH and ESP are also vehicles for access control, based on the distribution of cryptographic keys and the management of traffic flows relative to these security protocols. Also note that full protection from traffic analysis is not provided by any of the two IPSP (sub)protocols. At the most, tunnel mode ESP can provide a partial traffic flow confidentiality service. In fact, the ESP protocol can be used to create a secure tunnel between two security gateways. In this case, anyone eavesdropping on the communications between the security gateways is not able to see what hosts are actually sending and receiving IP packets from behind the security gateways. Nevertheless, it is fair to mention that only a few Internet users worry about traffic analysis at all.

A final word should be said about the interdependence between data compression and encryption. Note that when encryption is employed at the Internet layer, it prevents effective data compression by lower protocol layers. Unfortunately, the suite of IPsec protocols in its current form does not provide support for a data compression service (contrary to most transport layer security protocols). Such a service may be provided by higher layer protocols, or, in the future, by IP itself. The IETF IP payload compression protocol (IPPCP) WG has the charter to develop protocol specifications that make it possible to perform lossless data compression on individual payloads before the payload is processed by a protocol that encrypts it.

5.3.3   Internet Key Management Protocol

As mentioned before, the IP security architecture mandates support for both manual and automated SA and cryptographic key management (using an IKMP). For several years, the IETF IPsec WG has been struggling with competing proposals for such an IKMP:

- IBM has proposed a modular key management protocol (MKMP) for its IP secure tunnel protocol (IPST) [42];

- Sun Microsystems has proposed and is further elaborating on its simple key-management for Internet protocols (SKIP) [43]. In short, SKIP uses predistributed and authenticated Diffie-Hellman parameters to have two parties share an implicit master key from which session keys may be derived;

- Phil Karn from Qualcomm has proposed a Photuris key management protocol that is conceptually similar to the station-to-station (STS) protocol originally proposed by Diffie, van Oorshot, and Wiener [44]. It combines an ephemeral Diffie-Hellman key exchange with a subsequent authentication step to thwart the man-in-the-middle attack. In order to protect against clogging attacks, Karn has introduced an initial cookie exchange. The rationale behind this cookie exchange is beyond the scope of this book and further addressed in [45];

- Hugo Krawczyk from IBM has proposed a variation and generalization of the Photuris protocol, called Photuris Plus or SKEME [46];

- Hilarie Orman from the University of Arizona has proposed another variation and generalization of the Photuris protocol, called the OAKLEY key determination protocol [47]. In this protocol, several parameters are negotiable, including the authentication method and the mathematical structure in which the Diffie-Hellman key exchange is actually performed;

- Last but not least, the NSA Office of INFOSEC Computer Science has proposed an Internet security association key management protocol (ISAKMP). A domain of interpretation (DOI) specifies the application of ISAKMP in the context of the IP security architecture.

The protocol proposals and their trade-offs are overviewed and fully discussed in [3]. In September 1996, the IETF Security Area Director posted a document to the Internet to end the controversy. In this document, he reviewed the two contenders for IKMP status, SKIP and ISAKMP/OAKLEY, and concluded that ISAKMP/OAKLEY should be the mandatory standard, and that SKIP could still become an elective Internet standard. The main arguments for this decision were that ISAKMP/OAKLEY provides perfect forward secrecy (PFS),[15] whereas SKIP — at least in its native form — does not provide PFS, and that given an arbitrarily chosen pair of hosts, it is likelier that an ISAKMP/OAKLEY approach will result in a working SA than SKIP. Furthermore going back to the original IPsec WG chapter, the ISAKMP/OAKLEY approach seems to more closely follow the goals established in the charter of the IKMP portion of the IPsec work.

According to this decision, a set of RFCs has been written to further refine the ISAKMP/OAKLEY approach [33 – 35]. Meanwhile, this approach has also been renamed to become the *Internet key exchange* (IKE), and this acronym is likely to replace IKMP in the future. The RFCs that specify the IKE have entered the Internet standards track ultimately resulting in a protocol that is elective for IPv4 implementations and mandatory for IPv6 implementations. Another set of RFCs is being written to further refine the SKIP approach. These RFCs are intended to follow the IETF standards track ultimately resulting in a protocol that is elective for both IPv4 and IPv6 implementations.

---

[15]In short, PFS refers to the property of a key establishment protocol that the compromise of a long-term secret does not necessarily reveal all session keys that have been (will be) established in the past (future). For all practical purposes, PFS requires a key agreement protocol, such as a Diffie-Hellman key exchange.

5.3.4   Implementations

There are currently three ways in which IPsec is implemented in hosts and/or security gateways:

- The most simple and straightforward way is to integrate the suite of IPsec protocols into a native IP implementation. This is applicable to hosts and security gateways, but requires access to the corresponding source code.

- Another way is provided by so-called "bump-in-the-stack" (BITS) implementations. In these implementations, IPsec is implemented underneath an existing IP stack, between the native IP implementation and the local network drivers. Source code access for the IP stack is not required in this case, making it appropriate for use with legacy systems. This approach, when it is adopted, is usually employed with hosts.

- A somewhat related way is provided by so-called "bump-in-the-wire" (BITW) implementations. Similar to BITS implementations, source code access for the IP stack is not required for BITW implementations. But in addition to BITS implementations, additional hardware in the form of outboard cryptographic processors are typically used. This is a common design feature of network security systems used by the military, and of some commercial systems as well. BITW implementations may be designed to serve both hosts and security gateways.

As of this writing, most IPsec implementations are either BITS or BITW. This is expected to change in the future, since more and more vendors of networking software are integrating the suite of IPsec protocols into their products (including Cisco and Microsoft).

The IP security architecture as discussed in this section is not an overall security architecture for the Internet. It addresses security only at the Internet layer, provided through the use of the IPsec protocols. Related topics, such as securing the routing infrastructure, the domain name system (DNS), and network management, are further addressed in [25]. Also, the current status of the IP security architecture does not even address all aspects of Internet layer security. Topics for further study include the use of Internet layer security protocols in conjunction with network address translation (NAT), a more complete support for IP multicast, issues related to interoperability, as well as benchmark testing. Note that the evolving nature of the IP architecture and the corresponding suite of IPsec protocol specifications make true interoperability hard to achieve. Also note that the throughputs of IPsec implementations usually decrease with the number of SAs that are established and maintained simultaneously. Consequently, this should be reflected by adequate methods for IPsec benchmark testing.

Implementing the IPsec protocols is mandatory for IPv6 and therefore likely to become widespread during the next couple of years. However, there are advantages and disadvantages related to providing security at the Internet layer:

- The main advantage is that applications must not be changed to use the suite of IPsec protocols. Another advantage is that providing security at the Internet layer works for both TCP- and UDP-based applications. This is advantageous because a steadily increasing number of applications (especially in realtime and multicast communications) is based on UDP that is hard to secure at the transport layer.

- The main disadvantage is that IP stacks must either be changed or extended. Due to the inherent complexity of the IKE specifications, the changes or extensions are not at all trivial. In the long term, high-speed networking may also provide a performance problem. As of this writing, it is not clear whether encryption rates and key agility properties will be sufficient to compete with data throughputs of future high-speed networks.

Due to the disadvantages of providing security at the Internet layer, some alternative approaches have appeared in the past (as discussed in the other sections of this chapter). The current trend in industry suggests that the IPsec protocols will primarily be used for virtual private networking and connecting mobile users to corporate intranets.

5.4 TRANSPORT LAYER SECURITY PROTOCOLS

In this section, we focus on the security protocols that have been proposed and partly implemented for the transport layer. Again, the idea of having a standardized transport layer security protocol is not new, and several protocols had been proposed before the IETF TLS WG even started to meet:

- The security protocol 4 (SP4) is a transport layer security protocol that was developed by the NSA and NIST as part of the secure data network system (SDNS) suite of security protocols [48].

- The transport layer security protocol (TLSP) was developed and standardized by the International Organization for Standardization (ISO) [49].

In addition, Matt Blaze and Steven Bellovin from AT&T Bell Laboratories have developed an encrypted session manager (ESM) software package [50]. As this package resembles the secure shell overviewed and discussed next, it is not further addressed in this book.

5.4.1   Secure Shell

The *secure shell* (SSH) is a relatively simple program that is used to securely log in to a remote machine, to execute commands on that machine, and to move files from one machine to another. SSH provides strong authentication and secure communications over insecure channels. As such, it is intended as a complete replacement for the Berkeley r-tools, such as `rlogin`, `rsh`, `rcp`, and `rdist`. It can also replace `telnet` in many cases. Furthermore, X11 and arbitrary TCP/IP connections can be secured using the integrated port forwarding feature of SSH. There is also support for SOCKS.

SSH was created mostly by one person, Tatu Ylönen from the Helsinki University of Technology, Finland [51]. There are currently two versions of SSH:

- A public version that has been freely available for various UNIX systems since July 1995. Source, documentation, and configuration scripts are publicly available and can be downloaded from the SSH homepage on the WWW.[16]

- A commercial version called *F-Secure SSH* that is available for various UNIX systems, as well as for Windows 3.x, Windows 95, Windows NT, OS/2, and MacOS. F-Secure SSH products are jointly developed and sold as part of a marketing and technology alliance between Data Fellows Ltd.[17] and SSH Communications Security Oy.[18] Data Fellows Ltd. is a privately held Finish software development company with subsidiaries in the United States and Estonia, whereas SSH Communications Security Oy is a small startup company founded by Ylönen. The commercial version of SSH is equipped with a number of additional features and utilities. For example, the encrypting data dumper (EDD) can be used to transparently encrypt arbitrary data streams (i.e., for backup purposes). Also, professional technical support and maintenance agreements are available only for the commercial version of SSH. F-Secure SSH is used and widely deployed on the Internet today.

---

[16] http://www.cs.hut.fi/ssh
[17] http://www.DataFellows.com or http://www.Europe.DataFellows.com
[18] http://www.ssh.fi

SSH and F-Secure SSH both utilize a generic transport layer security protocol. When used over TCP/IP, the server normally listens for TCP/IP connections on port 22. This port number has been registered with the IANA and is officially assigned for SSH. In short, the SSH protocol provides support for both host authentication and user authentication, together with data compression and data confidentiality and integrity protection. Disadvantageous is the fact that SSH uses manually distributed and preconfigured public keys instead of a certificate-based key management. This is notably the major disadvantage of SSH as compared to the SSL and TLS protocols addressed next.

5.4.2   Secure Sockets Layer and Transport Layer Security Protocols

In Internet application programming, it is common to use a generalized interprocess communications facility (IPC) to work with different transport layer protocols. Two popular IPC interfaces are BSD sockets and the transport layer interface (TLI), found on System V UNIX derivats. One idea that comes to mind first when trying to provide security services for TCP/IP applications is to enhance an IPC interface such as BSD Sockets with the ability to authenticate peer entities, to exchange secret keys, and to use these keys to authenticate and encrypt data streams transmitted between the communicating peer entities. Netscape Communications Corporation followed this approach when it specified a *secure sockets layer* (SSL) and the corresponding SSL protocol. The idea was later adopted by the IETF *transport layer security* (TLS) WG that is tasked to develop a security protocol for the transport layer. Due to their importance on the marketplace for network security solutions, we further address the SSL and TLS protocols in the following chapter.

5.5   APPLICATION LAYER SECURITY PROTOCOLS

Providing security at the application layer is often the most intrusive option. It is also the most flexible, because the scope and strength of the protection can be tailored to meet the specific needs of the application. In general, there are two approaches to provide security services at the application layer: either the services are integrated into each application protocol individually, or a generic security system is built that can be used to incorporate security services into arbitrary applications. In the following subsections, we overview and discuss both approaches.

5.5.1   Security-Enhanced Application Protocols

There are several application protocols that have been enhanced to provide integrated security services. Next, we address security enhancements for Telnet, electronic mail, WWW transactions, and some other applications.

Telnet

Several security-enhanced Telnet software packages have been developed. Examples include the following packages:

- The `slogin` utility of the SSH software package;

- The secure Telnet software replacement for 4.4BSD UNIX developed at AT&T Bell Laboratories;

- The secure RPC authentication (SRA) software package was developed at Texas A&M University (TAMU) [52];

- Secure Telnet (STEL) is another secure Telnet software package for UNIX systems that was developed at the University of Milan in cooperation with the Italian CERT [53].

Again, the software packages are further described in [3]. In summary, it is important to use a secure Telnet software package as a replacement for `rlogin` and `telnet` in a corporate intranet environment (mainly to protect against password sniffing attacks from insiders). It is even more important to use such a replacement if users regularly connect to intranet hosts from the outside world, such as the Internet. In the case of `rlogin`, the use of address-based authentication lends itself to IP spoofing attacks. In the case of `telnet`, passwords are transmitted in the clear that are subject to passive eavesdropping and replay attacks.

Electronic Mail

The basis for electronic mail (e-mail) on the Internet is the simple mail transfer protocol (SMTP) specified in RFC 821, the text and ASCII message syntax specified in RFC 822, and the MIME specified in RFCs 2045 to 2049. The major problem addressed by the MIME specification is that e-mail messages typically consist of 7-bit ASCII text, whereas multimedia applications generate data streams that consist of arbitrary binary 8-bit patterns. Consequently, there must be a way to turn these 8-bit patterns into printable characters that can be passed unscathed through various software processes, such as e-mail handlers, and that would otherwise be interpreted as control or illegal characters. One obvious consequence of this encoding (or filtering) step is message expansion. Products that conform to the MIME specification permit sending more than 7-bit ASCII text by providing conventions for making part of a message some kind of 8-bit encoding. More precisely, the MIME specification provides a general structure for the content type of an e-mail message and allows extensions for new content types. For example, MIME can be used to encapsulate electronic data interchange (EDI) objects, as further described in RFC 1767.

Neither SMTP nor the corresponding message syntax provide support for security services. It is, in general, easy to modify a message content or to forge either the sender address or routing information. Also, picking off e-mail messages on public networks, such as the Internet, has become a documented art. The same hosts and routers that efficiently move e-mail messages along their delivery paths can also be turned against their users to perform massive searching and sorting. A tremendous amount of information about users and organizations can be gathered with traffic analysis, even without a human around. In addition, anyone who can intercept an e-mail message can potentially also launch an active attack and tamper with it at will. Even small alterations, such as changing a date or moving a decimal point in a floating point number, can sometimes have disastrous impacts.

It is commonly agreed that widespread use of e-mail messages for commercial applications will require the provision of security services, such as those enumerated in the OSI security architecture. Data confidentiality services are required to ensure that the content of an e-mail message is not revealed to unauthorized parties, whereas data integrity, message authentication, and non-repudiation of origin services are required to provide the assurance that a message has not been tampered with during transmission. It is also commonly agreed that the enabling technique for providing this kind of end-to-end security for e-mail messages is digital enveloping. What this basically means is that the sender of an e-mail message randomly selects a transaction key, encrypts the message body with this key, and appends the transaction key encrypted with the recipient's public key to the message. The recipient, in turn, uses his or her private key to decrypt the transaction key, and then uses this transaction key to decrypt the original message. If the message is addressed to several recipients, then the sender must iterate the encryption of the transaction key. More precisely, the sender must generate an appendix for each recipient. This appendix contains the transaction key encrypted with this recipient's public key. Additionally, the sender can also use his or her private key to digitally sign the message. In this case, the recipient uses the sender's public key to verify the digital signature.

During the past few years, three primary schemes for e-mail security have emerged on the Internet:

- Privacy enhanced mail (PEM) [54 – 58];

- Pretty Good Privacy (PGP) [59 – 61];

- Secure MIME (S/MIME) [62,63].

Again, the schemes are overviewed and briefly discussed in [3]. As of this writing, S/MIME is the emerging standard for e-mail security. In fact, S/MIME has been recognized by commercial software vendors, including Microsoft and Netscape Communications, and is being deployed at a large scale in the marketplace. As of this writing, many products already released to the marketplace, such as Netscape Messenger and Microsoft Outlook Express, provide support for S/MIME [64]. S/MIME builds on top of three public key cryptography standard (PKCS) de facto standard formats, namely PKCS #1 [65], PKCS #10 [66], and PKCS #7 [67]. As such, the application of S/MIME is not limited to e-mail. In fact, any application protocol that transports MIME objects can leverage S/MIME security services. For example, because HTTP transports MIME objects, it can also use S/MIME to secure communications between a browser and a Web server (instead of SSL or TLS). Similarly, S/MIME has also been applied to exchange digitally signed EDI data over the Internet.

WWW Transactions

The *secure hypertext transfer protocol* (S-HTTP) was developed and originally proposed by Eric Rescorla and Allan Schiffman of Enterprise Integration Technologies (EIT) Corporation on behalf of the CommerceNet consortium.[19] S-HTTP supports WWW transaction security by incorporating cryptographic enhancements to HTTP traffic at the application layer. S-HTTP version 1.0 was publicly released in June 1994 and distributed by the CommerceNet consortium. Since 1995, the S-HTTP specification has been developed and further refined under the auspices of the IETF

---

[19]Launched in 1994 as a nonprofit organization, CommerceNet is dedicated to advancing electronic commerce on the Internet. Its nearly 250 member companies and organizations seek solutions to technology issues, sponsor industry pilots, and foster market and business development. CommerceNet is available online and can be reached at URL http://www.commerce.net

WTS WG. In March 1997, the S-HTTP specification was upgraded to version 1.3. As such, S-HTTP defined an extension of HTTP that was used to provide end-to-end security services for WWW transactions. The protocol emphasized flexibility in choice of key management mechanisms, security policies, and cryptographic algorithms by supporting option negotiation between an S-HTTP-capable client and an S-HTTP-capable server. For example, S-HTTP did not require the use of client certificates. If a client had a certificate, then it was used. If, however, a client did not have a certificate, then other security techniques were employed. This is important because it meant that spontaneous WWW transactions could occur even without requiring users to have public key certificates. S-HTTP could also be used with manually distributed and configured shared secret keys or Kerberos tickets instead of public key certificates. While S-HTTP was able to take advantage of a PKI, its deployment would not require it.

Unfortunately, S-HTTP has sunk into oblivion in the last couple of years. As of this writing, the SSL and TLS protocols are the major technologies to provide security for WWW transactions.

5.5.2 Authentication and Key Distribution Systems

During the past few years, a considerable amount of work has been done to develop authentication and key distribution systems that can be used by arbitrary applications to incorporate security services. Examples include the following authentication and key distribution systems:

- Kerberos, originally developed at MIT;

- Network Security Program (NetSP), developed by IBM;

- SPX, developed by DEC;

- The Exponential Security System (TESS), designed and developed at the University of Karlsruhe.

In addition, there are several extensions to the basic Kerberos authentication system, such as those provided by Yaksha, SESAME (secure European system for applications in a multivendor environment), and the Distributed Computing Environment (DCE) developed by the Open Group.[20] In this section we are not going

---

[20] The Open Group was formed in early 1996 by the consolidation of two open systems consortia, namely the Open Software Foundation (OSF) and the X/Open Company Ltd. The Open Group includes a large number of computer vendors, including IBM, DEC, and Microsoft.

to describe and discuss the authentication and key distribution systems mentioned above. Instead we refer to the companion book, *Authentication Systems for Secure Networks*, also published by Artech House [2] (or to [68] as in the case of the Kerberos authentication system).

Although the idea of building an authentication and key distribution system that may serve several applications is promising, the proliferation of these systems has turned out to be rather slow. One reason for that is because the specification of the GSS-API has come rather late. Also, more work is needed to standardize and eventually simplify the GSS-API. More recently, Microsoft has announced support for the Kerberos authentication system in its upcoming new version 5 of Windows NT operating system (also known as Windows 2000). In short, Kerberos is used as a single sign-on (SSO) system to log into an NT domain. The NT domain controller, in turn, acts as a Kerberos KDC, including the authentication server and the ticket granting server in Kerberos terminology. As of this writing, it is planned that Kerberos service tickets will also be used to feed the SAD of a corresponding IPsec implementation. Unfortunately, Microsoft uses again some proprietary enhancements of the basic Kerberos authentication protocol to carry authorization information within the service tickets. These enhancements are similar but not compatible to the enhancements of SESAME and DCE.

5.6   CONCLUSIONS

In this chapter we overviewed and briefly addressed some cryptographic protocols that have been developed, proposed, and partly implemented to provide communication security services for TCP/IP-based networks. While most of these protocols are similar in terms of security services they provide as well as cryptographic algorithms and techniques they employ, they vary fundamentally in the manner in which they provide the security services and their placement within the TCP/IP communications protocol suite. In particular, we have seen protocols for the network access, Internet, transport, and application layer.

So far, the question of which layer is best suited to provide security services has not been addressed. This simple question has turned out to be rather difficult to answer. Remember that the OSI security architecture has not been specific about this question either, and has proposed several possibilities for proper placement within the OSI reference model and its layered protocol stack instead. In general, there are arguments to provide security services either at the lower or higher layers:

- The proponents of placing security lower in the protocol stack argue that lower-layer security can be implemented transparently to users and application programs, effectively killing many birds with a single stone.

- Contrary to the above, proponents of placing security higher in the protocol stack argue that lower-layer security attempts to do too many things simultaneously, and that only protocols that work at the application layer or above can actually meet application-specific security requirements and provide corresponding services.

Unfortunately, both arguments are somewhat true, so there is no generally agreed upon best layer to provide security services. The best layer actually depends on the security services required and the application environment in which the services must be deployed.

In summary, the question of which layer(s) is (are) best suited to provide communication security services is not an "either or" decision, but rather an "and" decision, actually traversing and encompassing multiple layers. For example, bulk data cryptographic transformations, such as message authentication, integrity checking, and data encryption, are well suited to be performed at the network or Internet layer, which is usually tightly coupled with the operating system kernel and thus allows for efficient implementation and scheduling of potentially available dedicated hardware, random number generators, and other components. At the same time, security policies that may be defined for a site or corporate intranet may be enforced without individual users being able to circumvent them. This has to be supplemented by an API and other utilities residing in application space. The API and the utilities are to provide applications with information about the level of authenticity a connection actually has, and what algorithms for data encryption and authentication should be used. Finally, the concept of user involvement in the provision of security services is very important, but has not been sufficiently addressed in the past. Currently, each application takes care of its cryptographic keys individually, but this is certainly not the way to go for future applications. From the user's point of view, it would be convenient to have some sort of a key agent that securely stores his or her cryptographic keys and provides the applications with the keys required in order to act on the user's behalf. With regard to digital signature keys, the concept of user involvement is even more important since the application and use of these keys may create liability.

REFERENCES

[1] R. Oppliger, "Internet Security: Firewalls and Beyond," *Communications of the ACM*, Vol. 40, No. 5, May 1997, pp. 92 – 102.

[2] R. Oppliger, *Authentication Systems for Secure Networks*, Artech House, Norwood, MA, 1996.

[3] R. Oppliger, *Internet and Intranet Security*, Artech House, Norwood, MA, 1998.

[4] J. Romkey, "A Nonstandard for Transmission of IP Datagrams over Serial Lines: SLIP," Request for Comments 1055.

[5] W. Simpson, "The Point-to-Point Protocol (PPP)," Request for Comments 1661, STD 51, July 1994.

[6] IEEE 802.10, "IEEE Standards for Local and Metropolitan Area Networks: Interoperable LAN/MAN Security (SILS)," 1998.

[7] IEEE 802.10c, "Supplements to IEEE Std 802.10, Interoperable LAN/MAN Security (SILS): Key Management (Clause 3)," 1992.

[8] A. Valencia, M. Littlewood, and T. Kolar, "Cisco Layer Two Forwarding (Protocol) L2F," Request for Comments 2341, May 1998.

[9] Microsoft Corporation, "Understanding Point-to-Point Tunneling Protocol (PPTP)," White Paper, 1997.

[10] C. Scott, P. Wolfe, and M. Erwin, *Virtual Private Networks*, O'Reilly & Associates, Sebastopol, CA, 1998.

[11] S. Hanks, T. Li, D. Farinacci, and P. Traina, "Generic Routing Encapsulation (GRE)," Request for Comments 1701, October 1994.

[12] D. Rand, "The PPP Compression Control Protocol (CCP)," Request for Comments 1962, June 1996.

[13] B. Lloyd, and W. Simpson, "PPP Authentication Protocols," Request for Comments 1334, October 1992.

[14] G. Meyer, "The PPP Encryption Control Protocol (ECP)," Request for Comments 1968, June 1996.

[15] L. Blunk, and J. Vollbrecht, "PPP Extensible Authentication Protocol (EAP)," Request for Comments 2284, March 1998.

[16] G. Zorn, and S. Cobb, "Microsoft PPP CHAP Extensions," Request for Comments 2433, October 1998.

[17] G.S. Pall, and G. Zorn, "Microsoft Point-to-Point Encryption (MPPE) Protocol," Request for Comments 2118, April 1998.

[18] B. Schneier, and P. Mudge, "Cryptanalysis of Microsoft's Point-to-Point Tunneling Protocol," *Proceedings of ACM Conference on Communcations and Computer Security*, November 1998.

[19] B. Schneier, and P. Mudge, "Cryptanalysis of Microsoft's PPTP Authentication Extensions (MS-CHAPv2)," http://www.counterpane.com/pptpv2-paper.html, June 1999.

[20] R.J. Atkinson, "Security Architecture for the Internet Protocol," Request for Comments 1825, August 1995.

[21] R.J. Atkinson, "IP Authentication Header," Request for Comments 1826, August 1995.

[22] R.J. Atkinson, "IP Encapsulating Security Payload," Request for Comments 1827, August 1995.

[23] P. Metzger, and W. Simpson, "IP Authentication Using Keyed MD5," Request for Comments 1828, August 1995.

[24] P. Karn, P. Metzger, and W. Simpson, "The ESP DES-CBC Transform," Request for Comments 1829, August 1995.

[25] R.J. Atkinson, "Towards a More Secure Internet," *IEEE Computer*, Vol. 30, January 1997, pp. 57 – 61.

[26] R. Oppliger, "Security at the Internet Layer," *IEEE Computer*, Vol. 31, No. 9, September 1998, pp. 43 – 47.

[27] S. Kent, and R. Atkinson, "Security Architecture for the Internet Protocol," Request for Comments 2401 (obsoletes RFC 1825), November 1998.

[28] S. Kent, and R. Atkinson, "IP Authentication Header," Request for Comments 2402 (obsoletes RFC 1826), November 1998.

[29] C. Madson, and R. Glenn, "The Use of HMAC-MD5-96 within ESP and AH," Request for Comments 2403, November 1998.

[30] C. Madson, and R. Glenn, "The Use of HMAC-SHA-1-96 within ESP and AH," Request for Comments 2404, November 1998.

[31] C. Madson, and N. Doraswamy, "The ESP DES-CBC Cipher Algorithm With Explicit IV," Request for Comments 2405, November 1998.

[32] S. Kent, and R. Atkinson, "IP Encapsulating Security Payload (ESP)," Request for Comments 2406 (obsoletes RFC 1827), November 1998.

[33] D. Piper, "The Internet IP Security Domain of Interpretation for ISAKMP," Request for Comments 2407, November 1998.

[34] D. Maughan, M. Schertler, M. Schneider, and J. Turner, "Internet Security Association and Key Management Protocol (ISAKMP)," Request for Comments 2408, November 1998.

[35] D. Harkins, and D. Carrel, "The Internet Key Exchange (IKE)," Request for Comments 2409, November 1998.

[36] R. Glenn, and S. Kent, "The NULL Encryption Algorithm and Its Use With IPsec," Request for Comments 2410, November 1998.

[37] R. Thayer, and N. Doraswamy, "IP Security Document Roadmap," Request for Comments 2411, November 1998.

[38] R. Nelson, "SDNS Services and Architecture," *Proceedings of National Computer Security Conference*, 1987, pp. 153 – 157.

[39] ISO/IEC 11577, *Information Technology - Telecommunications and Information Exchange Between Systems - Network Layer Security Protocol*, Geneva, Switzerland, 1993.

[40] J. Ioannidis, and M. Blaze, "The Architecture and Implementation of Network-Layer Security Under Unix," *Proceedings of USENIX UNIX Security Symposium*, October 1993, pp. 29 – 39.

[41] M. Oehler, and R. Glenn, "HMAC-MD5 IP Authentication With Replay Prevention," Request for Comments 2085, February 1997.

[42] P.C. Cheng, J.A. Garay, A. Herzberg, and H. Krawczyk, "A Security Architecture for the Internet Protocol," *IBM Systems Journal*, Vol. 37, No. 1, 1998, pp. 42 – 60.

[43] G. Caronni, H. Lubich, A. Aziz, T. Markson, and R. Skrenta, "SKIP – Securing the Internet," *Proceedings of WET ICE '96*, Workshops on Enabling Technologies: Infrastructure for Collaborative Enterprises, June 1996, pp. 62 – 67.

[44] W. Diffie, P.C. van Oorshot, and M.J. Wiener, "Authentication and Authenticated Key Exchanges," *Designs, Codes and Cryptography*, Kluwer Academic Publishers, 1992, pp. 107 – 125.

[45] R. Oppliger, "Protecting Key Exchange and Management Protocols Against Resource Clogging Attacks," *Proceedings of Communications and Multimedia Security*, September 1999.

[46] H. Krawczyk, "SKEME: A Versatile Secure Key Exchange Mechanism for Internet," *Proceedings of Internet Society Symposium on Network and Distributed System Security*, February 1996.

[47] H. Orman, "The OAKLEY Key Determination Protocol," Request for Comments 2412, November 1998.

[48] R. Nelson, "SDNS Services and Architecture," *Proceedings of National Computer Security Conference*, 1987, pp. 153 – 157.

[49] ISO/IEC 10736, *Information Technology - Telecommunications and Information Exchange Between Systems - Transport Layer Security Protocol*, Geneva, Switzerland, 1993.

[50] M. Blaze, and S.M. Bellovin, "Session-Layer Encryption," *Proceedings of USENIX UNIX Security Symposium*, June 1995.

[51] T. Ylönen, "SSH — Secure Login Connections Over the Internet," *Proceedings of USENIX UNIX Security Symposium*, July 1996.

[52] D.R. Safford, D.K. Hess, and D.L. Schales, "Secure RPC Authentication (SRA) for TELNET and FTP," *Proceedings of USENIX UNIX Security Symposium*, October 1993, pp. 63 – 67.

[53] D. Vincenzetti, S. Taino, and F. Bolognesi, "STEL: Secure Telnet," *Proceedings of USENIX UNIX Security Symposium*, June 1995.

[54] J. Linn, "Privacy Enhancement for Internet Electronic Mail: Part I — Message Encryption and Authentication Procedures," Request for Comments 1421, February 1993.

[55] S.T. Kent, "Privacy Enhancement for Internet Electronic Mail: Part II — Certificate-Based Key Management," Request for Comments 1422, February 1993.

[56] D. Balenson, "Privacy Enhancement for Internet Electronic Mail: Part III — Algorithms, Modes, and Identifiers," Request for Comments 1423, February 1993.

[57] B. Kaliski, "Privacy Enhancement for Internet Electronic Mail: Part IV — Key Certification and Related Services," Request for Comments 1424, February 1993.

[58] S.T. Kent, "Internet Privacy Enhanced Mail," *Communications of the ACM*, 36(8), August 1993, pp. 48 – 60.

[59] P.R. Zimmermann, *The Official PGP User's Guide*, The MIT Press, Cambridge, MA, 1995.

[60] P.R. Zimmermann, *PGP Source Code and Internals*, The MIT Press, Cambridge, MA, 1995.

[61] S. Garfinkel, *PGP: Pretty Good Privacy*, O'Reilly & Associates, Sebastopol, CA, 1995.

[62] S. Dusse, P. Hoffman, B. Ramsdell, L. Lundblack, and L. Repka, "S/MIME Version 2 Message Specification," Request for Comments 2311, March 1998.

[63] S. Dusse, P. Hoffman, B. Ramsdell, and J. Weinstein, "S/MIME Version 2 Certificate Handling," Request for Comments 2312, March 1998.

[64] J. Feghhi, J. Feghhi, and P. Williams, *Digital Certificates: Applied Internet Security*, Addison-Wesley Longman, Reading, MA, 1999.

[65] B. Kaliski, "PKCS #1: RSA Encryption Version 1.5," Request for Comments 2313, March 1998.

[66] B. Kaliski, "PKCS #10: RSA Encryption Version 1.5," Request for Comments 2314, March 1998.

[67] B. Kaliski, "PKCS #7: RSA Encryption Version 1.5," Request for Comments 2315, March 1998.

[68] B. Tung, *Kerberos: A Network Authentication System*, Addison-Wesley, Reading, MA, 1999.

Chapter 6

SSL and TLS Protocols

In this chapter, we further elaborate on two transport layer security protocols that we briefly introduced in Chapter 5: the SSL and TLS protocols. More specifically, we introduce the topic in Section 6.1, overview and briefly discuss the two protocols in Sections 6.2 and 6.3, and address SSL and TLS certificates in Section 6.4. Finally, we elaborate on firewall tunneling in Section 6.5, and draw some conclusions in Section 6.6.

6.1 INTRODUCTION

In general, there are several possibilities to cryptographically protect HTTP data traffic. For example, in the early 1990s the CommerceNet[1] consortium proposed S-HTTP that was basically a security-specific enhancement of HTTP (refer to [1] for an overview about S-HTTP). An implementation of S-HTTP was made publicly available in a modified version of the NCSA Mosaic browser that users had to purchase (contrary to the "normal" NCSA Mosaic browser that was publicly and freely available on the Internet).

---

[1]http://www.commerce.net

At the same time, however, Netscape Communications introduced SSL and a corresponding protocol with the first version of Netscape Navigator.[2] Contrary to the CommerceNet consortium, Netscape Communications did not charge its customers for the implementation of its security protocol. Consequently, SSL became the predominant protocol to provide security services for HTTP data traffic after 1994, and S-HTTP silently sank into oblivion.

So far, there have been three versions of SSL:

- SSL version 1.0 was used internally only by Netscape Communications. It contained some serious flaws and was never released in public.

- SSL version 2.0 was incorporated into Netscape Navigator versions 1.0 through 2.x. It had some weaknesses related to specific incarnations of the man-in-the-middle attack. In an attempt to leverage public uncertainty about SSL's security, Microsoft also introduced the competing *private communication technology* (PCT) protocol in its first release of Internet Explorer in 1996.

- Netscape Communications responded to Microsoft's PCT challenge by introducing SSL version 3.0 that addressed the problems in SSL 2.0 and added some new features. At this point, Microsoft backed down and agreed to support SSL in all versions of its TCP/IP-based software (although its own software still supports PCT for backward compatibility).

The latest specification of SSL 3.0 was officially released in March 1996.[3] It is implemented in both Netscape Navigator 3.0 (and higher) and Microsoft Internet Explorer 3.0 (and higher). As discussed later in this chapter, SSL 3.0 has also been adapted by the IETF TLS WG. In fact, the TLS 1.0 protocol specification is a derivative of SSL 3.0. Again, refer to [1] for a comprehensive overview and comparison of the SSL, PCT, and TLS protocols. In the following two sections, we focus only on the SSL and TLS protocols; the PCT protocol is not further addressed in this book.

---

[2] On August 12, 1997, Netscape Communications was granted U.S. patent 5,657,390 entitled "Secure socket layer application program apparatus and method" for the technology employed by the SSL protocol.

[3] The SSL 3.0 specification was drafted by Alan O. Freier and Philip Karlton of Netscape Communications, as well as Paul C. Kocher of Cryptography Research.

6.2   SSL PROTOCOL

The architecture of SSL and the corresponding SSL protocol are illustrated in Figure 6.1. According to this figure, SSL refers to an intermediate (security) layer between the transport and the application layer. Consequently, SSL is layered on top of a reliable transport service, such as provided by TCP. As such, it is conceptually able to provide security services for arbitrary TCP/IP application protocols, not just HTTP. As a matter of fact, one major advantage of transport layer security protocols in general, and the SSL protocol in particular, is that they are application-independent, in the sense that they can be used to transparently secure any TCP/IP application protocol layered on top of them. Figure 6.1 illustrates several exemplary application protocols, including NSIIOP, HTTP, FTP, Telnet, IMAP, IRC, and POP3. They can all be secured by layering them on top of SSL (the appended letter "s" in the corresponding protocol acronyms indicates the use of SSL).

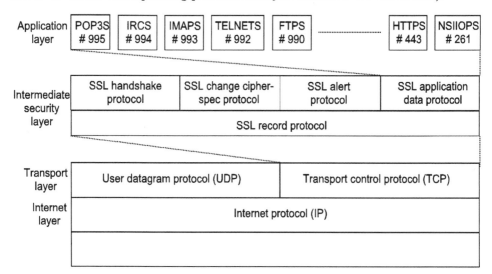

Figure 6.1   The architecture of SSL and the SSL protocol.

In short, the SSL protocol provides communication security that has three basic properties:

• First, the communicating parties (both the server and the client) can authenticate each other using public key cryptography;

• Second, the confidentiality of the data traffic is protected, as the connection is transparently encrypted after an initial handshake and session key negotiation has taken place;

- Third, the authenticity and integrity of the data traffic is also protected, as messages are transparently authenticated and integrity-checked using MACs.

Nevertheless, it is important to note that SSL does not protect against traffic analysis. For example, by examining the unencrypted source and destination IP addresses and TCP port numbers, or examining the volume of transmitted data, a traffic analyst can still determine what parties are interacting, what types of services are being used, and sometimes even recover information about business or personal relationships. We have already mentioned in this book that users generally consider the threat of traffic analysis to be relatively low, and so the developers of SSL have not attempted to address it either.

In order to make use of SSL protection, the client and the server must know that the other side is also using SSL. In general, there are three possibilities to address this issue:

- The first possibility is to use dedicated port numbers reserved by the IANA. In this case, a separate port number must be assigned for every application protocol that may be secured with SSL;

- The second possibility is to use the normal port number for every application protocol, and to negotiate security options as part of the (now slightly modified) application protocol;

- Finally, the third possibility is to use a TCP option to negotiate the use of a security protocol, such as the SSL or TLS protocol, during the normal TCP connection establishment phase.

The application-specific negotiation of security options (the second possibility mentioned above) has the disadvantage of requiring each application protocol to be modified to understand the negotiation process. Also, defining a TCP option (the third possibility mentioned above) would be a fine solution, but has not been seriously discussed in the past. In practice, separate port numbers have been reserved and assigned by the IANA for every application protocol that may run on top of SSL or TLS (the first possibility mentioned above).[4] Note, however, that

---

[4]http://www.isi.edu/in-notes/iana/assignments/port-numbers

Table 6.1

Port Numbers Assigned for Application Protocols That Run on Top of TLS/SSL

Keyword	Port	Description
nsiiops	261	IIOP name service over TLS/SSL
https	443	HTTP over TLS/SSL
smtps	465	SMTP over TLS/SSL (former ssmtp)
nntps	563	NNTP over TLS/SSL (former snntp)
ldaps	636	LDAP over TLS/SSL (former sldap)
ftps-data	989	FTP (data) over TLS/SSL
ftps	990	FTP (control) over TLS/SSL
telnets	992	TELNET over TLS/SSL
imaps	993	IMAP4 over TLS/SSL
ircs	994	IRC over TLS/SSL
pop3s	995	POP3 over TLS/SSL (former spop3)

the use of separate port numbers has the disadvantage of requiring two TCP connections if the client does not know what the server supports (first the client must connect to the secure port, and then to the unsecure port, or vice versa). It is very possible that future protocols will abandon this approach and go for the second possibility. For example, the simple authentication and security layer (SALS) defines a method for adding authentication support to connection-based application protocols [2]. According to SALS, the use of specific authentication mechanisms is negotiable between the client and the server of a specific application protocol. As of this writing, the use of SALS is primarily used to secure IMAP4 communications.

The port numbers assigned by the IANA for application protocols that run on top of TLS/SSL are summarized in Table 6.1 and partly illustrated in Figure 6.1. Note that some acronyms for application protocols that run on top of SSL/TLS have changed since the publication of [1]. Today, the "s" indicating the use of SSL is consistently appended (postfixed) to the acronyms of the corresponding application protocols.

In general, an SSL session is stateful and the SSL protocol is to initialize and maintain the session state information on both the client and the server side. The corresponding session state information elements are overviewed and briefly described in Table 6.2. Several connections may be derived from an SSL session and the corresponding connection state information elements are overviewed and briefly described in Table 6.3. Note that communicating parties may have multiple simultaneous sessions as well as sessions with multiple simultaneous connections.

Table 6.2
SSL Session State Information Elements

Element	Description
Session ID	Identifier chosen by the server to identify an active or resumable session state.
Peer certificate	X.509 version 3 certificate of the peer entity.
Compression method	Algorithm used to compress data prior to encryption.
Cipher spec	Specification of the data encryption and MAC algorithms.
Master secret	48-byte secret shared between the client and server.
Is resumable	Flag that indicates whether the session can be used to initiate new connections.

As illustrated in Figure 6.1, the SSL protocol consists of two main parts: the SSL record protocol and several SSL subprotocols that are layered on top of the SSL record protocol:

- On the one hand, the SSL record protocol is layered on top of a connection-oriented reliable transport service, such as provided by TCP, and provides message origin authentication, data confidentiality, and data integrity services (including such things as replay protection).

- On the other hand, the SSL subprotocols are layered on top of the SSL record protocol and provide support for SSL session establishment and management.

Notably, the most important SSL subprotocol is the SSL handshake protocol. This is an authentication and key exchange protocol that also negotiates, initializes, and synchronizes security parameters and corresponding state information located at either endpoint of an SSL session or connection. After the SSL handshake protocol completes, application data is sent via the SSL record protocol according to the negotiated security parameters and state information elements. The SSL record and handshake protocols are overviewed next.

6.2.1   SSL Record Protocol

As mentioned above, the *SSL record protocol* receives data from higher layer SSL subprotocols and addresses data fragmentation, compression, authentication, and encryption. More precisely, the protocol takes as input a data block of arbitrary size, and produces as output a series of SSL data fragments (further referred to

Table 6.3
SSL Connection State Information Elements

Element	Description
Server and client random	Byte sequences that are chosen by the server and client for each connection.
Server write MAC secret	Secret used for MAC operations on data written by the server.
Client write MAC secret	Secret used for MAC operations on data written by the clie
Server write key	Key used for data encryption by the server and decryption the client.
Client write key	Key used for data encryption by the cli᾿ and decryption by the server.
Initialization vector	Initialization state for a block ipher ir CBC mode. This field is first initialized by the SSL andshake protocol. Thereafter, the final ciphertext block from each record is preserved for use with the following record.
Sequence number	Each party maintains separate sequence numbers for transmitted and received messages for each connection.

as "SSL records") of maximal $2^{14} - 1 = 16,383$ bytes each. The various steps of the SSL record protocol that lead from a raw data fragment to an SSLPlaintext (fragmentation step), SSLCompressed (compression step), and SSLCiphertext (encryption step) record are illustrated in Figure 6.2. Finally, each SSL record contains the following information fields:

- Content type;

- Protocol version number;

- Length;

- Data payload (optionally compressed and encrypted);

- MAC.

The content type defines the higher layer protocol that must be used to subsequently process the SSL record data payload (after proper decompression and decryption). The protocol version number determines the SSL version in use (typically 3.0). Each SSL record data payload is compressed and encrypted according to the current compression method and cipher spec defined for the SSL session. At the start of each SSL session, the compression method and cipher spec are usually defined as null. They are both set during the initial execution of the SSL handshake protocol. Finally, a MAC is appended to each SSL record. It provides message origin authentication and data integrity services. Similar to the encryption algorithm, the algorithm that is used to compute and verify the MAC is defined in the cipher spec of the current session state. By default, the SSL record protocol uses a slightly modified version of the HMAC construction specified in RFC 2104 [3]. The modification refers to the inclusion of a sequence number in the message before hashing in order to protect against specific forms of replay attacks. Finally, note that the MAC is always computed and appended to the SSL record before the data payload is encrypted.

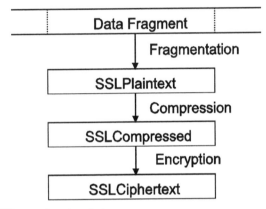

Figure 6.2   The SSL record protocol steps.

As mentioned above, several SSL subprotocols are layered on top of the SSL record protocol. Each subprotocol may refer to specific types of messages that are sent using the SSL record protocol. The SSL 3.0 specification defines the following three SSL protocols:

- Alert protocol;

- Handshake protocol;

- ChangeCipherSpec protocol.

In short, the SSL Alert protocol is used to transmit alerts via the SSL record protocol. Alerts are a specific type of message that consist of two parts: an alert level and an alert description. The SSL handshake protocol is notably the major SSL subprotocol. As such, it is overviewed and briefly discussed in the following subsection. Finally, the SSL ChangeCipherSpec protocol is used to change between one cipher spec and another. Although the cipher spec is normally changed at the end of an SSL handshake, it can also be changed at any time. In addition to these SSL subprotocols, an SSL application data protocol is used to directly pass application data to the SSL record protocol. From the application's (and user's) point of view, this is probably the major use of SSL.

6.2.2 SSL Handshake Protocol

As mentioned above, the *SSL handshake protocol* is the main SSL subprotocol that is layered on top of the SSL record protocol. Consequently, SSL handshake messages are supplied to the SSL record layer, where they are encapsulated within one or more SSL records, which are processed and transmitted as specified by the compression method and cipher spec of the current SSL session, and the cryptographic keys of the corresponding SSL connection. The aim of the SSL handshake protocol is to have a client and server establish and maintain state information that is used to secure communications. More specifically, the protocol is to have the client and server agree on a common SSL protocol version, select the compression method and cipher spec, optionally authenticate each other, and create a master secret from which the various session keys for message authentication and encryption will be derived. An execution of the SSL handshake protocol between a client C and a server S can be summarized as follows (the messages that are put in square brackets are optional):

$$
\begin{array}{rlll}
1 : & C \longrightarrow S & : & \text{CLIENTHELLO} \\
2 : & S \longrightarrow C & : & \text{SERVERHELLO} \\
: & & : & [\text{CERTIFICATE}] \\
: & & : & [\text{SERVERKEYEXCHANGE}] \\
: & & : & [\text{CERTIFICATEREQUEST}] \\
: & & : & \text{SERVERHELLODONE} \\
3 : & C \longrightarrow S & : & [\text{CERTIFICATE}] \\
: & & : & \text{CLIENTKEYEXCHANGE} \\
: & & : & [\text{CERTIFICATEVERIFY}] \\
: & & : & \text{CHANGECIPHERSPEC} \\
: & & : & \text{FINISHED} \\
4 : & S \longrightarrow C & : & \text{CHANGECIPHERSPEC} \\
: & & : & \text{FINISHED}
\end{array}
$$

When client C wants to connect to server S, he or she establishes a TCP connection to the HTTP port (not included in the protocol description) and sends a CLIENTHELLO message to the server in step 1 of the SSL handshake protocol execution. The client can also send a CLIENTHELLO message in response to a HELLOREQUEST message or on its own initiative in order to renegotiate the security parameters of an existing connection. The CLIENTHELLO message includes the following fields:

• The number of the highest SSL version understood by the client (typically 3.0);

• A client-generated random structure that consists of a 32-bit timestamp in standard UNIX format, and a 28-byte value generated by a pseudorandom number generator;

• A session identity the client wishes to use for this connection;

• A list of cipher suites that the client supports;

• A list of compression methods that the client supports.

Note that the session identity field should be empty if no SSL session currently exists or if the client wishes to generate new security parameters. In either case, a nonempty session identity field is to specify an existing SSL session between the client and the server (a session whose security parameters the client wishes to reuse). The session identity may be from an earlier connection, this connection, or another currently active connection. Also note that the list of supported cipher suites, passed from the client to the server in the CLIENTHELLO message, contains the combinations of cryptographic algorithms supported by the client in order of preference. Each cipher suite defines both a key exchange algorithm and a cipher spec. The server will select a cipher suite or, if no acceptable choices are presented, return an error message and close the connection accordingly. After having sent the CLIENTHELLO message, the client waits for a SERVERHELLO message. Any other message returned by the server except for a HELLOREQUEST message is treated as an error at this point.

In step 2, the server processes the CLIENTHELLO message and responds with either an error or SERVERHELLO message. Similar to the CLIENTHELLO message, the SERVERHELLO message includes the following fields:

• A server version number that contains the lower version of that suggested by the client in the CLIENTHELLO message and the highest supported by the server;

- A server-generated random structure that also consists of a 32-bit timestamp in standard UNIX format, and a 28-byte value generated by a pseudorandom number generator;

- A session identity corresponding to this connection;

- A cipher suite selected by the server from the list of cipher suites supported by the client;

- A compression method selected by the server from the list of compression algorithms supported by the client.

If the session identity in the CLIENTHELLO message was nonempty, the server looks in its session cache for a match. If a match is found and the server is willing to establish the new connection using the corresponding session state, the server responds with the same value as supplied by the client. This indicates a resumed session and dictates that both parties must proceed directly to the CHANGE-CIPHERSPEC and FINISHED messages as addressed further below. Otherwise, this field contains a different value identifying a new session. The server may also return an empty session identity field to indicate that the session will not be cached and therefore cannot be resumed later. Also note that in the SERVERHELLO message, the server selects a cipher suite and a compression method from the corresponding lists provided by the client in the CLIENTHELLO message. The key exchange, authentication, encryption, and message authentication algorithms are determined by the cipher suite selected by the server and revealed in the SERVERHELLO message. The cipher suites that have been defined for the SSL protocol are essentially the same as the ones that are specified for the TLS protocol (as summarized in Tables 6.4 to 6.7).

In addition to the SERVERHELLO message, the server may also send other messages to the client. For example, if the server is using certificate-based authentication (which is currently almost always the case), the server sends its own site certificate to the client in a corresponding CERTIFICATE message. The certificate type must be appropriate for the selected cipher suite's key exchange algorithm, and is generally an X.509v3 certificate. The same message type will be used later for the client's response to the server's CERTIFICATEREQUEST message. In the case of X.509v3 certificates, a certificate may actually refer to an entire chain of certificates, ordered with the sender's certificate first followed by any CA certificates proceeding sequentially upward to a root CA (that will be accepted by the client). The use of SSL (and TLS) certificates is further addressed in Section 6.4 of this book.

Next, the server may send a SERVERKEYEXCHANGE message to the client if it has no certificate, a certificate that can be used only for verifying digital signatures, or uses the FORTEZZA token-based key exchange algorithm (KEA). Obviously, this message is not required if the site certificate includes an RSA public key that can be used for encryption. Also, a nonanonymous server can optionally request a personal certificate in order to authenticate the client. It therefore sends a CER-TIFICATEREQUEST message to the client. The message includes a list of the types of certificates requested, sorted in order of the server's preference, as well as a list of distinguished names for acceptable CAs. At the end of step 2, the server sends a SERVERHELLODONE message to the client in order to indicate the end of the SERVERHELLO and associated messages.

Upon receipt of the SERVERHELLO and associated messages, the client verifies that the server provided a valid site certificate,[5] if required, and checks that the security parameters provided in the SERVERHELLO message are indeed acceptable. If the server has requested client authentication, it then sends a CERTIFICATE message that includes a personal certificate for the user's public key to the server in step 3. Next, the client sends a CLIENTKEYEXCHANGE message, whose format depends on the key exchange algorithm selected by the server:

- If RSA is used for server authentication and key exchange, the client generates a 48-byte premaster secret,[6] encrypts it with the public key found in the site certificate or the temporary RSA key from the SERVERKEYEXCHANGE message, and sends the result back to the server in the CLIENTKEYEXCHANGE message. The server, in turn, uses the corresponding private key to decrypt the premaster secret. We will come back to this key exchange algorithm later in this section when we talk about a specific attack.

- If FORTEZZA tokens are used for key exchange, the client derives a token en-cryption key (TEK) using the KEA. The client's KEA calculation uses the public key from the server certificate along with some private parameters in the client's token. The client sends public parameters needed for the server to also generate the TEK, using its private parameters. It generates a premaster secret, wraps it using the TEK, and sends the result together with some initialization vectors to the server as part of the CLIENTKEYEXCHANGE message. The server, in turn,

---

[5]A site certificate is considered to be valid if its server's common name field entry matches the host part of the URL the client wants to access.

[6]The premaster secret is 48 bytes long and consists of 2 bytes specifying the protocol version and 46 bytes of randomly generated data.

can decrypt the premaster secret accordingly. This key exchange algorithm is not widely used in practice.

- If a Diffie-Hellman key exchange is performed, the server and client exchange their public parameters as part of the SERVERKEYEXCHANGE and CLIENT-KEYEXCHANGE messages. Obviously, this is only required if the Diffie-Hellman public parameters are not included in the site and personal certificates. The negotiated Diffie-Hellman key can then be used as premaster secret. It is assumed that this key exchange algorithm will be more widely used in the future.

For RSA, FORTEZZA, and Diffie-Hellman key exchange, the same algorithms are used to convert the premaster secret into a 48-byte master secret (that is stored in the corresponding SSL session state), and to derive session keys for encryption and message authentication from this master secret. Nevertheless, some key exchange algorithms, such as FORTEZZA token-based key exchange, may also use their own procedures for generating encryption keys. In this case, the master secret is only used to derive keys for message authentication. The procedures to derive master and session keys, as well as initialization vectors, are fully described in the SSL protocol specification and are not further addressed in this book.

If client authentication is required, the client also sends a CERTIFICATEVERIFY message to the server. This message is used to provide explicit verification of the user's identity based on the personal certificate. It is only sent following a client certificate that has signing capability (all certificates except those containing fixed Diffie-Hellman parameters). Finally, the client finishes step 3 by sending a CHANGE-CIPHERSPEC message and a corresponding FINISHED message to the server. The FINISHED message is always sent immediately after the CHANGECIPHERSPEC message to verify that the key exchange and authentication processes were successful. As a matter of fact, the FINISHED message is the first message that is protected with the newly negotiated algorithms and session keys. It can only be generated and verified if these keys are properly installed on both sides. No acknowledgment of the FINISHED message is required; parties may begin sending encrypted data immediately after having sent the FINISHED message. The SSL handshake protocol execution finishes up by also having the server send a CHANGECIPHERSPEC message and a corresponding FINISHED message to the client in step 4.

After the SSL handshake is complete, a secure connection is established between the client and the server. This connection can now be used to send application data that is encapsulated by the SSL record protocol. More precisely, application data may be fragmented, compressed, encrypted, and authenticated according to the SSL record protocol, as well as the session and connection state information that is now established (according to the execution of the SSL handshake protocol).

As mentioned previously, the SSL handshake protocol can be shortened if the client and server decide to resume a previously established (and still cached) SSL session or duplicate an existing SSL session. In this case, only three message flows and a total of six messages is required. The corresponding message flows are summarized as follows:

```
1 : C  ⟶  S : CLIENTHELLO
2 : S  ⟶  C : SERVERHELLO
    :           : CHANGECIPHERSPEC
    :           : FINISHED
3 : S  ⟶  C : CHANGECIPHERSPEC
    :           : FINISHED
```

In step 1, the client sends a CLIENTHELLO message to the server that includes a session identity to be resumed. The server, in turn, checks its session cache for a match. If a match is found, and the server is willing to resume the connection under the specified session state, it returns a SERVERHELLO message with the same session identity in step 2. At this point in time, both the client and the server must send CHANGECIPHERSPEC and FINISHED messages to each other in steps 2 and 3. Once the session reestablishment is complete, the client and server can begin exchanging application data.

In summary, the SSL protocol can be used to establish secure TCP connections between clients and servers. In particular, it can be used to authenticate the server, to optionally authenticate the client, to perform a key exchange, and to provide message authentication, as well as data confidentiality and integrity services for arbitrary application protocols layered on top of TCP. Although it may seem that not providing client authentication goes against the principles that should be espoused by a secure system, an argument can be made that the decision to optionally support it helped SSL gain widespread use in the first place. Support for client authentication requires public keys and personal certificates for each client, and since SSL support for HTTP must be embedded in the corresponding browser software, requiring client authentication would involve distributing public keys and personal certificates to every user on the Internet. In the short term, it was believed to be more crucial that consumers be aware of with whom they are conducting business than to give the merchants the same level of assurance. Furthermore, since the number of Internet servers is much smaller than the number of clients, it is easier and more practical to first outfit servers with the necessary public keys and site certificates. As of this writing, however, support for client-side public keys and personal certificates is growing very rapidly. We will further address SSL (and TLS) certificates in Section 6.4.

A comprehensive security analysis of SSL 3.0 was performed by Bruce Schneier from Counterpane Systems and David Wagner from the University of California at Berkeley [4]. Except for some minor flaws and worrisome features that could be easily corrected without overhauling the basic structure of the SSL protocol, they found no serious vulnerability or security problem in their analysis. Consequently, they concluded that the SSL protocol provides excellent security against eavesdropping and other passive attacks, and that people implementing the protocol should be aware of some sophisticated active attacks.

More recently, Daniel Bleichenbacher from Bell Laboratories found an adaptive chosen ciphertext attack against protocols based on the public key cryptography standard (PKCS) #1 [5]. In short, an RSA private key operation (a decryption or digital signature operation) can be performed if the attacker has access to an oracle that, for any chosen ciphertext, returns only 1 bit telling whether the ciphertext corresponds to some unknown block of data encrypted using PKCS #1 [6]. Since this attack is quite sophisticated and requires some basic understanding of cryptanalysis, you may skip the following paragraphs and continue to read the next subsection that addresses currently available SSL implementations.

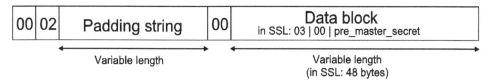

Figure 6.3   PKCS #1 block format for encryption.

In order to understand the Bleichenbacher attack, it is necessary to have a look at PKCS #1. In fact, there are three block formats specified in PKCS #1: block types 0 and 1 are used for RSA digital signatures, and block type 2 is used for RSA encryption. Remember from our previous discussion that — if the RSA algorithm is used for server authentication and key exchange — the client randomly generates a 46-byte premaster secret, prepends the two bytes 03 (the SSL protocol version number) and 00 to the premaster secret, encrypts the result using the public key of the server, and sends it in a CLIENTKEYEXCHANGE message to the server. As such, the CLIENTKEYEXCHANGE message carrying the encrypted premaster secret must conform to the format specified in PKCS #1 block type 2. The format is illustrated in Figure 6.3.

Now, assume there is an attacker who can send an arbitrary number of randomly looking messages to an SSL server, and the server responds for each of these messages with a bit indicating whether a particular message is correctly encrypted and encoded according to PKCS #1 (the server thus acts as an oracle). Under this assumption, Bleichenbacher developed an attack to illegitimatly perform an RSA operation with the private key of the server (either a decryption or a digital signature operation). When applied to decrypt a premaster secret of a previously sent CLIENTKEYEXCHANGE message, the attacker can rebuild the premaster secret and the session keys that are derived from it accordingly. Consequently, the attacker can then decrypt the entire session (if he or she has monitored and stored the data stream of that session).

The attack is primarily of theoretical interest. Note that experimental results have shown that typically between 300,000 and 2,000,000 chosen ciphertexts are required to actually perform the (decryption or digital signature) operation. To make things worse, the attack can only be launched against an SSL server that is available online (since it must act as an oracle). From the attacker's point of view, it may be difficult to send this huge number of chosen ciphertexts to the SSL server without causing the server administrator to become suspicious.

There are several possibilities to protect against the Bleichenbacher attack. First of all, it is not necessary for the server to respond with an error message after having received a CLIENTKEYEXCHANGE message that does not conform to PKCS #1. Another possibility is to change the PKCS #1 block format for encryption and to remove the leading 00 and 02 bytes, as well as the 00, 03, and 00 bytes in the middle of the message (as illustrated in Figure 6.3). Finally, another possibility is to use plaintext-aware encryption schemes, such as the one proposed by Mihir Bellare and Phillip Rogaway [7], or any other public key cryptosystem that is (provably) secure against adaptive chosen ciphertext attacks [8].[7] For example, in the aftermath of the publication of Bleichenbacher's results, IBM launched a marketing initiative to promote such a cryptosystem jointly developed by Ronald Cramer and Victor Shoup [9].

Before Bleichbacher published his attack in the summer of 1998, he had been working with RSA Laboratories to update PKCS #1 and to specify a version 2 that is secure against adaptive chosen ciphertext attacks [10]. Meanwhile, all major vendors of SSL servers have incorporated and implemented PKCS #1 version 2

---

[7] Note that plaintext-awareness always implies security against chosen ciphertext attacks.

into their products. As a result, this attack does not work anymore due to recent releases of SSL server software.

Finally, it may be interesting to know that most banks that offer their services over the Internet have their corresponding home banking client software based on SSL. This decision also conforms to the strategic view of the European Committee for Banking Standards (ECBS) [11]. As of this writing, the SSL protocol is by far the most pervasive security protocol for the Internet in general and the WWW in particular. This trend still continues. Some exemplary implementations of SSL are overviewed next.

6.2.3   Implementations

In the recent past, many Web servers and browsers have been modified to make use of SSL. For example, the Apache Web server has been modified to incorporate the SSLeay implementation addressed below [12]. However, the most widely deployed and heavily used implementations of SSL are found in commercial Web server and browser software. For example, there are several commercial Web servers available that support SSL (and TLS). Typically, these servers are called "secure" or "commerce servers." Note, however, that these servers are not necessarily more secure than any other Web server; they just support SSL to secure the data traffic that is transmitted between the client and the server. On the client side, most browsers support SSL. In particular, Netscape Navigator and Microsoft Internet Explorer both provide support for SSL. Most of these products support the RC4 algorithm for encryption and the MD2 and MD5 one-way functions for hashing.

As of this writing, there are three major implementations of SSL: SSLref, SSLeay, and SSL Plus. In addition, there is an increasingly large number of SSL implementations based on the Java programming language (e.g., the SSLava Toolkit developed and marketed by the Phaos Technology Corporation[8]). This is particularly interesting, since it allows Java applets that implement the SSL protocol to be dynamically downloaded to the browser.

SSLref

After the development of Netscape Navigator, Netscape Communications produced a reference implementation of SSL that would be distributable within the United States and Canada. The implementation was written entirely in the C programming language and was named *SSLref*. The 2.0 reference implementation was published

---

[8]`http://www.phaos.com`

in 1995. The SSLref source code is distributed freely for noncommercial use. Parties interested in using SSLref in a commercial product require a license from Netscape Communications.

Note, however, that SSLref does not include implementations of either the RC2 or RC4 encryption algorithms. To make things worse, many programs that use SSL, such as Netscape Navigator, contain only the RC2 or RC4 encryption algorithms. Consequently, for a program based on SSLref to be interoperable with a program such as Netscape Navigator, it is necessary to separately license the RC2 or RC4 encryption algorithms from RSA Data Security, Inc. These algorithms are a standard part of RSA Data Security's BSAFE toolkit. Also note that SSLref additionally uses the RSA encryption algorithm, which must also be licensed directly or indirectly from RSA Data Security, Inc. for use within the United States.

SSLeay

SSLeay refers to an independent implementation of SSL 2.0, SSL 3.0, and TLS 1.0 (as of the release of SSLeay-0.9.0) originally developed by Eric Young in Australia. The software is publicly and freely available around the world on a number of anonymous FTP sites. Since SSLeay was entirely developed outside the United States, its distribution is not restricted by U.S. export controls.

SSLeay uses implementations of the RC2 and RC4 encryption algorithms based on the algorithms that were anonymously posted to the Usenet in September 1994 (in the case of RC2) and February 1996 (in the case of RC4). Beyond the RC2 or RC4 encryption algorithms, SSLeay also includes implementations of the DES, Triple-DES, IDEA, and Blowfish encryption algorithms. Further information on SSLeay and SSLapps (a collection of SSL-enhanced application programs) can be found in the SSLeay and SSLapps FAQ document at URL http://www.psy.uq.oz.au/~ftp/Crypto/.

SSL Plus

The *SSL Plus* Security Toolkit[9] developed by Consensus Development Corporation[10] is currently the leading commercial implementation of SSL 3.0 in the marketplace. It is licensed and used by several leading companies to deploy security using public key cryptography and digital certificates for their applications.

---

[9]http://www.consensus.com/sslplus/
[10]http://www.consensus.com

6.2.4   Performance Considerations

For obvious reasons, the use of SSL slows down the speed of a browser interacting with an HTTPS server. This performance degradation is in fact noticeable by the user. It is primarily due to the public key encryption and decryption operations that are required to initialize the SSL session and connection state information elements between the browser and the server. In practice, users experience an additional pause of a few seconds between opening a connection to the HTTPS server and retrieving the first HTML page from it. Because SSL is designed to cache the master secret between subsequent sessions, this delay affects only the first SSL connection between the browser and the server. Compared to the session establishment, the additional overhead of encrypting and decrypting the data traffic using one of the supported encryption algorithms, such as DES, RC2, or RC4, is practically insignificant (and not necessarily noticeable by the user). Consequently, for users that have a fast computer and a relatively slow network connection to an HTTPS server, the overhead of SSL is insignificant, especially if a large amount of data is sent afterward over the SSL session or over multiple SSL sessions that use a shared master secret. On the other hand, administrators of very busy SSL servers should consider getting either extremely fast computers or hardware assistance for the public key operations.

To minimize the performance degradation and impact of SSL, some organizations transmit the bulk of their data in the clear, and use SSL only for encrypting sensitive data. Unfortunately, this leaves the user open to specific attacks, because the unencrypted HTML can be modified in transit as it is sent from the server to the client and vice versa by a sophisticated packet filtering and malicious data injection program. In fact, a group of graduate students at the University of California at Berkeley have demonstrated how such a program can modify an executable program delivered on the fly over the network. Also consider the example that the action tag in an HTML form is changed so that instead of posting a credit card number to a transaction processing system, it is instead posted to a pirate system. Assuming that the pirate system's administrators can get a site certificate for their HTTPS server, it may be very difficult for users duped in this manner to detect that they were actually the victim of such an attack.

6.3   TLS PROTOCOL

Early in 1996, the IETF chartered a TLS WG within the Security and Transport Areas. The objective of the TLS WG was to write Internet standards track RFCs for a TLS protocol using the currently available specifications of SSL (2.0 and 3.0), PCT (1.0), and SSH (2.0) as a basis.[11] Shortly before the IETF meeting in December 1996, a first TLS 1.0 document was released as an Internet Draft. The document was essentially the same as the SSL 3.0 specification. In fact, it was the explicit strategy of the IETF TLS WG to have the TLS 1.0 specification be based on SSL 3.0, as opposed to SSL 2.0, PCT 1.0, SSH 2.0, or any other transport layer security protocol proposal. There were at least three major modifications suggested for SSL 3.0 to be incorporated into TLS 1.0:

- First, the HMAC construction developed in the IETF IPsec WG should be adopted and consistently used in TLS 1.0;

- Second, the FORTEZZA token-based KEA should be removed from TLS 1.0, since it refers to a proprietary and unpublished technology. Instead, a DSS-based key exchange mechanism should be included in TLS 1.0;

- Third, the TLS record protocol and the TLS handshake protocol should be separated out and specified more clearly in related documents.

After having adopted these modifications, the resulting TLS protocol was specified in a series of Internet Drafts. In January 1999, the TLS protocol version 1.0 was then specified in Internet Standards Track RFC 2246 [13]. The differences between TLS 1.0 and SSL 3.0 are not huge, but they are significant enough that TLS 1.0 and SSL 3.0 do not easily interoperate. Nevertheless, TLS 1.0 does incorporate a mechanism by which a TLS implementation can back down to SSL 3.0.

Similar to the SSL protocol, the TLS protocol is a layered protocol that consists of a TLS record protocol and several TLS subprotocols that are layered on top of it:

- On the lower layer, the *TLS record protocol* takes messages to be transmitted, fragments them into manageable data blocks (so-called "TLS records"), optionally compresses them, computes and appends a MAC to each record, encrypts the result, and transmits it. Again similar to SSL, the resulting records are called TLSPlaintext, TLSCompressed, and TLSCiphertext. A received TLSCiphertext record, in turn, is decrypted, verified, decompressed, and reassembled before it is delivered to the application protocol. A TLS connection state is the operating

---

[11]Note that at this point in time the SSH protocol had been investigated by the IETF TLS WG, and that the IETF later chartered a SECSH WG to update and standardize the SSH protocol independently of the TLS protocol.

environment of the TLS record protocol. It specifies compression, encryption, and message authentication algorithms, and determines parameters for these algorithms, such as encryption and MAC keys and IVs for a connection in both the read and write directions. There are always four connection states outstanding: the current read and write states and the pending read and write states. All records are processed under the current read and write states. The security parameters for the pending states are set by the TLS handshake protocol, and the handshake protocol selectively makes either of the pending states current, in which case the appropriate current state is disposed of and replaced with the pending state; the pending state is then reinitialized to an empty state.

- On the higher layer, there are several TLS subprotocols layered on top of the TLS record protocol. For example, the *TLS handshake protocol* is used to negotiate session and connection information elements that comprise a session identifier, a peer certificate, a compression method, a cipher spec, a master key, and a flag whether the session is resumable and can be used to initiate new connections. These items are used to create security parameters for use by the TLS record protocol when protecting application data. In addition, there is a *TLS change cipher spec protocol* and a *TLS alert protocol*. Both are similar to the corresponding SSL protocols (and are not further addressed in this section).

After a TLS handshake has been performed, the client and server can exchange application data messages. These messages are carried by the TLS record protocol and fragmented, compressed, authenticated, and encrypted accordingly. The messages are treated as transparent data to the TLS record layer.

The cipher suites that are specified for TLS 1.0 are summarized in Table 6.4. The key exchange and encryption mechanisms, as well as the one-way hash function that are used in a particular cipher suite, are all encoded in its name. For example, the cipher suite TLS_RSA_WITH_RC4_128_MD5 uses RSA public key encryption for key exchange, RC4 with 128 bit session keys for encryption, and MD5 for computing one-way hash function results. Similarly, the cipher suite TLS_DH_DSS_WITH_3DES_EDE_CBC_SHA uses the Diffie-Hellman key exchange algorithm (DH) for key exchange, the Digital Signature Standard (DSS) to compute and verify digital signatures, Tripe-DES in CBC mode for encryption, and SHA-1 for computing one-way hash function results. Consequently, a TLS cipher suite is always named TLS_X_WITH_Y_Z, where X refers to the key exchange algorithm, Y to the encryption algorithm, and Z to the one-way hash function that is being used. The key exchange and encryption algorithms, as well as the one-way hash

functions that are specified in TLS 1.0 are itemized and further explained in Tables
6.5 to 6.7.

Table 6.4
TLS 1.0 Cipher Suites as Specified in [13]

Cipher Suite	Exportable
TLS_NULL_WITH_NULL_NULL	yes
TLS_RSA_WITH_NULL_MD5	yes
TLS_RSA_WITH_NULL_SHA	yes
TLS_RSA_EXPORT_WITH_RC4_40_MD5	yes
TLS_RSA_WITH_RC4_128_MD5	no
TLS_RSA_WITH_RC4_128_SHA	no
TLS_RSA_EXPORT_WITH_RC2_CBC_40_MD5	yes
TLS_RSA_WITH_IDEA_CBC_SHA	no
TLS_RSA_EXPORT_WITH_DES40_CBC_SHA	yes
TLS_RSA_WITH_DES_CBC_SHA	no
TLS_RSA_WITH_3DES_EDE_CBC_SHA	no
TLS_DH_DSS_EXPORT_WITH_DES40_CBC_SHA	yes
TLS_DH_DSS_WITH_DES_CBC_SHA	no
TLS_DH_DSS_WITH_3DES_EDE_CBC_SHA	no
TLS_DH_RSA_EXPORT_WITH_DES40_CBC_SHA	yes
TLS_DH_RSA_WITH_DES_CBC_SHA	no
TLS_DH_RSA_WITH_3DES_EDE_CBC_SHA	no
TLS_DHE_DSS_EXPORT_WITH_DES40_CBC_SHA	yes
TLS_DHE_DSS_WITH_DES_CBC_SHA	no
TLS_DHE_DSS_WITH_3DES_EDE_CBC_SHA	no
TLS_DHE_RSA_EXPORT_WITH_DES40_CBC_SHA	yes
TLS_DHE_RSA_WITH_DES_CBC_SHA	no
TLS_DHE_RSA_WITH_3DES_EDE_CBC_SHA	no
TLS_DH_anon_EXPORT_WITH_RC4_40_MD5	yes
TLS_DH_anon_WITH_RC4_128_MD5	no
TLS_DH_anon_EXPORT_WITH_DES40_CBC_SHA	no
TLS_DH_anon_WITH_DES_CBC_SHA	no
TLS_DH_anon_WITH_3DES_EDE_CBC_SHA	no

Note that Tables 6.4 and 6.6 also indicate whether a particular implementation
of a cipher suite or encryption algorithm is exportable from the U.S. In Table 6.6,
the type of a cipher indicates whether it is a stream cipher or a block cipher running
in CBC mode. Similarly, the key length indicates the number of bytes that are used
for generating the encryption keys, whereas the expanded key length indicates the
number of bytes actually fed into the encryption algorithm. Finally, the effective key

bits measure how much entropy is in the key material being fed into the encryption routine, and the IV size measures how much data needs to be generated for the IV.

Table 6.5
TLS 1.0 Key Exchange Algorithms as Specified in [13]

Key Exchange Algorithm	Description	Key Size Limit
DHE_DSS	Ephemeral DH with DSS signatures	None
DHE_DSS_EXPORT	Ephemeral DH with DSS signatures	DH = 512 bits
DHE_RSA	Ephemeral DH with RSA signatures	None
DHE_RSA_EXPORT	Ephemeral DH with RSA signatures	DH = 512 bits
DH_anon	Anonymous DH, no signatures	None
DH_anon_EXPORT	Anonymous DH, no signatures	DH = 512 bits
DH_DSS	DH with DSS-based certificates	None
DH_DSS_EXPORT	DH with DSS-based certificates	DH = 512 bits
DH_RSA	DH with RSA-based certificates	None
DH_RSA_EXPORT	DH with RSA-based certificates	DH = 512 bits
NULL	No key exchange	N/A
RSA	RSA key exchange	None
RSA_EXPORT	RSA key exchange	RSA = 512 bits

TLS 1.0 has been submitted to the IESG for consideration as a proposed standard. In addition, there are proposals to improve and further enhance the TLS protocol. One proposal, for example, is to use Kerberos as an additional authentication method.[12] The idea is that Kerberos could be used as an alternative to RSA- and DH/DSS-based key exchange mechanisms in situations where Kerberos is already put in place. The premaster secret would then be sent protected with a Kerberos session key. Another proposal is to fit password-based authentication into the TLS protocol. The reasoning behind this proposal is that passwords are still in widespread use today, as opposed to public key certificates. The result of this effort is a *shared key authentication protocol* (SKAP). Current working items of the IETF TLS WG also address elliptic curve cryptosystems (ECC)[13] cipher suites to the TLS protocol, the use of HTTP over TLS,[14] as well as extensions for attribute certificate-based authorization[15] and an Internet attribute certificate profile for authorization.[16] In fact, there is a lot of refinement work being done within the

---

[12]draft-ietf-tls-kerb-cipher-suites-*.txt

[13]draft-ietf-tls-ecc-*.txt

[14]draft-ietf-tls-https-*.txt

[15]draft-ietf-tls-attr-cert-*.txt

[16]draft-ietf-tls-ac509prof-*.txt

IETF TLS WG. Let's see where this work is going to lead us.

Table 6.6
TLS 1.0 Encryption Algorithms as Specified in [13]

Cipher	Exportable	Type	Key Length	Expanded Key Length	Effective Key Bits	IV Size	Block Size
NULL	Yes	Stream	0	0	0	0	N/A
IDEA_CBC	No	Block	16	16	128	8	8
RC2_CBC_40	Yes	Block	5	16	40	8	8
RC4_40	Yes	Stream	5	16	40	0	N/A
RC4_128	No	Stream	16	16	128	0	N/A
DES40_CBC	Yes	Block	5	8	40	8	8
DES_CBC	No	Block	8	8	56	8	8
3DES_EDE_CBC	No	Block	24	24	168	8	8

Table 6.7
TLS 1.0 One-Way Hash Funtions as Specified in [13]

Hash Function	Hash Size	Padding Size
NULL	0	0
MD5	16	48
SHA	20	40

6.4 SSL AND TLS CERTIFICATES

When Netscape Communications released its first version of Netscape Navigator with SSL support, it was faced with a very practical problem: the SSL protocol required the existence of one or several CAs to make it work, but there were no CAs offering their services to the general public. Consequently, Netscape Communications turned to RSA Data Security, Inc., which had supplied the public key technology software on which Netscape Navigator was actually based. For several years RSA Data Security, Inc. ran its own CA called RSA Certification Services. The CA's primary reason for existence was to enable protocols that required certification services, such as PEM [1]. In 1995, RSA Data Security, Inc. spun off its certification services division to a new company called VeriSign, Inc.[17]

---

[17]http://www.verisign.com

Since then, each successive version of Netscape Navigator has added technology to allow for the creation of a marketplace for commercial CAs and CA services. The first version contained a certificate for a single root CA. The second version still came with support for only a single root CA, but it allowed other root CAs to be dynamically loaded with the user's permission. Netscape Navigator 3.0 came preloaded with certificates for 16 root CAs. In addition, the browser also contained a user interface for viewing the currently loaded certificates, deleting certificates, and adding more. The number of preconfigured and loaded certificates has even increased in the more recent releases of Netscape Navigator. For example, version 4.05 came preconfigured and loaded with public key certificates for 35 root CAs (the list starting with AT&T Certificate Services). The corresponding user panel to configure certificate signers' certificates is illustrated in Figure 6.4.

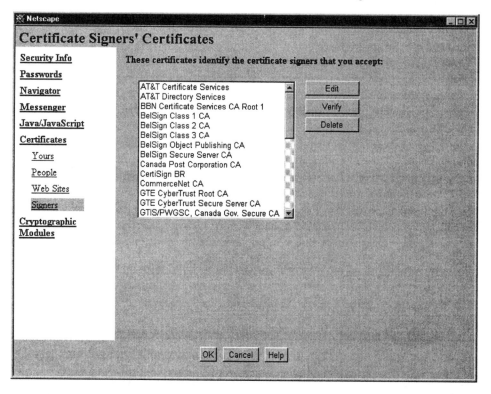

Figure 6.4   Netscape Navigator user panel to configure certificate signers' certificates. © 1999 Netscape Communications Corporation.

Note that you can edit, verify, or delete the certificates of the root CAs by pressing the corresponding buttons on the right side of the user panel. The left panel of Figure 6.4 also illustrates that Netscape Navigator distinguishes between four classes of certificates:

- **Yours:** This class includes personal certificates that have been issued by a CA for the user of the browser. In the current version of Netscape Navigator, it is not possible to distinguish between different users of the browser.

- **People:** This class includes personal certificates that have been issued for other users mainly for the purpose of secure messaging (using a S/MIME compliant e-mail client or user agent).

- **Web Sites:** This class includes site certificates that have been issued for HTTPS servers and that have been accepted by the current user.

- **Signers:** This class includes certificates for root CAs that the user accepts and implicitly trusts. This is important, since it is this class of certificates that determines what root CAs a user is going to accept (if he or she doesn't change the configuration to better suit his or her needs).

In the following two subsections we further address personal certificates (certificates from the "Yours" class in the terminology of Netscape Navigator), as well as CA and site certificates (certificates from the "Signers" and the "Web Sites" classes in the terminology of Netscape Navigator). Note that certificates from the "People" class are primarily used for secure messaging and are not further addressed in this book. Also note that the use of certificates is further addressed in Chapter 8, when we talk about certificate management.

6.4.1   Personal Certificates

Personal certificates are used by browsers to authenticate clients acting on behalf of particular users to HTTPS servers (as well as e-mail software to authenticate S/MIME messages). Unfortunately, the processes for users to request and receive personal certificates are addressed by Netscape Communications and Microsoft in different ways. In either case, the procedure for creating a personal certificate involves HTML forms. These forms include client specific features, such as special HTML form tags or dedicated programs, as well as CGI scripts that call certificate handling operations on the server side.

In short, the general steps for creating a personal certificate are as follows:

- First, the user requests an HTML document that displays a specific fill-out form (the form includes all the information that is required to generate a public key certificate request);

- Second, the user provides the information that is required by the fill-out form;

- Third, the submission of the fill-out form causes the browser to generate a public key pair, the private key to be stored by the browser (in a secure way), the public key to be sent together with other identification information to the server, and the server to actually run a CGI script that creates the requested certificate and loads it down to the browser.

The HTML form includes fields for the different distinguished name attributes to be used in the personal certificate (as illustrated in Figure 4.4), information allowing the browser to generate a public key pair, and a hidden field used to return this information to the CGI script. Unfortunately, the HTML form tags and the information that is encoded in the hidden field depends on the browser in use.

- In Netscape Navigator, the fill-out form contains a dedicated and nonstandard HTML KEYGEN form tag. The tag has the following format:

```
<KEYGEN NAME="SPKAC"
        CHALLENGE="challenge"
        KEYTYPE="type"
        PQG="pqg-pars">
```

As of this writing, Netscape Navigator returns a signed public key and challenge (SPKAC) public key when the KEYGEN tag is encountered. Consequently, the NAME parameter must always be set to SPKAC. In addition, the CHALLENGE parameter is used by CAs to verify a user's request for a certificate revocation operation. The challenge is usually chosen by the user before the HTML document containing the KEYGEN tag is generated and sent to the browser. Also, the KEYTYPE parameter is used to specify what type of key is to be generated. Valid values are "RSA," which is the default, and "DSA." Both values refer to the corresponding digital signature algorithms. Finally, the PQG parameter is only used for DSA keys and not further addressed in this book (since the commonly used keytype is "RSA"). From the user's point of view, the fill-out form looks like a normal form where the user can enter his or her name and other X.500-related information. In addition, there is a field that can be used to select the keylength. In general, international versions only support 512-bit RSA keys, whereas domestic U.S. versions support 512-bit, 768-bit, and 1024-bit RSA keys.

- In Microsoft Internet Explorer, the HTML fill-out form is more complicated, because it requires a simple program (written either in JavaScript or Visual Basic) in the document to use an ActiveX control to generate a key pair and create a corresponding PKCS #10 certificate request. The program is downloaded with the HTML document, and called when the Submit form button is pressed. The program then calls the `GenReqForm` method of the `certenr3` ActiveX control (also called certHelper), passing to it the distinguished name values from the form. The PKCS #10 certificate request produced by the ActiveX control is then loaded into a hidden field of the form, and returned with the form values of the server CGI script.

In either case, the CGI script running on the server is responsible for turning the certificate request information into a valid PKCS #10 certificate request and forwarding it to the CA. After the CA has received a PKCS #10 personal certificate request, it generates an X.509v3 certificate and encodes it according to the DER in the case of binary data, or PEM format in the case of ASCII data. In the second case, the Base64-encoded certificate is placed between the following two lines:

```
-----BEGIN CERTIFICATE-----
-----END CERTIFICATE-----
```

Downloading the certificate from the CA works the same way for both Netscape Navigator and Microsoft Internet Explorer (the certificate is downloaded to the browser as MIME type `application/x-x509-user-cert` in the Content-type HTTP header). In either case, the browser checks that the downloaded certificate matches a previously sent certificate request. If it matches, the certificate will be locally installed and activated.

A final word is due about the way in which the private keys that correspond to personal certificates are stored and protected in current browsers. In general, there are four possibilities:

- The simplest way to store and protect a private key is to encrypt it using a key that is derived from a password or pass phrase chosen by the user. This is the way that most browsers, including Netscape Navigator and Microsoft Internet Explorer, protect the users' private keys. The advantage is that it is simple and convenient to use. The disadvantage is that if someone gains access to the computer and knows the appropriate password or pass phrase, he or she can also access and use the private key. And since the private key must be decrypted in order to be used, it is also vulnerable to attacks inside the computer's memory by a software attack, such as employed by a computer virus, Trojan horse, or any other rogue program.

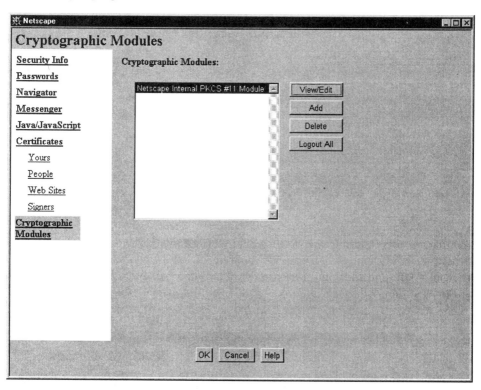

Figure 6.5 Netscape Navigator's interface to configure cryptographic modules. © 1999 Netscape Communications Corporation.

- A slightly more secure way to store and protect a private key is to keep it encrypted on some removable media, such as a floppy disk or CD-ROM. With this technique, an attacker must have both the media and knowledge of the password or pass phrase to decrypt and actually access the private key. Unfortunately, to use the private key, the computer must decrypt the private key and put a copy of it in its memory; this still leaves the key vulnerable to software attacks.

- A more secure way is to store the private key in a smartcard or any other "smart" device. The smartcard has a microprocessor and actually creates the public key pair. Ideally, the private key never leaves the smartcard. Instead, if a user wants to sign or decrypt a piece of information, that piece of information has to be transmitted into the card, and the signed or decrypted answer transmitted off the card. Consequently, an attacker cannot use the private key unless he or she has possession of the smartcard. And, unlike storing the private key on a floppy disk, a rogue program running inside the computer can't surreptitiously make a copy of the private key, because the key itself is never placed in the computer's memory. However, the input/output stream to the smartcard may still be subject to some sophisticated attacks.

- Finally, the most secure way is to use dedicated hardware that performs all computation and controls all input/output operations.

As of this writing (and as mentioned above), most browsers support the simplest way by having the private key locally stored in encrypted form. The key that is used to encrypt the private key(s) is derived from a password or pass phrase. In order to export and import private keys, it is possible to keep them on removable media. In the future, it is planned to use smartcards to store and protect private keys. For example, Netscape Navigator comes along with a panel to configure cryptographic modules, such as the Netscape Internal PKCS #11 Module (as illustrated in Figure 6.5).

Smartcards provide an interesting and promising security technology. They can be programmed to require a PIN, password, or pass phrase before they will perform a cryptographic function. This helps protect its key(s) in the event that the card is stolen. They can also be programmed so that if many PINs are tried in succession, the key(s) is (are) automatically erased. Finally, smartcards can be built to additionally use biometrics. Unfortunately, smartcards also have disadvantages. For example, some of them are fragile. Furthermore, if a card is lost, stolen, or damaged, the key(s) it contains is (are) gone and no longer available to the user. Thus, it is necessary to have some form of card duplication or replication system to prevent key loss. This is especially important for keys that are used to decrypt stored data. Finally, it is also the case that smartcards are not completely tamperproof. For example, Ross Anderson and Markus Kuhn showed how to break the security of a smartcard that was widely used for security mechanisms in 1996 [14]. Later that year, a group of researchers at Bellcore announced a theoretical attack against smartcards that perform encryption. Other researchers quickly entered the fray and published a variety of attacks on hardware-based encryption systems.

6.4.2   Site and CA Certificates

When a browser connects to an SSL or TLS-enabled Web server (an HTTPS server), the server returns a site certificate in the CERTIFICATE message immediately following the SERVERHELLO message. If this certificate is issued by a root CA that is preconfigured and loaded in the browser, it can be verified immediately. If, however, the certificate is issued by a CA that is not preconfigured and loaded in the browser, an additional step is required. In this case, the browser pops up a dialog box to warn the user about the unknown status of the certificate. It is up to the user to decide what to do. In general, the user can select among the following options:

- Deny the connection;

- Accept the connection for this time only;

- Accept the connection anyway and memorize the certificate of the server (not of the signing CA), so next time the server is accessed, the question is not asked again.

In addition, the browser also compares the common name (CN) field entry of the certificate with the host part of the URL that follows the prefix `https://`. If they do not match, the browser pops up a dialog box telling the user that the server certificate's common name does not match the URL and that a masquerade could be in progress.

Instead of accepting individual site certificates, it is also possible to configure the browser to accept all site certificates that have been issued by specific CAs (as mentioned before, several root CAs come preconfigured in standard browser software distributions). In this case, the user has to install corresponding CA certificates (which will be self-signed) in his or her browser. Note, however, that if you use a CA that is not preconfigured and loaded into browsers by default, it is necessary to load the CA certificate into the browser, enabling the browser to validate site certificates signed by that CA. Doing so may be dangerous, since once loaded, the browser will accept all certificates signed by that particular CA.

On the technical side, the browser can be made to access a specific link to download data of the `application/x-x509-ca-cert` MIME type.[18] In this case,

---

[18]The main complication of this is that while Netscape Navigator accepts CA certificates in various formats, including the PEM format, Microsoft Internet Explorer recognizes certificates only in the binary DER format. To support Microsoft Internet Explorer, any PEM-encoded CA certificate must be transformed into DER format. There are several tools that can be used for this transformation (e.g., SSLeay).

the browser recognizes this data as the certificate of a new CA. If the CA were already known, the user would be informed that the corresponding CA certificate is already stored in the database. Otherwise, the user is asked if he or she wants to introduce and trust the new CA. Note at this point that the user has no simple way to check whether he or she has received a correct certificate, and that he or she is not protected against the man-in-the-middle attack accordingly. In principle, the user should press the "More Info" button and compare the resulting fingerprint[19] of the certificate with a previously published version of the fingerprint that is received by some trusted way. For obvious reasons, this is seldom done in practice. After having accepted the certificate, the user can limit the scope of the certificate for SSL, secure messaging, or code signing. The user can also enter a nickname of his or her choice under which the CA will appear in the corresponding list.

6.5   FIREWALL TUNNELING

As of this writing, SSL and TLS in general, and HTTPS in particular, are widely used and deployed within the Internet and the WWW. Unfortunately, the protocols do not easily interoperate with proxy-based firewalls (either dual-homed or screened subnet configurations as addressed in Chapter 3). Note that an SSL or TLS connection is always established on an end-to-end basis, and that any proxy server working at the firewall (between the client and the origin server) must be considered as a man-in-the-middle (or something similar) accordingly. Also note that different protocols have different requirements for proxy servers. Some are handled fundamentally differently by the proxy server, while others fit well into the generic framework used by proxy servers. In general, a protocol can either be proxied or tunneled through a proxy server [15]:

- When we say that a protocol is being proxied, we actually mean that the corresponding proxy server is aware of the specifics of the protocol and can understand what is happening on the protocol level. This allows such things as protocol-level filtering, access control, and logging. Examples of protocols that are usually proxied include Telnet, FTP, and HTTP.

- Contrary to that, we say that a protocol is being tunneled when we actually mean that the corresponding proxy server (which is basically acting as a circuit-level gateway) is not aware of the specifics of the protocol and can't understand what is

---

[19]In this case, the term "fingerprint" refers to a hash value, most commonly generated with MD5.

happening on the protocol level accordingly. It is simply relaying, or "tunneling," the data between the client and the server, and does not necessarily understand the protocol being used. Consequently, it cannot perform such things as protocol-level filtering, access control, and logging to the same extent as is possible for a full-fledged proxy server. Examples of protocols that are usually tunneled by proxy servers or circuit-level gateways include SSL-enhanced protocols, such as HTTPS, as well as the Internet inter-ORB protocol (IIOP) used for CORBA applications.[20]

In an early attempt to address the problem of having SSL or HTTPS traffic going through a proxy-based firewall, Ari Luotonen from Netscape Communications proposed an *SSL tunneling protocol* that basically allows an HTTP proxy server to act as a tunnel for SSL-enhanced protocols.[21] As such, the protocol allows an SSL (or HTTPS) client to open a secure tunnel through an HTTP proxy server that resides on the firewall. When tunneling SSL, the proxy server must not have access to the data being transferred in either direction (for the sake of confidentiality). The proxy server must merely know the source and destination addresses (IP addresses and port numbers), and possibly, if the proxy server supports user authentication, the name of the requesting user. Consequently, there is a handshake between the client and the proxy server to establish the connection between the client and the remote server through the intermediate proxy server. In order to make the SSL tunneling extension be backward compatible, the handshake must be in the same format as normal HTTP/1.0 requests, so that proxy servers without support for this feature can still determine the request as impossible for them to service, and provide proper error notifications. As such, SSL tunneling isn't really SSL specific. It's rather a general way to have a third party establish a connection between two endpoints, after which bytes are simply copied back and forth by this intermediary.

In SSL tunneling, the client connects to the proxy server and uses the CONNECT method to specify the hostname and the port number to connect to (the hostname and port number are separated by a colon). The `host:port` part is then followed by a space and a string specifying the HTTP version number (e.g., HTTP/1.0 or HTTP/1.1), and the line terminator. After that, there is a series of zeros or more of HTTP request header lines, followed by an empty line. After this empty line, if the handshake to establish the connection was successful, SSL can actually transfer data. Consequently, an SSL tunneling sequence may look as follows:

---

[20]In short, IIOP has both SOCKS and SSL tunneling options for traversing a firewall.
[21]`draft-luotonen-ssl-tunneling-*.txt`

```
CONNECT www.ifi.unizh.ch:443 HTTP/1.0
User-agent: Mozilla/4.05 [en] (WinNT; U)
```

... SSL data ...

The SSL tunneling handshake is freely extensible using arbitrary HTTP/1.0 headers. For example, to enforce client authentication, the proxy may use the 407 status code and the Proxy-authenticate response header to ask the client to provide some authentication information to the proxy. Consequently, the SSL tunneling sequence looks as follows:

```
HTTP/1.0 407 Proxy authentication required
Proxy-authenticate: ...
```

... SSL data ...

In this case, the client would send the required authentication information in a message that looks as follows:

```
CONNECT www.ifi.unizh.ch:443 HTTP/1.0
User-agent: Mozilla/4.05 [en] (WinNT; U)
Proxy-authorization: ...
```

... SSL data ...

Note that the CONNECT method provides a lower level function than the other HTTP methods. Think of it as some kind of an "escape mechanism" for saying that the proxy server should not interfere with the transaction, but merely serve as a circuit-level gateway and forward the data stream. In fact, the proxy server should not need to know the entire URL that is being requested, only the information that is actually needed to serve the request, such as the hostname and port number of the origin Web server. Consequently, the proxy server cannot verify that the protocol being spoken is really SSL, and the proxy server configuration should therefore explicitly limit allowed (tunneled) connections to well-known SSL ports, such as 443 for HTTPS or 563 for NNTPS (the port numbers are assigned by the IANA). As of this writing, SSL tunneling is supported by most HTTP proxy servers and browsers that are commercially available, including Netscape Navigator and Microsoft Internet Explorer on the client side.

The primary use of SSL tunneling is to let internal users within a corporate intranet access external HTTPS servers on the Internet (in this case, it is seldom necessary to check the destination port number, because outbound HTTP connections are allowed in most security policies). Nevertheless, SSL tunneling can also be used in the opposite direction, namely to make internal HTTPS servers visible and accessible to the outside world (to the users located on the Internet). In this case, however, the proxy server acts as an inbound proxy[22] for the SSL data traffic. What this basically means is that HTTPS connections originated from the outside world are simply relayed by the inbound proxy to the internal HTTPS servers, where the requesting users should be strongly authenticated. Therefore, the internal Web servers must implement the SSL or TLS protocol. Unfortunately, this is not always the case and most internal Web servers are still not SSL or TLS-enabled (and don't represent HTTPS servers accordingly). In this case, the inbound proxy must authenticate the requesting clients and connect them to the appropriate internal Web servers. To make this possible (and to make these servers visible to the outside world), the idea of using a combination of SSL client authentication (at the inbound proxy) and URL rewriting techniques was originally developed at the DEC Systems Research Center in a technology called "secure Web tunneling" [16].

The core of the resulting secure Web tunneling system is a specialized server, which has been named the *Web tunnel*. In short, the Web tunnel controls external access to internal HTTP servers and acts as inbound proxy for all HTTP requests targeted at a protected intranet server. The Web tunnel executes within the protection of the corporate firewall and is logically part of the firewall. The firewall permits HTTP and HTTPS connections to the Web tunnel from the outside world, and can make HTTP connections to servers inside the firewall. According to the proposed design, the Web tunnel consists of the following three components:

- The *authenticator* is to authenticate the client to the proxy (several user authentication schemes can be supported at this point);

- The *redirector* processes incoming HTTP requests, and maps HTTP URLs to HTTPS URLs (the HTTPS URLs are then returned to the client in HTTP redirect response messages);

---

[22]In the literature, inbound proxies are called reverse proxies most of the time. In this book, however, we use the term "inbound proxy," since there is no reverse functionality involved. In fact, a reverse proxy is doing nothing differently than a normal proxy server. The only difference is that it primarily serves inbound connections (instead of outbound connections).

- Upon receipt of one of these HTTPS URLs, the client establishes a secure connection to the *proxy* for transmitting the redirected request. The proxy relays the original request as HTTP on the intranet, and returns any response over the secure connection back to the client. Note that the internal HTTP server must not reauthenticate the client, since the client has already been authenticated at the firewall. One problem arises because many URLs embedded in the HTTP resources include relative URLs. These URLs must be extended at the firewall using URL rewriting techniques.

In firewall parlance, the Web tunnel actually represents an application-level gateway. A similar design was developed and is being implemented by the IT Security Group of the Swiss Federal Strategy Unit for Information Technology (FSUIT). The design is simpler because it does not use a separate redirector. Instead, the user is required to map HTTP URLs to HTTPS URLs.

Finally, the use of SSL (or any other encryption technologies) for HTTP data traffic also negatively influences the usefulness of proxy servers for caching. Once again, the security administrator is in conflict with the network administrators who want to make the proxy servers as efficient as possible through the extensive use of cache memory. This memory, however, is essentially worthless when it comes to HTTPS data traffic (since the data traffic is encrypted with a specific session key).

6.6   CONCLUSIONS

In this chapter, we elaborated on two transport layer security protocols that were briefly introduced in Chapter 5: the SSL and TLS protocols. Both protocols are well suited to provide communication security services for TCP-based applications. In fact, the user community of the SSL and TLS protocols is growing very rapidly. In the previous section, we saw that there is a practical difficulty in tunneling SSL and TLS data traffic through a firewall (this difficulty is due to the fact that the SSL and TLS protocols are end-to-end protocols, and that any firewall represents a man-in-the-middle). Unfortunately, the protocols have two additional problems that are even more difficult to address:

- First, none of the two protocols (neither SSL nor TLS) provides a viable solution for the security-related problems of UDP-based applications;

- Second and more important, the deployment of SSL and TLS-based solutions is seriously limited by the currently existing U.S. export controls.

With regard to the first problem, remember that the SSL and TLS protocols both require a TCP connection before the handshake may be performed. Consequently, if no TCP connection is established at all (as in the case of UDP-based applications), neither the SSL nor the TLS protocol can be used. In the long term, this may pose some problems, since an increasingly large number of applications make use of UDP as a transport layer protocol. This is essentially true for realtime communications and multicast applications.

With regard to the second problem, remember from Chapter 4 that the United States controls the export of cryptographic hardware and software. Due to these export controls, users outside the United States and Canada can usually only obtain international versions of SSL or TLS-enabled products (both browsers and servers). What this basically means is that the international versions of these products will incorporate weak cryptography. In particular, most international versions of U.S. browser and Web server products support RC4 encryption with an effective key-length restricted only to 40 bits.[23] This is accomplished by encrypting only 40 bits of the 128-bit RC4 session key and sending the remaining 88 bits of the key in the clear. It is commonly agreed today that 40-bit keys are far too weak to be used in serious applications [17]. Also, certificate chains containing one or more 512-bit RSA key(s) or signatures may not be appropriate in these environments.

For users outside the United States and Canada, there are currently three approaches to circumvent weak encryption technology in their browsers:

- The first approach is to use a browser that has been developed and marketed outside the United States and Canada;

- The second approach is to use tools to upgrade browsers employing weak cryptography to the full-grade cryptographic strength (this is not always possible, since it is difficult to get U.S. export approval for products that implement cryptographic techniques that can easily be replaced);

- Finally, the third approach is to use the international version of a browser, but to additionally use a personal proxy server[24] that provides support for SSL with

---

[23]Recent legislation allows for registered U.S. companies to export software that uses 56-bit keys, but only if they allow the U.S. government to access the data under certain circumstances.

[24]According to [15], personal proxy servers are trimmed-down proxy servers intended for individual use. They typically run on the same system as the browser. In general, the distinction between features of the browser and personal proxy servers is vague, and one might argue that the functionality of a personal proxy server should be completely integrated into the corresponding browser.

strong encryption. In this case, weak encryption is used between the client and the personal proxy server, and strong encryption is used between the personal proxy server and the origin server. In essence, the personal proxy server acts as an encryption amplifier between the local client and the origin server.

The first approach is somewhat difficult, since there are not many software products available that have been developed and are being marketed outside the United States and Canada. Therefore, the second and third approaches are more realistic. For example, a software package called Fortify can be used to upgrade the browser's cryptographic strength.[25] In addition, there are several products that support the third approach. Examples include the SafePassage Web Proxy,[26] the Secure Socket Relay (SSR[27]), and the SecureNet client software that is being used in Switzerland for Internet banking. In addition, Baltimore Technologies Ltd. has developed a set of Java applets called WebSecure that provide essentially the same functionality.[28] On the client side, WebSecure works with WWW browsers that support Java 1.0.2 or greater. A similar approach is being followed by the X◊PRESSO software that was developed by a German company named Brokat Systeme.[29]

More recently, the concept of *server gated cryptography* (SGC) was proposed by Microsoft.[30] In short, SGC defines a mechanism for negotiating strong crypto-graphic security for SSL or TLS sessions based on the presence of a special server-side certificate (a so-called "SGC certificate"). The rationale behind SGC is very different from key escrow and key recovery. In fact, in SGC session keys are not escrowed. Instead, SGC certificates are only issued to institutions that are assumed to be trustworthy and willing to cooperate with authorized national bodies. Examples include banks and other financial institutions, as well as other proponents of e-commerce applications. Distribution of SGC certificates is controlled in accordance with an export license from the U.S. Department of Commerce (DoC). As of this writing, VeriSign is the only company that is authorized to issue SGC certificates.

---

[25]http://www.fortify.net
[26]http://stronghold.ukweb.com/safepassage/
[27]http://www.medcom.se/ssr/
[28]http://www.baltimore.ie/websecur.htm3summary
[29]http://www.brokat.de
[30]http://www.microsoft.com/security/tech/sgc/

REFERENCES

[1] R. Oppliger, *Internet and Intranet Security*, Artech House, Norwood, MA, 1998.

[2] J. Myers, "Simple Authentication and Security Layer," Request for Comments 2222, October 1997.

[3] H. Krawczyk, M. Bellare, and R. Canetti, "HMAC: Keyed-Hashing for Message Authentication," Request for Comments 2104, February 1997.

[4] D. Wagner, and B. Schneier, "Analysis of the SSL 3.0 Protocol," *Proceedings of 2nd USENIX Workshop on Electronic Commerce*, USENIX Press, November 1996, pp. 29 – 40.

[5] D. Bleichenbacher, "Chosen Ciphertext Attacks Against Protocols Based on the RSA Encryption Standard PKCS #1," *Proceedings of CRYPTO '98*, August 1998, pp. 1 – 12.

[6] RSA Data Security, Inc., *PKCS #1: RSA Encryption Standard*, Redwood City, CA, November 1993.

[7] M. Bellare, and P. Rogaway, "Optimal Asymmetric Encryption," *Proceedings of EURO-CRYPT '94*, 1994, pp. 92 – 111.

[8] M. Bellare, A. Desai, D. Pointcheval, and P. Rogaway, "Relations Among Notions of Security for Public-Key Encryption Schemes," *Proceedings of CRYPTO '98*, August 1998.

[9] R. Cramer, and V. Shoup, "A Practical Public Key Cryptosystem Provably Secure Against Adaptive Chosen Ciphertext Attack," *Proceedings of CRYPTO '98*, August 1998, pp. 13 – 25.

[10] B. Kaliski, and J. Staddon "PKCS #1: RSA Cryptography Specifications Version 2.0," Request for Comments 2437, October 1998.

[11] European Committee for Banking Standards (ECBS), *Secure Banking Over the Internet*, March 1997.

[12] B. Laurie, and P. Lauried, *Apache: The Definitive Guide*, O'Reilly & Associates, Sebastopol, CA, 1997.

[13] T. Dierks, and C. Allen, "The TLS Protocol Version 1.0," Request for Comments 2246, January 1999.

[14] R. Anderson, and M. Kuhn, "Tamper Resistance — a Cautionary Note," *Proceedings of 2nd USENIX Workshop on Electronic Commerce*, USENIX Press, November 1996, pp. 18 – 21.

[15] A. Luotonen, *Web Proxy Servers*, Prentice Hall PTR, Upper Saddle River, NJ, 1998.

[16] M. Abadi, A. Birrell, R. Stata, and E. Wobber, "Secure Web Tunneling," *Proceedings of 7th International World Wide Web Conference*, April 1998, pp. 531 – 539.

[17] H. Abelson, R. Anderson, S.M. Bellovin, J. Benaloh, M. Blaze, W. Diffie, J. Gilmore, P.G. Neumann, R.L. Rivest, J.I. Schiller, and B. Schneier, *The Risks of Key Recovery, Key Escrow, and Trusted Third-Party Encryption*, May 1997.

Chapter 7

Electronic Payment Systems

In this chapter, we overview and briefly discuss some electronic payment systems that can be used in e-commerce applications for the Internet and the WWW. After a short introduction in Section 7.1, we elaborate on electronic cash systems, electronic checks, electronic credit card payments, and micropayment systems in Sections 7.2 to 7.5. Finally, we draw some conclusions in Section 7.6. Note that some parts of this chapter are taken from [1]. Also note that the descriptions that are given in this chapter are simplified and rather superficial. This is because a detailed description of currently available electronic payment systems would fill a book of its own. In fact, there are many books that address electronic payment systems and their application in e-commerce. Among these books, I particularly recommend [2]. Refer to this book for a more comprehensive and thorough treatment of the topic. To keep this chapter sufficiently small, several cross-references to various parts of this book are included.

7.1 INTRODUCTION

The exchange of goods conducted face-to-face between two or more entities dates back to before the beginning of recorded history. Eventually, as trade became more

171

complicated and inconvenient, human beings invented some increasingly abstract forms of representation for value. Consequently, we (or rather our predecessors) have experienced a progression of value transfer systems, starting from barter arrangements, through commodity money, coins and bank notes, payment orders, checks, and credit cards.

More recently, the progression of value transfer systems has culminated in *electronic payment systems*. In fact, the growing importance of electronic commerce (e-commerce) and corresponding applications has resulted in the introduction of a variety of different and partly competing electronic payment systems [3,4]. Within currently available electronic payment systems, payments are done electronically, but the mapping between the electronic payments and the transfer of "real value" is still guaranteed by banks through financial clearing systems. These clearing systems are built on the closed networks of financial institutions that are considered comparatively more secure than open networks, such as the Internet.

It is important to note that all abstract forms of representation for value and corresponding value transfer systems suffer from well-known (and probably also some unknown) security problems. For example, money can be counterfeited, signatures on checks can be forged, and checks can be bounced. Electronic payment systems retain the same or similar security problems and may eventually pose additional risks. For example, unlike paper, digital data (representing monetary value) can be copied perfectly and arbitrarily often, digital signatures can be counterfeited perfectly by anybody who knows the private key, and a customer's name can be associated with every payment, effectively eliminating the anonymity of conventional cash. Thus, without new security mechanisms and techniques being developed, implemented, and deployed, widespread use of electronic payment systems and corresponding e-commerce applications is not likely to take off.

All currently available electronic payment systems differ in details, but have the same basic purpose of facilitating the transfer of monetary value between multiple parties. In general, electronic payments involve a *buyer* (the party that wants to buy goods or services) and a *merchant* (the party that wants to sell goods or services). In the terminology of electronic payment systems, a buyer is often called a *payer*, and a merchant is often called a *payee*. Obviously, the intent of an electronic payment system is to safely and securely transfer monetary value from the payer to the payee. Transfer is accomplished by electronic payment protocols. These protocols are general in nature and must not depend on the actual transport media in use. As a matter of fact, a payment protocol may be implemented as part of a Web application using HTTP, as part of an e-mail application using SMTP, or as part of any other application protocol. In either case, it must be ensured that the data involved in an electronic payment protocol execution is safe and secure, even if the medium is not. In the case that the medium is attacked, nothing more than a useless data stream must be obtained by the attacker. To provide this kind of safety and security, most electronic payment systems make use of some more or less sophisticated cryptographic techniques.

Note, however, that there is no obligation to use cryptographic techniques at all. For example, it has been possible for a long time to make credit card payments without requiring the customer and merchant to be colocated. Credit card companies have allowed orders to be taken either by post or telephone. These orders are collectively referred to as *mail order/telephone order* (MOTO) transactions, and special rules have been imposed by the credit card companies on how these transactions are to be processed. In fact, cardholders are asked to provide some additional information, such as their names and addresses, that are used to verify their identity. Also, if goods that require physical delivery are being ordered, they must be sent to the address associated with the cardholder. Although there are many possibilities for fraud associated with MOTO transactions, it is still very popular today (for certain applications the benefits simply outweigh the risks).

Using credit cards to make payments across computer networks has similar associated risks as are experienced with MOTO transactions. Attackers eavesdropping on network traffic may intercept data and capture credit card and associated verification information. What makes the risks considerably higher than MOTO transactions is the open nature of computer networks and the speed in which transactions can be conducted in these networks. Against this background, there are only a few electronic payment systems for the Internet that don't make use of cryptographic techniques. For example, one of the earliest credit-card-based payment system was the product of a company called First Virtual Holdings, Inc.[1] In October 1994, the company commenced operation of a noncryptographic payment system called the *VirtualPIN*. The goal of the VirtualPIN system was to allow the selling of low-value information goods across the Internet without the need for special-purpose client hardware or software to be put in place.

In the VirtualPIN system, both the customers and merchants had to register with First Virtual (FV) before any transactions could take place.

- A customer registering with FV had to forward credit card information and an e-mail address to the FV server and in exchange received a pass phrase, called a

---

[1]More recently, First Virtual Holdings, Inc. has changed its name to MessageMedia, Inc. As such, the company provides solutions for e-mail security. The homepage of MessageMedia, Inc. can be found at URL http://www.messagemedia.com.

VirtualPIN. This initial part of the exchange could take place across the Internet, with the user filling out a form and inventing the first part of a pass phrase. The FV server acknowledged this and added a suffix to the pass phrase to actually form the VirtualPIN. The customer then made a telephone call to FV to tender credit card information. This allowed FV to establish a link between the VirtualPIN and the pass phrase on the one hand and the customer's credit card information on the other hand without ever using this information on the Internet.

• Merchants had to go through a similar registration procedure in which they gave bank account information to FV and then were given a merchant VirtualPIN.

After a customer had properly registered with FV, he or she could browse any Web site on which a FV merchant was selling goods. The customer selected the item(s) he or she wished to purchase and was asked to enter the VirtualPIN (representing his or her FV account identifier). The VirtualPIN was then forwarded to the merchant, and the merchant checked that it was valid by querying a corresponding FV server. If the customer's VirtualPIN was not blacklisted, the merchant delivered the information to the customer and forwarded information about the transaction, including the customer's VirtualPIN, to the FV server. No payment was made at this point, since the system was based on a "try before you buy" philosophy. Consequently, the next step was for the FV server to send an e-mail message to the customer asking whether he or she accepted or rejected the goods. In addition, the customer could also indicate that a fraud was going on (as a third option). Upon receipt of this message, the FV server would immediately blacklist the customer's VirtualPIN. At the end of every 90 days, the customer's credit card account was debited for the charges that had accumulated during the time period, and the corresponding merchant's checking account was credited with payments for the items sold. FV performed the accounting for both the customer and merchant, taking a percentage of each transaction as commission fee.

It is obvious that if a VirtualPIN was compromised by an attacker eavesdropping on network data traffic, bogus purchases could be made from then until the VirtualPIN was blacklisted. Since payment authorization requests were sent to the customer by e-mail, this time period could range from a few minutes to perhaps a couple of days. Furthermore, degradation-of-service and denial-of-service attacks on the e-mail system could be used to prolong this period substantially. Consequently, the actual security of the FV payment system was not based on the VirtualPIN and the pass phrase, but rather on the customer's ability to revoke each payment within a certain period of time. In other words, there was no definite authorization during payment. Until the end of the clearing period (typically 90 days as mentioned above), the merchant had to take the entire risk.

As of this writing, FV is no longer offering its service to the general public. The FV system is further addressed in Section 4.3 of [2]. Also, *collect all relevant information* (CARI) is a payment system similar to FV that does not make use of cryptographic techniques. The CARI system is described in Section 4.4 of [2] and is not further addressed in this book.

In the remaining part of this chapter, we focus on electronic payment systems that make use of cryptographic techniques. Most of these systems require at least one financial institution, such as a bank, that links the data exchanged in the payment protocol to corresponding transfers of monetary value. Typically, banks participate in electronic payment protocols in two roles:

- As an *issuer* (interacting with the customer or payer);

- As an *acquirer* (interacting with the merchant or payee).

In addition, there may be some form of *arbiter* to settle disputes. In most electronic payment systems, the presence of an arbiter is not explicit. Even if the necessary pieces of evidence are produced, disputes must be handled outside the payment systems. In many cases, dispute handling is not even specified. This is about to change, since contemporary research in electronic payment systems also addresses dispute handling. Finally, certain payment systems may involve more players, such as registration authorities (RAs), CAs, or any other form of TTPs.

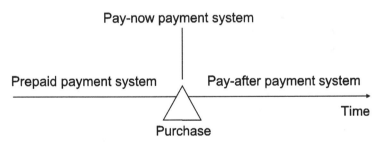

Figure 7.1   Prepaid, pay-now, and pay-after payment systems.

In general, electronic payment systems are classified according to the relationship between the time the payment initiator (the customer) considers the purchase as finished and the time the corresponding monetary value is actually taken from his or her account. As illustrated in Figure 7.1, one can distinguish among prepaid, pay-now, and pay-after payment systems:

- In a *prepaid payment system*, a certain amount of money is taken away from the customer (for example, by debiting his or her bank account) before any purchase is made. This amount of money can afterward be used for payments. Smart card-based electronic purses and wallets, electronic cash, and certain bank checks (such as certified checks) fall into this category.

- In a *pay-now payment systems*, the customer's account is debited exactly at the time of the purchase. Certain debit cards fall into this category.[2]

- Finally, in a *pay-after payment system*, the merchant's bank account is credited the amount of the purchase before the customer's account is debited. Obviously, normal credit cards fall into this category.

Note that any prepaid payment system is conceptually similar to physical cash. Consequently, they are sometimes also referred to as *cashlike payment systems*. Also note that the later two payment systems (pay-now and pay-after payment systems) are also similar in nature. In either case the payer must have some sort of "account" with the bank, and a payment is always done by sending some form, such as a check or credit card slip, from the customer to the merchant. Consequently, these two categories of payment systems are sometimes collectively referred to as *checklike payment systems*. Note that a key difference between cashlike and checklike payment systems is also due to the fact that providing anonymity in a cashlike payment system is possible and conceptually simple, whereas anonymity in a checklike payment system is inherently more difficult to provide.

In the field of electronic payment systems, the notions online and offline refer to a specific property of the corresponding payment protocol. Although the payment protocol is functionally a protocol between two parties (the customer and the merchant) many payment systems require that the merchant contact a TTP acting as a central authority (e.g., a bank, a credit card company, or an acquirer) before accepting a payment. If that is the case, the system is called an *online payment system*. In this case, the communication between the merchant and the central authority may be using any communication medium (not necessarily the Internet). If such a contact with a TTP is not required during the payment protocol, the system is called an *offline payment system*. In an offline payment system, merchants are required to contact their acquirer on a regular basis for clearing all received payments.

---

[2]For example, Switch debit cards are very common in the United Kingdom. They are issued by banks and are used like credit cards, although the money is deducted from the customer's bank account immediately.

In general, online payment systems are more appropriate to adequately secure the merchant and the bank against customer fraud, since every payment must be approved. The primary disadvantage of online authorization is the associated per transaction cost, imposed by the requirement for a highly reliable and efficient clearing system at the customer's bank. Consequently, offline payment systems have been designed (and still continue to be designed) to lower the cost of transactions by delaying the clearing to a batch process. Offline systems, however, suffer from the potential of double spending, whereby the electronic currency is duplicated and spent repeatedly. Thus, offline protocols concentrate on preventing or detecting and limiting fraud, and in catching the fraudulent party in the second case. Offline systems that detect and limit fraud are generally suitable only for low-value transactions where accountability after the fact is sufficient to deter abuse.

In the remaining part of this chapter, we overview and briefly discuss some exemplary electronic cash systems, electronic checks, electronic credit card payments, and micropayment systems. Finally, we conclude with some more general remarks regarding the future and further deployment of electronic payment systems.

7.2 ELECTRONIC CASH SYSTEMS

Almost all statistical investigations show that consumers make extensive use of cash. Depending on the country involved, somewhere between 75% and 95% of all financial transactions are paid with cash, even though the value of these transactions are for the most part quite low. As mentioned previously in this chapter, prepaid or cashlike payment systems provide an electronic analog for physical cash. In short, a bank issues *electronic cash* (e-cash), and customers use e-cash to purchase goods or services from merchants that accept this form of payment. Consequently, there are three parties involved in an e-cash system:

- An e-cash issuing bank;

- A customer (representing the payer);

- A merchant (representing the payee).

Typically, the customer and merchant have accounts with the same bank. However, the customer and merchant may also have accounts with other banks. In this case, these banks are referred to as the customer's bank or issuer and the merchant's bank or acquirer (as mentioned before).

Given this cast, an e-cash transaction typically takes place in three distinct and independent phases:

- In the first phase, the customer withdraws some e-cash. He or she therefore requests his or her bank to transfer some monetary value from his or her account to the e-cash issuing bank. Following this value transfer, the bank issues[3] and sends a corresponding amount of e-cash to the customer. The customer, in turn, stores the e-cash locally (e.g., on his or her hard disk or smart card).

- In the second phase, the customer uses the e-cash to purchase some goods or services. In particular, he selects goods or services and transfers the corresponding amount of e-cash to the merchant. The merchant, in turn, delivers the goods or services to the customer.

- In the third phase, the merchant redeems the e-cash he or she has just received from the customer. He or she therefore transfers the e-cash to the issuing bank. Alternatively, the merchant may also transfer the e-cash to his or her bank (the merchant's bank), and this bank may, in turn, redeem the money from the e-cash issuing bank. In this case, the issuing bank transfers money to the merchant's bank for crediting the merchant's account.

It is commonly agreed that e-cash should satisfy some general properties. For example, e-cash should be independent in the sense that its existence must not depend on a particular system platform or location. Probably one of the distinguishing features of physical cash (at least in the case of coins) is anonymity, meaning that cash must not provide information that can be used to trace previous owners. One can reasonably argue that e-cash must also provide this form of anonymity. Consequently, e-cash should be transferable from one person to another, and this transfer should occur without leaving any trace of who has been in possession of the e-cash before. In this case, however, it must be ensured that each owner can spend the e-cash only once and that double spending can be prevented or at least be detected in one way or another. Furthermore, e-cash should be available in several denominations and be divisible in a way similar to physical cash. Finally, e-cash should be available in such a way so it can be securely stored on various media, such as hard disks or smart cards.

Not all e-cash systems that have been proposed in the past satisfy all of these properties. For example, the anonymity property is still very controversial today, since it leads to the undesired possibility of illegal money laundering, or hiding of black market and blackmail money. This has led to the development of fairly

---

[3]In general, e-cash is issued by having the bank mint digital coins. The digital coins, in turn, are minted by digitally signing an item, such as a serial number for the coin, with a private key that is characteristic for the actual denomination of the coin.

anonymous e-cash systems, in which the customer's anonymity may leak under certain conditions. Fairly anonymous e-cash systems are an active area of research and are not further addressed in this book.

In the following subsections, we elaborate on some exemplary electronic cash systems, such as eCash, CAFE, NetCash, CyberCoin, Mondex, and EMV cash cards. Note that there are many other electronic cash systems that have been proposed in the past (and that will be proposed in the future). Also note that all systems mentioned above are further described and fully discussed in Chapter 6 of [2].

7.2.1   eCash

In the early 1980s, David Chaum developed a mechanism to blind RSA signatures that can be used to issue anonymous e-cash [5 – 7]. The explanations that follow are intended for the reader who's familiar with the mathematical principles of the RSA public key cryptosystem (refer to reference [21] in Chapter 4 for the RSA cryptosystem).

Let d be the private and (n, e) the public RSA key of an e-cash issuing bank (for one particular digital coin size, such as one dollar). In this case, n is the modulus and e and d are the exponents that correspond to each other; that is, for all x holds, $x^{de} \equiv x^{ed} \equiv x \pmod{n}$. The customer generates a serial number m for a digital coin and a random number r that serves the role of a blinding factor. He or she then computes $x = mr^e \pmod{n}$ and sends x to the e-cash issuing bank. Note that the bank cannot recognize m or r from x. The bank digitally signs x by calculating $y = x^d \pmod{n}$ and sends y back to the customer. At the same time, the bank also charges the customer's account with the corresponding amount of money (one dollar in this case). Obviously, this happens in the same way as if the customer would personally withdraw money from his or her bank account. The customer then divides y by r. This yields the bank's digital signature z of the digital coin's serial number m:

$$
\begin{aligned}
z &= y/r \\
&\equiv x^d/r \\
&\equiv (m(r^e))^d/r \\
&\equiv (m^d r^{ed})/r \\
&\equiv (m^d r)/r \\
&\equiv m^d \pmod{n}
\end{aligned}
$$

The pair (m, z) represents a digital coin that can be used by the customer to buy goods or services from a merchant that accepts this form of payment. More specifically, if the customer transfers (m, z) to the merchant, the merchant can use (n, e) — the public key of the issuing bank — to verify the digital signature z for the digital coin referenced by m. If the signature is valid, the merchant can assume that the coin has originally been issued by the bank. However, it may still be the case that the coin has already been spent previously. To prevent double spending, the merchant hence contacts the issuing bank and asks whether the coin referenced by m has already been spent. Obviously, this requires an online communications link between the merchant and the bank. It also requires a database that includes the serial numbers of all previously spent coins.[4] If the coin has not been spent yet, the merchant accepts it as a payment. If, however, the coin has already been spent previously, the merchant refuses to accept the coin as payment. If the merchant accepts the payment, he or she delivers the goods or services to the customer and redeems the coin from the issuing bank.

Chaum founded DigiCash, Inc.[5] to market the anonymous online e-cash scheme overviewed above under the name *eCash*. In the eCash system, digital coins are stored locally on the customer's computer system. An eCash trial using a virtual currency called *cyberbucks*, was launched on the Internet in October 1994. By early 1996, over 30,000 participants had taken part in the trial and registration for new participants was closed. The Mark Twain Bank of St. Louis was the first bank to issue eCash worth real monetary value (U.S. dollars). Meanwhile, several banks have followed the Mark Twain Bank. In fact, current eCash issuers include the Deutsche Bank in Germany, NetPay AG in Switzerland, EUnet in Finland, St.George in Australia, Den norske Bank in Norway, and the Bank Austria. In addition, eCash has also been licensed by the Japanese Nomura Research Institute.

7.2.2 CAFE

In addition to DigiCash's eCash system, the idea of anonymous e-cash was further explored in a European ESPRIT project called *Conditional Access for Europe* (CAFE).[6] The project began in 1992 and lasted for three years. As its name suggests, the aim of the project was to develop a system to administer conditional access rights for customers of e-commerce applications. The most significant out-

---

[4]Note, however, that the size of the database can at least be bounded through the use of expiration times in digital coins. Unfortunately, this also breaks the analogy with physical cash.

[5]http://www.digicash.com

[6]http://www.cwi.nl/cwi/projects/cafe.html

come of the project was the development of an anonymous offline electronic cash system of the same name.

The assumption of this project was that online examinations of digital coins (as in the eCash system) are not always possible, and that offline electronic cash systems provide a somewhat better approach for widespread use. However, one problem that arises immediately in an offline system is the double-spending problem. How can one ensure that a digital coin is not used twice? Note that in an offline system there is typically no possibility for the merchant to contact the issuing bank in order to verify the coin. In general, there are two approaches to address this problem:

- The first approach is to use some sophisticated cryptographic techniques to make sure that the identity of the owner of a digital coin that has been spent twice can be revealed. In this case, the owner of the coin provides a part of his or her identification characteristics during the payment process, which alone gives no further information about his or her identity. Only in combination with another part of his or her identification characteristics can the identity of the owner be revealed. This approach was first proposed in [8].

- The second approach is to use dedicated hardware devices that store the coins and make sure they are spent only once.

Obviously, the two approaches are not mutually exclusive and can even be combined to improve security. Such a hybrid approach was actually being followed in the CAFE project [9]. The first line of defense was provided by the second approach mentioned above (the use of dedicated hardware). Protecting against double spending was guaranteed as long as the tamper resistance of the hardware device was not compromised. The second line of defense, however, was provided by the first approach mentioned above. Consequently, the CAFE system had a cryptographic fallback mechanism that allowed the financial institutions to detect double spending of digital coins and blacklist suspected customers.

There are various hardware devices that can be used in the CAFE system to store digital coins, perform cryptographic operations, and make payments to merchants:

- The simplest hardware device is a smart card that is used in the CAFE α system.

- The more sophisticated hardware device is the *electronic wallet* that consists of two parts that work in conjunction with each other:

  - One part is known as an *observer* (or *guardian* as it is called in CAFE terminology) and protects the issuing bank's interests, namely that digital coins can be spent only once;

– The other part is known as the *purse* and protects the customer's interests, namely that digital coins are protected and that no information leaks from the electronic wallet.

The purse includes a keyboard and a display. This further protects the customer as he or she can enter his or her PIN on the purse and does not have to trust any third-party input device (this point is further explored in [4]). Furthermore, all communications between the wallet and the outside world are done exclusively through the purse, guaranteeing that the observer module cannot divulge any secret information to the bank without the customer's knowledge.[7] The use of a two-button wallet leads to the CAFE α^+ system, whereas the use of a full wallet leads to the CAFE Γ system.

Refer to Section 6.2 of [2] for a comprehensive description of the protocols used in the CAFE α, α^+, and Γ systems. In summary, the CAFE system is a very interesting anonymous offline electronic cash system. It is interesting mainly from a theoretical point of view. For all practical purposes, however, the CAFE electronic cash system is not very important (since it is not widely used and deployed). One reason for this astonishing fact is certainly its requirement for dedicated hardware.

7.2.3   NetCash

NetCash[8] is a research prototype of an online electronic cash system that was developed at the Information Sciences Institute of the University of Southern California [10]. The NetCash system consists of customers, merchants, and currency servers. Since there are multiple currency servers, a customer can choose one that is physically close and trustworthy. A currency server provides the following four services to customers and merchants:

- Issuing coins in return for electronic check payments;

- Verifying coins (to detect and prevent double spending);

- Buying back coins, giving an electronic check in return;

- Exchanging valid coins for new ones (to provide some form of weak anonymity).

---

[7]Note that the customer has to trust the purse manufacturer in this point.
[8]http://gost.isi.edu/info/netcash/

Consequently, the currency servers issue coins to the customers, accepting electronic checks in payment for them. The NetCheque system as introduced later in this chapter is used to provide the electronic check infrastructure required to bring monetary value into and out of the NetCash system. Not only can customers buy and sell NetCash coins in exchange for electronic checks, but NetCash servers can also use electronic checks to settle debts between them.

In the NetCash system, a digital coin is a piece of data representing monetary value. It is minted by a currency server and includes the name and address of the minting currency server, an expiration date, a serial number that is unique for the coins minted by the server, and a value that specifies the amount the coin is worth. Each coin is digitally signed with the minting currency server's private key. To prevent double spending, a currency server maintains a list of the serial numbers of every coin minted by it that is in current circulation. During a purchase, the merchant verifies that the coins he or she has received from a customer haven't been double spent by querying the corresponding currency server. The currency server, in turn, checks that a coin's serial number is present in its database. If it is, the coin is valid. If it is not, it has either been spent before and removed from the databse or it may have expired (serial numbers that have expired are removed from the database to bound its size and to allow serial numbers to be reused).

To make a purchase using the NetCash system, a customer first obtains digital coins from a currency server, buying them, for example, with an electronic check. Some of the purchased coins are then sent to the merchant in payment for an item. To protect against double spending, the merchant will verify the coins, either directly with the minting currency server or indirectly through a currency server of his or her choice (in the second case, the contacted currency server must query the minting currency server on the merchant's behalf). In either case, this verification must be done online. In exchange for valid coins received by the customer, the merchant can receive new coins, minted by the server he or she has contacted, or an electronic check. A digitally signed receipt from the merchant, and possibly the purchased item, may finally be sent to the customer.

Refer to Section 6.3 of [2] for a more comprehensive overview and description of the NetCash system and the corresponding protocols. Due to its origin, the NetCash system is not widely used and deployed outside universities and prototype environments.

7.2.4   CyberCoin

CyberCash, Inc.[9] was founded in August 1994 to provide software and service solutions for all types of financial transactions and payments over the Internet. In 1996, CyberCash launched an online electronic cash system called *CyberCoin*.[10] The CyberCoin system is proprietary and the details of the corresponding payment protocols have not been published so far. Nevertheless, the CyberCoin system is widely used and deployed in many e-commerce applications.

Customers buy electronic cash from a CyberCash server, charging the amount of money to their credit card or bank account. The CyberCoin cash is stored in a special area of a software called CyberCash wallet (this is the same piece of software that can be used to make CyberCash credit card payments as addressed later in this chapter). When a customer decides to pay a merchant, he or she forwards a payment message to the merchant who verifies it with the CyberCash server. If the transaction is successful, the merchant delivers the requested goods or services to the customer. The CyberCoin cash, having already been verified, is later deposited into the merchant's bank account via the CyberCash server.

Note that while a merchant does not necessarily know the identity of the customer, the CyberCoin system is not anonymous, as the CyberCash server will have records of each customer's transactions. Also, in the CyberCoin system, the digital coin metaphor is a lot weaker than in other tokenized systems, such as eCash or NetCash, in which pieces of data actually represent monetary value. When a customer buys CyberCoin cash, an account is established with the CyberCash server. Making a payment is similar to authorizing an amount of money to be transferred from this account to a merchant's account.

7.2.5   Mondex

The approach taken by researchers to electronic cash and that taken by the banking industry are quite different. The trend in the banking industry has been toward the use of more sophisticated payment cards to effect payment in the retail context. During the last decade, a number of schemes have been tried out that involve preloading a smart card with value that could then be spent at retail outlets. These schemes are generally referred to as prepayment cards and one of the more successful of them is the *Mondex* electronic cash card.

The concept of the Mondex card was developed in 1990 at NatWest, a major

---

[9]http://www.cybercash.com

[10]http://www.cybercash.com/cybercash/services/cybercoin.html

banking organization in the United Kingdom. After several field trials, a separate company, called Mondex International Ltd.,[11] was formed in 1996 to promote the technology through a series of further trials in many different locations around the world. Today, Mondex International is a subsidiary of MasterCard International. As of this writing, little is publicly known about the security features used in the Mondex electronic cash cards. Consequently, the cards have not been subject to public scrutiny.

7.2.6   EMV Cash Cards

EMV is a consortium consisting of Europay International together with the two major credit card companies (Visa International and MasterCard). Since 1994, EMV has been working on common specifications for prepayment cards and the applications thereof. In June 1996, a three-volume specification was released defining the following components:

- The physical and electrical characteristics of prepayment cards and terminals;

- The architecture for a multiapplication card reader terminal;

- An application specification for handling transactions.

Europay International was the first to launch a cash card according to the EMV specifications. Also, Visa International uses cards complying with these specifications as the basis for their *VISA Cash* electronic purses. These cards were first used in public trials at the 1996 Atlanta Olympic Games, and subsequently in many other locations around the world. Finally, MasterCard has also announced that it will market a similar electronic purse, called *MasterCash* purse, based on the EMV specifications. More recently, Visa International and MasterCard have started to collaborate with some banking organizations to allow VISACash and MasterCash to run on the same hardware. This will be important for the further deployment of both VISACash and MasterCash purses.

7.3   ELECTRONIC CHECKS

Since the use of checks is widely deployed in the real world (at least in the United States), electronic checks may also provide an interesting payment scheme for e-commerce applications. A payment system for electronic checks includes the following parties:

---

[11] http://www.mondex.com

- A customer and a customer's bank;

- A merchant and a merchant's bank;

- A clearinghouse to process checks among different banks.

From a technical point of view, electronic checks are rather simple. An electronic check may simply consist of a document that is digitally signed with the customer's private key. The receiver (the merchant or the merchant's bank) uses the customer's public key to verify the digital signature accordingly. More specifically, an electronic check transaction is executed in three phases:

- In the first phase, the customer purchases some goods or services and sends a corresponding electronic check to the merchant. The merchant, in turn, validates the check with his or her bank for proper payment authorization. If the check is valid, the merchant accomplishes the transaction with the customer (and delivers the goods or services).

- In the second phase, the merchant forwards the electronic check to his or her bank for deposit. This action may take place at the discretion of the merchant.

- In the third phase, the merchant's bank forwards the electronic check to the clearinghouse for cashing it. The clearinghouse, in turn, cooperates with the customer's bank, clears the check, and transfers the money to the merchant's bank, which updates the merchant's account accordingly. The customer's bank also updates the customer with the corresponding withdrawal information.

Compared with paper checks and some other real-world payment systems, electronic checks provide several advantages. For example, electronic checks can be issued without needing to fill out, mail, or deliver checks. It also saves time in processing the checks. With paper checks, the merchant typically collects all the checks and collectively deposits them at the bank. With electronic checks, the merchant can instantly forward the checks to the bank and get them credited to his or her account. As such, electronic checks can greatly reduce the time from the moment a customer writes a check to the time when the merchant receives the deposit. In addition, electronic check systems can be designed in such a way that the merchant gets proper authorization from the customer's bank before accepting a check. This is very similar to the concept of a cashier's check.

The Financial Services Technology Consortium (FSTC) is a group of American banks, research agencies, and government organizations that have come together to assist in enhancing the competitiveness of the U.S. financial service industry.[12] While the FSTC has been formulating a strategy for banks to deal with electronic checks, the research community has also been formulating alternative electronic check systems for the Internet. Three exemplary systems — NetBill, NetCheque, and PayNow — are overviewed next. Refer to Chapter 5 of [2] for further information regarding the payment protocols and corresponding message formats of the NetBill and NetCheque systems.

7.3.1   NetBill

NetBill is an online checklike electronic payment system originally developed at Carnegie Mellon University in 1994 [11,12].[13] Similar to many other electronic payment systems, NetBill is optimized for the selling and buying of low-priced information goods. Unlike many other electronic payment systems, however, NetBill aims to provide a total system, from price negotiation to goods delivery. As such, its main contributions are:

- An atomic certified delivery method so that a customer pays if and only if he or she receives the requested information goods intact;

- A credential mechanism that allows customers to prove membership in groups (for example, to support group membership discounts);

- A structure for constructing pseudonyms to protect the identities of customers.

The NetBill transaction model involves three parties: the customer, the merchant, and the NetBill transaction server that also maintains accounts for both the customer and merchant. Again, these accounts can be linked to traditional accounts in financial institutions. When a customer purchases information goods, his or her NetBill account is debited by the appropriate amount of money, and the merchant's account is credited with the value of the goods. Furthermore, the NetBill system guarantees that a customer pays for only the goods that he or she successfully receives. In the basic scheme, a NetBill transaction requires eight messages to be exchanged. There are many variations within NetBill that allow, for example, the customer to hide his or her identity from the merchant, for price negotiation to take place, for limited spending authority to be given to others, and for disputes of all

---

[12]http://www.fstc.org

[13]More recently, CyberCash, Inc. has acquired the rights to use the NetBill technology from Carnegie Mellon University.

kinds to be settled. Refer to Section 5.2 of [2] for a comprehensive description of the NetBill transaction protocol and its variations.

From the technical point of view, the NetBill system makes use of a modified version of the Kerberos authentication system [13]. The modification is due to the use of public key cryptography to decrease the Kerberos server dependency by allowing public keys to be used in certain parts of the protocol message exchanges. Furthermore, NetBill provides transaction support through libraries integrated with the client and server. The client library is called the *checkbook* and the server library is called the *till*. The checkbook and till libraries, in turn, communicate with the client and server application programs. All network communication between the checkbook and the till is encrypted to protect against potential adversaries. Unfortunately, all transactions must involve the NetBill server before they can be completed. This turns the NetBill server into the bottleneck of the system.

7.3.2   NetCheque

NetCheque, developed at the Information Sciences Institute of the University of Southern California, is another online checklike electronic payment system that is based on the use of Kerberos [14,15].[14] Roughly speaking, a NetCheque check (or NetCheque for short) is represented by a Kerberos ticket that allows an authorized bearer to withdraw funds from the NetCheque issuer's account and prevents an unauthorized bearer from depositing a NetCheque not issued to him or her.

More specifically, NetCheque is a distributed accounting service consisting of a hierarchy of NetCheque servers that are used to clear checks and settle interbank accounts. A hierarchy is used to make the system scalable. It also allows customers to select the bank of their choice. A NetCheque account is similar to a conventional bank account against which customers (account holders) can write electronic checks. To make use of the NetCheque system, a customer must have registered with a NetCheque accounting server and obtained the corresponding client software. Refer to Section 5.3 of [2] for a comprehensive description and discussion of the NetCheque system.

7.3.3   PayNow

As mentioned previously in this chapter, CyberCash was founded to provide software and service solutions for all types financial transactions and payments over the

---

[14]http://gost.isi.edu/info/NetCheque/

Internet. PayNow is CyberCash's scheme for electronic checks.[15] In the PayNow system, a CyberCash server acts as a gateway server that links the customer wallet and merchant software to the existing financial infrastructure. Again, the protocols that are used to handle electronic checks in the PayNow system have not been published by CyberCash. Consequently, it's difficult to argue about the security properties of the system.

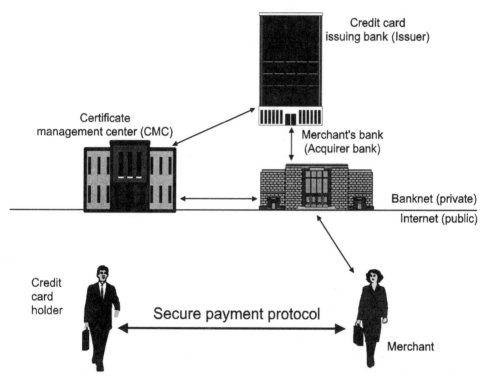

Figure 7.2   The parties involved in a secure electronic credit card payment scheme.

7.4   ELECTRONIC CREDIT CARD PAYMENTS

In the recent past, credit card payment systems have become the payment instrument of choice for Internet users and customers. There are several security requirements that these systems must address. For example, a mechanism must

---

[15]http://www.cybercash.com/cybercash/services/paynow.html

be provided to authenticate the various parties involved, such as customers and merchants, as well as participating banks. Another mechanism must be provided to protect the credit card and payment information during transmission over the Internet. Finally, a process must be instituted to resolve credit card payment disputes between the various parties involved. Several electronic credit card payment systems have been designed to address these requirements. Most of these schemes have additional properties. For example, in some schemes the credit card information can be prevented from disclosure to the merchant. This property is not inherent in traditional credit card systems. Consequently, an electronic credit card payment scheme may provide a higher level of security than a traditional credit card payment scheme. Also, an electronic credit card payment scheme can be designed to obtain almost instant payments to the merchants from credit card sales. For traditional credit card schemes, it takes a significant amount of time for the merchant to deliver the credit card receipts to the bank, and for the bank to settle the payments (this advantage is similar to electronic checks). Figure 7.2 overviews the parties involved in a secure electronic credit card payment scheme. There are five parties involved:

- A credit card holder;

- A merchant;

- A merchant's bank;

- A certificate management center (CMC);

- A credit card issuing bank.

The credit card holder uses his or her credit card to purchase goods or services from the merchant. The merchant, in turn, interacts with his or her bank, called the merchant's bank, the acquirer bank, or simply the acquirer. In an electronic credit card payment scheme, the acquirer typically refers to a financial institution that has an account with a merchant and processes credit card authorizations and corresponding payments. In this setting, a payment gateway is a device operated by the acquirer to handle merchant payment messages. A very important party for a secure electronic credit card payment system is the CMC that issues and revokes public key certificates to the parties involved. In addition, there are usually two networks involved in an electronic credit card payment scheme:

- A public network (typically the Internet);

- A private network owned and operated by the banking community (therefore referenced as the "Banknet" in Figure 7.2).

The basic assumption is that data transmissions across the Banknet are sufficiently secure (since the Banknet is a private network), whereas data transmissions across the the Internet are inherently insecure and must be cryptographically protected. Consequently, an electronic credit card payment protocol mainly focuses on the communications that takes place over the Internet and does not address communications that takes place over the Banknet.

In the recent past, several electronic credit card payment schemes have been designed, proposed, and implemented. We briefly overview the most important schemes next. Again, further information regarding the corresponding payment protocols and message formats can be obtained from Chapter 4 of [2].

7.4.1   CyberCash

As mentioned previously in this chapter, CyberCash was founded to provide software and service solutions for all types of financial transactions and payments over the Internet. We have already overviewed and briefly discussed CyberCash's CyberCoin and PayNow systems. In addition, CyberCash has also developed and deployed a credit card-based payment system for the Internet.[16] The resulting CyberCash card-based payment system uses special wallet software on the client side to enable customers to make secure purchases using major credit cards from CyberCash-affiliated merchants. The software runs alongside any Web browser and uses 56-bit DES and 768-bit RSA for protecting the credit card information stored on the customer's hard disk and during transmission in the CyberCash payment protocol. Since the cryptographic software is only used to protect the financial data, it has been approved for international export from the U.S. government. This allows CyberCash to deploy its system globally. In fact, the CyberCash system was originally launched in April 1995 and is in widespread use today. Many Internet service providers have adopted the CyberCash system to provide Internet payment solutions to their customers.

In the CyberCash credit card-based payment system, a CyberCash server acts as a gateway server that links the customer wallet and merchant software to the existing financial infrastructure. As such, the CyberCash server is connected to the Internet on one side and to many banks and bank transaction processors on the other side. Purchase messages containing a customer's credit card information

---

[16]http://www.cybercash.com/cybercash/services/credit.html

are forwarded through this gateway from a merchant at the time of purchase. The actual credit card purchase is authorized and captured in the banking network. The results of the transaction are forwarded back through the CyberCash server to the merchant. If the transaction was successful, the merchant can ship the goods to the customer. Consequently, CyberCash does not act as an acquirer, issuer, or bank, but rather provides the gateway as a means of securely passing messages between the Internet and the Banknet and vice versa. The CyberCash messages, in turn, are transport-independent so that they can be sent using HTTP, SMTP, or any other transport or application protocol. They are overviewed and fully discussed in Section 4.6 of [2].

7.4.2 iKP

The term iKP (where $i = 1, 2$, or 3) refers to a family of Internet keyed payments protocol (or i-key-protocol) developed at the IBM Research Division to securely transfer electronic payments over the Internet [16]. The protocols are based on public key cryptography and differ from each other based on the number of parties that possess a public key pair. More precisely, the value of i determines the number of parties that hold a public key pair and a corresponding public key certificate. So, 1KP is the simplest protocol where only the acquirer gateway possesses a public key. For 2KP, the acquirer gateway, as well as the merchant, possess a public key. Finally, the 3KP protocols require each of the three parties involved in a transaction (the customer, the merchant, and the acquirer gateway) to possess a public key. The 3KP has been the starting point for many electronic credit card payment protocols, including the ones that are addressed in the rest of this section. Refer to Section 4.7 of [2] to get a comprehensive overview about the 1KP, 2KP, and 3KP.

7.4.3   SEPP and STT

A consortium chaired by MasterCard embedded and expanded the 3KP into an application context with key management and a more concrete clearing process, which was specified by the name *secure electronic payment protocol* (SEPP). Apart from IBM and MasterCard, some other companies also participated in the SEPP development, including Netscape Communications, GTE, and CyberCash. The SEPP specification was launched in October 1995. SEPP is further addressed in Sections 4.8 of [2].

Soon after the publication of the SEPP specification, another consortium chaired by Visa International and Microsoft publicly announced a different credit card-based network payment protocol that was called *secure transaction technology* (STT). SEPP and STT were conceptually similar, but differed in detail.

7.4.4 SET

The simultaneous publication of the SEPP and STT specifications led to the unfortunate situation where the two major credit card companies were each backing an independent solution for credit card payments over the Internet. In January 1996, MasterCard and Visa International announced that they would come together with some new partners (including, for example, SAIC, Terisa, and VeriSign) to develop a unified system that would be called *secure electronic transaction* (SET). It soon became clear that SET would become the standard for electronic credit card-based payments over the Internet, and that browsers would eventually provide support for SET by either incorporating the protocol in the browser or by downloading it in the form of an ActiveX control, Java applet, or plug-in (refer to Chapter 9 for an overview of these technologies).

A preliminary version of the SET specification was published in February 1996, and a second version in June 1996. This version was then extensively used in field trials and had an enormous impact on the specification of SET version 1.0 that was released on May 31, 1997. The SET specification is publicly and freely available from many Internet sites, including, for example, `http://www.setco.org` which is the official Web site of the SET Secure Electronic Transaction LLC (commonly referred to as "SETCo"). SETCo was formed by Visa International and MasterCard in December 1997 to implement the SET 1.0 specification. Refer to Section 4.9 of [2] or [17,18] for a comprehensive overview and discussion of the SET specification.

In short, SET addresses the interactions between credit card holders, merchants, and acquirer banks (or acquirer gateways). Referring to the *i*KP terminology, the SET protocol refers to a 3KP, meaning that all parties possess a public key pair and a corresponding public key certificate. More precisely, most parties possess two public key pairs:

- A public key pair for key exchange;

- A public key pair for digital signatures.

The credit card holder and the merchant obtain their public key certificates when they register prior to doing any transaction. Consequently, the use of SET requires the existence of a fully operable X.509-based PKI, including such things as certificate revocation mechanisms as further addressed in Section 8.4 of this book.

It is commonly agreed that an electronic credit card payment protocol should provide the merchant only with the order information, such as the purchased items and their respective sale prices, and the acquirer only with the credit card information. In particular, the merchant should not require access to the customer's credit card information as long as the acquirer authorizes the payment. Similarly, there is no need for the acquirer to know the details of the purchased items, except in the case of some very expensive goods, such as luxury cars and houses. In such a case, the acquirer may want to make very sure that the customer is able to refund the payment. This separation of available information is achieved by a simple and effective cryptographic mechanism known as *dual signature*. In short, two parts of a message are dually signed by hashing them separately, concatenating the two hash values, hashing the result once more and digitally signing it. One recipient gets the plaintext of the first part of the message and the hash value of the second, and the other recipient gets the hash value of the first part of the message and the plaintext of the second part. In this way, each recipient can verify the authenticity and integrity of the complete message, but can only read the plaintext of the part of the message specifically intended for him or her. The other part remains as a hash value, which conceals its actual content.

Let's assume that a credit card holder has selected some items to purchase and wants to initiate a corresponding credit card payment to the merchant. Therefore, the credit card holder constructs two sets of information:

- The *order information* (OI);

- The *payment instructions* (PI).

In short, the OI includes some information that is related to the items purchased, such as the goods or services and their sale prices, whereas the PI includes some information that is related to the credit card payment, such as the credit card number and the expiration date of the credit card. Next, the credit card holder generates two random session keys K_1 and K_2. He or she digitally envelopes the OI with the first session key K_1 and the merchant's public key exchange key k_M (resulting in $\{OI\}K_1, \{K_1\}k_M$), and the PI with the second session key K_2 and the acquirer's public key exchange key k_A (resulting in $\{PI\}K_2, \{K_2\}k_A$). In addition, he or she computes $h(OI)$ and $h(PI)$, and uses a private signature key to generate a dual signature for the two hash values. Consequently, the credit card holder uses a private key k_C^{-1} to generate the dual signature $\{h(h(OI), h(PI))\}k_C^{-1}$. He or she sends the digitally enveloped OI and PI (namely $\{OI\}K_1, \{K_1\}k_M$ and $\{PI\}K_2, \{K_2\}k_A$), $h(OI)$ and $h(PI)$, as well as the dual signature to the merchant. The merchant, in turn, is able to decrypt the first digital envelope with the private key exchange key k_M^{-1} and retrieve the OI accordingly. He or she forwards $\{PI\}K_2, \{K_2\}k_A$ (the digitally enveloped PI), $h(OI)$, $h(PI)$, and the dual signature to the acquirer. The acquirer, in turn, is able to decrypt the other digital envelope with the private key exchange key k_A^{-1}, and retrieve the PI accordingly. He or she checks with the credit card issuer whether the payment is authorized. The corresponding communication may take place over the Banknet and doesn't need any further protection. In either case, the acquirer returns the issuer's decision about the payment authorization to the merchant, and the merchant informs the credit card holder whether he or she is going to accept the credit card payment.

Finally, we want to reemphasize that due to the use of dual signatures, a merchant does not learn the credit card information of his or her customers. For all practical purposes this is very important, since it relieves the customers from having to care about host and site security issues at the merchant's site. Note that a lot of credit card fraud is enabled by the fact that credit card information is being stored in many database systems without adequate security controls.

7.5 MICROPAYMENT SYSTEMS

An important factor in the evaluation of electronic payment systems is the cost of the overhead involved in collecting payments as compared to the actual amount of money being transferred. Apart from the overhead costs incurred in the extra transactions required to implement the payment protocol, there is also another set of costs that banks may charge for their services. These bank service or transaction fees may be charged when an account or credit card is accessed and may contribute a large component to the overall costs of a payment system.

Of the conventional payment instruments of cash, check, and credit card, the one most suited for low-value transactions is cash. Nevertheless, the use of cash is limited in that no transaction can involve less than the value of the smallest coin (e.g., one cent). There are many e-commerce applications where this limitation poses a serious problem. Examples include obtaining a quotation of the current price of a share on the stock market or making a single query in a database system. In conventional commerce, the solution to this problem has been to use a subscription mode of payment, where the customer pays in advance and can access the product or service for a fixed period of time. While this ensures that the provider is paid, it seals off what is in many cases a large customer base of people who may only wish to use a service occasionally. To make things worse, it also restricts the ability of people to simply try out a service.

Following this line of argument, it is clear that the subscription mode of payment does not adequately solve the problem, and that there is need for payment systems that efficiently transfer very small amounts of money, perhaps less than one cent, in a single transaction. These payment systems are collectively referred to as *micropayment systems*, and their design is still a research-grade problem. To achieve the required efficiency, micropayment systems must not involve computationally expensive cryptographic operations. The basic idea is to replace the use of public key cryptography with keyed one-way hash functions. The main advantage of this replacement is efficiency, whereas the main disadvantage is the inability to provide non-repudiation services. However, since micropayments typically do not exceed a few cents, the merchant may carry the risk that a customer later denies having committed to a payment.

In the following subsections, we overview and briefly describe some exemplary micropayment systems that have been proposed in the past. Again, refer to Chapter 7 of [2] for a more comprehensive treatment of these systems. Because micropayment systems have many applications in e-commerce (examples include such things as usage metering, usage-based charging, and discount coupons), it is very likely that more systems will be proposed by cryptographic researchers and e-commerce application developers in the future (recent examples include the Agora [19] and NetCents [20] micropayment protocols). In fact, many micropayment protocols can be implemented as an extension to HTTP and are particularly well suited for paying for Web content. As of this writing, no large-scale trials have been undertaken with any of the micropayment systems. So it is not clear what systems will eventually endure in the long term.

7.5.1   Millicent

Millicent is a micropayment system developed by a group of researchers at Digital Equipment Corporation (DEC) early in 1995 [21,22]. The basic idea of the Millicent system is to use a keyed one-way hash function to authenticate and verify digital coins. Note that the secret key that is used to key the one-way hash function must be known only to the issuer of the coins and the merchants who verify and eventually accept the coins. So if the coins are merchant-specific, the secret key that is used to verify the coins must be known only to the issuer of the coins and the merchant that actually accepts them. This allows a merchant to easily detect double spending (since every coin can be uniquely identified through a serial number). Also note that the use of a keyed one-way hash function is much more efficient than the use of digital signatures that are computationally more expensive, but also universally verifiable (assuming a corresponding PKI is put in place). The result of the Millicent design is a micropayment system in which a merchant can verify the authenticity of a digital coin without having to contact a TTP for every single transaction.

In their original design, the developers of the Millicent system have proposed the use of the MD5 one-way hash function that is keyed in secret suffix mode (meaning that the key is appended to the data of a digital coin before it is hashed with MD5). In Millicent terminology, the merchant-specific currency is called *Scrip*, and the parties that issue and actually sell scrip are called Millicent *brokers*. One of the core functions of a broker is to provide all the different merchant scrip needs of a customer in return for a single macropayment. The broker will have an agreement with each merchant whose scrip he or she sells. In principle, there are two ways a broker gets the merchant scrip that he or she sells:

- First, the broker may buy many pieces of scrip from the merchant. The scrip is stored and then sold piece by piece to different customers. In this case, the broker does not need the secret key that is used to mint and issue scrip.

- Second, the broker may be licensed to generate the scrip on behalf of the merchant. Obviously, this possibility is more efficient. In this case, however, the broker also needs the secret key that is used to mint and issue scrip.

The overall idea of the Millicent micropayment system is to have a customer buy merchant-specific scrip from a broker, and to have the customer use this scrip to buy some low-value information goods from that merchant. Repeated payments at a specific merchant are highly efficient with regard to network connections. In fact, if a customer already has valid scrip for that merchant, only a single network and no interaction with the broker is required. More specifically, the current implementation of the Millicent system provides support for three different possibilities to send scrip over a network:

- First, the customer may send the scrip unprotected across the network to the merchant;

- Second, the customer may send the scrip over an encrypted network connection to the merchant;

- Third, the customer may authenticate the scrip and send it across the network to the merchant. Again, keyed one-way hash functions are used for authentication.

In the second and third possibility, additional cryptographic keys are required. Refer to Section 7.1 of [2] to get a more comprehensive overview and description of the Millicent payment protocols, the message formats, and various extensions.

7.5.2   SubScrip

SubScrip is a very simple micropayment scheme that was developed at the University of Newcastle in Australia [23]. It is a prepaid system with no need for user identification. As such, it was originally designed for efficient pay-per-view payments on the Internet.

SubScrip uses techniques similar to the ones used in the Millicent micropayment system to achieve low transaction costs. As with Millicent, a SubScrip micropayment can be verified locally by a merchant without the need for any online clearance with a third party. Similarly, there is an initial overhead associated with making payments to a new merchant. Both micropayment schemes are optimal for repeated payments to the same merchant over a short period of time. However, unlike Millicent, the SubScrip micropayment scheme does not use a broker to mediate between customers and merchants. Instead, an existing macropayment system may take over this role.

More specifically, a customer chooses a macropayment system that a merchant accepts as a form of payment. The customer then makes a payment large enough to cover the macropayment transaction costs to the merchant. This payment will typically be of a few dollars and is used to set up a temporary account at the merchant. In order to make micropayment purchases against the temporary account, the customer needs some type of account identifier. Within the SubScrip scheme, this account identifier is encoded in a *SubScrip ticket* (in addition to the account identifier, the SubScrip ticket also includes a value field that holds the amount of money remaining in the account and and expiration date). The merchant maintains a database of valid SubScrip tickets and corresponding account identifiers.

To make a purchase, the customer sends a SubScrip ticket to the merchant. The merchant, in turn, verifies that the ticket is valid by checking the corresponding entry in his or her database. The micropayment amount is deducted from the account balance. A new random account identifier and a matching SubScrip ticket with the new balance is then generated for the account and returned to the customer along with the purchased information or service result. The customer stores the new SubScrip ticket for further purposes. A more detailed description of the SubScrip micropayment scheme can be found in Section 7.2 of [2].

7.5.3   PayWord

PayWord is a credit-based micropayment scheme that was jointly developed by Ronald L. Rivest and Adi Shamir [24]. The scheme uses chains of hash values — so-called *paywords* — to represent user credit. The paywords are merchant-specific and can be sent by the customer to the merchant as payment. They are backed by commitments that are digitally signed by the customer to honor payments for them. Furthermore, brokers mediate between customers and merchants and maintain accounts for both. They vouch for customers by issuing a PayWord certificate allowing that customer to generate paywords. They redeem spent payword chains from merchants, transferring the amount of money spent from the customer's account to the merchant's account. It is not necessary for both a customer and a merchant to have an account at the same broker.

More specifically, a PayWord certificate authorizes a customer to generate payword chains, and guarantees that a specific broker will actually redeem them. Customers obtain a PayWord certificate when they initially set up an account with a PayWord broker. Any electronic payment system (e.g., a credit card payment) can be used to actually feed the account. To limit fraud, PayWord certificates typically expire after a relatively short period of time, such as one month. A PayWord certificate includes identifiers for both the broker and the customer, the customer's delivery address (e.g., IP address, e-mail address, or physical mailing address), the customer's public key, the expiration date, and some additional information, such as user- or broker-specific details, as well as credit limits per merchant. The certificate is digitally signed with the broker's private key. So if a broker wanted to verify the authenticity of a PayWord certificate, he or she would have to securely obtain that broker's public key in some way. Furthermore, he or she would have to check whether the PayWord certificate was revoked by this broker in the meantime. Consequently, the deployment of the PayWord micropayment scheme requires existing and fully operational infrastructures for both public key and PayWord certificates.

We have already mentioned that a payword chain (chain of hash values) represents customer credit at a specific merchant. Each payword (hash value) in the chain has the same value, such as one cent. To generate a new payword chain, the customer first decides on the length n of the chain (a payword chain of length $n=10$ will be worth 10 cents if the payword value is one cent). The chain value should be greater than the amount one is likely to spend at the merchant site (unused paywords in a chain can be safely discarded). Next, the customer selects a random number W_n and computes n repeated one-way hash values of W_n. Assuming that h is the one-way hash function currently in use, the customer computes $h(W_n), h^2(W_n), \ldots, h^n(W_n)$ and the final payword chain will be $W = \{W_0 = h^n(W_n), W_1 = h^{n-1}(W_n), W_2 = h^{n-2}(W_n), \ldots, W_{n-1} = h(W_n), W_n\}$. Finally, the customer digitally signs a commitment to the payword chain W to authorize the merchant to redeem any paywords from the committed chains. It allows the merchant to be confident that he or she will be paid for the paywords accepted from the customer. The commitment is signed with the customer's private key. It includes the name of the merchant (remember that a payword chain is merchant-specific), the customer's PayWord certificate, the value W_0 (that represents the root of the payword chain), an expiration date for the commitment, and some additional information.

When a customer encounters a merchant from whom he or she wishes to purchase goods or services, he generates a new payword chain and commitment as discussed above. The commitment is then sent to the merchant to indicate the customer's intentions of spending paywords there. To make a one-cent payment (or whatever the denomination of the PayWord system is), the customer sends the first payword (W_1) to the merchant. The merchant, in turn, verifies the payword by hashing it, and verifying that the one-way hash value actually matches the root of the payword chain (W_0) found in the customer's commitment. This works because only the customer posseses the valid W_1 payword, and because it is computationally hard to generate a value that would hash to W_0 due to the nature of one-way hash function in use. Consequently, knowing W_0 does not allow anybody (an attacker or a cheating merchant) to generate valid paywords in the chain.

To make a further one-cent payment, the customer sends the second payword (W_2) to the merchant. The merchant, in turn, compares the value obtained by taking the one-way hash of W_2, namely $h(W_2)$, to the previously received payword W_1. If the payword W_2 is valid, then the values match. Payments of values greater than one cent can be made by sending paywords further down the chain, without having sent skipped-over paywords. For example, to make a five-cent payment after having spend W_2, the seventh payword, namely W_7, can be sent. Consequently, the actual payment message P consists of a payword W_i and its index i in the chain: $P = (W_i, i)$. This allows the merchant to know how many hashes should be performed. The customer's name (or another identifier) may also have to be included in the payment message P to allow the merchant to identify the customer, depending on implementation details. The merchant is responsible for recording the last valid payword in a chain accepted from a customer, and to keep corresponding state information accordingly.

Note that the broker does not need to be contacted during a payment, and that the paywords can be verified locally by the merchant. To receive payment a merchant redeems payword chains with the appropriate broker, perhaps at the end of each day (or during the night). For each chain, the merchant must send the signed customer commitment for that chain and the highest indexed payword spent to the broker. The broker, in turn, verifies the highest indexed payword spent, W_l, by performing l hashes on it. The value obtained must match W_0 in the customer's commitment if W_l is valid. If both the digital signature on the customer commitment and W_l are valid, the broker debits the spent amount of money from the customer's account and pays it to the merchant (e.g., by crediting the merchant's account).

The PayWord micropayment scheme is further addressed in Section 7.3 of [2]. Similar to other micropayment schemes, the PayWord scheme tries to minimize communication costs for a transaction. Unlike the Millicent system, a broker does not have to be contacted for a new payment, nor is there any need for scrip change or the returning of unused merchant-specific scrip to the broker. On the down side, however, the PayWord scheme also provides more opportunities for fraud than the Millicent system, especially if a customer's private key is compromised.

7.5.4 μ-iKP and MiniPay

The authors of the *i*KP suite of protocols have also developed a credit-based micropayment scheme that can be used in conjunction with *i*KP [16]. The resulting scheme is named μ-iKP and has been prototyped in a system called *MiniPay* [4].[17] Similar to PayWord, the μ-iKP scheme is based on the creation of a chain of hash values using a cryptographically strong one-way hash function. The hash values are called coupons (instead of paywords as in the case of the PayWord scheme). The resulting μ-iKP scheme and its protcols are further addressed in Section 7.4 of [2].

7.5.5 MicroMint

Similar to PayWord, *MicroMint* is a micropayment scheme that was jointly developed by Ronald L. Rivest and Adi Shamir [24]. Unlike PayWord, the MicroMint micropayment scheme is based on a unique form of identified (nonanonymous) offline electronic cash that does not make use of public key cryptography. Remember from our previous discussions that in most electronic cash systems, such as the ones described in Section 7.2, a digital coin is signed by the issuing bank to show that it is authentic. However, to sign and verify each coin in this way is too computationally expensive for a micropayment scheme. That's why most micropayment schemes use one-way hash functions instead of public key cryptography. For their MicroMint scheme, however, Rivest and Shamir have proposed another cryptographic construction to authenticate coins. The aim was to find a construction that makes it computationally difficult for anyone except the broker to mint valid coins, but to make it efficient for anybody to verify a coin.

---

[17]`http://www.ibm.net.il/ibm_il/int-lab/mpay`

In the MicroMint scheme, a coin is represented by a k-way hash function collision. Remember that a one-way hash function h maps a value x to another value $y = h(x)$ of a specified length. A (two-way) collision of h occurs when two different values for x (e.g., x_1 and x_2) map to the same value of y, meaning that $h(x_1) = h(x_2) = y$. More generally, a k-way hash function collision occurs when k different input values $x_1, x_2, \ldots, x_k$ map to the same value of y, meaning that $h(x_1) = h(x_2) = \ldots = h(x_k) = y$.

In the MicroMint scheme, k is set to 4, and a MicroMint coin is represented by a four-way hash function collision. Each coin is worth a certain amount of money (e.g., one cent), and a coin C consists of four input values x_1, x_2, x_3, and x_4 that collide to the same value y when the hash function is applied:

$$C = \{x_1, x_2, x_3, x_4\}$$

To mint a MicroMint coin involves finding multiple values of x that hash to the same value of y. The computational costs of finding such values depends on the bit length of both the values of x and the value of y. The computational costs of minting coins are further discussed in [24]. In short, it is computationally expensive to mint the first few coins, whereas it becomes progressively cheaper to mint more coins afterwards. Using special-purpose hardware, a broker may be able to compute a very large number of hash values in a relatively short period of time when minting coins.

In either case, the authenticity of a MicroMint coin C is verified by the following three steps:

1. Ensuring that each $x_i (i = 1, \ldots, 4)$ is different;

2. Performing the four hashes $h(x_1), h(x_2), h(x_3)$, and $h(x_4)$;

3. Verifying that all hash values map to the same y value.

Note, however, that this verification procedure only proves that a coin is authentic. It cannot be used to detect double spending. To do this, the broker must maintain a copy of each coin already spent to check against.

In the MicroMint micropayment scheme, digital coins are minted by a broker who sells them to customers. Similar to many other micropayment schemes, the broker maintains customer and merchant accounts that can be settled using macropayment systems. A customer can buy MicroMint coins from a broker and spend them at any merchant who accepts MicroMint coins. Since the MicroMint scheme is offline, the merchant does not contact a bank or broker for verification at the time of purchase. Instead, he or she collects all coins during a day and redeems them at the end of a day. Consequently, double spending is possible and a customer can spend coins at multiple merchants. However, because the MicroMint micropayment scheme is identified, a broker may record which coins are issued to a customer. Double-spending will be detected, after the fraud, at the end of the day when merchants redeem spent coins with a broker. Customers whose coins are repeatedly double spent will be blacklisted and excluded from the system. A more detailed description and discussion of the the MicroMint micropayment scheme and its extensions can also be found in Section 7.5 of [2].

Due to its offline operation and universal nature of its digital coins, the overall security provided by the MicroMint micropayment scheme is less than that of PayWord (the other micropayment scheme proposed by Rivest and Shamir). While some small-scale fraud is possible, large-scale fraud is designed to be computationally difficult (since it requires finding four-way hash function collisions). The major advantage of MicroMint is that it allows customers to make micropayments to many different merchants (whereas paywords are merchant-specific in the PayWord micropayment scheme).

7.6 CONCLUSIONS

In the recent past, the growing importance of electronic commerce (e-commerce) and corresponding applications has resulted in the introduction of a variety of different and partly incompatible electronic payment systems. In this chapter, we overviewed and briefly discussed the basic principles of some exemplary electronic cash systems, electronic checks, electronic credit card payments, and micropayment systems.

For business application developers, this variety implies the need to understand the details of different systems, to adapt the code of the application programs as soon as new electronic payment systems are introduced, and to provide a way of picking a suitable payment system for every transaction. More recently, a group of researchers headed by IBM has tried to unify the different payment mechanisms in a common framework with corresponding APIs [3]. This allows application programs to be developed independent of specific payment systems, with the additional benefit of providing a central point of control for payment information and policies. This work has been carried out as part of the Secure Electronic Marketplace for Europe (SEMPER) project aimed at building a secure electronic marketplace in Europe [25].

In spite of the many electronic payment systems that have been designed, developed, proposed, and partly implemented in the past, a certain degree of convergence will occur in the industry (where systems that address the same needs will compete and one will emerge as a victor). As with any payment system, a major factor in its success is consumer trust and acceptance. Any system backed by big-name banking organizations or indeed the banking industry as a whole will easily build this level of consumer trust and acceptance. It is possible and very likely that SET will emerge as a standard way of doing credit card payments over the Internet. With regard to the other categories of payment systems, such as electronic cash systems, electronic checks, and micropayment systems, it's more difficult to predict the future.

Similar to the various payment systems used in the Middle Ages, it is possible and very likely that we will use many electronic payment systems in the future (although it is hard to tell which ones). Consequently, there is need for a negotiation layer on top of the corresponding electronic payment systems. In December 1995, the World Wide Web Consortium (W3C) and the CommerceNet consortium jointly launched the *Joint Electronic Payment Initiative* (JEPI) to bring the key industry players together to ensure that multiple payment schemes, protocols, and transport mechanisms will work together and interoperate over the Internet. JEPI is intended to enable automated payment negotiation, where computers perform negotiations and users make final decisions [1]. More recently, JEPI has slowed down and a W3C Electronic Commerce Interest Group has been founded as a forum designed to allow its members to share information related to e-commerce.[18]

Last but not least, there are also some banking and other regulations pertaining to handling electronic payments. For example, who is authorized to issue electronic money? Can every bank issue its own currency and mint its own digital coins? If so, how is fraud prevented, and who's in charge of monitoring the banking operations to protect the customers? Note that conventional payment instruments have, in the past at least, been operated by banks who are subject to regulation by their national central bank. Typically, a bank must be licensed to operate, and in the course of obtaining this license will subject itself to scrutiny. As of this writing, it is not clear what regulations should be imposed on electronic payment systems, and how the above-mentioned concerns should be addressed. Several parties have become active in this field, including the Group of Ten (G-10) working party on electronic money. A corresponding report was published in 1997 [26].

REFERENCES

[1] R. Oppliger, *Internet and Intranet Security*, Artech House, Norwood, MA, 1998.

---
[18]http://www.w3.org/ECommerce/

[2] D. O'Mahony, M. Peirce, and H. Tewari, *Electronic Payment Systems*, Artech House, Norwood, MA, 1997.

[3] J.L. Abad Peiro, N. Asokan, M. Steiner, and M. Waidner, "Designing a Generic Payment Service," *IBM Systems Journal*, Vol. 37, No. 1, 1998, pp. 72 – 88.

[4] N. Asokan, P.A. Janson, M. Steiner, and M. Waidner, "The State of the Art in Electronic Payment Systems," *IEEE Computer*, Vol. 30, No. 9, September 1997, pp. 28 – 35.

[5] D. Chaum, "Blind Signatures for Untraceable Payments," *Proceedings of CRYPTO '82*, August 1982, pp. 199 – 203.

[6] D. Chaum, "Security Without Identification: Transaction Systems to Make Big Brother Obsolete," *Communications of the ACM*, Vol. 28, No. 10, October 1985, pp. 1030 – 1044.

[7] D. Chaum, "Achieving Electronic Privacy," *Scientific American*, August 1992, pp. 96 – 101.

[8] D. Chaum, A. Fiat, and M. Naor, "Untraceable Electronic Cash," *Proceedings of CRYPTO '88*, August 1988, pp. 319 – 327.

[9] D. Chaum, and T. Pedersen, "Wallet Databases With Observers," *Proceedings of CRYPTO '92*, August 1992, pp. 89 – 105.

[10] G. Medvinsky, and B.C. Neuman, "NetCash: A Design for Practical Electronic Currency on the Internet," *Proceedings of ACM Conference on Computer and Communications Security*, 1993.

[11] B. Cox, J.D. Tygar, and M. Sirbu, "NetBill Security and Transaction Protocol," *Proceedings of USENIX Workshop on Electronic Commerce*, July 1995.

[12] M. Sirbu, and J.D. Tygar, "NetBill: An Internet Commerce System Optimized for Network Delivered Services," *IEEE Personal Communications*, August 1995, pp. 6 – 11.

[13] R. Oppliger, *Authentication Systems for Secure Networks*, Artech House, Norwood, MA, 1996.

[14] B.C. Neuman, and G. Medvinsky, "Requirements for Network Payment: The NetCheque Perspective," *Proceedings of IEEE Compcon*, March 1995.

[15] B.C. Neuman, and G. Medvinsky, "Internet Payment Services," *Proceedings of MIT Workshop on Internet Economics*, March 1995, pp. 401 – 415.

[16] M. Bellare, J.A. Garay, R. Hauser, A. Herzberg, H. Krawczyk, M. Steiner, G. Tsudik, and M. Wiener, "iKP — A Family of Secure Electronic Payment Protocols," *Proceedings of USENIX Workshop on Electronic Commerce*, July 1995.

[17] L. Loeb, *Secure Electronic Transactions: Introduction and Technical Reference*, Artech House, Norwood, MA, 1998.

[18] M.S. Merkow, and J. Breithaupt, *Building SET Appliactions for Secure Transactions*, John Wiley & Sons, New York, NY, 1998.

[19] E. Gabber, and A. Silberschatz, "Agora: A Minimal Distributed Protocol for Electronic Commerce," *Proceedings of the 2nd USENIX Workshop on Electronic Commerce*, 1996.

[20] T. Poutanen, H. Hinton, and M. Stumm, "NetCents: A Lightweight Protocol for Secure Micropayments," *Proceedings of the 3rd USENIX Workshop on Electronic Commerce*, August 1998.

[21] M. Manasse, "The Millicent Protocols for Electronic Commerce," *Proceedings of the 1st USENIX Workshop on Electronic Commerce*, July 1995.

[22] S. Glassman, M. Manasse, M. Abadi, P. Gauthier, and P. Sobalvarro, "The Millicent Protocol for Inexpensive Electronic Commerce," *Proceedings of 4th International World Wide Web Conference*, December 1995, pp. 603 – 618.

[23] A. Furche, and G. Wrightson, "SubScrip — An Efficient Protocol for Pay-Per-View Payments on the Internet," *Proceedings of International Conference on Computer, Communications and Networks (ICCCN '96)*, October 1996, pp. 603 – 618.

[24] R.L. Rivest, and A. Shamir, "PayWord and MicroMint," *RSA Laboratories' CryptoBytes*, Vol. 2, No. 1, Spring 1996, pp. 7 – 11.

[25] M. Waidner, "Development of a Secure Electronic Marketplace for Europe," *Proceedings of 4th European Symposium on Research in Computer Security (ESORICS '96)*, 1996, pp. 98 – 106.

[26] Group of Ten, *Electronic Money: Consumer Protection, Law Enforcement, Supervisory and Cross Border Issues*, Report of the G-10 Working Party on Electronic Money, April 1997.

Chapter 8

Managing Certificates

In this chapter, we address the problem of how to manage certificates in a corporate environment. In particular, we introduce the topic in Section 8.1, elaborate on possibilities to establish a corporate PKI in Section 8.2, overview and briefly discuss the current offerings of two exemplary certification service providers in Section 8.3, address the problems related to certificate revocation and authorization in Sections 8.4 and 8.5, and draw some conclusions in Section 8.6. Note that this chapter requires a thorough understanding of public key cryptography and corresponding infrastructural requirements. We have introduced the fundamentals in Section 4.4 of this book. Further information can be found in [1,2].

8.1 INTRODUCTION

According to Webster's dictionary, the term "certificate" refers to a document stating the truth. In the digital world we live in today, the term "certificate" refers to "a collection of information to which a digital signature has been affixed by some authority who is recognized and trusted by some community of certificate users" [1]. According to this definition, there may exist various types of certificates that potentially serve many purposes.

Historically, the term "certificate" was first used by Loren M. Kohnfelder to refer to a digitally signed record holding a name and a public key [3]. In such a certificate, a public key is securely attributed to a principal, such as a person, a hardware device, or any other network entity. Consequently, the corresponding certificates are called *public key certificates*. In Section 4.4, we have introduced the notion of public key certificates. We have also argued that the use of public key cryptography requires the existence of a PKI, and that a PKI, in turn, consists of one or several CAs that issue and revoke public key certificates for users or other CAs.

In a more general sense, the term "certificate" refers to a digitally signed testimony to whom it may concern, stating some fact or granting some form of privilege. As we have seen, one possibility for a certificate is to bind a public key to a name. However, there are many other facts a certificate may state. For example, a certificate may also grant some general attributes to its owner. This is actually the aim of an *attribute certificate* (AC) as discussed later in this section. Similar to public key certificates, ACs bind characteristics of an entity, called attributes, to that particular entity by the signature of a TTP that is now called *attribute authority* (AA). Consequently, the major difference between a public key certificate and an attribute certificate is that the former includes a public key (the key that is certified), whereas the latter simply includes a more general form of attribute (the attribute that is certified).

Many standardization bodies have been working in the field of public key certificates and PKIs. First and foremost, the Telecommunication Standardization Sector of the International Telecommunication Union (ITU-T) has released and is periodically updating a corresponding recommendation that is commonly referred to as X.509 [4]. As mentioned in Section 4.4, the current release is X.509 version 3 (X.509v3). Meanwhile, the ITU-T recommendation X.509 has also been adopted by many other standardization bodies, including, for example, the International Organization for Standardization in ISO/IEC 9594-8. Since we have already overviewed and discussed the format of X.509v3 certificates in Section 4.4 (refer to Figure 4.4 and related explanations), we are not going to repeat it in this chapter.

More recently, the IETF has also recognized the importance of certificates, and has chartered two WGs to design and actually build a PKI for the Internet community:

- On the one hand, the IETF *Public Key Infrastructure X.509* (PKIX) WG has been tasked to design and build a PKI based on ITU-T X.509;

- On the other hand, the IETF *Simple Public Key Infrastructure* (SPKI) WG has been tasked to produce a certificate infrastructure and operating procedure to meet the needs of the Internet community for trust management in as easy, simple, and extensible a way as possible.

The reason that has motivated the IETF to task two WGs is that some participants of the IETF believed that the task of building an X.509-based PKI for the Internet community may be too big. Note that the IETF Privacy Enhanced Mail (PEM) WG failed to establish an X.509-based PKI for secure messaging a couple of years ago [5]. Nevertheless, it is only fair to mention that this failure was also due to product immaturity at this time, and that the situation has changed fundamentally in the meantime. As of this writing, there are several working systems in operation that effectively make use of X.509-based PKIs.

The solutions that have been and are being proposed by the two IETF WGs (the IETF PKIX WG and the IETF SPKI WG) are fundamentally different, and we are going to overview and briefly discuss the work that is being done in the two WGs next. Note, however, that from a practical point of view, the work that is being done in the IETF PKIX WG is much more important, and that the work that is being done in the IETF SPKI WG is primarily of theoretical interest (as such, it may become important for practical purposes only in the long term). If you are a network practitioner, you may skip the corresponding SPKI-related subsection 8.1.2 without losing context. In either case, you should read Section 8.1.3 that addresses attribute certificates.

8.1.1 IETF PKIX WG

As mentioned above, the IETF *Public Key Infrastructure X.509* (PKIX) WG has been tasked to design and build a PKI for the Internet community based on the ITU-T recommendation X.509.[1] As such, the IETF PKIX WG has come up with a family of RFC documents that address the management of ITU-T X.509v3 public key certificates and corresponding certificate revocation lists (CRLs).

The operational model of the IETF PKIX WG consists of subjects and end entities,[2] CAs, and RAs.[3] The functions which the RA may carry out will vary from

---

[1]http://www.ietf.org/html.charters/pkix-charter.html

[2]In the specifications of the IETF PKIX WG, the term "end entity" is used rather than the term "subject" to avoid confusion with the X.509v3 certificate field of the same name (again, refer to Section 4.4 and Figure 4.4 for a description of the X.509v3 certificate format).

[3]Other terms are used elsewhere for the functionality of an RA. For example, the term local registration agent (LRA) is used in ANSI X9 standards, local registration authority (also acronymed as LRA) is used in [1], organizational registration agent (ORA) is used in certain U.S. government

case to case but may include personal authentication, token distribution, certificate revocation reporting, name assignment, key generation, and key archival. In any PKI architecture, RAs are optional components that are transparent to the end entities (when they are not present, the CA is assumed to be able to carry out the RAs' functions so that the PKI management protocols are the same from the end entities' point of view). Finally, the certificates generated by the CAs are made publicly available in certificate repositories (e.g., network services that are available online).

According to this operational model, the family of RFC documents produced by the IETF PKIX WG can be summarized as follows (note that some RFCs are submitted for the Internet standards track, whereas other RFC documents are just for informational purposes):

- Standards track RFC 2459 [6] profiles the format and semantics of X.509v3 certificates and X.509v2 CRLs for use on the Internet. As such, it describes in detail the X.509v3 certificate format and its standard and Internet-specific extension fields, as well as the X.509v2 CRL format and a required extension set. Finally, the RFC also describes an algorithm for X.509 certificate path validation and provides ASN.1 specifications for all data structures that are used in the profiles.

- Standards track RFC 2510 [7] describes the various certificate management protocols that are supposed to be used in an X.509-based PKI for the Internet.

- More specifically, standards track RFC 2511 [8] specifies the syntax and semantics of the Internet X.509 certificate request message format (CRMF) that is used to convey a request for a certificate to a CA (possibly via an RA) for the purpose of X.509 certificate production. The request typically includes a public key and some related registration information.

- Informational RFC 2527 [9] presents a framework to assist the writers of certificate policies and certificate practice statements (CPS) for CAs and PKIs. More specifically, the framework provides a comprehensive list of topics that potentially need to be covered in a certificate policy definition or CPS. Note that the framework needs to be customized in a particular operational environment.

- Informational RFC 2528 [10] profiles the format and semantics of the field in X.509v3 certificates containing cryptographic keys for the KEA.[4]

---

specifications, and registration agent (RA) has also been used elsewhere.

[4]The KEA is a key exchange algorithm that was originally proposed by NIST for use

- Standards track RFC 2559 [11] addresses requirements to provide access to certificate repositories for the purpose of retrieving PKI information and managing that information. The mechanism is based on the lightweight directory access protocol (LDAP) as specified in RFC 1777 [12], defining a profile of LDAP for use within the X.509-based PKI for the Internet. In addition, RFC 2587 [13] defines a minimal schema to support PKIX in an LDAPv2 environment, as defined in RFC 2559.

- Standards track RFC 2585 [14] specifies the conventions for using FTP and HTTP to obtain certificates and CRLs from certificate repositories.

- Finally, standards track RFC 2560 [15] specifies a protocol useful in determining the current status of a digital certificate.

In summary, the above-summarized family of RFC documents specifies an X.509-based PKI for the Internet. This evolving PKI is sometimes also referred to as *Internet X.509 public key infrastructure* (IPKI). The number of RFC documents that specify various aspects of the IPKI will certainly grow in the future, since a lot of work is being done to further refine the IPKI and its operational protocols and procedures. In fact, the number of RFC documents specifying the IPKI will certainly have increased by the time you read this book (e.g., for the provision of certificate validation and timestamping services). Refer to the IETF PKIX WG homepage that is indicated in footnote 1 to get a comprehensive overview about the RFC and Internet Draft documents currently available. The current trend in industry is to make commercial PKI products "PKIX compliant," and this trend is most likely to continue.

8.1.2   IETF SPKI WG

As mentioned above, the IETF *Simple Public Key Infrastructure* (SPKI) WG has been tasked to produce a certificate infrastructure and operating procedure to meet the needs of the Internet community for trust management in as easy, simple, and extensible a way as possible.[5] As such, the SPKI WG has first established a list of things one might want to do with certificates and summarized that list in a

---

together with the Skipjack encryption algorithm in Clipper and Fortezza chips. Refer to http://csrc.nist.gov/encryption/skipjack-kea.htm for a specification of the Skipjack and KEA algorithms.

[5]http://www.ietf.org/html.charters/spki-charter.html

corresponding Internet Draft.[6] According to these requirements and the experiences made in the IETF PEM WG, the participants of the IETF SPKI WG realized that any X.509-based PKI has to deal with two fundamental problems:

- First, the recommendations of the ITU-T X.500 series (including X.509) are based on a global name space.[7] Consequently, the names of the entities are intended to have a mapping to globally unique names. For example, it is generally possible to refer to an X.500 entity with its globally unique distinguished name (DN). Similarly, my PGP name is `Rolf Oppliger <rolf.oppliger@bfi.admin.ch>`. It is a string in the global name space of PGP (the set of all PGP keys). Unfortunately, the assumption that names are valid identifiers remains true in much of daily life, but is not necessarily true on a global scale [16]. In fact, practical experience has shown that the assumption of a global name space is seldom realistic,[8] and that the original X.500 plan is unlikely ever to come to fruition. Certain collections of directory entries, such as employee or customer lists, are considered valuable or even confidential by those owning the lists and are therefore not likely to be published in the form of X.500 directory subtrees. Consequently, globally unique names may be inappropriate for the global Internet (they may even be politically undesirable). Nevertheless, we use names all the time, but the names we use are local ones. These are the names we write in personal address books or use as nicknames in e-mail user agents. Local names do not need to be globally unique. Rather, they need to be unique only for the principal that maintains the local name space.

- Secondly, a globally unique distinguished name (DN) is supposed to uniquely define an X.500 entity, and a corresponding X.509-based certificate is supposed to bind this name to a public key. Consequently, an X.509-based public key certificate doesn't (or, at least, it didn't initially) say anything about the authorizations of that particular keyholder. Again, practical experience has shown that a PKI should not only be used for authentication, but also for authorization [17]. A PKI that enables applications to decide who signed a request isn't immediately useful on its own. Rather, one needs an infrastructure that also allows the verifier of a digital signature to decide whether the signer has the authority to do what he or she wants to do.

---

[6]`draft-ietf-spki-cert-req-*.txt`

[7]In short, a global name space refers to a set of names that is known worldwide.

[8]The only exception is the domain name system (DNS), which is a global name space that works. In fact, without an operational DNS, the Internet would probably crumble.

In spite of the fact that both problems can be addressed (and solved) in the latest versions of X.509, the resulting technologies become very complex. For example, X.509v3 permits general extension fields, and these extension fields can be used to carry authorization information. Another possibility to address the authorization problem is to use attribute certificates as discussed in the following subsection. Note, however, that attribute certificates are much more immature than public key certificates. In fact, the use of attribute certificates is a currently active area of research.

In an attempt to address the two problems mentioned above — the global name space problem and the authorization problem — Ronald L. Rivest and Butler Lampson developed and proposed a *simple distributed security infrastructure* (SDSI) [18]. Instead of X.509v3 certificates, the SDSI uses S-expressions as the standard format for certificates. In short, an S-expression is recursively defined as being either an octet-string (a finite sequence of 8-bit octets), or a finite list of simpler S-expressions [19].[9]

Contrary to the philosophy of X.500 and X.509, an SDSI principal refers to its public key[10] (and not to a string that may be associated with the principal that holds the corresponding private key), and the main feature of the SDSI is its extensive use of local name spaces. In short, a local name space is defined relative to a particular key, which can later be dereferenced to a key or another SDSI name. A SDSI name, in turn, is a sequence of arbitrary length consisting of a public key followed by zero or more identifiers. An example of a SDSI name is (K_{Rolf} Isabelle Sister). It begins with the key K_{Rolf} that refers to my public key. The identifier Isabelle following the principal K_{Rolf} is understood to be equivalent to another SDSI name ($K_{Isabelle}$) in the name space of K_{Rolf}. Subsequently, the identifier Sister is defined in the name space defined by the key that is bound to Isabelle. In this example, Sister can be dereferenced to Caroline who's actually my sister-in-law (or the sister of my wife Isabelle, respectively). Obviously, this scheme can be generalized and SDSI's local name spaces can be linked to form arbitrary chains [20]. Further information about the SDSI versions 1.0 and 2.0 can be found on the Web by following the URL http://theory.lcs.mit.edu/~cis/sdsi.html. Also, there are several implementations of SDSI [21,22], as well as an efficient certificate discovery algorithm using SDSI 2.0 certificates [23].

---

[9]People familiar with the LISP programming language will have no problem and even feel comfortable with S-expressions used in SDSI.

[10]If there exists a collision-resistant one-way hash function, then a hash value of the public key may also serve as a globally unique identifier for the keyholder. The advantage is that the one-way hash value is probably shorter than the public key.

The participants of the IETF SPKI WG soon realized that SDSI met their requirements and merged the two approaches into a collaborative effort. As such, the IETF SPKI WG has done some work and come up with a number of Internet Drafts:

- An Internet Draft that specifies the SPKI certificate theory;[11]

- An Internet Draft that specifies the structure of a SPKI certificate;[12]

- An Internet Draft that gives some examples.[13]

These Internet Drafts are certainly going to be published as informational RFC documents later on. Due to its immaturity, we are not going to further address the SDSI/SPKI effort in this book. Note, however, that it is important to stay tuned for future results of the IETF SPKI WG (since they may change the way we think about certificates and PKIs in the long term).

8.1.3   Attribute Certificates

As mentioned previously in this section, an X.509v3 public key certificate can also convey authorization information about its owner. This information can be encoded in one of the X.509v3 standard or extension fields. Note, however, that there are at least two reasons why caution should be taken in using X.509v3 public key certificates for conveying authorization information [1]:

- First, the authority that is most appropriate for verifying the identity of a person associated with a public key may not be appropriate for certifying the corresponding authorization information. For example, in a company the corporate security or human resources departments may be the appropriate authorities for verifying the identities of persons holding public keys, whereas the corporate finance office may be the appropriate authority for certifying permissions to sign on behalf of the company.

- Second, the dynamics of the two types of certificates may be different. For example, the persons authorized to perform a particular function in a company may vary monthly, weekly, or even daily. Contrary to that, public key certificates are

---

[11]draft-ietf-spki-cert-theory-*.txt

[12]draft-ietf-spki-cert-structure-*.txt

[13]draft-ietf-spki-cert-examples-*.txt

typically designed to be valid for a much longer period of time (e.g., one or two years). If it becomes necessary to revoke and reissue public key certificates frequently because of changing authorizations (that are encoded into the public key certificates), this may have a severe impact on the performance characteristics of the resulting certificate management system.

Recognizing that public key certificates are not always the best vehicle to carry authorization information, the U.S. American National Standards Institute (ANSI) X9 committee developed an alternative approach known as *attribute certificates* (ACs). Meanwhile, this approach has also been incorporated into both the ANSI X9.57 standard and the X.509-related standards and recommendations of both ITU-T and ISO/IEC. More recently, the IETF TLS WG has also started to work on AC-based authorization as a possible extension to the TLS protocol.[14]

In essence, an attribute certificate binds one or more pieces of additional information to the certificate owner (as specified in the subject field).[15] As such, the attribute certificate may contain group membership, role, clearance, or any other form of authorization or access control-related information associated with its owner. In conjunction with authentication services, attribute certificates may provide the means to securely transport authorization information to the application programs. Consequently, attribute certificates are particularly well suited to control access to system resources, and to implement role-based authorization and access controls accordingly [24]. Note that attribute certificates are conceptually similar to *privilege attribute certificates* (PACs) as used in the European SESAME project and adapted in the Open Group's DCE [25] and Microsoft's Windows 2000 operating system.[16]

Anyone can define and register attribute types and use them in attribute certificates. The certificate is digitally signed and issued by an AA. AAs, in turn, are assumed to be certified by CAs, so that a single point of trust — namely a trusted public key of a root CA — can be used to validate the certificates of AAs, other CAs, and end users. Apart from differences in content, an attribute certificate is managed the same way as a public key certificate. For example, if an organization already runs a directory service to distribute public key certificates and CRLs, this

---

[14] As discussed in Chapter 6, the TLS protocol is a slightly enhanced version of Netscape's SSL protocol. As of this writing, there are two Internet Drafts that address AC-based authorization for SSL and TLS: `draft-ietf-tls-attr-cert-*.txt` and `draft-ietf-tls-ac509prof-*.txt`.

[15] Again, the major difference between a public key certificate and an attribute certificate is that the former includes a public key (the key that is certified), whereas the latter simply includes an attribute (that is certified).

[16] Unfortunately, SESAME, DCE, and Windows 2000 use incompatible formats for PACs.

service can also be used to distribute attribute certificates. Note that — similar to public key certificates — attribute certificates can be used in either the "push" or "pull" model:

- In the "push" model, the attribute certificates are pushed from the client to the server;

- In the "pull" model, the attribute certificates are pulled by the server from an online network service (either the attribute certificate issuer or a directory service that is fed by the attribute certificate issuer).

An attribute certificate infrastructure should support both models, since some applications work best when a client pushes the attribute certificate to the server, whereas for other applications it is more convenient for the client simply to authenticate to the server and for the server to request the client's attribute certificate from a corresponding network service or attribute certificate repository. Note that this is somehow contradictory to Proposition 2 of [26], where it is claimed that "the signer can (and should) supply all evidence the acceptor needs, including recency information." While this proposition holds in most situations, there are also some situations that require a server to handle specific tasks on the client's behalf (e.g., thin clients or, more generally, devices with small computing power).

According to the specifications of the ANSI X9 committee, an attribute certificate may consist of the following fields [1]:

- *Version:* This field indicates the version of the attribute certificate format in use (currently version 1).

- *Subject:* This field identifies the principal with which the attributes are being associated. Identification can be either by name or by reference to an X.509 public key certificate.[17]

- *Issuer:* This field identifies the AA that issued the attribute certificate.

- *Signature:* This field indicates the digital signature algorithm used to sign the attribute certificate.

- *Serial Number:* This field contains a unique serial number for the attribute certificate. The number is assigned by the issuing AA and used in a CRL to identify the attribute certificate.

---

[17]Such a reference comprises a combination of an X.509 issuer name and a corresponding certificate serial number.

- *Validity:* This field may contain a set of possibly overlapping time periods during which the attribute certificate is assumed to be valid.

- *Attributes:* This field contains information concerning the owner of the attribute certificate (the owner is the principal that is referred to in the subject field). The information may be supplied by the subject, the AA, or a third party, depending on the particular attribute type in use.

- *Issuer Unique Identifier:* This field contains an optional bit string used to make the issuing AA name unambiguous in the case that the same name was reassigned to different principals through time.

- *Extensions:* This field allows for the addition of new fields to the attribute certificate. It basically works the same way as the extensions field of an X.509 public key certificate.

Note that attribute certificates constitute a general-purpose mechanism that potentially has many uses, and that distribution of authorization information is just one use. Also note that the above-mentioned format for an attribute certificate is just one proposal (the one from the ANSI X9 committee), and that other competing formats have been and will probably continue to be proposed and submitted for standardization. For example, we have already said that the IETF TLS WG is looking into possibilities to use AC-based authorization for TLS. Unfortunately, the format currently suggested in the corresponding Internet Drafts differs from the one mentioned above.

In summary, attribute certificates represent an important technology for authorization in e-commerce applications [24]. Unfortunately, the technology is still immature and there are many open issues related to its use and wide deployment. For example, attribute certificates and AC services must be standardized in one way or another. At the time of this writing, this is not yet the case (there are standards that address the format of attribute certificates, but these standards are neither commonly agreed nor widely deployed). To make things worse, some vendors use attribute certificates with proprietary formats. Also, the use of attribute certificates must be supported in custom client (and server) software. In particular, a client must be able to send appropriate attribute certificates together with public key certificates. Eventually, the TLS protocol specification must be adapted to make use of ACs. This work is currently under way. Finally, there are also some legal challenges to be addressed. For example, it is not immediately clear at the moment what (national or international) bodies are to certify the AAs of the organizations that want to make use of ACs. Unless all of these issues are resolved, it is assumed that ad-hoc solutions will be used to address the authorization problem for Internet-based e-commerce applications.

8.2   ESTABLISHING A PUBLIC KEY INFRASTRUCTURE

As of this writing, many companies and organizations face the problem of how to get the X.509v3 certificates they need for emerging technologies, such as SSL and TLS or S/MIME (refer to Chapters 5 and 6 if these acronyms do not mean anything to you). In general, there are two possibilities:

- The companies and organizations can either establish a PKI of their own;

- Or, they can outsource certification services and buy corresponding X.509v3 certificates from one (or several) commercial certification service provider(s).

The first possibility is addressed in this section, whereas the second possibility is addressed in the following section.

If a company or organization wants to establish a PKI of its own, it can either buy a commercial PKI solution or develop a solution of its own:

- In the first case, there are many commercial PKI solutions available on the marketplace. Examples include Entrust/PKI[18] from Entrust Technologies, UniCERT[19] from Baltimore, Notary[20] from Entegrity Solutions, Xcert Sentry[21] from Xcert International, and Blueprint[22] from PC Security. Refer to the trade press to get a more comprehensive and up-to-date overview about currently available PKI solutions and corresponding products.

- In the second case, there is public domain software available that is used to develop a PKI solution that meets the requirements of a specific company or organization. The most important example is the SSLeay software package[23] that also incorporates some certificate management functions.

---

[18]http://www.entrust.com/products/pki.htm
[19]http://www.baltimore.com/products/unicert/
[20]http://www.entegrity.com/Products/notary.htm
[21]http://www.xcert.com
[22]http://www.pcsl.com/bprint.htm
[23]Refer to Chapter 6 for an overview about the SSLeay software package.

If a company or organization wants to build and establish a PKI of its own, it can follow either a centralized or a decentralized approach. Following a centralized approach means to establish one (or several) CA(s) that is (are) to receive certificate requests, authenticate the corresponding users, and finally issue, distribute, and possibly revoke public key certificates. It is obvious that the CA(s) will very likely become the bottleneck(s). This is mainly due to the fact that the task of authenticating users can't be automated beyond a certain degree.

As a viable alternative to a centralized approach, the use of a single CA plus several RAs is a decentralized approach. In the remaining part of this section, we overview and briefly discuss an architecture for a corresponding *distributed certificate management system* (DCMS) [27]. In addition to following a decentralized approach, the DCMS architecture was also designed to support the notion of group-based access controls. In fact, the aims of the DCMS architecture are twofold:

- On the one hand, the DCMS is to provide a high degree of delegation and decentralization with regard to providing certification services in a corporate environment (the underlying assumption is that delegated and decentralized certification services can be provided more effectively and efficiently than its centralized counterparts, and that they are also less subject to overheated political discussions about who provides the CA services);

- On the other hand, the DCMS is to support the notion of group memberships and to provide support for group-based access controls accordingly (this aim is similar to the use of attribute certificates, as discussed earlier in this chapter).

In addition to these two aims, the DCMS architecture was also designed to minimize the need for special hardware and software. In the optimal case, the user interface for the DCMS is a normal browser that also supports SSL/TLS, such as Netscape Navigator or Microsoft Internet Explorer.

In essence, the DCMS architecture consists of three main components:

- A DCMS core;

- One or several decentralized DCMS frontends;

- A DCMS database that is maintained by the DCMS core. Data that is collected by the DCMS frontends are periodically uploaded to the DCMS core, processed by the core, and redistributed to the frontends accordingly.

The DCMS core is the component that represents the CA. As such, it holds the private key that is used to digitally sign and issue public key certificates. The DCMS core is assumed to run in a physically secure environment and operated offline by DCMS administrators with corresponding privileges. The DCMS core is connected online only to communicate with the DCMS frontends for a relatively short period of time (e.g., a few times per day).

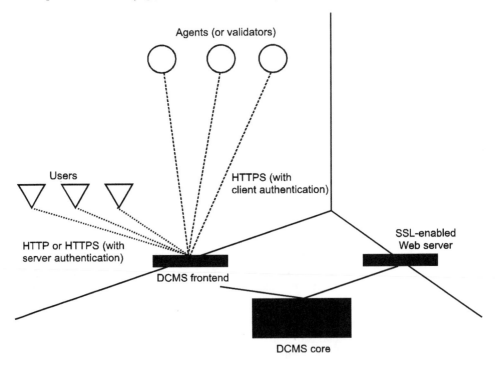

Figure 8.1   The DCMS architecture and a possible deployment.

Contrary to the DCMS core, the DCMS frontends are provided by Web servers that are operated by corresponding system administrators. In fact, DCMS frontends can either run as normal Web servers or SSL/TLS-enabled server-only authenticated Web servers (which is notably the preferred configuration). The same DCMS frontend can even run on a fully operable SSL/TLS-enabled Web server (including client authentication), which then allows certain users, called DCMS agents or validators, to perform specific tasks within the DCMS database. In short, a DCMS agent is a user who has been granted special privileges with regard to the verification of user identities or the confirmation of their appropriate group memberships.

It is up to the DCMS administrators to nominate users as DCMS agents. These agents are equipped with public key certificates that allow them to strongly authenticate themselves to a DCMS frontend (that supports client authentication). Consequently, any communications between a DCMS agent and the frontend are secured through the use of SSL/TLS. Similarly, communications between the DCMS core and the frontends must be secured either by physical means or by using cryptographic security protocols, such as the ones described in Chapters 5 and 6 of this book. Note that the DCMS topology is a star, simplifying the task of key management (for the cryptographically secured communication between the DCMS core and its frontends) and database synchronization considerably. Figure 8.1 illustrates the DCMS architecture and a possible deployment with one DCMS core and SSL-enabled Web servers that actually represent the DCMS frontends.

As mentioned above, the DCMS supports group-based access controls, and as such it is centered around the notion of a "group." In essence, a certificate may be granted group membership, in which case the certificate owner obtains the privileges related to this group. In general, there are several possibilities to link a certificate to one (or more) group(s). One possibility is to encode group membership information into the certificate that is issued by the certification system. The problem with this approach is that group membership may change frequently, and that the corresponding certificates must be frequently reissued. In this situation, one can argue that group membership information is better stored and maintained within a database system. In fact, the DCMS architecture follows this line of argument. It uses a database system to store and maintain certificates as well as to link them to specific groups. This has the advantage of having public key certificates in a relatively constant and permanent form, whereas all transient group membership information is stored and dynamically maintained in the database system (notably the DCMS database). Access to the database is protected through the use of strong authentication and encryption technologies (using SSL/TLS). The list of available groups is determined by the DCMS administrators and can be changed at will.

The DCMS architecture as described so far has been prototyped by the IT Security Group of the Swiss Federal Office of Information Technology and Systems (BFI), using Perl 5.0 and the database module Sprite. The resulting implementation is called PECAN, an acronym derived from PErl Certification Authority Network. A PECAN frontend is accessible from the Internet by following the URL https://ca.admin.ch.

8.3   CERTIFICATION SERVICE PROVIDERS

In this section, we elaborate on the possibility to outsource certification services and buy corresponding X.509v3 certificates from one (or several) certification service provider(s). As two exemplary certification service providers, we focus on VeriSign, Inc. located in the United States and Swisskey Ltd. located in Switzerland. Note, however, that there are many other companies (in addition to VeriSign and Swisskey) that offer comparable certification services to the general public. You can look at your browser software and the root CA certificates that come preconfigured with it to verify this statement (you can also refer to Figure 6.4). In fact, the number of commercial certification service providers is expected to increase in the future (as public key cryptography is being deployed in e-commerce applications).

8.3.1   VeriSign

Historically, the first commercial certification service provider was VeriSign, Inc.[24] As we already mentioned in Chapter 6, VeriSign was founded by RSA Data Security, Inc. in 1995, when the first version of Netscape Navigator with SSL support appeared on the marketplace.

As of this writing, VeriSign is offering individual digital certificates and server digital certificates, as well as code signing certificates to the general public:

- *Individual digital certificates* (digital IDs) are primarily intended for Web users. A class 1 certificate is tied to a unique e-mail address and is suitable for securing correspondence to that address, whereas a class 2 certificate is tied to an actual name and personal identity. A class 1 certificate is priced at $ 9.95 (U.S. dollars) per year, whereas a class 2 certificate is intended to be priced at $ 19.95 (U.S. dollars) per year.

- *Server digital certificates* (server IDs) are primarily intended for Web servers. There are several categories of server digital certificates, ranging from $ 349.00 to $ 1295.00 (U.S. dollars). Refer to URL http://www.verisign.com/server/ for a comprehensive overview about the various classes of server IDs available from VeriSign.

- Finally, *code signing certificates* are available for individual (class 2 digital IDs) and commercial software publishers (class 3 digital IDs). Individual software publisher digital IDs are currently available only in the United States and are priced

---

[24]http://www.verisign.com

at \$ 20.00 (U.S. dollars) per year, whereas commercial software publisher digital IDs are globally available and priced at \$ 400.00 (U.S. dollars) per year. Code signing certificates are available for Microsoft Authenticode, Netscape Object Signing, and Marimba Castanet.[25]

More recently, VeriSign has also started to offer certification services that are conceptually similar to the ones provided by an implementation of the DCMS architecture. The corresponding service is named VeriSign OnSite[26] [2].

8.3.2 Swisskey

Swisskey Ltd.[27] was established in the spring of 1998 as a joint-venture between Swisscom, Telekurs Holding, and DigiSigna.[28] Since October 1998, Swisskey has been selling digital certificates to the general public.

Similar to VeriSign, Swisskey is offering certificates for personal (currently priced at 35.00 Swiss francs per year), corporate (currently priced at 150.00 Swiss francs per year), and server IDs (currently priced at 650.00 Swiss francs per year). In addition, Swisskey is also offering customer branded CA services. With these services, customers can make use of Swisskey's infrastructure to issue certificates according to their own CPSs. Consequently, certificates issued by a customer branded CA are digitally signed with a private key that actually belongs to the customer.

Unlike VeriSign and other commercial certification service providers that operate on a global scale, Swisskey requires its customers to appear at a physical RA for proper authentication (using some legitimate passport or identification card). Currently, there are a number of chambers of commerce that act as RAs for Swisskey. For the future, it is intended to establish a mesh of geographically distributed RAs. Possible candidate RAs are bank offices as well as the branches of the Post (the now private postal delivery service in Switzerland).

Note that this is usually the place where several books on applied cryptography and public key certificates fill many pages with screenshots that illustrate the graphical user interfaces (GUIs) of the certification service providers, such as VeriSign or

---

[25] In short, Marimba's Castanet is a set of technologies which distributes and maintains applications and services within a corporate intranet or across the Internet. It ensures that subscribers always and automatically have the most up-to-date tools and information available at their desktops.

[26] http://www.verisign.com/onsite/

[27] http://www.swisskey.ch

[28] DigiSigna is an association of the chambers of commerce throughout Switzerland and Lichtenstein.

Swisskey. There are at least two reasons why we don't want to follow this tradition in this book:

- First, the educational value of these screenshots is considerably low;

- Second, the GUIs of the certification service providers tend to change very rapidly (and they would certainly look different by the time you read this book).

Furthermore, the GUIs of the certification service providers are generally intuitive enough to be followed without further information. Just follow the instructions that are summarized on the homepages of the corresponding certification service providers.

8.4   CERTIFICATE REVOCATION

The term *certificate revocation* refers to the process of publicly announcing that a certificate[29] has been revoked and should no longer be used. In practice, there may be several reasons that require certificate revocation. For example, a user's or a CA's private key may be compromised, or a user may no longer be registered and certified by a particular CA.

In general, the certification and revocation of (public key) certificates involves three parties:

- The certificate-issuing authority (namely the CA);

- The certificate repository, such as a networked directory service (that may even be replicated several times);

- The users of the CA and the certificate repository.

In this setting, the CA does not necessarily provide online certificate status information to the users. Instead, it may operate offline and update the certificate repository only on a periodic basis. The certificate repository, in turn, operates online and is permanently available and accessible to the users. In general, it must be assumed that the CA is trusted, whereas the certificate repository and the users

---

[29]In this section, we assume that attribute certificates expire relatively quickly, and that there is no need to revoke attribute certificates accordingly. So when we talk about certificate revocation, we actually refer to the revocation of public key certificates. If attribute certificates had a long lifetime, essentially the same revocation mechanisms could also be used to revoke them.

may not be. A user who contacts the directory doesn't only want to retrieve a certificate, but may also want to get some kind of proof of validity for the certificate at this particular point in time.

From a theoretical point of view, certificate revocation refers to a challenging problem, and there are several approaches to address it:

- The first approach is to make certificates automatically time out after a certain amount of time and to require periodic renewals of certificates;

- The second approach is to list all nonrevoked certificates in an online directory service, and to accept only certificates that are found there;

- The third approach is to have CAs periodically issue CRLs that itemize the certificates that have been revoked and should no longer be used;

- Finally, the fourth approach is to provide an online certificate status checking mechanism that informs users whether a specific certificate is still valid or has been revoked.

Note that the approaches are not mutually exclusive, but can be combined to come up with more efficient or more effective certificate revocation schemes. Also note that all approaches have advantages and disadvantages. For example, the first approach has the advantage of not requiring explicit certificate revocation (since the certificates time out after a certain amount of time). The disadvantages of this approach are due to the fact that time-outs only provide a slow revocation mechanism, and that it depends on servers having accurate clocks. Someone who can trick a server into turning back its local clock can still use expired certificates (the security of the certificate revocation mechanism thus depends on the security of the timing service). Similarly, the second approach has the advantage that it is almost immediate, whereas the disadvantages are that the availability of authentication is only as good as the availability of the directory service, and that the security of the certificate revocation mechanism as a whole is only as good as the security of the directory service. Furthermore, users tend to cache certificates they have retrieved from the directory service for performance reasons, and the use of such a cache actually defeats the original purpose of the directory service (to provide timely status information).

For all practical purposes, the third and fourth approaches are the ones that are being followed and most widely deployed. For example, the ITU-T recommendation

X.509 follows the third approach,[30] and recommends that each CA periodically issues a CRL that itemizes all certificates that have been revoked and should no longer be used. A user receiving a certificate would first check in the appropriate CRL whether the certificate has been revoked. In addition to the use of CRLs as proposed in the ITU-T recommendation X.509, the IETF PKIX WG is specifying and standardizing an online certificate status protocol (OCSP). CRLs and the use of OCSP are further addressed in the remaining part of this section. Afterward, we elaborate on some alternative certificate revocation schemes that are primarily of theoretical interest.

8.4.1   CRLs

The classical and simplest solution to the certificate revocation problem is the use of CRLs. As mentioned above, this approach is being followed by the ITU-T recommendation X.509 [4]. In this approach, a CA periodically issues and digitally signs a message that lists all certificates that have been revoked and should no longer be used. This message is called a CRL and it is made available through the certificate repository. Users who want to make sure that a particular certificate has not been revoked must query the repository and retrieve the latest CRL. If the CRL does not include the certificate, the user can assume that the certificate has not been revoked (at least until the time the CRL was issued and digitally signed).

The major advantage of using CRLs is simplicity. A user of a certificate is required to retrieve the latest CRL from the appropriate CA or the repository and check whether the certificate has been revoked. Only if the certificate is not included in the CRL (and has not been revoked accordingly) is the user authorized to accept and use the certificate. Obviously, the consequence of this scheme is that the user has to periodically retrieve the latest CRLs from all of the CAs he or she uses and accepts certificates from. This introduces some communication costs between the CA and the certificate repository, and high communication costs between the repository and the users (since CRLs may be very long). Another disadvantage is that a user does not receive succinct proof for the validity of a particular certificate.

Finally, note that a CRL is a negative statement. It is the digital equivalent of the little paper books of bad checks or bad credit cards that were distributed to cashiers in the 1970s and before. These have been replaced in the retail world by

---

[30]The X.509 CRL format is an ITU-T and ISO/IEC standard, first published in 1988 as version 1 (X.509v1 CRL). Similar to the ITU-T X.509 certificate format, the X.509v1 CRL was subsequently modified to allow for extension fields, resulting in X.509 version 2 CRL (X.509v2 CRL) format. Again, the X.509v2 CRL format is overviewed and discussed in [1,2].

positive statements in the form of online validation of a single check, ATM card, or credit card. The digital equivalent to this online validation of a certificate is provided by the OCSP (or a similar protocol).

8.4.2 OCSP

Instead of or as a supplement to checking against periodically issued CRLs, it may be necessary to obtain timely information regarding a certificate's current status. Examples include high-value funds transfer or large stock trades. Consequently, the IETF PKIX WG has specified and standardized an OCSP in RFC 2560 [15]. In short, the OCSP enables a user to determine the status of an identified certificate. An OCSP client issues a status request to an OCSP responder and suspends acceptance of the certificate in question until the responder provides a response (whether the certificate in question is good, revoked, or is in an unknown state for the responder). A certificate-issuing authority can either respond to OCSP requests directly or have one (or several) delegated OCSP responder(s) providing OCSP responses to the requesting entities on its behalf.

As of this writing, the use of OCSP is not yet widely deployed on the Internet.[31] Nevertheless, it is assumed and very likely that future CAs and certificate repositories will provide support for both certificate revocation mechanisms (CRLs and OCSP queries). It is also possible and very likely that the value of an e-commerce transaction will finally determine whether a check in a CRL is sufficient enough, or whether an OCSP query must be invoked.

8.4.3 Alternative Certificate Revocation Schemes

We have seen that the use of CRLs introduces some communication costs between the CA and the certificate repository, and high communication costs between the repository and the users (since CRLs may be very long), and that using CRLs, a user does not receive succinct proof for the validity of a particular certificate. We have also seen that the OCSP can be used to address the second problem.

More recently, some alternative certificate revocation schemes have been proposed that try to address both problems mentioned above. In this subsection, we address some of these schemes. In particular, we address Silvio Micali's certificate

---

[31]Note that browsers do not currently check the revocation status of any certificate at all. The only time a browser knows that a site certificate has been revoked is when it eventually expires. It is possible and very likely that this behavior will change in the future, and that certificate revocation checking will be adapted in one way or another.

revocation system (CRS), Paul Kocher's certificate revocation trees (CRTs), and a new certificate revocation and update scheme proposed by Moni Naor and Kobbi Nissim. Note that the following explanations are interesting mainly from a theoretical point of view, and that they may not be relevant for all practical purposes.

Certificate Revocation System

In order to address the problems mentioned above, Silvio Micali from the Massachusetts Institute of Technology (MIT) has proposed a CRS [28]. The underlying idea is to sign a message for every certificate stating whether it was revoked, and to use special signature schemes, such as on-line/off-line signature schemes[32] [29], to reduce the cost of periodically updating these signatures.

According to Micali's CRS proposal, the CA associates with each certificate two numbers — N and Y_{365} — that are signed along with the "normal" certificate data. The CA therefore randomly selects two numbers, N_0 and Y_0, and uses a one-way function f to compute $N = f(N_0)$ and $Y_{365} = f^{365}(Y_0)$.[33] After this initialization step, the directory is updated daily by the CA by sending it a number C for each certificate as follows:

- For a revoked certificate, $C = N_0$.

- For a non-revoked certificate, the CA reveals one application of f (i.e., $C = Y_{365-i} = f^{365-i}(Y_0)$), where i is a daily incremented counter ($i = 0$ on the date of issue).

---

[32]On-line/off-line signature schemes were originally introduced as a means to speed up the signing process in applications where computing resources are limited and time to sign is critical. In short, they combine one-time digital signatures and digital signatures arising from public key cryptography. The offline portion of the signature generation is to create a set of validation parameters for a one-time signature scheme, and to hash this set and sign the resulting hash value using a public key signature scheme. Since the public key signature scheme is computationally more expensive, it is done offline. The offline computations are independent of the messages to be signed. The online portion is to sign the message using the one-time signature scheme and the validation parameters which were constructed offline; this part of the signature scheme is very efficient. The resulting signatures are much longer than would be the case if only the public key signature scheme were used to sign the message directly and, consequently, bandwidth requirements are a disadvantage of the on-line/off-line signature schemes.

[33]To be precise, a stronger assumption is required for f, namely that f is one-way on all of its iterates (i.e., that given $y = f^i(x)$, it is infeasible to find an x' such that $y = f(x')$). This is automatically guaranteed if f is a one-way permutation.

According to this scheme, the most updated value for C serves as a short proof that a certain certificate was or was not revoked at a certain point in time. This value may then be provided by the directory in reply to a user requesting a particular certificate.

The advantage of the CRS as compared to the use of CRLs is in its low communication costs between the directory and the users (the users don't have to periodically download potentially very long CRLs). Another advantage of the CRS is that each user may hold a succinct transferable proof of the validity of the requested certificate. Directory accesses are saved when users hold such proofs and present them along with their certificates. However, the main disadvantage of the CRS is the increase in the computation costs for the CA and the increase in the communication costs between the CA and the directory. Due to the computational power of the CA and the high throughput between the CA and the directory, this doesn't pose a serious problem.

Certificate Revocation Trees

In order to enable a user to get proof that a specific certificate has not been revoked, Paul Kocher has suggested the use of *certificate revocation trees* (CRTs) [30].[34] In short, a CRT is a binary hash tree as originally proposed by Ralph C. Merkle [31], with leaves corresponding to a set of statements about the validity of the certificates (produced from the set of revoked certificates of every CA). The CRT provides information about whether a particular certificate is revoked (or whether its current status is unknown to the CRT issuer). In general, a certificate revocation system based on CRTs consists of three major components: CRT issuance, confirmation issuance (of certificate status), and verification of such confirmation.

To issue a CRT, one must first obtain a set of all revoked certificates from the CAs under consideration. These would typically come from CRLs issued by the CAs, but revocations could also come from other sources, such as users revoking their own certificates (actual revocation policies are generally determined by each CA). For any CA, there may be zero or more revoked certificates. Any revoked certificate is uniquely identified by the following information:

- The CA's public key (or a hash value of it);

- The certificate serial number (issued by the corresponding CA).

---

[34]The technology is being marketed by ValiCert, a company co-founded by Kocher. Additional information is available on the WWW by following the URL http://www.valicert.com

Afterward, the CRT issuer builds a set of statements that collectively specifies the revoked certificates. For this purpose, there are two types of statements:

- Statements specifying ranges of unknown CAs (type 1 statements);

- Statements specifying ranges of certificate serial numbers of which only the certificate with the lower serial number has been revoked (type 2 statements).

Table 8.1
An Exemplary Set of Statements

1	if $-\infty < CA_X < CA_1$	then Unknown CA
2	if $CA_X = CA_1$ and $-\infty \leq X < 156$	then X is revoked if and only if $X = -\infty$
3	if $CA_X = CA_1$ and $156 \leq X < 343$	then X is revoked if and only if $X = 156$
4	if $CA_X = CA_1$ and $343 \leq X < 344$	then X is revoked if and only if $X = 343$
5	if $CA_X = CA_1$ and $344 \leq X < \infty$	then X is revoked if and only if $X = 344$
6	if $CA_1 < CA_X < CA_2$	then Unknown CA
7	if $CA_X = CA_2$ and $-\infty \leq X < \infty$	then X is revoked if and only if $X = -\infty$
8	if $CA_2 < CA_X < CA_3$	then Unknown CA
9	if $CA_X = CA_3$ and $-\infty \leq X < 987$	then X is revoked if and only if $X = -\infty$
10	if $CA_X = CA_3$ and $987 < X < \infty$	then X is revoked if and only if $X = 987$
11	if $CA_3 < CA_X < \infty$	then Unknown CA

The following example has been taken from [30]. Consider the situation in which there are three CAs with public key hash values $CA_1 < CA_2 < CA_3$. In this situation, CA_1 has revoked three certificates (156, 343, 344), CA_2 has revoked no certificates, and CA_3 has revoked one certificate (987). The numbers in brackets refer to the serial numbers of the revoked certificates. In this situation, the CRT issuer can make 11 statements about a certificate with serial number X from a CA whose public key hash is CA_X. The resulting statements are summarized in Table 8.1. Statements 1, 6, 8, and 11 are of type 1, whereas statements 2, 3, 4, 5, 7, 9, and 10 are of type 2. Note that for any CA_X and certificate X, there is a single appropriate statement above which provides all known information about whether X is revoked. Also note that the existence of an unknown CA implies that also the revocation status is unknown, and that ∞ refers to infinity.

Having in mind the statements summarized in Table 8.1, the CRT issuer builds a binary hash tree with hash values of the statements as leaf nodes. In our example, there would be eleven leaf nodes ($N_{0,0}, ..., N_{0,10}$), where $N_{0,i}$ is the hash value of the statement number $i + 1$. Figure 8.2 illustrates the binary hash tree for our example. Wherever two arrows converge on a single node (such as $N_{2,1}$ is produced from $N_{1,2}$ and $N_{1,3}$), the right-hand node is computed as the hash value of the left-hand two nodes with the upper node put first. For example, $N_{2,1}$ would equal $h(N_{1,2}, N_{1,3})$, where the comma denotes concatenation. Also, a node with a single arrow is equal to the node to its left (i.e., $N_{3,1} = N_{2,2}$. According to this scheme, the root node $N_{4,0}$ is a function of all leaf nodes $(N_{0,0}, ..., N_{0,10})$. After producing the entire hash tree, the CRT issuer digitally signs the root node along with some supporting information, such as the date and time of the CRT issuance).

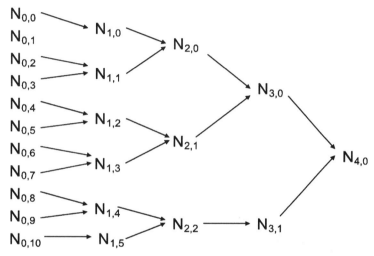

Figure 8.2   An exemplary binary hash tree.

To determine the revocation status of a certificate, the user needs the appropriate statement and proof that the statement is correct. The role of a confirmation issuer is to provide a user these two components:

- Expressing the statement is easy; it's just the appropriate statement that is represented by a leaf node in the binary hash tree.

- To assure the statement's validity, the user needs cryptographic proof that the leaf representative of the revocation status of the certificate is the leaf in a properly signed CRT. This assurance consists of the signed root node and a set of intermediate nodes that cryptographically bind the appropriate leaf node to the root node.

For example, in our example the appropriate statement for certificate 600 from CA_1 is statement number 5. The user can hash this statement to get $N_{0,5}$. The supporting nodes in this example are $N_{0,4}$, $N_{1,3}$, $N_{2,0}$, and $N_{3,1}$. The user can now use h to compute:

$$N_{1,2} = h(N_{0,4}, N_{0,5})$$
$$N_{2,1} = h(N_{1,2}, N_{1,3})$$
$$N_{3,0} = h(N_{2,0}, N_{2,1})$$
$$N_{4,0} = h(N_{3,0}, N_{3,1})$$

Finally, the user can check that $N_{4,0}$ was properly signed by the CRT issuer (at an acceptable date and time).

The main advantages of using a CRT instead of one (or several) CRL(s) are that the entire CRL(s) is (are) not needed for verifying the validity of a specific certificate, and that a user may hold succinct proof of the validity of the certificate. Note that this provides some scalability advantages as compared to the use of CRLs. Also note that in spite of the fact that CRTs work independently from CRLs, currently existing CRLs can still be used to actually build one (or several) CRT(s). Consequently, the two technologies are not mutually exclusive, but can rather be used to complement each other. On the other side, the main disadvantages of using a CRT is in the computational work needed to periodically build the CRT. Any change in a set of revoked certificates may result in a need to recompute the entire CRT.

Naor-Nissim Certificate Revocation Scheme

So far, we elaborated on the use of simple lists and binary trees to maintain certificate revocation state. The resulting certificate revocation schemes (e.g., CRLs, CRS, and CRTs) are comparably simple and efficient. More recently, theoretical work has addressed the question of using alternative (authenticated) data structures to improve the efficiency of the resulting certificate revocation schemes. For example, Moni Naor and Kobbi Nissim from the Weizmann Institute of Science have proposed authenticated data structures based on search trees [32]. More precisely, they have proposed the use of a 2-3 tree with leaves corresponding to the revoked certificates' serial numbers in increasing order. In a 2-3 tree, every interior node has two or three children and the paths from root to leaves all have the same length

[33]. The main property of 2-3 trees that is used in the Naor-Nissim certificate revocation scheme is that membership queries, insertions, and deletions involve only changes to nodes on a search path (i.e., every change is local and the number of affected paths is small). This is different from CRTs, where most operations require the recomputation of the entire tree.

In the Naor-Nissim certificate revocation scheme, every tree node is assigned a value according to the following procedure:

- If the node is a leaf, it stores a revoked certificate serial number as its value.

- If the node is not a leaf (but an internal node), it is computed by applying a collision-resistant hash function h, such as MD5 or SHA-1, to the values of its children.

During tree update (deletions or insertions), some new nodes may be created or some nodes may be deleted due to the balancing of the 2-3 tree. The important thing is that these nodes occur only on the search path. Finally, the CA vouches for the authenticity of the data structure by signing a message containing the tree root value and the tree height. A proof that there exists a leaf in the tree with a certain value consists of all node values on a path (of length equal to the tree height) from the root to a leaf, plus the values of these nodes' children. The proof is verified by checking the values of the given path and its length. Proving that a certificate was revoked or proving that a certificate was not revoked both reduce to proving the existence of certain leaves in the tree:

- Proving that a certificate was revoked is equivalent to proving the existence of a leaf corresponding to it;

- Proving that a certificate was not revoked is equivalent to proving the existence of two certificates corresponding to two neighboring leaves in the tree. One of these certificates has a lower serial number than the queried certificate, and the other has a higher serial number.

Note that finding a fallacious proof for the existence of a leaf in the tree amounts to breaking the collision resistance of h. Also note that the Naor-Nissim certificate revocation scheme is closer in spirit to CRLs and CRTs than to the CRS, since it maintains a list of only the revoked certificates. For a simpler implementation of the authenticated data structure, Naor and Nissim have also suggested the use of random treaps [34] instead of 2-3 trees. Similarly, it is assumed that many other data structures will be proposed in the future for efficiency reasons.

8.5 AUTHORIZATION

In the recent past, a lot of work has been done in establishing PKIs for e-commerce applications. Unfortunately, existing PKIs can only be used to authenticate the participants of e-commerce applications; they can't be used to properly authorize the participants and to control access to system resources accordingly. Consequently, the existing PKIs address only half of the problem with regard to e-commerce applications, and some complementary technologies are required to address the authorization problem [17].

As of this writing, the following technologies can be used to address the authorization problem [35]:

- The use of public key certificates with authorization information (encoded in X.509 standard or extension fields);

- The use of SDSI/SPKI certificates (as addressed in Section 8.1.2);

- The use of attribute certificates (as addressed in Section 8.1.3);

- The use of database systems to store authorization information (as, for example, employed by the DCMS architecture overviewed in Section 8.2).

Each authorization method has its own advantages and disadvantages. For example, certificate-based authorization is simple and straightforward. As such, it is well suited for applications that don't require sophisticated access control decisions. The use of attribute and SDSI/SPKI certificates, as well as the use of database systems are appropriate for applications that require intelligent and more sophisticated access control decisions. The more static the authorization information is, the more advantageous is the use of attribute and SDSI/SPKI certificates. Contrary to that, the use of database systems is better suited for situations in which the authorization information is transient and changes very dynamically. Consequently, there is no single best authorization method for e-commerce applications, and different applications may require different authorization methods. The question which method is best suited in a given situation primarily depends on the temporal characteristics of the corresponding authorization information:

- If the authorization information is transient and changes very dynamically (let's say each couple of minutes or hours), the use of a database system is appropriate;

- If the authorization information changes less frequently (let's say each couple of hours or days), the use of attribute and SDSI/SPKI certificates is appropriate;

- Finally, if the information is permanent and not subject to frequent changes, the use of public key certificates with encoded authorization information is certainly the easiest way to go.

In the near future, it is assumed that several competing authentication and authorization technologies and methods will be developed, explored, and further investigated. For example, some researchers at AT&T have broadened the scope of designing and building a PKI to *trust management*. According to the terminology introduced in their *PolicyMaker* system [36,37], trust management refers to a unified approach to specifying and interpreting security policies, credentials, access control, and authorization. Consequently, a trust management system consists of five basic components:

- A mechanism for identifying principals;

- A language for describing actions (operations with security consequences that are to be controlled by the system);

- A language for specifying application policies (policies that govern the actions that principals are authorized to perform);

- A language for specifying credentials (data records that allow principals to delegate authorization to other principals);

- A compliance checker (component that provides a service to applications for determining how an action requested by one or several principals should be handled, given a policy and a set of credentials).

Any application that makes use of a trust management system can ask the compliance checker whether a requested action should be allowed. More recently, the AT&T researchers have also designed a simple and flexible trust management system to work with various TCP/IP-based applications. The resulting trust management system has been named *KeyNote*. Version 2 of the KeyNote trust management system is further described in a preliminary document that is intended to be published as an informational RFC.[35]

---

[35]`ftp://ftp.research.att.com/dist/mab/knrfc.txt`

8.6   CONCLUSIONS

In this chapter, we addressed the problem of how to manage (public key and attribute) certificates in a corporate environment. In particular, we have introduced the topic, elaborated on possibilities to establish a corporate PKI, overviewed and briefly discussed the current offerings of two exemplary certification service providers, namely VeriSign and Swisskey, and addressed the problems related to certificate revocation and authorization in some detail.

A final (and more critical) word should be said about the overall cost of public key cryptography. Note that the original claim of public key cryptography was to minimize the initiation cost of a secure communication path between parties that share no prior administrative relationship. It was assumed that this would be the major reason why public key cryptography would dominate e-commerce applications in the first place. Note, however, that with no shared administrative structure to connect the parties, we must invent many things, such as certificate chaining, certificate revocation, and certificate directory services. Put in other words, we have to invent the very thing that public key cryptography claimed not to need, namely administrative overhead. This point was first made by Aviel D. Rubin, Daniel Geer, and Marcus J. Ranum [38]. In fact, they don't argue against public key cryptography in general, but they argue that much of the implied cost savings of public key cryptography over secret key cryptography is nothing more than an illusion. To further clarify this point, they argue that the sum of the cost for cryptographic key issuance and the cost for cryptographic key revocation is more or less constant (for both public key cryptography and secret key cryptography). There is some truth in this statement, considering the difficulty and pain we experience today in establishing a fully operational PKI. Note, for example, that the certificate revocation problem makes it necessary to have an online component permanently available for otherwise offline CAs.

Following this line of argument (and contrary to the original claim of public key cryptography), it is more likely that the first users of public key cryptography are groups that have some prior relationship and are simply moving from paper-based or private network-based communications to open networks, such as the Internet. In this situation, an existing and fully operational PKI allows a server to strongly authenticate users who contact across the Internet. Furthermore, the PKI allows to use digital signature schemes that are essential for the provision of non-repudiation services. There are signs that indicate that normal users will use public key cryptography much later on (if at all) and only when the problems related to authorization (as outlined in the previous section) have been resolved.

REFERENCES

[1] W. Ford, and M.S. Baum, *Secure Electronic Commerce: Building the Infrastructure for Digital Signatures & Encryption*, Prentice Hall PTR, Upper Saddle River, NJ, 1997.

[2] J. Feghhi, J. Feghhi, and P. Williams, *Digital Certificates: Applied Internet Security*, Addison-Wesley Longman, Reading, MA, 1999.

[3] L.M. Kohnfelder, "Towards a Practical Public-key Cryptosystem," Bachelor's thesis, Massachusetts Institute of Technology (MIT), Cambridge, MA, May 1978.

[4] ITU-T, Recommendation X.509: The Directory — Authentication Framework, 1988.

[5] S.T. Kent, "Internet Privacy Enhanced Mail," *Communications of the ACM*, Vol. 36, No. 8, August 1993, pp. 48 – 60.

[6] R. Housley, W. Ford, W. Polk, and D. Solo, "Internet X.509 Public Key Infrastructure Certificate and CRL Profile," Request for Comments 2459, January 1999.

[7] C. Adams, "Internet X.509 Public Key Infrastructure Certificate Management Protocols," Request for Comments 2510, March 1999.

[8] M. Myers, C. Adams, D. Solo, and D. Kemp, "Internet X.509 Certificate Request Message Format," Request for Comments 2511, March 1999.

[9] S. Chokhani, and W. Ford, "Internet X.509 Public Key Infrastructure Certificate Policy and Certification Practices Framework," Request for Comments 2527, March 1999.

[10] R. Housley, and W. Polk, "Internet X.509 Public Key Infrastructure Representation of Key Exchange Algorithm (KEA) Keys in Internet X.509 Public Key Infrastructure Certificates," Request for Comments 2528, March 1999.

[11] S. Boeyen, T. Howes, and P. Richard, "Internet X.509 Public Key Infrastructure Operational Protocols — LDAPv2," Request for Comments 2559, April 1999.

[12] Y. Yeong, T. Howes, and S. Kille, "Lightweight Directory Access Protocol," Request for Comments 1777, March 1995.

[13] S. Boeyen, T. Howes, and P. Richard, "Internet X.509 Public Key Infrastructure LDAPv2 Schema," Request for Comments 2587, June 1999.

[14] R. Housley, and P. Hoffman, "Internet X.509 Public Key Infrastructure Operational Protocols: FTP and HTTP," Request for Comments 2585, May 1999.

[15] M. Myers, R. Ankney, A. Malpani, S. Galperin, and C. Adams, "X.509 Internet Public Key Infrastructure Online Certificate Status Protocol — OCSP," Request for Comments 2560, June 1999.

[16] C. Ellison, "Establishing Identity Without Certification Authorities," *Proceedings of USENIX Security Symposium*, July 1996.

[17] J. Feigenbaum, "Towards an Infrastructure for Authorization," Position Paper, *Proceedings of USENIX Workshop on Electronic Commerce*, 1998.

[18] R.L. Rivest, and B. Lampson, "SDSI — A Simple Distributed Security Infrastructure," April 1996.

[19] R.L. Rivest, "S-Expressions," `http://theory.lcs.mit.edu/~rivest/sexp.txt`, May 1997.

[20] M. Abadi, "On SDSI's Linked Local Name Spaces," *Proceedings of 10th IEEE Computer Security Foundations Workshop*, June 1997, pp. 98 – 108.

[21] M.H. Fredette, "An Implementation of SDSI — the Simple Distributed Security Infrastructure," Master's thesis, Massachusetts Institute of Technology (MIT), Cambridge, MA, May 1997.

[22] A. Morcos, "A Java Implementation of Simple Distributed Security Infrastructure," Master's thesis, Massachusetts Institute of Technology (MIT), Cambridge, MA, May 1998.

[23] J.-E. Elien, "Certificate Discovery Using SPKI/SDSI 2.0 Certificates," Master's thesis, Massachusetts Institute of Technology (MIT), Cambridge, MA, May 1998.

[24] R. Oppliger, G. Pernul, and C. Strauss, "Using Attribute Certificates to Implement Role-based Authorization and Access Control Models," work in progress.

[25] R. Oppliger, *Authentication Systems for Secure Networks*, Artech House Publishers, Norwood, MA, 1996.

[26] R.L. Rivest, "Can We Eliminate Certificate Revocation Lists?" *Proceedings of Financial Cryptography*, 1998.

[27] R. Oppliger, A. Greulich, and P. Trachsel, "A Distributed Certificate Management System (DCMS) Supporting Group-based Access Controls," *Proceedings of Annual Computer Security Applications Conference (ACSAC '99)*, December 1999, work in progress.

[28] S. Micali, "Efficient Certificate Revocation," Massachusetts Institute of Technology (MIT), Technical Memo MIT/LCS/TM-542b, 1996.

[29] O. Goldreich, S. Goldwasser, and S. Micali, "On-line/Off-Line Digital Signatures," *Journal of Cryptology*, Vol. 9, 1996, pp. 35 – 67 (an earlier version of the paper was presented at CRYPTO '89).

[30] P. Kocher, "A Quick Introduction to Certificate Revocation Trees (CRTs)."

[31] R.C. Merkle, "A Certified Digital Signature," *Proceedings of CRYPTO '89*, 1989, pp. 234 – 246.

[32] M. Naor, and K. Nissim, "Certificate Revocation and Certificate Update," *Proceedings of 7th USENIX Security Symposium*, January 1998.

[33] A.V. Aho, J.E. Hopcroft, and J.D. Ullman, *Data Structures and Algorithms*, Addison-Wesley, 1983.

[34] R.G. Seidel, and C.R. Aragon, "Randomized Search Trees," *Proceedings of 30th Annual IEEE Symposium on Foundations of Computer Science*, 1989, pp. 540 – 545.

[35] R. Oppliger, "Authorization Methods for E-Commerce Applications," *Proceedings of 18th IEEE Symposium on Reliable Distributed Systems*, October 1999.

[36] M. Blaze, J. Feigenbaum, and J. Lacy, "Decentralized Trust Management," *Proceedings of IEEE Conference on Security and Privacy*, 1996, pp. 164 – 173.

[37] M. Blaze, J. Feigenbaum, and M. Strauss, "Compliance-Checking in the PolicyMaker Trust-Management System," *Proceedings of Financial Cryptography*, 1998, pp. 251 – 265.

[38] A.D. Rubin, D. Geer, and M.J. Ranum, *Web Security Sourcebook*, John Wiley & Sons, Inc., New York, NY, 1997.

Chapter 9

Executable Content

In this chapter, we focus on potential risks related to executable (or active) content. After a brief introduction in Section 9.1, we elaborate on binary mail attachments in Section 9.2, helper applications and plug-ins in Section 9.3, scripting languages in Section 9.4, Java applets in Section 9.5, and ActiveX controls in Section 9.6. Finally, we elaborate on the implications for firewalls in Section 9.7, and draw some conclusions in Section 9.8. As of this writing, one can reasonably expect the problems related to executable content as outlined in this chapter to become more and more important in the future (as the report on security issues related to mobile code and agent-based systems in Chapter 11 of this book also suggests).

9.1 INTRODUCTION

One of the most dangerous things that can be done with a computer system connected to the Internet is to download an arbitrary piece of software and execute it locally. That's because many operating systems place no limits on what a program can do once it starts running. Consequently, when a user downloads an arbitrary piece of software and executes it locally, the user places himself or herself entirely in the hands of the corresponding program author and software developer (note that

241

this is not only true for downloaded programs, but for any program as well). In practice, most programs that are downloaded behave as expected. But the point is that they don't have to and some don't. Many programs have bugs that may cause computers to crash. Also, some programs are malicious and can do damaging things, such as erasing a hard disk or transmitting confidential data to secret locations somewhere on the Internet.

In general, the ultimate goal of a (software) attacker is to be able to execute a program of choice on a computer system of choice without the corresponding victim's knowledge. Once this ability is achieved, any other attack is technically feasible and can follow. The easiest way for an attacker to accomplish this goal is to provide the computer system with a program to execute. One would think that an easy way to protect a computer system against this type of attack is to inspect all downloaded programs to see if they contain malicious code. Unfortunately, it's impossible to determine what a computer program will do without actually running it. What's possibly even more worrisome is the fact that it's often impossible to determine what a program is doing while or after it is running. Programs may have many ways of hiding their actual operations (we will take up this point in Section 11.3 when we talk about technologies to protect mobile code against potentially hostile runtime environments, such as time-limited blackbox security or computing with encrypted functions). Even sophisticated operating systems with memory protection and other security features, such as UNIX and Windows NT, offer users little protection against malicious programs that they download and execute locally. That's because once the program is running, it inherits all the privileges and corresponding access rights from the user who invoked it. No commercially available operating system allows users to create a restricted area in which potentially suspicious programs could be executed (similar to the Java sandbox addressed later in this chapter). To make things worse, Internet users have been told for years to download various programs and execute them locally without asking any further questions. For example, browsers as well as helper applications and plug-ins are typically distributed by having users download, execute, and install particular files. The same is true for bug-fixes and software patches. This user behavior automatically leads to security problems.

In general, executable or active content embraces a large collection of technologies that make Web pages more interesting and interactive, but also more dangerous. In short, executable or active content is downloaded into a browser where it is run on the local computer system. Examples of executable or active content include binary mail attachments, data files for word processors or other office automation programs, Java applets, ActiveX controls, as well as scripts written in specific languages, such as JavaScript or VBScript. Well-written executable or active content may enhance Web pages with animations, interactive games, and serious applications, such as database browsers or groupware applications. In fact, the entire idea of *network computing* is centered around the idea of well-written (and well-intended) executable or active content. However, one question that arises immediately is how to decide whether executable or active content is well-written (and well-intended) or not. If the content is not well-written or buggy, it may contain security holes that may compromise the user's privacy or the integrity of the data stored on the computer system. Even more worrisome, executable or active content written for malicious purposes may attempt to damage the computer system or seek to gain illegitimate access to the local area network. Unfortunately, it has been shown that deciding whether an arbitrary piece of software is malicious is a hard problem. Again, this point will be further addressed in Chapter 11 (in Section 11.1 to be precise).

From a theoretical point of view, the security problems related to executable or active content arise because there is no fundamental difference between a program (representing an active component) and data (representing a passive component) with regard to its internal representation within a computer system. In fact, it has been a fundamental principle in computer science that programs and data are treated equally and stored in the same memory.[1] This allows a program to modify both data and programs (eventually modifying itself). For example, most computer viruses take advantage of the fact that they can manipulate and directly modify program code. But in spite of these theoretical considerations, we have become accustomed to the clear distinction between active programs and passive data. Unfortunately, this distinction has been blurred in the recent past. Things that we used to assume are safe, such as data files for word processors, can now launch macro virus attacks against our computer systems. As a matter of fact, macro viruses that infect data files (or rather the macro programming features of these files) are spreading very rapidly throughout the Internet and the WWW. To make things worse, Web pages can contain executable or active content that is entirely transparent and invisible for the casual Web user.

The WWW and the deployment of executable or active content on the Web has fundamentally changed the notion of buying shrink-wrapped software from a trusted neighborhood store. Nowadays, it is more common to download potentially unsafe content from Web sites around the world. The Web sites may be good or

---

[1]This principle is generally attributed to John von Neumann. You may refer to the URL http://www-groups.dcs.st-andrews.ac.uk/ history/Mathematicians/Von_Neumann.html to get a comprehensive overview about John von Neumann's work.

bad, and it may be hard to tell the difference. Consequently, by the time executable or active content reaches a browser it may already be contaminated by computer viruses. Also, there is hardly any traceability or accountability in the contemporary model of downloading executable or active content from the Web. Against this background, Web surfing is fundamentally different from watching television. After a user leaves a Web site, downloaded active content may still continue to run on his or her computer system, potentially carrying out improper activities. The WWW and the deployment of executable or active content on the Web has indeed shifted the security problem from protecting the server against potentially malicious clients to protecting the client against potentially malicious servers. This problem is more difficult to address.

In this new environment, the use of secure software distribution systems, such as *Bellcore's Trusted Software Integrity System* (BETSI) [1,2], may provide a viable solution for the secure software distribution problem. BETSI is an interim solution, one that has been in place for a couple of years and can be expected to prevail until a more rigorous security infrastructure displaces it. The system requires users to obtain an authentic public key and some widely available cryptographic software, such as PGP and an implementation of the MD5 one-way hash function. In BETSI, there are authors and users:

- Authors are people or companies (e.g., Microsoft) who wish to securely distribute software on the Internet;

- Users are people who wish to download software with authenticity and integrity guarantees.

Authors must register with BETSI in advance. Once they are registered, they can communicate securely with a BETSI server because they will share authentic and valid copies of one another's PGP public keys. When an author has a file (e.g., a software package) to distribute, he or she creates an integrity certificate request for the file. The request contains information, such as the author's name, the file's name, and the MD5 hash value of the file. The author then digitally signs the request using PGP software and a private key, and sends the result to the BETSI server. The server, in turn, receives the request and verifies the PGP signature. At this point, the message is verified as being authentic and as having integrity. BETSI then replies to the author with a signed integrity certificate, which states that the named author is indeed registered and that he or she has requested a certificate linking a certain hash value to the specific file (or filename). The author verifies that the certificate is valid and makes it available with the distribution of the file.

Consequently, the user obtains a copy of the certificate along with the file. He can verify that the file has not been (intentionally or unintentionally) modified by verifying the integrity certificate with BETSI's public key and computing the hash value of the corresponding file. If the integrity certificate is valid, the user can be sure that the file is authentic and has integrity. Unfortunately, the use of BETSI or other integrity protection tools has never really taken off in the commercial world of the Internet. This will hopefully change in the future.

In the following sections, we overview and briefly discuss the potential problems related to the various classes of executable or active content. In particular, we elaborate on binary mail attachments, helper applications and plug-ins, scripting languages, Java applets, and ActiveX controls.

9.2 BINARY MAIL ATTACHMENTS

A *binary mail attachment* is an attachment to an e-mail message that contains some binary data that may encode anything (from random data to executable program code). As such, binary mail attachments represent the simplest class of executable or active content. The sender of an e-mail message simply attaches one (or several) binary data file(s) to the message, and the receiver (manually or automatically) executes the file(s) upon reception.

It is common practice today to use binary mail attachments to distribute simple animation programs over the Internet. In general, these programs are executed on the receiver's side without thinking about possible security implications. For example, it would be a fairly simple exercise for a software developer to write a program that automatically deletes all files a user running the program has access to and is authorized to delete. In fact, several programs that illustrate this possibility have already been distributed over the Internet for educational purposes. These programs are to increase the awareness of the problem of binary mail attachments to common e-mail users. Unfortunately, these programs are not very effective in this task, and users are busily redistributing binary mail attachments they personally like to their colleagues and friends.

9.3 HELPER APPLICATIONS AND PLUG-INS

Not so long ago, most browsers could only render and display ASCII and HTML text, as well as images in either the GIF or the JPEG format. While these four data types provided a good basis and starting point for the Web to emerge, there are many kinds of data types that can't be readily translated into these types.

Consequently, Web developers had to think about possible ways to extend the ability of browsers to understand, render, and display additional data types.

An obvious way to extend a browser is through the use of so-called *helper applications* (also known as *external viewers*). In short, a helper application is a special program that is run automatically by the Web browser[2] when a data type other than ASCII, HTML, GIF, or JPEG is downloaded. Using helper applications is a flexible and extensible way through which practically any kind of information can be downloaded, rendered, and displayed. For example, the widely used and deployed RealAudio system works by designating the RealAudio player software as a helper application for Web browsers. When a user clicks on a corresponding HTML link, a file is downloaded to the user's computer system. The RealAudio player then reads the file and determines where on the Internet it should go to actually download the audio program. This program is then fetched, and the sound is played.

Motivated by the work that had been done in the field of helper applications, Netscape Communications developed a similar system called *plug-ins*. In short, a plug-in is a module that is loaded directly into the address space of the corresponding browser and is automatically run when documents of a particular data type are downloaded. One of the simplest uses for plug-ins is to replace helper applications used by browsers. Instead of requiring that data be specially downloaded, saved in a file, and processed by a helper application, the data can be left in the browser's memory pool and processed directly by the appropriate plug-in. Plug-ins are manually downloaded by Web users and stored in a directory called `Plugins` (typically located in Netscape Navigator's program directory). The browser scans this directory when it starts up to discover what plug-ins are available. As of this writing, most popular helper applications have been rewritten as plug-ins, including the Adobe Acrobat reader to display PDF files, the RealAudio player to play sound files, and the Macromind Shockwave player to play animated video sequences.[3]

In spite of their advantages in terms of browser extensibility, helper applications and plug-ins can also be the source for some security problems. That's because the helper applications and plug-ins run on the user's computer system, but take their input from arbitrary Web sites. If a helper application or plug-in has sufficiently powerful features, a rogue Web site can use it against the user's own interests. An obvious danger is that there is no way for a user downloading a helper application or

---

[2]This section is equally applicable to e-mail, as we have moved from SMTP (ASCII data) to MIME (any application data). Consequently, helper applications can also be configured into e-mail clients to handle arbitrary application data.

[3]Plug-ins have been developed by Netscape Communications. Although Microsoft Internet Explorer can run Netscape plug-ins, they are deprecated in favor of ActiveX controls.

plug-in to be sure that he or she is actually downloading an authentic copy, and not a version that has been modified to incorporate some undocumented and critical features. Again, a secure software distribution system, such as BETSI, would help a lot at this point.

One of the most powerful application programs is an interpreter for a general-purpose programming language. Given the appropriate input, an interpreter can open, read, modify, or delete any file on a computer system. To make things worse, many programming languages allow programs to open network connections, allowing them to scan for vulnerabilities and security loopholes on other computers. Because they are so powerful, interpreters for general-purpose programming languages should never be used or configured as helper applications. This includes Microsoft Word and Excel (unless the macros feature is turned off), since they are both equipped with the Visual Basic scripting language. According to [3], the following programs should never be used or configured as helper applications:

- Any other program that includes Microsoft's Visual Basic scripting language;

- The scripting languages Perl, Python, and Tcl/Tk;

- UNIX shells, such as `sh`, `csh`, `tcsh`, or any other UNIX shell;

- The DOS command shell `COMMAND.COM`;

- Any PostScript interpreter other than GhostView.[4]

If you configure a browser to automatically run one of these programs as a helper application when a document of a certain MIME type is downloaded, you are implicitly trusting the authors of the Web pages that you are browsing to be friendly with your computer. This level of implicit trust may not always be justified and is very dangerous.

More recently, a group of researchers at the University of California at Berkeley (UC Berkeley) presented an approach to limiting the damage from untrusted helper applications in the Solaris operating system [4]. The idea is to limit the access that a helper application has to the system calls at the operating system level. They used the term "sandboxing" to represent the idea that a program can play around in its own confined area, without having access to anything outside. As such, the approach is conceptually similar to the sandbox approach used for Java applet security (as addressed later in Section 9.5).

---

[4]Note that there are PostScript commands to open, read, and delete files, as well as to execute arbitrary commands. However, these commands are disabled by default when GhostView is run in "safe" mode.

9.4   SCRIPTING LANGUAGES

In this section, we address two scripting languages that are in widespread use today: JavaScript and VBScript. Note that Netscape's JavaScript language is available for both Netscape Navigator and Microsoft Internet Explorer, whereas VBScript runs only on Microsoft Internet Explorer. However, both scripting languages have a similar rationale. While fully fledged programming languages for the Web, such as Java, offer great power and flexibility, their capabilities can only be exploited by technically skilled programmers. The creation of Java applets from scratch is beyond the capabilities of many HTML authors. Also, a full-blown Java applet is also overkill for most applications. If an HTML author needs only to confirm that the value typed into a field of a form corresponds to a correct telephone number, it would be overkill to develop an applet for that purpose. In this situation, scripting languages offer an intermediate solution between HTML authoring and Java applet (or other technology) development.

9.4.1   JavaScript

It is important to note that Java and JavaScript[5] are not the same, and that they are in fact two different programming languages (with different syntaxes, different semantics, different user communities, and different security implications). In fact, *JavaScript* is a simple scripting language that Netscape Communications developed to make animation and other forms of interaction more convenient, whereas Java is a full-fledged general-purpose programming language developed by Sun Microsystems (overviewed in the following section). But in spite of their differences, Java and JavaScript also have some things in common:

- They (obviously) have similar names;

- They are both languages that are primarily used to add interactivity to Web pages;

- They can both run on either a Web server or a browser (or even standalone);

- They both have a syntax that resembles the C^{++} programming language.

The situation would be less confusing if JavaScript would have been given a completely different name (or at least a name that is less similar to Java).

---

[5]JavaScript was first named LifeScript. Also, Microsoft incorporated a very similar scripting language, technically known as JScript, into its browsers beginning with Internet Explorer 3.0.

JavaScript code resides inside HTML files, usually surrounded by `<SCRIPT>` and `</SCRIPT>` (so that they are recognized by JavaScript-enabled browsers) and HTML comment tags (so that they can be ignored by browsers that do not understand JavaScript). In addition, the language within the `<SCRIPT>` tag can be set to JavaScript (`<SCRIPT language = Javascript>`).

In practice, JavaScript code is most often used to command a browser. For example, it can be used to create new windows, check or fill out fields in forms, jump to new URLs, process image maps locally, change the content of an HTML file, compute mathematical results, or perform other functions. JavaScript has many built-in functions specifically designed to modify the appearance of a browser. For example, it can make visual elements of the browser appear or disappear, or it can make messages appear in the status line of a browser. In fact, some of the earliest JavaScript applications displayed moving banners across the browser's status line.

In theory, JavaScript code is inherently more secure than code written in any other programming language, mainly for two reasons:

- First, there are no JavaScript methods that can be used to directly access the file system on the client side;

- Second, there are no JavaScript methods that can be used to open network connections to other computer systems.

But JavaScript, like many other components of the Web, is changing very rapidly. For example, Netscape Communications has developed and is deploying a capabilities-based system that relies on digital signatures to determine which privileges JavaScript code should have. In this system, the security implications are similar to the ones related to Java applets and ActiveX controls (as further discussed in Sections 9.5 and 9.6). In addition to the security problems that will emerge from this capabilities-based system, JavaScript has also been the source of both denial-of-service and privacy violation attacks:

- JavaScript can be used to mount denial-of-service attacks against browsers and their corresponding clients. These attacks can be resident on Web pages or they can be sent to users with JavaScript-enabled e-mail readers. For example, the JavaScript attack code can iteratively open a large number of windows on the screen or it can try to solve a computationally expensive problem.

- Because JavaScript code runs inside the browser, it potentially has access to the same information. If the JavaScript code (maliciously or not) leaks this information, a privacy violation may occur. Early JavaScript implementations featured a variety of problems that could lead to loss of confidentiality or user privacy. For example, JavaScript could be used to create forms that automatically filled themselves with private data and send these data to a remote attacker's e-mail account. Similarly, JavaScript code segments had access to the browser's history file. This allowed a Web site to discover the URLs of all of the other Web pages that a user had visited before. Finally, a JavaScript code segment running in one window could monitor the URLs of Web pages displayed on other windows. Most of these problems have been corrected in newer versions of Netscape Navigator and Microsoft Internet Explorer. However, new problems will probably have been discovered as this book hits the shelves of the bookstores.

To make things worse, JavaScript can also be used to launch electronic versions of social engineering attacks. For example, a JavaScript code segment can be used to request the name and password from a Web user. Figure 9.1 illustrates a corresponding password prompt produced by a JavaScript code segment. Although this window looks official, it can be generated with the following simple segment of JavaScript code:

```
<SCRIPT LANGUAGE=JavaScript>
    password = prompt("You have lost your dial-up connection.\n
                    Please reenter your password","");
</SCRIPT>
```

It is possible and very likely that a common Web user will fill out the field and reveal his or her password accordingly. A slightly enhanced version of the JavaScript code segment could then take care of the password, and send it, for example, to a remote e-mail account.

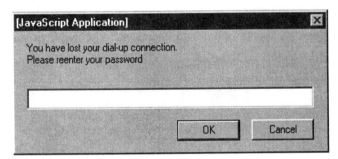

Figure 9.1   A password prompt produced by a JavaScript code segment. © 1999 Netscape Communications Corporation.

Similarly, the status line of a browser normally displays the URL that will be retrieved if the user clicks on an HTML link. By using JavaScript, a user can also be made to believe that one URL actually points someplace else. For example, the following HTML link will display `http://www.realshop.com` when the mouse is moved over the link, but clicking on the link will actually have the browser jump to the Web site located at `http://www.fakedshop.com`:

```
Click <A href="http://www.fakedshop.com"
      onMouseover="window.status='http://www.realshop.com';
      return true">here</A> to enter the real shop.
```

Obviously, the two technologies (and many others) can be combined to maliciously mislead users.

JavaScript's security history is not reassuring, and there is nothing to suggest that the rate at which vulnerabilities and bugs are discovered will slow down in the future. The use of code and object signing technologies will help a little, but it won't be able to completely solve the problem. Anybody who is concerned with potential abuses of JavaScript should therefore disable JavaScript in his or her browser (Figure 9.2 illustrates the corresponding Netscape Navigator Preferences menu).

9.4.2   VBScript

As mentioned earlier in this section, the scripting language VBScript is conceptually similar to JavaScript, but is currently available only for Microsoft browsers. In fact, it made its appearance in Internet Explorer version 3.0. VBScript is a dialect of Visual Basic and draws on the popularity of that programming language in Microsoft Windows environments [5].

VBScript, in contrast to JavaScript, has been subject to far less scrutiny by the Internet community. Consequently, fewer security holes are being reported. Similar to JavaScript, VBScript code segments can be used to make annoying denial-of-service and privacy violation attacks. In addition, they can also be used to launch electronic versions of social engineering attacks.

9.5   JAVA APPLETS

Although *Java* is widely thought of as a language for writing programs that are downloaded over the Internet to browsers (so-called *Java applets*), it wasn't designed for that purpose. In fact, Java's history started in 1991 when a group of engineers at Sun Microsystems were working on a stealth project aimed at developing a new programming language that could be used in the world of consumer electronics.

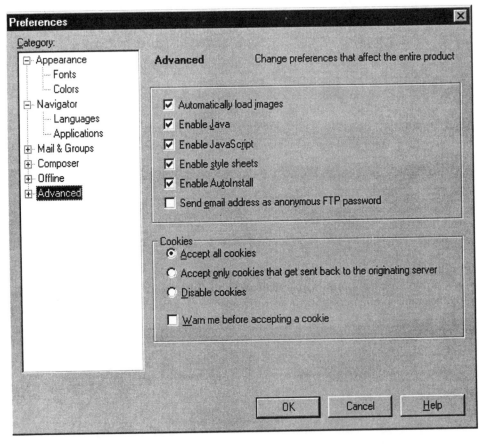

Figure 9.2   The Netscape Navigator Preferences menu to enable or disable Java. © 1999 Netscape Communications Corporation.

The idea was to make it possible for consumer electronics devices to download their control programs over a network. The key was a new computer language called *Oak* that had been developed by James Gosling. Instead of being compiled for a specific microprocessor, Oak was designed to be compiled into an interpreted bytecode that would run on a virtual machine. The use of portable bytecode would allow a consumer electronic manufacturer to change its microprocessor without losing compatibility with existing programs.

In the early 1990s, Oak was tested for interactive cable TV decoder boxes, CD-ROMs, and multimedia publishing. But right around that time, another multi-platform phenomenon was sweeping the computer industry: the WWW. The Oak team quickly realized that they had a language that was designed to be small and portable, and that they could use the Web to download programs to end users' computer systems and to have the programs run instantly there. This was actually the birth of the idea of network computing. In July 1994, a first Web browser was implemented to demonstrate the idea. Within a month, the browser was rewritten from scratch in Oak, and a system for running downloaded programs was designed and implemented. Eight months later, Sun officially announced Java and its HotJava browser at the 1995 SunWorld tradeshow, and Netscape announced its intention to license Java for use in Netscape Navigator.

In essence, Java is an object-oriented, general-purpose programming language that has a syntax similar to C^{++}, dynamic binding, garbage collection, and a simple inheritance model [6]. Instead of being compiled for a particular microprocessor, Java programs (both applications and applets) are compiled into a processor-independent bytecode. This bytecode is loaded into a computer's memory by the Java Class Loader. Finally, the bytecode is run on a Java virtual machine (JVM). The JVM can run Java programs directly on an operating system, such as UNIX, Windows, or MacOS. Alternatively, the JVM can be embedded inside a browser, allowing Java applets to be executed as they are downloaded from the Web. The JVM can execute the Java bytecode directly using an interpreter. Alternatively, it can use a "just-in-time" compiler to convert the Java bytecode into the native machine code of the particular computer system on which it is actually running. Finally, Java can also be compiled directly into machine code and run on the target system. Used this way, however, Java loses its major advantage of being able to run on any computer and any operating system that has a JVM.

Right from the beginning, the Java development team wanted to create a language that would encourage programmers to write code that was inherently reliable. In fact, they sought to increase the safety of the language and the sanity of the programs written in it. The main way that Java achieves this is by providing automatic memory management (including garbage collection), exception handling, and built-in bounds checking on all strings and arrays. In addition, Java doesn't have pointers, only has single inheritance, and is strongly typed. All of these features (and some others) combine to make Java a comparably safe programming language. What this basically means is that Java programs rarely behave badly when given data that is slightly unexpected. Similarly, because most security problems are the result of bugs and programming errors, it is commonly believed that Java programs will be inherently more secure than programs written in other general-purpose programming languages, including C and C^{++}.

But in spite of the security properties mentioned above, Java was not originally designed to be a secure programming language. In fact, under Java's original vision, programs would only be downloaded by an equipment manufacturer or an approved content provider. Java was designed for a closed community and for a somewhat constrained set of target environments. But when Java was repositioned for the WWW, security immediately became a major concern. By design, the Web allows any user to download anything from anyone on the Internet, whether it is from an approved content provider or not. If Web users can download and run a program by simply clicking on an HTML link on a Web page, then there needs to be some mechanisms for protecting users and their computer systems from malicious and poorly coded programs. Note that having a safe programming language protects users from many traditional security problems (that are related to bugs and programming errors). But a safe programming language alone cannot protect users from programs that are intentionally malicious. To provide protection against these types of attack, it's necessary to place limits on what downloaded programs can do. In fact, Java employs a variety of techniques to limit what a downloaded Java applet can do. The main ones are the Java sandbox, security manager, bytecode verifier, and class loader as briefly addressed next.

Sandbox: Java applets run on a JVM inside a restricted runtime environment. As such, the Java applets are prohibited from doing dangerous things, such as making direct calls to the computer's operating system. Sun Microsystems termed this approach to security the Java "sandbox." In fact, the Java programming language is quite notable for its sandbox approach toward warding off the threats of Java applets downloaded into browsers from arbitrary Web sites.

Security Manager: If all Java applets were restricted so that they couldn't send information over a network, couldn't access the local file system, and couldn't manipulate the computer's input/output devices, they would probably be nearly safe. After all, there would be little damage an applet could do. Unfortunately, these restrictions would also make Java a much less exciting programming language and programming environment. In the Java security model, there is a special class, called the `SecurityManager` class, which is designed to be called before any potentially dangerous operation is executed. The `SecurityManager` class is to determine whether a specific operation should be allowed or not. The

SecurityManager class, in turn, identifies a number of access control methods called by various methods in the Java system libraries before they perform any potentially unsafe operations. In general, any program can instantiate its own security manager (as an instance of the SecurityManager class). For example, Netscape Navigator and Microsoft Internet Explorer both have their own instantiation of the SecurityManager class.

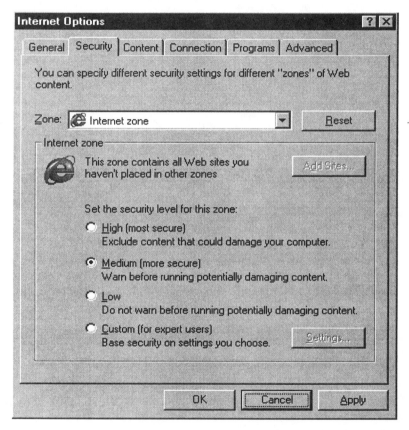

Figure 9.3   The Security tab of the Internet Microsoft Explorer Internet Options menu. © 1999 Microsoft Corporation.

Class Loader: Because most of the security checks in the Java programming environment are written in the Java language itself, it's important to ensure that a malicious piece of code can't disable these checks. For example, one way to launch such an attack would be to have a malicious Java program disable the standard **SecurityManager** class or replace it with a more permissive version. Such an attack could be carried out by a downloaded piece of machine code or a Java applet that exploited a bug in the Java runtime system. To prevent these types of attack, the Java class loader examines classes to make sure that they do not violate the runtime system.

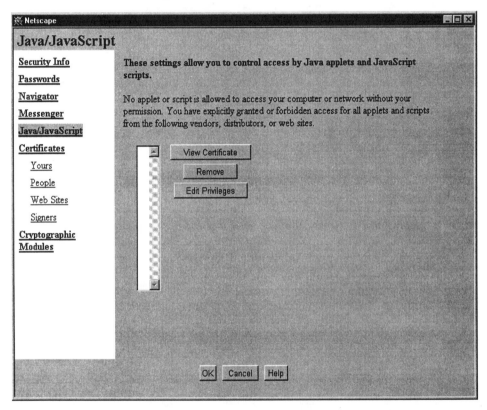

Figure 9.4   The Netscape Navigator Security Java/JavaScript menu. © 1999 Netscape Communications Corporation.

Bytecode Verifier: To further protect the Java runtime system, Java employs a bytecode verifier. The verifier is to ensure that downloaded bytecode could only have been created by compiling a valid Java program. For example, it is supposed to assure that a downloaded program doesn't violate access restrictions or object types, and doesn't forge pointers. The bytecode verifier is implemented as a series of ad hoc checks.

In general, the Java sandbox, security manager, bytecode verifier, and class loader collectively implement a security policy. The Java security policy, in turn, is complicated by the fact that the Java programming language is dual-use:

- On the one hand, Java is a general-purpose programming language for creating any kind of application software;

- On the other hand, Java is also a programming language for creating applets that perform some particular tasks on the user's machine.

Obviously, these different purposes require fundamentally different security policies and the dual nature leads to a more complicated security model, which in turn leads to more difficulty in enforcement. For example, Java's original implementors envisioned three different security policies that could be enforced by browsers that implemented the Java programming language:

1. Do not run Java programs at all.

2. Run Java programs with different privileges depending on their actual sources. For example, Java applets downloaded from remote Web sites would run with severe restrictions, whereas Java programs loaded off the local file system would be considered trustworthy and would have no such restrictions (they would have full access to all the system resources).

3. Run Java programs with no restrictions at all.

Note that the policies enumerated above are only examples, and that many other policies can be defined. This is especially true for the security model of Java version 1.2 [7,8].

Sun's HotJava browser implemented all three of these policies, and the choice was left to the user (most users actually chose the second policy). Netscape and Microsoft also followed this simplistic approach to Java security policy. In fact, Netscape Navigator and Microsoft Internet Explorer both allow the user to enable or disable Java, and both restrict applets that are downloaded from the Internet more severely than applets that are loaded from the local file system. Figures 9.2 and 9.3 illustrate the Netscape Navigator Preferences menu to enable or disable

Java and the corresponding Microsoft Internet Explorer View > Internet Options > Security menu where security zones can be specified (as explained below).

The sandbox model does safeguard sensitive computer resources from the threats of malicious Java applets, but it does so at the expense of severely constraining the execution environments and their capabilities. A Java applet confined to a sandbox cannot generally read from local files or write to a file, and it cannot establish network connections except to the originating system that served the applet. In fact, it turns out that a sandboxed Java applet is not capable of doing many interesting things that we usually associate with executable or active content (e.g., a Java applet implementing a word processor). The developers of browser software have been well aware of this problem. In fact, since Internet Explorer 3.0 and Netscape Navigator 4.0, they have made the Java sandbox configurable to allow downloaded Java applets more functionality and flexibility in a way that can be carefully monitored and controlled by the user.

For obvious reasons, software distributed over the Internet is not shrink-wrapped like software found in retail stores. Consequently, it is not at all obvious who published a piece of software or whether it has been tampered with during the distribution process. To authenticate the publisher and to protect the integrity of a specific piece of software, digital signatures can be used. In short, the software publisher digitally signs the software and anybody who knows the software publisher's public key can verify the authenticity and integrity of the software accordingly. Consequently, code signing technologies bind a piece of software to the identity of the corresponding publisher. The aim is to trace back a malicious piece of software downloaded into a browser to its original publisher, who may then be held accountable and be subject to litigation.[6] Microsoft calls this application of digital signatures *Authenticode*; it serves as a "digital" or "virtual shrink-wrap" for software distributed over the Internet.[7] In fact, code-signed software published on the Internet is analogous to shrink-wrapped software sold in retail stores. A user can download signed code, view, and verify the publisher's certificate, and then assume the same level of trust in the quality and reliability of the code as if he or she had

---

[6]Note, however, that it is very difficult to hold a software publisher accountable for unsigned code because the publisher can always claim not to have published the code or argue that it was tampered with during the download.

[7]Authenticode was publicly announced in 1996 as part of Microsoft's Internet Explorer 3.0 and ActiveX technologies. Microsoft has been promoting its trademarked Authenticode technology as an open industry standard. To accomplish this goal, Microsoft has also published the specifications to promote cross-platform developments, submitted the Authenticode proposal to W3C, embraced industry standards, and sought the participation of other software industry members and standards bodies.

bought shrink-wrapped software from the same publisher (note that the level of trust may even be better, since it is generally more difficult to counterfeit a digital signature than it is to counterfeit a shrink-wrapped software package). Based on whether a user is familiar with and has trust in a particular software publisher, he or she can decide whether or not to install and run a software that may include Java applets or ActiveX controls.

As of this writing, Microsoft's Authenticode technology is based on commercially available certificates, such as those provided by VeriSign. More recently, Microsoft released Authenticode 2.0 that also includes a timestamping feature. The aim of the timestamping feature is to establish that a piece of software was properly signed during the valid lifetime of a software publisher's public key certificate.

First, Microsoft Internet Explorer 3.0 could be configured so that Java applets digitally signed with a (individual or commercial) software publisher's key and approved by the user could also have full access to the local computer and file system. This approach was later adapted by Netscape's *object signing system* for Navigator 4.0. Similar to Microsoft's Authenticode technology, Netscape's object signing system addresses the distribution of reliable content over the Internet by identifying the publisher of signed content, ensuring the integrity of downloaded signed content, and automatically updating signed software components. Furthermore, it provides a mechanism for downloading signed Java applets or JavaScript code to step out of the sandbox and request privileges to access specific system resources. In fact, Netscape Navigator 4.0 identifies a variety of different kinds of privileges that a Java applet might need. These privileges can then be given to a Java applet on a case-by-case basis. Similar to Microsoft's Authenticode technology, Netscape Navigator 4.0 further allows Java classes to be digitally signed by software publishers. Giving Java programs capabilities in this way allows the Java environment to satisfy the "principle of least privilege," meaning that programs should have the privileges necessary to perform the tasks that are expected of them, and nothing more. The Netscape Navigator Security Java/JavaScript menu where arbitrary Java capabilities can be configured is illustrated in Figure 9.4. It's an open question whether it is possible to educate users to properly configure Java capabilities.

Obviously, Netscape's object signing system exploits the same underlying techniques as Microsoft's Authenticode technology to achieve its goals. In fact, it also uses public key cryptography, X.509v3 certificates, digital signatures, and PKCS standards to digitally sign objects. However, Netscape Communications refers to the technology as *object signing* instead of *code signing*, mainly to convey the fact that the technology can sign any kind of file and to explicitly distinguish itself from Microsoft's Authenticode technology. Furthermore, Netscape Communications refers to X.509v3 certificates required for signing as *object signing certificates* as opposed to *software publisher certificates*, in the case of Microsoft's Authenticode technology (Netscape Communications, however, also supports the distinction between individual and commercial object signing certificates).

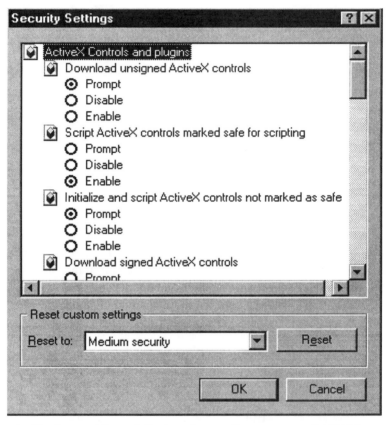

Figure 9.5   The Internet Microsoft Explorer Security Settings menu. © 1999 Microsoft Corporation.

As of this writing, object signing certificates can be purchased from VeriSign,[8] BelSign,[9] and Thawte Certification.[10] In addition, it's also possible to issue ob-

---

[8]http://digitalid.verisign.com/nosintro.htm

[9]http://www.belsign.com/

[10]http://www.thawte.com/

ject signing certificates using Netscape's Certificate Server. Further information on Netscape's object signing system and corresponding resources is available on the Web.[11]

Meanwhile, Internet Explorer 4.0 has also introduced a more sophisticated capabilities-based system that uses code signing to extend additional privileges to Java applets. More specifically, a user can divide the Web into security zones and have Microsoft Internet Explorer provide different levels of trust, depending on which zone he or she has assigned a Web site to. Against this background, a *security zone* refers to a group of Web sites in which a user has the same level of trust. You can think of Internet Explorer's security zones as visas that some countries issue to travelers. If the country trusts you, they stamp your passport so you can travel anywhere you like during your stay. If for some reason the country doesn't trust you, it strictly limits where you can go and what you can do during your visit.

In principle, security zones work the same way, except that you are in the role of the country deciding how much access to allow to your visitors (or active content) on your computer. For example, it's likely that you fully trust Web sites on your corporate intranet, so you'll probably want to allow all types of active content (including, for example, Java applets) to run there. At the same time, however, you may not feel so confident about arbitrary Web sites you may visit while browsing through the Internet, so you can assign them to the untrusted zone, where you can prevent active content from being run and prevent code from being downloaded to your system in the first place. The advantage of security zones is that they provide advanced protection for your computer and your privacy without interrupting you with repeated warnings while you're visiting Web sites that you've already decided you can trust. From the user's point of view, Microsoft's security zones seem to be more intuitive and easier to understand than a full-fledged system to configure Java capabilities, such as that employed by Netscape Navigator.

Microsoft Internet Explorer 4.0 comes along with the following four security zones that are predefined:

- Internet;

- Local intranet;

- Trusted sites;

- Restricted sites.

---

[11]`http://developer.netscape.com/docs/manuals/signedobj/overview.html`

The *local intranet zone* is for Web sites within a local area network, usually protected by a firewall. You may consider these internal Web sites to be trustworthy and grant them unrestricted access privileges to your computer system. The *trusted sites zone* includes sites that are on the Internet, but you have a high level of trust in their integrity and are willing to give them access to some of the resources on your computer system. The Web sites of your brokerage, your bank, and your friends are good examples of trusted Web sites. Contrary to that, the *restricted sites zone* is the black list. It houses sites that contain damaging active content. In general, you are not willing to grant these sites any privileges. Finally, the *Internet zone* contains everything else on the Internet. In general, you neither trust nor distrust these sites.

As illustrated in Figure 9.3, the View > Internet Options > Security menu can be used to set the security level for each zone. For each security zone, a High, Medium, Low, or Custom security setting can be chosen. The Custom option gives advanced users and administrators more control over all security options, including, for example, access to files, ActiveX controls, and scripts, the level of capabilities given to Java applets, or whether sites must be authenticated through the use of SSL. The corresponding option menu is illustrated in Figure 9.5.

Due to the Authenticode technology, Internet Explorer 4.0 can identify who published a piece of software to help users decide whether to download it. More precisely, Internet Explorer 4.0 has introduced some certificate management capabilities that let network administrators control which Java applets and ActiveX controls are allowed to run on their networks, based on who published the Java applets or the ActiveX control. For example, an administrator can allow users to open and run all internally created Java applets, but keep all applets that originate from outside the corporate firewall from loading and running on an internal machine. The security zones and certificate management capabilities on a user's computer can be configured with Microsoft's Internet Explorer Administration Kit (IEAK). The IEAK can also be used to configure the Internet Explorer in a way that blocks users from downloading other (not preconfigured) certificates. This has the following benefits:

- Administrators have greater control over what can be downloaded onto a user's computer;

- Users are presented with fewer warnings and choices for downloading executable or active content.

Issues related to trust management in Netscape Navigator and Microsoft Internet

Explorer are further addressed in [9]. Also, many things that we have said in this section are equally true for ActiveX controls that are addressed next.

9.6   ACTIVEX CONTROLS

Unlike Java, which is an entirely new programming language designed from the bottom up to be suitable for Web applications, Microsoft's *ActiveX* technology is just a repackaging of existing technologies. In fact, ActiveX is a stripped-down version of Microsoft's object linking and embedding (OLE) and component object model (COM) architectures, two highly successful Windows programming components that allow multiple programs to interact, exchange data, and share each other's windows. As such, ActiveX is also a system and a corresponding API for downloading executable code over the Internet. The code is bundled into a single file called *ActiveX control*. In general, a file carrying an ActiveX control has the extension .ocx.

ActiveX controls are small programs that can be written in any programming language, including Java. They are automatically downloaded and installed as needed, then automatically deleted when no longer required. Consequently, an ActiveX control is conceptually similar to a dynamic plug-in that is downloaded along with its data and run, and then discarded. However, in spite of the similarities between ActiveX controls and dynamic plug-ins, there are at least two fundamental differences:

- Whereas plug-ins are usually used to extend a browser so that it can accommodate a new document type, most ActiveX controls used to date have brought a new functionality to a specific Web page just like Java applets;

- Also like Java applets, most ActiveX controls are downloaded and run automatically, whereas Netscape plug-ins must be manually installed.

ActiveX controls can be digitally signed using Microsoft's Authenticode technology (as explained in the previous section). Microsoft Internet Explorer, for example, can be configured to disregard any ActiveX control that isn't properly signed, to run only ActiveX controls that have been signed by specific software publishers, or to accept ActiveX controls signed by any registered software publisher.

Like Java applets, ActiveX controls are typically displayed within the browser window as live inline images. They can do all the things that Java applets can do, including simple tasks, such as creating animations, acting as viewers for data of specific MIME types, interacting with mouse and keyboard, creating windows, reading and writing data from the user's clipboard, scanning the hard disk, or even turning off the computer.

The syntax for incorporating an ActiveX control into an HTML document is similar to that for incorporating a Java applet. In fact, the <OBJECT> tag is used to identify the name of the ActiveX control, the URL of the directory that contains it, an ID attribute that contains a unique hexadecimal serial number, and some other parameters. The serial number allows an ActiveX control to be downloaded automatically from one of several ActiveX control archives and repositories that are located all over the world. Like inline images and Java applets, ActiveX controls developed and maintained at one site can be incorporated into HTML documents on another site. Also like Java applets, the ActiveX control is passed as runtime information in a series of <PARAM> tags. This allows the developer to customize the behavior of an ActiveX control.

In general, there are two kinds of ActiveX controls: the ones that contain native machine code and the ones that contain Java bytecode. The first controls are written in programming languages, such as C, C++, or Visual Basic. The control's source code is compiled into an executable that is downloaded to the browser and executed on the client machine. Contrary to that, the second controls are written in Java or any other programming language that can be compiled into Java bytecode. These controls are downloaded to the browser and executed in the browser's JVM. Note that the two different kinds of ActiveX controls have fundamentally different security implications.

- In the first case, the ActiveX technology is simply a means to download and run a native machine code program on the client machine. It is up to the programmer to decide whether to follow the ActiveX APIs, whether to use the operating system APIs, or whether to attempt direct manipulation of the computer system's resources. In general, there is no easy way to properly audit the ActiveX control functions on contemporary operating systems.

- In the second case, ActiveX controls that are downloaded as Java bytecode can be subject to all of the same restrictions that normally apply to Java applets. Consequently, these controls can be run by the browser within a sandbox. Alternatively, a browser can grant these controls specific privileges, such as the ability to read and write within a specific directory or to initiate network connections to specific IP addresses. Perhaps most importantly, the actions of such an ActiveX control can be properly audited (if the Java runtime environment allows such auditing).

In spite of the fact that ActiveX support has been ported to a variety of plat forms (in addition to Microsoft Windows), ActiveX controls that are downloade as machine code are processor and operating system dependent. These control are typically compiled for a particular processor and with a particular set of APIs Contrary to that, ActiveX controls that are written in Java can be processor and operating system independent.

In practice, ActiveX controls that are downloaded as machine code are predomi- nant. From the point of view of software developers and Web users, they have three important advantages [10]:

- First and foremost, developers can use the programming languages and compilers with which they are familiar;

- Second, developers can draw on their existing repository of application programs, OLE components, and libraries, allowing them to bring ActiveX controls to mar- ket faster;

- Third, ActiveX controls can do anything (meaning that they are not restricted by a sandbox).

Obviously, the third point illustrates that ActiveX controls are risky from a security point of view. If the ActiveX controls can do anything, they can also trash files (or entire file systems), reformat hard disks, probe firewalls, install viruses, or do anything an attacker may dream of. Once an ActiveX control is running on a system, it has the ability to do anything that any other full-fledged program can do. While this makes ActiveX controls very powerful, it also makes them potentially very dangerous. An ActiveX control written for malicious purposes may compromise the users' privacy or damage computer systems in overt or subtle ways. In fact, the risks of ActiveX controls have been demonstrated on several occasions. Refer to [3] for an overview of some security-related incidents. The most prominent incident that shocked many users of the ActiveX technology occurred in February 1997, when Lutz Donnerhacke, a member the famous Chaos Computer Club (CCC) located in Germany, demonstrated an ActiveX control that could initiate electronic funds transfers using the European version of the Quicken software for home banking. With this version of Quicken, it is possible to initiate a transfer directly from one bank account to another. Donnerhacke's ActiveX control started up a copy of Quicken on the user's computer and recorded an electronic funds transfer in the user's checking account ledger. Written in Visual Basic as a demonstration tool for a German television station, the ActiveX control did not attempt to hide its actions. Consequently, it is possible and very likely that sooner or later similar ActiveX controls will occur that are made more stealthy.

As introduced in Section 9.5, Authenticode is a technology and a fully operational system developed by Microsoft to let users verify the identity of the author of a particular ActiveX control, and to let them determine whether the control has been modified since the first time it was distributed. The Authenticode technology makes use of digital signatures and public key certificates. More precisely, Authenticode describes a series of file formats for signing Microsoft 32-bit `.exe`, `.cab`, `.dll`, and `.ocx` files (Authenticode cannot be used to sign Windows `.com` files or 16-bit `.exe` files). A signed file contains the original unsigned file, the digital signature, and an X.509v3 digital certificate for the public key needed to verify the Authenticode signature. To publish software with Authenticode support, it is necessary to have a copy of the Microsoft ActiveX Software Developer's Kit (SDK).

Authenticode signatures can be used for different purposes depending on whether the ActiveX control is distributed in binary machine code or JVM bytecode:

- For ActiveX controls distributed in binary machine code, an Authenticode signature can be used to enforce a simple decision: either download the control or do not download the control;

- For ActiveX controls distributed in JVM bytecode, an Authenticode signature can additionally be used to determine what access permissions are given to the Java bytecode when it is running in the JVM.

If an ActiveX control mixes binary machine code and JVM bytecode, or if both binary machine code and JVM bytecode controls are resident on the same Web page, the capabilities-controlled access permitted by the Java system is disabled. Also, Authenticode signatures are only verified when a control is downloaded from the Internet. If the control resides on the local file system, it is assumed to be trustworthy and safe to run. In this case, the ActiveX control is given unrestricted access to the system.

Obviously, code signing as implemented by the Authenticode technology (or the object signing system in Netscape Communication's terminology) is an important tool for certifying the authenticity and integrity of program code. However, code signing does not provide "safety," as it is implied by Microsoft Internet Explorer's control panel. It is important to note that code signing does not provide users with a safe environment where they can run their program code. Instead, it provides users with some audit trail, so that if a program misbehaves, it should be possible to interrogate the signed program code and decide whom to sue. Unfortunately, security through code signing is not that simple and has many shortcomings.

- First, the damage that an ActiveX control does may not be immediately visible. In fact, an ActiveX control may be used to install a trapdoor (a hidden access to secret data or services);

- Second, the Authenticode technology does not protect a user against bugs and software manipulations (e.g., computer viruses);

- Third, the Authenticode software (and its validation routines), as well as the audit trails, are vulnerable in the sense that once a signed ActiveX control is running, it may erase the audit trail that would allow the user to identify the author (unless the "prompt" option had been chosen where the user would be told beforehand who had signed it).

Earlier in this chapter, we said that the aim of code signing technologies is to trace back a malicious piece of software downloaded into a browser to its original publisher, who may be held accountable and be subject to litigation. We should mention that the degree to which a user of maliciously signed code can litigate against a software vendor heavily depends on the supporting legal structure, the type of certificate the vendor used to digitally sign the code, and a number of other factors. For example, on June 17, 1997, Fred McLain released an ActiveX control called Exploder Control on one of his personal Web pages.[12] When downloaded to a computer that has a power conservation BIOS, the Exploder Control shuts down Windows 95, and turns off the computer. Later, McLain obtained an Individual Software Publisher Digital ID from VeriSign, signed his ActiveX control, and reposted it on the Web page. McLain was soon to lose his certificate. Because he violated his contractual agreements associated with his software publisher certificate when he used it to sign malicious code, VeriSign unilaterally revoked the software publisher certificate. Note, however, that this was a futile act since very few people bother to retrieve and actually check CRLs at all. Consequently, hardly anyone knew that McLain's software publisher certificate was revoked. Also note that McLain's Exploder Control incited a flurry of controversy about the usefulness and effectiveness of code and object signing technologies. In fact, it showed that without automatic certificate revocation checking, these technologies are almost valueless (refer to Section 8.4 for a comprehensive overview about certificate revocation techniques).

---

[12]`http://www.halcyon.com/mclain/ActiveX/welcome.html`

9.7   IMPLICATIONS FOR FIREWALLS

The main thesis of this chapter is that executable or active content is a dangerous thing, and that one should try to avoid it in the first place. Unfortunately, it is not always possible to avoid executable or active content. In this case, one should at least think about strategies and possibilities to block executable or active content at a corporate firewall. Note that if intranet users run executable or active content obtained from outside the firewall (e.g., through the use of binary mail attachments, executable or active content that is retrieved through HTTP requests that are not blocked at the firewall, or even through the use of floppy disks), the firewall must treat insiders as adversaries. This changes the firewall's role in the overall security landscape dramatically.

Against this background, several strategies have been developed and are being implemented to block executable or active content at the firewall. For example, in the case of a proxy-based firewall, *response content filtering* may be used [11]. In response content filtering, the proxy server actually looks at the content of HTTP response messages. Typically, content filters are designed specifically for a certain type of executable content, and are invoked only if the MIME content type matches one of the content types for which the filter has been configured.

The following examples illustrate some possible response blocking and content filtering mechanisms:

- *Java applet blocking* mechanisms prevent Java applets from being downloaded to computer systems located behind a firewall. A simple strategy takes advantage of the fact that all Java class files begin with the 4-byte hex signature **CA, FE, BA,** and **BE** (according to the JVM specification). The strategy is to prevent all inbound files beginning with this signature from being forwarded by the firewall. By proxying HTTP, FTP, and Gopher, such transfers can be detected and blocked. Another commonly-suggested strategy is to reject all browser requests via HTTP, FTP, and Gopher for files with names ending in .`class`. This strategy once enjoyed most of the advantages of the previous strategy, even though there was never any requirement in the JVM specification that class files actually have the suffix .`class`. Unfortunately, both strategies can block neither JavaScript code nor ActiveX controls. Because of JavaScript's inline nature, blocking JavaScript code at the firewall turns out to be difficult.

- *HTML tag filtering* mechanisms allow certain HTML tags to be removed from HTML documents (applicable for documents of MIME type `text/html`). This is used in the same way as other filtering mechanisms to prevent the exploitation of known security holes and bugs. For example, it is possible to filter out embedded objects from HTML documents, such as Java applets, ActiveX controls, or JavaScript code. In the case of Java applets, for example, it is possible to scan the HTML documents for `<APPLET>` tags and rewrite them in a more benign form. The firewall toolkit originally developed by Trusted Information Systems, Inc. (TIS) has been extended accordingly [12]. Similarly, it is possible to scan the HTML documents for tags that are used to incorporate JavaScript code and ActiveX controls.

- *Virus scanning* allows downloaded programs to be scanned for known computer viruses (applicable for documents of MIME type `application/octet-stream`). By restricting the application of this technology, HTML and ASCII text transfer performance remains unaffected by computer virus scanning.

- Similar to virus scanning, various forms of *code scanning* allow specialized analysis of executable content, such as Java applets and ActiveX controls, inspecting what function calls are made and determining whether they are allowed or not. For example, a software called SurfinGate (developed by Finjan Software[13]) performs this sophisticated type of filtering. Unfortunately, it is not easily decidable whether a specific code segment is malicious or not (we will restate this fact at several places throughout the book).

Each of these strategies is most easily implemented in an application-level gateway or proxy server. None of the strategies can be implemented with a packet filter alone, since each requires interpreting a part of the data stream that must be found by context. Also, none of the strategies can prevent applets already available through the client's file system from running. Finally, it is important to note that encrypted data traffic cannot be parsed or scanned by a proxy server. This poses some interesting problems with regard to the simultaneous use of cryptographic security protocols, such as IPsec or SSL/TLS, and scanning and filtering technologies. In the long term, one can reasonably expect the problem related to downloadable, executable, or active content to be dealt with at the end systems (similar to the problems related to computer viruses).

9.8 CONCLUSIONS

In this chapter, we focused on potential risks related to executable (or active) content. Fortunately, these risks represent more a potential problem than a real one.

---

[13]`http://www.finjan.com`

In fact, a variety of malicious Java applets and ActiveX controls have been demonstrated, but few serious attacks have actually been reported so far. This will probably change as knowledge on programming executable or active content becomes more common and widespread. One can reasonably expect executable or active content to be essential for the next generation of intranet software and groupware applications.

Most incidents that have occurred in practice have launched a denial-of-service attack. Note that any programming or scripting language or environment that allows systemwide resources to be allocated, and then places no limitations on the allocation of these resources, is subject to denial-of-service attacks. But the languages addressed in this chapter seem to be especially suitable for denial-of-service attacks, apparently because their authors have not considered denial-of-service attacks to be serious threats, and because it is very difficult (if not impossible) to fully protect against denial-of-service attacks. In Section 11.2 we briefly address a programming language for mobile code called Telescript that controls the use of systemwide resources by giving each process a limited supply of funds (so-called "teleclicks"), and requiring a process to expend a certain quantity of teleclicks in order to accomplish specific results, such as spawning new copies of itself. This approach can at least be used to protect against certain denial-of-service attacks. The languages addressed in this chapter do not make use of this (or a similar) concept. In fact, code segments written in these languages can easily command large amounts of system resources, and there are few possibilities for a user who is under attack to regain control of the system. To make things worse, there is nothing even resembling process control within most Web browser environments. The only way to interrupt a running piece of code is generally to kill and shut down the browser (this is a suitable protection mechanism).

In the spring of 1996, a group of researchers at Princeton University searched for and found a number of security problems in the Java programming language. The team christened themselves the *Secure Internet Programming* (SIP) group and has published several bulletins informing users of the problems they found.[14] They also worked with Sun Microsystems, Microsoft, and Netscape Communications to correct the problems they discovered. An overview about the bugs in the Java runtime system and some early design flaws in the Java language itself are overviewed in [3]. While most of the basic implementation flaws have been fixed, new features and releases will eventually bring new bugs. Note, for example, that the size of the JDK software distribution steadily increases, and that the probability for new

---

[14]http://www.cs.princeton.edu/sip/

bugs behaves similarly. Also, other programming languages addressed earlier in this chapter have similar problems. In general, software manufacturers need to be more open with their internal reviews, and they need to slow down the pace of development so that software can be evaluated more rigorously before it is used on a global scale. But in practise the opposite is happening due to market forces (this argument is recapitulated later in this book). Meanwhile, users who view security as a primary concern are well advised to disable executable content by their browsers. This is especially true for new and evolving technologies, such as provided by dynamic HTML, extensible markup language (XML[15]), and virtual reality modeling language (VRML[16]). The security implications of these technologies have not yet been thoroughly investigated.

REFERENCES

[1] A.D. Rubin, "Location-Independent Data/Software Integrity Protocol," Request for Comments 1805, June 1995.

[2] A.D. Rubin, "Trusted Distribution of Software Over the Internet," *Proceedings of Internet Society Symposium on Network and Distributed System Security*, February 1995, pp. 47 – 53.

[3] S. Garfinkel, and E.H. Spafford, *Web Security & Commerce*, O'Reilly & Associates, Sebastopol, CA, 1996.

[4] I. Goldberg, D. Wagner, R. Thomas, and E.A. Brewer, "A Secure Environment for Untrusted Helper Applications," *Proceedings of USENIX Security Symposium*, July 1996, pp. 1 – 13.

[5] P. Lomax, *Learning VBScript*, O'Reilly & Associates, Sebastopol, CA, 1997.

[6] D. Flanagan, *Java in a Nutshell*, 2nd Edition, O'Reilly & Associates, Sebastopol, CA, 1997.

[7] S. Oaks, *Java Security*, O'Reilly & Associates, Sebastopol, CA, 1998.

[8] J. Knudsen, *Java Cryptography*, O'Reilly & Associates, Sebastopol, CA, 1998.

[9] J. Feghhi, J. Feghhi, and P. Williams, *Digital Certificates: Applied Internet Security*, Addison-Wesley Longman, Reading, MA, 1999.

[10] L.D. Stein, *Web Security: A Step-by-Step Reference*, Addison-Wesley, Reading, MA, 1998.

[11] A. Luotonen, *Web Proxy Servers*, Prentice Hall PTR, Upper Saddle River, NJ, 1998.

[12] D.M. Martin, S. Rajagopalan, and A.D. Rubin, "Blocking Java Applets at the Firewall," *Proceedings of Internet Society Symposium on Network and Distributed System Security (SNDSS '97)*, February 1997.

---

[15]http://www.w3.org/XML/
[16]http://vrml.sdsc.edu/

Chapter 10

CGI and API Scripts

In this chapter, we address CGI and API scripts as well as their security implications for Web servers. In particular, we introduce the topic in Section 10.1, address safe CGI and API programming in Section 10.2, elaborate on configuring CGI and API scripts in Section 10.3, overview and discuss server-side includes (SSIs) in Section 10.4, and conclude with some final remarks in Section 10.5. Further information on the topic can also be found in many books on Web security. Again, I particularly recommend [1 – 3].

10.1 INTRODUCTION

As we have already mentiond in Chapter 1, a Web server can also run programs in response to incoming HTTP request messages. Originally, these programs were invoked using CGI. In common Web parlance, the term CGI is used to refer to two things:

- On the one hand, CGI refers to a specific programming interface that is used to invoke some additional functionality on the server side;

- On the other hand, CGI also more generally refers to the idea of enabling a given URL to return something dynamic rather than something static.

273

According to its first use, CGI was the first and remains the most popular means of extending the functionality of a Web server. Its syntax is a loosely de facto standard handed down from the NCSA Web server, but CGI has also had a number of proprietary enhancements here and there.

As of this writing, CGI scripts have been written for many applications, including the following:

- To perform database queries and display results;

- To allow Web users to "chat" with one another across the Internet;

- To perform complex financial calculations.

In fact, literally every innovative and interactive use of the WWW was originally written using CGI scripts. Examples range from conventional search engines to more sophisticated Web applications, such as FedEx's tracking system for postal deliveries.[1]

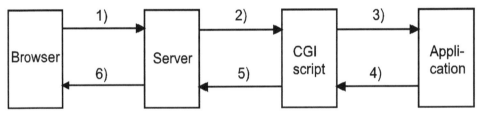

Figure 10.1   The architectural placement of a CGI script between a Web server and a corresponding application.

Figure 10.1 illustrates the architectural placement of a CGI script as an intermediate between a Web server and an application. On the left side we have a browser that wants to make use of a specific application (one that is invoked though a CGI script). In step 1, the browser connects to the Web server and requests a URL that invokes a CGI script. In step 2, the Web server invokes the CGI script, and in step 3, the CGI script invokes the requested application. The application, in turn, may produce some output as a result. This output is then returned to the CGI script, the Web server, and the browser in steps 4, 5, and 6.

In general, CGI scripts may be written in any programming language. All that is required is that they be able to read from the standard input (**stdin**), write to the standard output (**stdout**), and have access to arguments that the

Web server prepares. Most CGI scripts are written in interpreted scripting and programming languages that are supposed to be fast and easy to use, such as Perl,[2] the Tool Control Language (Tcl), Java, and Python.[3] As of this writing, Perl is by far the most popular language for CGI scripting (note that when evaluating a language for CGI scripting, security is usually not the only criterion that is taken into consideration).

Table 10.1

CGI Environment Variables from Web Server to CGI Script (in Alphabetical Order)

Environment Variable	Meaning
GATEWAY_INTERFACE	Revision of the CGI specification
SERVER_NAME	Hostname, DNS alias, or IP address of the Web server
SERVER_SOFTWARE	Name and version of the Web server software
AUTH_TYPE	User authentication method
CONTENT_LENGTH	Length of content data
CONTENT_TYPE	Type of content data
PATH_INFO	Anything left after the CGI script name from URL
PATH_TRANSLATED	PATH_INFO mapped to physical path
QUERY_STRING	String that follows the question mark in the URL (undecoded)
REMOTE_ADDR	IP address of the host making the request
REMOTE_HOST	Name of the host making the request
REMOTE_IDENT	Remote username (where applicable)
REQUEST_METHOD	Requested method, such as GET or POST
SCRIPT_NAME	Virtual path to the CGI script
SERVER_PORT	Port number of the request
SERVER_PROTOCOL	Name and revision of the requesting protocol

Contrary to Figure 10.1, a CGI script typically runs as subtask of the Web server that hosts it. Arguments are supplied in environment variables to the script's standard input, whereas results are returned on the script's standard output. The CGI environment variables sent from the Web server to the CGI are summarized in Table 10.1. The first three environment variables are set for all HTTP requests, whereas all other environment variables are set for specific HTTP requests. In addition, the browser may also send HTTP headers of its own to the CGI script running on the Web server. If the browser does so, the server packages the browser inputs into CGI environment variables with the prefix "HTTP_" followed by the header name and

---

[2]http://www.perl.com

[3]http://www.python.org

passes them right along with the CGI environment variables mentioned above. Incidentally, any dash character ("-") in the header name is changed to an underscore character ("_"). Table 10.2 summarizes the resulting CGI environment variables provided by the browser. Note, however, that the Web server is not required to handle all possible client headers. Though it will generally pass them through, the Web server is free to exclude any headers that it has already processed, and it may exclude any headers if including them would exceed system limits.

In addition to the CGI environment variables itemized in Tables 10.1 and 10.2, SSL-enabled Web servers generally set several additional environment variables when SSL is active. CGI scripts are free to use these variables for any purpose. For example, a CGI script that provides access to a database with confidential material could abort, unless a certain type of cipher suite were used. Refer to the manual of your SSL-enabled Web server for an overview of SSL-related environment variables.

Table 10.2
CGI Environment Variables from Browser to CGI Script (in Alphabetical Order)

Environment Variable	Meaning
HTTP_ACCEPT	Type and subtype list of acceptable MIME types
HTTP_USER_AGENT	Software and version as well as library and version of browser
HTTP_REFERER	Last visited URL
HTTP_*	Other variables sent by browser

Among the information the Web server provides to the CGI script is the one encoded in the QUERY_STRING environment variable. It usually contains information provided by the remote user and is the user's sole means for passing data to the CGI script. The contents of the QUERY_STRING environment variable is arbitrary. For example, it may contain a list of keywords for a search engine or an SQL expression for use by a database gateway. In either case, query strings may be sent to CGI scripts in two different ways:

- One way is to append the query strings directly to the CGI script's URL. An example may looks as follows:

```
http://www.testsite.com/cgi-bin/do_search?search=Rolf+Oppliger
```

In this URL, everything after the question mark ("?") includes the query string, in this case the phrase "search=Rolf+Oppliger." Because it is part of a URL, it has to follow the URL syntax rules, such as replacing spaces with the plus character ("+"). The CGI script, in turn, recovers the query string by examining the environment variable QUERY_STRING. This way of sending query strings to CGI scripts uses the standard HTTP GET method to request URLs and is typically used by older CGI scripts.

- Another way is to directly send the query string to the CGI script's URL using the HTTP POST method. In this case, the Web server sends the query string directly to the CGI script's standard input. The POST method is usually called in response to the user filling out and submitting an HTML form that basically looks as follows:

```
<FORM ACTION="/cgi-bin/do_search" METHOD=POST>
Search string: <INPUT TYPE="text" NAME="search"><P>
<INPUT TYPE="submit" VALUE="Search">
</FORM>
```

When this HTML code is received by a browser, a simple fill-out form is usually displayed. If the user types in "Rolf Oppliger" into the text field and presses the "Search" button, the contents of the form are submitted to the URL /cgi-bin/do_search, as indicated by the HTML form ACTION attribute, using the HTTP POST method, as indicated by the form's METHOD attribute. Afterwards, the CGI script finds the following query string on its standard input:

```
search=Rolf+Oppliger
```

In general, the Web server's configuration settings define how CGI scripts are executed. There are two ways of configuring a Web server: It is either configured so that a particular directory contains all CGI scripts, or a certain filename extension is declared to always identify executable CGI scripts (or both). For example, the typical installed Apache server will be looking for the subdirectory cgi-bin in the server root or for filenames ending with .cgi. This issue is what is known as "script-aliased CGI" versus "non-script-aliased CGI."

- *Non-script-aliased CGI* means that CGI programs may appear in any directory as long as the filename extension corresponds to the one defined in the server's configuration settings;

- Contrary to that, *script-aliased CGI* means that CGI programs may appear only in an explicitly configured directory, typically the subdirectory `./cgi-bin` in the root directory of the Web server.

For obvious reasons, script-aliased CGI is the more common approach for security-minded Web sites. Whenever you have the choice, make script-aliased CGI your standard configuration. Having only one directory to look for CGI scripts is better from a security point of view. To use script-aliased CGI, you must first specify the server root in the global Web server configuration file (using the `ServerRoot` directive), and then declare the use of script-aliased CGI (using the `ScriptAlias` directive).

Unfortunately, the use of CGI scripts is not very efficient because a separate process is started for each incoming HTTP request and Web transaction. Consequently, some vendors, including Microsoft and Netscape Communications, suggest that you do something else by the time you get to high-frequency applications. In fact, both vendors suggest that you compile and link your applications directly into the running Web server binaries via their proprietary application programming interfaces (APIs), namely ISAPI and NSAPI. As a result, the applications have access to the Web server's data structures and internal functions. This makes them faster and more powerful than common CGI scripts. Unfortunately, it also gives them the ability to crash the Web server if they are not properly written (unlike CGI scripts, user data is sent to the server directly in memory structures rather than through environment variables or standard input). In summary, compiling and linking application programs directly into a running Web server binary is mostly about avoiding the cost of restarting a CGI script over and over again. There is no intentional effect on what the previously scripted application can and cannot do. In essence, it just saves the overhead of process invocation at the cost of some reprogramming.

With regard to the security implications of API scripting (ISAPI, NSAPI, or any other API), it is important to note that data of all kinds are available to CGI-based applications on the Web server so long as the applications have sufficient privileges and rights to access the file system. In general, it is good practice to avoid an application reaching any file whose disclosure or modification could itself affect the security of the Web server (process). Against this background, API scripts pose some fairly serious security risks. In fact, security holes in a bound-in application will endanger the server, and security holes in the server will endanger the application. If any such hole is successfully exploited, any data owned or handled by the Web server is endangered as well. According to [2], binding applications into the running Web server is like roping mountain climbers together. If everyone is competent, it saves much. If anyone on the rope is a fool, all perish. There are at least two conclusions to draw:

- First, you should never bind your code into a running Web server of which you cannot inspect the internals;

- Second, if you are going to bind applications into a running Web server, then you have even stronger reason to run the server with few privileges.

In summary, CGI and API scripts are easy to write, easy to install, and easy to use. Popular Web sites make heavy use of them, and some have hundreds of custom scripts installed. But a CGI or API script's main blessing is also its biggest curse: the scripts are so easy to write that many of them are created by programmers with no prior experience in network programming and little appreciation of security issues. Consequently, the list of security holes in CGI and API scripts is long and steadily growing. In fact, many CGI and API scripts have had flaws that allowed attackers to compromise the security of Web servers or machines that hosted them. Some of these flaws have been found and corrected, whereas others still wait for their discovery and exploitation. Safe CGI and API programming is addressed next.

10.2 SAFE CGI AND API PROGRAMMING

Many people argue that secure CGI (and API) programming is contradictory, and that it's simply not possible to use the word "secure" in the same sentence as "CGI programming" or "API programming." They would say that if a program's arguments are supplied from unknown parties over the Internet, then surely there will be a security flaw in the program, and just as surely, there will be people that find it. Consequently, we are not going to address secure CGI and API programming, but rather focus on safe CGI and API programming in this section; this is easier to achieve.

According to [3], there are five problem areas and failure modes for CGI scripts. These areas are briefly discussed next.

- *Misusing interpreters as CGI scripts:* A number of Internet security incidents have been the result of Webmasters who carelessly installed a powerful command interpreter, such as a Perl, Tcl, or Java interpreter, a UNIX command shell, or a DOS/NT command interpreter, in the CGI scripts directory. For example, if you place a Perl interpreter in the CGI scripts directory, any user can execute Perl scripts by simply invoking them with corresponding URLs. More precisely, if you place a Perl interpreter `perl.exe` together with a Perl CGI script `search.pl` in the CGI scripts directory of the Web server hosted at `www.victim.com`, any user can invoke it through the following URL:

```
http://www.victim.com/cgi-bin/perl.exe?search.pl
```

Unfortunately, this configuration also allows anyone on the Internet to run arbitrary Perl commands on the Web server machine. In fact, anybody can request the following URL from the victim's Web server:

```
http://www.victim.com/cgi-bin/perl.exe?-e+%27unlink+%3C*%3E%27
```

Following the protocol for unescaping URLs, the Web server would transform this expression into the shell command `perl -e unlink '<*>'`, which represents a Perl command to delete all files in the current directory. Whether the command is successful depends on whether the server's user permissions allow it to make the delete operations. Consequently, all command interpreters, shells, and language interpreters should be excluded from the CGI scripts directory, and only programs designed to be CGI scripts should actually be installed there.

- *Flawed memory management:* Flawed memory management has been responsible for the opening of security holes in a number of Internet and Web server programs. For example, it was responsible for a hole in older versions of NCSA `httpd`. By requesting very long URLs to the server, remote users could execute arbitrary shell commands on the server. The most common example of a memory management flaw or bug is the use of a statistically allocated memory buffer, followed by the failure to check the length of a data structure before moving it into the buffer. In fact, this flaw or bug has a fairly long tradition within the Internet programming community. It is primarily the domain of compiled programs, such as C and C++ language executables. Programming languages that perform memory management internally, such as Perl, Java, and Python, are immune to this type of problem (provided the language interpreter itself is free of bugs).

- *Passing unchecked user input to command interpreters:* Authors of CGI scripts often assume that users behave properly and play by the rules (meaning that they type in only valid information, that file names will only contain legal characters, or that they won't peek at secret CGI parameters contained inside "hidden" form fields. Unfortunately, none of these assumptions is true, and the largest class of

CGI scripting bug involves failures to perform validity checking on user-supplied input data. The most serious ramification of this bug occurs when unchecked user input is passed to a command shell, allowing remote users to execute shell commands on the machine hosting the Web server. In fact, this bug has surfaced many times in both commercial and freeware software. A typical example of this bug crops up in Perl CGI scripts designed to send an e-mail message to an address entered in a fill-out form. In UNIX, it's comparably easy to do this by opening a pipe to the `mail` command and printing the body of the e-mail message to the pipe. Assume that `param` is a function that extracts named fields from the CGI query string, then a corresponding Perl script segment may look as follows (the example is taken from [3]):

```
$address = param('address');
$subject = param('subject');
$message = param('message');
open(MAIL,"| /bin/mail -s '$subject' $address");
print MAIL $message;
close MAIL;
```

The script segment first uses `param` to recover the e-mail address, subject line, and body of the message. It then opens a pipe to the `mail` command, using the `-s` flag to specify a subject line and passing the recipient's e-mail address on the command line. The script prints the body of the message to the pipe, then closes it. When the pipe is closed, the mail command delivers the message. The script is intended to be called from a fill-out form that may look as follows:

```
<FORM ACTION="/cgi-bin/handle_mail" METHOD=POST>
To: <INPUT TYPE="text" NAME="address"> <P>
Subject: <INPUT TYPE="text" NAME="subject"> <P>
Message: <TEXTAREA NAME="message" ROWS=5></TEXTAREA> <P>
<INPUT TYPE="submit" VALUE="Send Mail">
</FORM>
```

If the user types `rolf.oppliger@bfi.admin.ch` into the "To:" field, and `Test` into the "Subject:" field, the CGI script opens a pipe to the following command:

```
/bin/mail -s 'Test' rolf.oppliger@bfi.admin.ch
```

In this case, everything will work as anticipated and the e-mail message will be delivered to my e-mail account. Unfortunately, the script has a problem: it blindly trusts that the e-mail address and subject line provided by the user are valid. Now consider what happens when a malicious user types the string rolf.oppliger@bfi.admin.ch; cat /etc/passwd into the e-mail address field (on UNIX systems, the semicolon character is a metacharacter used to separate multiple commands). In this case, the shell command the script now executes looks as follows:

```
/bin/mail -s 'Test' rolf.oppliger@bfi.admin.ch; cat /etc/passwd
```

The effect of this is to run the anticipated mail command and then execute cat /etc/passwd. This command prints the content of the system password file to its standard output, which is transferred intact to the user's browser. Of course, there's no reason that the same or a similar technique couldn't be used to read the contents of any file on the server host, including HTML documents that are normally protected by access control mechanisms and encrypted in transmit through the SSL or TLS protocol. In fact, variants on this exploit can be used to do many (malicious) things on the host system.

Consequently, the most important thing to do from a security point of view is to sanitize user-supplied input data, and to perform some pattern-matching checks accordingly. For example, a security-minded server administrator should always be aware of shell escape characters in user-supplied input data. The meaning of "be aware" is to "unescape" any data received before it is handed to a command-line program. The "unescape" operation is a standard support program that comes along with Web servers descended from the Mosaic Web server. In this context, "unescape" means to quote the escape characters in the input stream and thereby remove their special "escape" functions. The unescaping process can also be done in specific scripting languages, such as Perl (for tainted variables).[4] Alternatively, it's also possible to just remove forbidden characters or refuse input containing them.

---

[4]The most important security feature of Perl is *taint checks*. When taint checks are turned on, Perl keeps track of all variables that contain information that came from "outside" the program. They are referred to as tainted variables. Any variable that comes into contact with a tainted variable itself becomes tainted. If a CGI script later tries to use a tainted variable in any of a variety of unsafe operations, Perl will complain and abort.

- *Opening files based on unchecked user input:* A somehow related class of security holes arises when unchecked user input is used to derive the name of a file to open for read or write operations. Remote users can exploit this bug to read files that aren't intended for the general public or to overwrite existing files. Again, refer to [3] for examples of programs that are buggy in this sense. As in the previous problem area, it's crucial to check user-supplied input for validity before opening any file (the correct check to perform depends on the operating system and CGI scripting language in use).

- *Writing unchecked user input to disk:* Finally, CGI scripts that autonomously update files in the Web server's document tree based on user input can also run into problems if they fail to check the input carefully. Again refer to [3] for exemplary exploitations of this bug and corresponding countermeasures.

If you take care to carefully address the five problem areas itemized above, you'll have significantly improved the safety and security of your CGI scripts. In addition, CGI scripts should also be written in a way to record all unusual events to an error log. Unusual events include such things as invalid user input, system calls that fail, or file system operations that return error codes.

Simson Garfinkel and Eugene H. Spafford have compiled a list of general principles and rules by which to code [1]. While many of these principles and rules generally apply to software engineering, some of them are especially true for CGI and API programming. The principles and rules are summarized in Table 10.3. In addition, [1] also gives more concrete rules for Perl and C programmers. These rules are not replicated in this book.

10.3 CONFIGURING CGI AND API SCRIPTS

The most important rule for configuring CGI and API scripts is that interpreters, shells, scripting engines, and other extensible programs must never be located on a computer system where they might be invoked by an HTTP request to the Web server. As mentioned before, this is especially true for the `cgi-bin` directory that is often used to collectively place CGI scripts. For example, on Windows-based systems the Perl executable `perl.exe` should never appear in the `cgi-bin` directory. Unfortunately, many Windows-based HTTP servers have been configured this way because it makes it easier to set up Perl scripts. As we've seen in the previous section, programs that are installed in this way allow attackers to run any program they wish on the computer system.

Table 10.3
General Principles and Rules for Safe CGI and API Programming*

No.	Principle or Rule
1	Carefully design the program before you start.
2	Check all values provided by the user.
3	Check arguments that you pass to operating system functions.
4	Check all return codes from system calls.
5	Have internal consistency-checking code.
6	Include lots of logging.
7	Make the critical portion of your program as small and as simple as possible.
8	Read through your code and data files.
9	Rather than depending on the current directory, set it yourself.
10	Test your program thoroughly.
11	Be aware of race conditions.
12	Don't have your program dump core except during your testing.
13	Do not create files in world-writable directories.
14	Don't place undue reliance on the source IP address in the packets of connections you receive (such items may be forged or altered).
15	Include some form of load shedding or load limiting in your server to handle cases of excessive load.
16	Put reasonable time-outs on the real time used by your CGI script while it is running.
17	Put reasonable limits on the CPU time used by your CGI script while it is running.
18	Do not require the user to send a reusable password in plaintext over the network connection.
19	Have your code reviewed by another competent programmer (or two, or even more).
20	Whenever possible, steal code.

* According to [1].

Another serious source of concern are CGI (and eventually API) scripts that are distributed with the Web server software and then later found to have bugs and security flaws. There are many buggy CGI scripts floating around on the Web. According to [3], there are three categories of risk from buggy CGI scripts:

- First, some buggy CGI scripts may unintentionally leak information that will help intruders to break into or gain access to sensitive data;

- Second, some buggy CGI scripts may be tricked into making unauthorized modifications to files on the Web site or the server host machine;

- Third, some buggy CGI scripts may be tricked into executing commands on the Web server hosting machine.

Even big software companies have published CGI scripts containing security holes in the past. To make things worse, Webmasters rarely delete files from the `cgi-bin` directories, making these dangerous scripts persist for a potentially long time. It is possible and very likely that some determined hackers will find and exploit them.

Carefully designed user accounts and corresponding privileges are the first line of defense against buggy CGI scripts. Note that whatever restrictions apply to a Web server apply to its CGI and API scripts, as well. For example, if a Web server runs on a UNIX system that uses a shadowed password file, the Web server user will be unable to read the password file. As a result, a buggy CGI script cannot be tricked into leaking passwords. As a corollary to this, a Web server must never be run with more privileges than it actually needs. A server running with root (in the case of UNIX) or administrator (in the case of Windows NT) privileges has unlimited powers, and so does each of the scripts it hosts. Consequently, controlling Web server privileges is a good first step, but it cannot protect you against all the ways that CGI or API scripts can go wrong. To be safe, scripts must be bug-free.

10.4   SERVER-SIDE INCLUDES

Similar to helper applications that are invoked on the client-side (refer to Section 9.3 for a comprehensive overview about helper applications and plug-ins), an SSI allows an HTML document on a Web server to have the output of arbitrary system commands inserted into it at the moment it is actually returned to the requesting browser. To turn on SSI, you must follow the steps indicated in the manual of your Web server software package.

In general, an SSI in an HTML document looks as follows:

```
<!-#operator arg1="x" arg2="y" ... ->
```

The operator and the various arguments are enumerated in Table 10.3. The security implications and concerns with SSIs are obvious. If an SSI executes a script at runtime with the privileges of the Web server, then the script must not represent a threat to the server. The simplest way to take advantage of a malicious script is through an insider — that is, an individual within the group of people who create and provide the documents for a Web server. Against this background, one of the first defenses against SSI security violations is just to deny access to the **exec** operator while leaving the rest of the SSI system intact. This is generally done by putting in the server options the directive **Options IncludesNOEXEC** rather than the simple directive `Options Includes`. By doing this, you will not be subject to abuse of the `exec` operator at the cost of interactivity and flexibility in SSI writing (the usual tradeoff for security). If, however, you decide to allow the exec operator to be used, then make sure you screen for silly mistakes with argument handling.

Table 10.3
Operators and Arguments for SSIs

Operator	Arguments (meaning)
echo	$DOCUMENT_NAME (echoes current filename)
	$DOCUMENT_PATH (echoes path to the current filename)
	$DATE_LOCAL (echoes current date and time on local host)
	$DATE_GMT (echoes current date and time in Greenwich time)
	$LAST_MODIFIED (echoes lastmod data on current filename)
	plus all the variables that are available to CGI scripts
include	virtual /x/y (includes file /x/y relative to document root)
	file /x/y (includes file /x/y relative to current directory)
fsize	x (echoes bytesize of file x)
flastmod	x (echoes last mod date of file x)
config	errmsg (configures generic error message for SSI failure)
	sizefmt (configures fsize format)
	timefmt (configures time format)
exec	cgi (string treated as path to a CGI script)
	cmd (string passed to **/bin/sh** and executed directly)

For example, as pointed out in [2], let's assume that you let the user input arguments directly to the following code segment:

```
<STRONG>Whom are you looking for?</STRONG>
<!-#exec cmd="finger $QUERY_STRING" ->
```

In this example, you rely on the $QUERY_STRING being consumed entirely by the finger command. Consider what happens if there is a semicolon in $QUERY_STRING. In this case, an arbitrary command could be encoded by the user feeding the SSI in the $QUERY_STRING. Consequently, if you are going to allow SSIs, make sure that you handle any escape characters that may be lurking in input data.

More recently, Jared Karro and Jie Wang from the University of North Carolina at Greensboro have investigated and analyzed security holes concerning the use of SSIs in some of the most widely used Web server software packages, including the latest versions of Apache, Stronghold, Netscape Fast-Track, and Zeus [4]. They empirically showed that, by exploiting the SSI features of these packages, one could seriously compromise the security of these Web servers.

10.5 CONCLUSIONS

In this chapter, we addressed CGI and API scripts as well as their security implications for Web servers. In summary, CGI and API scripts give Web developers and Webmasters the ability to extend the servers' functionalities in many ways. They can generate pages with dynamic content, provide interfaces to databases, run online games, and process customer orders. In fact, CGI and API scripts can do almost anything they like. They have as much access to the hardware devices, file system, and network as any other program, and the operating system itself imposes the main limitation on what a CGI or API script can do. When a script executes, it does so with the identity and privileges of the user account the Web server runs under.

Unfortunately, bugs in CGI scripts have also been a major concern and source of security breaches on the WWW. The scripts are yet seductively easy to write, but they are not easy to write well. In fact, a single bug in a CGI script may expose the Web server and its hosting machine to attack by malicious intruders. There are many buggy CGI scripts floating around on the WWW, and even big companies have occasionally published scripts containing security holes. Again, a general security rule applies to the use of CGI and API scripts: only install CGI and API scripts that are needed by the users of your Web server. Anything else poses an unnecessary security risk.

REFERENCES

[1] S. Garfinkel, and E.H. Spafford, *Web Security & Commerce*, O'Reilly & Associates, Sebastopol, CA, 1996.

[2] A.D. Rubin, D. Geer, and M.J. Ranum, *Web Security Sourcebook*, John Wiley & Sons, Inc., New York, NY, 1997.

[3] L.D. Stein, *Web Security: A Step-by-Step Reference*, Addison-Wesley, Reading, MA, 1998.

[4] J. Karro, and J. Wang, "Protecting Web Servers from Security Holes in Server-Side Includes," *Proceedings of Annual Computer Security Applications Conference (ACSAC '98)*, December 1998, pp. 103 – 111.

Chapter 11

Mobile Code and Agent-Based Systems

In this chapter, we elaborate on mobile code and agent-based systems, as well as their security implications. In particular, we briefly introduce the topic in Section 11.1, and address the two closely related problems of (a) how to protect an execution environment against potentially malicious mobile code and (b) how to protect the mobile code against potentially malicious hosts and execution environments in Sections 11.2 and 11.3. We will see that few technical solutions exist to address the problems. To make things worse, the solutions that exist are contradictory in the sense that some solutions for problem (b) make it more difficult to find appropriate solutions for problem (a). In Section 11.4, we finish up the chapter with some concluding remarks and an outlook.

Contrary to other parts of this book, this chapter is purely theoretical. If you are interested in future computing environments you will want to read on.

11.1 INTRODUCTION

In the recent past, *mobile code technology* has become a major driving force for new applications in computer networks and distributed systems. Making code mobile actually means that complete programs or program segments are exchanged between computer systems, and that the heterogeneity of execution support is hidden by a common language in which the programs or program segments are actually written. According to [1], currently existing mobile code technologies can be divided into two sets:

- *Weakly mobile technologies* allow an application to send (mobile) code to a remote site in order to execute it there, or to dynamically link (mobile) code retrieved from a remote site in order to execute it locally. The transferred code may be accompanied by some initialization data but no migration of execution state is actually involved. The most important example of a weakly mobile technology includes all forms of Java applets. In fact, Java is commonly seen as the programming language of choice for mobile code and agent-based systems (we have elaborated on the security implications of Java and other executable content in Chapter 9). Note, however, that the typical Java applet is mobile only in a very limited sense: it usually travels from a server to a client, executes locally, and disappears after execution. The Java applet itself has no identity and is not uniquely addressable. In particular, there is no execution state being migrated from one execution environment to another.

- Contrary to that, *strongly mobile technologies* allow an executing program or program segment that is running at a particular host to move to a different execution environment on another host. In this case, the execution of the program or program segment is stopped and its code and execution state are both marshaled into a message that is sent to the remote site. The remote site, in turn, resumes the program or program segment from the statement that follows the invocation of the migration primitive. Examples of strongly mobile technologies include Telescript [2], a programming language and architecture for mobile code and agent-based system originally developed at General Magic, Inc. in 1993, and Agent Tcl [3]. While Telescript itself was not commercially successful, the ideas it embodies helped prepare the ground for the Java programming language. Agent Tcl is still in use under its new name D'Agents. Note that strongly mobile technologies allow agents to have identities and be uniquely addressable.

Based on mobile code technology, it is possible to create distributed computing environments where programs or program segments can autonomously move from one computer system to another. Unlike Java applets that are downloaded at a user's request, such mobile software agents decide for themselves when and where to go. Also, they may take execution state with them as they roam through a computer network or distributed system. In the terminology introduced above, mobile software agents generally implement and represent strongly mobile technologies. Various systems have been built and are subject to ongoing research. Some of these systems are still based on the unmodified Java programming language, whereas others use alternative and more sophisticated programming languages.

The general idea behind an *agent-based system* is that principals can have delegated (mobile) agents acting autonomously on their behalf. Consequently, delegation is a fundamental principle when it comes to the wide deployment of agent-based systems.

Agent-based systems are being studied for both military and civil applications. Beyond simple information gathering tasks, mobile agents can also take over commercially relevant tasks, such as price negotiation, contract signing, and delivery of services and immaterial goods. Also, current computer networks and distributed systems are based on the exchange of passive data units. Contrary to that, in active networks each data unit can be replaced by an active mobile code unit that carries data but also instructions telling a network how to process the data unit. Although it induces some processing overhead, this instructional mode of data communications gives the most freedom for realizing customized communication architectures. In the recent past, active networks have become a new field of study in the computer networks and distributed systems area. In fact, the Defense Advanced Research Projects Agency (DARPA) is sponsoring several research and development projects that address this field of study [4].[1] In this book, we are not going to delve into the technical details of active networks. However, keep in mind that many of the things that we are going to say on mobile code and agent-based systems are also true for active networks.

In general, the use and wide proliferation of mobile code and agent-based systems is about to change the computing environments we use and depend on in our daily lifes:

- In the past, we have had centralized computer systems with "dumb" terminals permanently connected to mainframe computers for their applications;

- At present, we have client/server computing with programmed connectivity between user workstations that act as clients and corresponding application and data servers;

- In the future, it is possible that we will have mobile code and agent-based systems that provide support for dynamically brokered interactions between taskable agents and composable network services.

---

[1]http://www.darpa.mil/ito/ResearchAreas/ActiveNetsList.html

The transition from the present client/server computing environment to the future mobile code and agent-based systems environment is in progress. However, the transition progress is also hampered by some nontrivial security issues that arise when mobile code (with or without associated execution state) is moved among execution environments. Some of these issues have been studied in the context of computer networks and distributed system security for a long time. For example, in both the CHRISTMA EXEC incident in December 1987 and the Internet Worm in November 1988, programs overwhelmed the data networks of the time (namely the EARN and the Internet) simply by spawning copies of themselves in ways that the systems were not prepared to deal with. Both programs functioned by arranging them to be executed upon arrival (in the case of the Internet Worm) or upon some simple user action (in the case of CHRISTMA EXEC). Also, in both cases, the advice of the security community was the same:

"Do not allow programs to execute on arrival, and do not make it easy for users to execute programs received across the network."

In the aftermath of the first computer viruses and the two network-related incidents mentioned above, the consensus of the security community was:

"Don't let programs become mobile; it's too dangerous."

Unfortunately, the situation has changed fundamentally since the late 1980s. In fact, support for Java and other programming languages for mobile code and agent-based systems has become mandatory. It is no longer possible for the security community to simply say "don't do it." Instead, the community has to more thoroughly address the security issues related to mobile code and agent-based systems. In [5], David M. Chess points out that mobile code and agent-based systems raise new security issues because they violate a number of assumptions that underlie most existing computer security measures, and that in doing so, they also present a number of new challenges for the design and implementation of computer security systems. More precisely, the mechanisms and technologies that are used to provide access control and communication security services for static programs and program segments must be adapted to take into account mobility. It turns out that key security requirements for mobile code and agent-based systems are the ability to (a) protect the execution environment against potentially malicious mobile code, and (b) protect the mobile code against potentially malicious execution environments. The second requirement is particularly challenging since it is difficult (if not impossible) to protect a program being executed from the environment responsible for its execution. The two key requirements are overviewed and briefly discussed in the following sections.

11.2 PROTECTING THE EXECUTION ENVIRONMENT

The most obvious concern with regard to the security of mobile code and agent-based systems is related to the environment in which the code is assumed to execute. How can the execution environment be protected against potentially hostile actions of mobile code under execution? Our very first examples of mobile code attacks, namely the CHRISTMA EXEC and the Internet Worm incidents, have clearly demonstrated the power of simple replication techniques to cause security problems in computer networks and distributed systems. The problems and some partial solutions have been known for some time, but no perfect solution exists even when the objects being replicated are simple messages. For example, the original Telescript model of mobile code control involved giving each process a limited supply of funds (so-called "teleclicks"), and requiring a process to expend a certain quantity of teleclicks in order to accomplish specific results, such as spawning new copies of itself.[2] On the one hand, this puts some form of restriction on replication by out-of-control programs. On the other hand, however, it may also prevent desirable behavior, as when a process is requiring more funds than it is actually authorized to use.

In many respects mobile code resembles potentially malicious (static) code, such as provided by Trojan horses, computer viruses, and network worms. The good news is that any security technology that can be used to secure mobile code can also be used to secure static code (and vice versa). The bad news is that protection against malicious code (either static or mobile) is hard in theory and practice. For example, in his 1983 ACM Turing Award Lecture, Ken Thompson[3] showed that deciding whether an arbitrary code segment contains a Trojan horse is actually a hard problem [6]. Obviously, this statement also applies for code that is mobile. Consequently, there exists no general routine that can decide for every mobile code segment whether it contains malicious code, and the problem of protecting the runtime environment must be addressed alternatively.

In addition to the technologies that can be used to protect an execution environment against potentially malicious (static) code, such as access control and code

---

[2]Note that teleclicks are conceptually similar to the currencies used in micropayment systems.

[3]Ken Thompson was one of the main developers of the UNIX operating system at AT&T Laboratories.

verification mechanisms, there are only a few approaches that can be used to protect the execution environment against potentially malicious mobile code. In this section, we address sandboxing, digital "shrink-wraps," and the use of a technology called proof-carrying code (PCC). We have already heard about the former two approaches (sandboxing and digital "shrink-wraps") when we addressed security issues related to executable content in Chapter 9. All three approaches can be used individually or combined. It is likely and very possible that alternative approaches will be developed and used in the future. In fact, the field is wide open for further research and development.

11.2.1 Sandboxing

In Chapter 9 we saw that one possibility to protect an execution environment against a potentially malicious mobile code is to restrict the environment in terms of privileges and access rights for the mobile code. Consequently, the mobile code is executed in some sort of "sandbox" where it can damage only a few things. For example, the mobile code may be authorized to draw some funny pictures on the screen or launch animations, but it may not access the local file system or use the network to connect to remote sites.

As we have seen, Sun Microsystems and other vendors that support Java are following the sandboxing approach for the distribution of Java applets [7]. In general, Java applets are executed in a JVM that is controlled by a security policy. The JVM of common browsers, including Netscape Navigator and Microsoft Internet Explorer, is configured in a way that does not allow any access to the local file system for applets that are downloaded over network connections. Also, the security policy does not allow the establishment of TCP connections, except to the site the applet has been downloaded from. This is just a possible security policy, and other security policies may be put in place. As a matter of fact, in the new Java security model it has become possible for an applet to step out of a browser's sandbox under certain conditions (as explained in Chapter 9).

11.2.2 Digital "Shrink-Wrap"

In Chapter 9 we also saw that another approach to protect an execution environment against potentially malicious mobile code is to authenticate the mobile code before it is actually executed. This approach resembles the idea of a digital "shrink-wrap." Although it is not possible to decide whether a given piece of mobile code contains malicious code, one can at least determine whether it is authentically coming from its claimed source. This approach has been pioneered by Microsoft in its Authenticode technology. It has also been adapted by Netscape Communications for its object signing system. In short, a software publisher digitally signs the mobile code and distributes the code together with the certificate that is needed to verify the signature.

Note that the two approaches — sandboxing and digital "shrink-wraps" — are not mutually exclusive and can even be combined to come up with more sophisticated protection schemes (as demonstrated, for example, by Sun Microsystems in its new Java security model).

11.2.3 PCC

More recently, Peter Lee and George C. Necula from the Carnegie Mellon University developed and proposed an alternative technique to protect an execution environment against potentially malicious mobile code [8]. The technique is called PCC.[4] It enables a computer system to determine, automatically and with certainty, that (mobile) code provided by another system is safe to install and execute. The key idea behind PCC is that the system that produces the code (the *code producer*) provides an encoding of a proof that the code adheres to a safety policy defined by the recipient of the code (the *code consumer*).[5] The proof is encoded in a form that is transmitted to the consumer and then quickly validated using a specific proof-checking process.

PCC has many applications, and typical examples of code consumers include trusted applications and Internet hosts that must install and execute (mobile) code. More specifically, PCC is useful in any situation where the safety in the presence of newly installed code is paramount. Note that PCC is generic, and that it is up to the code consumer to define the safety policy. This policy is not limited to a particular notion of safety. It is specified once and for all by the code consumer, in advance of any interaction with mobile code. Once the safety policy is defined, PCC involves a two-stage interaction process:

- In the first stage, the code consumer receives the untrusted code and extracts from it a safety predicate that can be proved only if the execution of the code does not violate the safety policy. This predicate is then sent to the proof producer who proves it and returns its proof back to the consumer.

---

[4]http://foxnet.cs.cmu.edu/people/petel/papers/pcc/pcc.html

[5]In its most general form PCC involves, in addition to a code consumer and code producer, also a *proof producer*. In practice, it often turns out that the code producer and proof producer are the same.

- In the second stage, the code consumer checks the validity of the proof using a simple and fast proof checker. If the proof is found to be a valid proof of the safety predicate, then the untrusted code becomes trusted (not to violate the security policy). As such, it can safely be installed and executed.

A PCC session starts with the code producer preparing the untrusted code to be sent to the code consumer. As part of this preparation phase, the code producer adds annotations to the code (this can be done manually or automatically by a tool). The annotations contain information that helps the code consumer understand the safety-relevant properties of the code. The code producer then sends the annotated code to the code consumer, requesting its execution. Upon receiving the annotated code, the code consumer uses a tool to perform a first inspection of the code:

- First, the tool checks some simple safety properties of the code (for example, it is verified that all immediate jumps are within the code segment boundaries);

- Second, the tool watches for instructions whose execution might violate the safety policy. When such an instruction is found, the tool emits a predicate that expresses the conditions under which the instruction is safe. Such conditions are called *verification conditions* (and the tool can be seen as a verification condition generator as used in the field of automatic program verification). In principle, any program logic can be used to describe the verification conditions. In its current instantiation, however, PCC uses first-order predicate logic extended with predicate symbols as dictated by the safety properties to be proved. Consequently, this instantiation of PCC can be used to prove any safety or liveness property that can be expressed in first-order predicate logic.

The collection of all verification conditions, together with some additional control flow information, make up the *safety predicate*. A copy of the safety predicate is sent to the proof producer next. Upon receiving the safety predicate, the proof producer attempts to prove it. If the proof producer is successful, he or she sends an encoding of a formal proof back to the code consumer.[6] Upon receiving the formal proof, the code consumer validates the proof. This validation phase is performed using a program that basically implements a proof checker. In short, the proof checker verifies that each inference step in the proof is a valid instance of one of the axioms and inference rules specified as part of the safety policy. In addition, the

---

[6]Because the code consumer does not have to trust the proof producer, any system can act as a proof producer. In particular, the code producer can also act as the proof producer.

proof checker also verifies that the proof proves the same safety predicate generated previously (this prevents an attacker from circumventing PCC by submitting, for example, a valid proof of a trivial predicate). Finally, after the code has passed all checks, it is trusted not to violate the safety policy. Consequently, it can be safely installed and executed, without any further need for checking during its execution.

The process overviewed above and the details of the implementations of each component of PCC are further discussed in [8]. As such, PCC has the potential to free the execution environment from relying on run-time checking as the sole means of ensuring safety. Also, it provides a viable alternative to sandboxing and digital "shrink-wraps" as discussed earlier in this section. Consequently, PCC is an interesting technology mainly from a theoretical point of view. The major advantage of PCC is that it does not require trust relationships, meaning that the code consumer does not need to trust the code producer. In other words, the consumer does not have to know the identity of the producer, nor does he or she have to know anything about the process by which the code was produced. All of the information that is required to determine the safety or security of the code is included in the code and its proof. The major disadvantage of PCC (and similar technologies), however, is that it requires a thorough understanding of security vulnerabilities to specify adequate safety policies. This understanding is not always available.

11.3 PROTECTING THE MOBILE CODE

The fact that an execution environment may attack a program under execution hardly plays a role in classic computer security. This is because the party that maintains the execution environment generally also employs the program. This situation is fundamentally different in the case of mobile code and agent-based systems. In this case, the mobile code owner and the operator of the execution environment, are in most cases, different parties. This situation automatically leads to the problems of malicious hosts or execution environments and how to protect mobile code against them. In short, a malicious host or execution environment is defined in a general way as a party able to execute an agent that belongs to another party and that tries to attack that agent in some way. For example, the party may try to spy out or manipulate code, data, or control flow, masquerade as another host or execution environment, or return wrong results to system calls issued by the agent [9].

It is commonly agreed that protecting mobile code against malicious hosts and execution environments is not a "nice-to-have" feature but is crucial for agent-based systems to be useful at all. Against this background, it is often argued that mobile code cannot be effectively protected against the execution environment, because the environment has full access to the mobile code, its data, and its execution state. This seems to imply that mobile code requires strong guarantees on the trustworthiness of the executing computer, thus mobile code technology would underline the necessity of a trusted computing base (TCB).

So far, little research has been done on protecting mobile code against malicious hosts and corresponding execution environments. The resulting approaches are classified in three groups:

- The first group of approaches tries to circumvent the problem by not allowing mobile code to move to hosts that are not trusted. According to these approaches, an agent-based system is not open in the sense that everybody can open a host, but only trustworthy parties can operate hosts. The main problem of these approaches is that it is not always clear in advance whether a specific host is trusted. Also, trust may not always be a binary decision (it may happen that only some specific information should be hidden from an otherwise trusted host).

- The second class of approaches uses specialized, tamper-resistant hardware to ensure the integrity of the runtime environments and to protect the mobile code accordingly. Obviously, these approaches require the usage of special hardware in every host, which is currently a too-restrictive (and usually too expensive) requirement.

- Finally, the third class of approaches tries to solve some of the problems related to mobile code protection by setting up restricted environments, deploying cryptographic protocols between the mobile code and a cryptographically "safe haven," and by frustrating potential adversaries by making mobile code tampering difficult. For fairly obvious reasons, these approaches are expensive in terms of computation and communication costs.

Unfortunately, most of these approaches are insufficient because they are either too restrictive or too unreliable. According to [10], the main challenge for mobile code protection is to find answers to the following questions:

- Can mobile code detect if it has been tampered with?

- Can mobile code protect itself against tampering by a malicious host?

- Can mobile code conceal the function it wants to have executed?

• Can mobile code remotely sign a document without disclosing the user's private key?

Currently existing solutions to the problem of protecting mobile code against attacks originating from its execution environment are aimed at prevention or detection. In the following subsections, we briefly overview three approaches that have been proposed so far. The former two — time-limited blackbox security and computing with encrypted functions — are aimed at prevention, whereas the last — cryptographic traces — is aimed at detection. Again, the field is wide open for further research and development.

11.3.1   Time-Limited Blackbox Security

The notion of *blackbox security* to protect mobile code against malicious hosts was first proposed by Fritz Hohl from the University of Stuttgart [9]. The central idea of blackbox security is to generate executable code from a given agent specification that cannot be attacked by read or modification attacks. According to Hohl, an agent is considered to be a blackbox, if at any time the agent code cannot be attacked in the above-mentioned sense, and if only its input and output behavior can actually be observed by the attacker. Unfortunately, there is no known algorithm that can be used to provide this kind of blackbox security (even though the approach addressed in the following subsection — computing with encrypted functions — points in that direction).

Since full blackbox security does not seem possible today, Hohl has redefined the blackbox property definition in a way that differs in the statement about how long the blackbox property should actually be valid. In the revised definition, it is not assumed that the blackbox protection holds forever, but only for a certain known time interval. According to this definition, an agent has the time-limited blackbox property if for a certain known time interval it cannot be attacked in the above-mentioned sense. To make the protection time interval explicit, an expiration time or date may also be attached to the blackbox.

In order to achieve the time-limited blackbox property for mobile agents, Hohl has proposed several conversion algorithms. In short, the task of a conversion algorithm is to generate a new agent out of an original agent, which differs in code and representation but yields the same results. In addition, the newly generated agent is assumed to be hard to analyze. In this context, "hard" means that the analysis required to understand the agent's functionality should take as much time as possible for an arbitrary attacker. Such conversion algorithms are sometimes also called obfuscating or mess-up algorithms. Note that the new agents are then used to replace the old ones. Also note that limited blackbox security does not assume that it is impossible for an attacker to analyze an agent, the analysis only takes a certain amount of time. More specifically, the assumption is that a lower bound for the time interval can be determined and that this lower bound is long enough for most agents to securely reside on one host.

Blackbox security in general, and time-limited blackbox security in particular, is a new approach to address the problem of how to protect mobile code against malicious hosts and runtime environments. As such, it does not protect against every possible attack. For example, it is still possible for the host to deny the execution or to return wrong system call results. Also, it is still possible for an attacker to read or manipulate data and code, but as he or she cannot determine the role of these elements for the application, the attack results are random. However, there remain two problems to be solved for the limited blackbox security approach:

- The first problem is that the protection intervals have to be of "useful" lengths, whereas the attribute "useful" depends on the application in use;

- The second problem is related to the question of how to determine a lower bound for protection intervals from the conversion algorithms.

More recently, Fritz Hohl and Kurt Rothermel also proposed a protocol that can be used to prevent blackbox testing attacks against time-limited blackbox protected mobile agents. In short, a blackbox testing attack executes an agent several times with varying input parameters. After each execution, the attacker observes the effect of the various input parameters. The proposed protocol requires a network registration service running on a trusted host. This requirement makes the deployment of the protocol rather difficult. Refer to [11] for a description of this protocol.

11.3.2   Computing with Encrypted Functions

More recently, Tomas Sander and Christian F. Tschudin further elaborated on the notion of blackbox security and found some interesting results. In two of their papers [10,12], they argue that any cryptographic solution for the mobile code protection problem should be subject to the following constraints:

- Mobile code should be allowed to execute in untrusted environments but still have guarantees for its correct execution;

- Mobile code should run autonomously (i.e., without interaction with its originating site);

- Mobile code protection mechanisms should be provably secure.

The twist that shows ways to protect mobile agents according to these requirements is to move away from the assumption that a mobile agent consists of plaintext code and data. There is no intrinsic reason why program must be executed in plaintext form. In the same sense that one can send ciphertext without understanding it, one can have a computer execute a cipherprogram without necessarily understanding it. Sander and Tschudin therefore claim that the general belief about a mobile agent's vulnerabilities is wrong simply because it assumes that a mobile agent consists of plaintext code and data.

Similar to the problem of *computing with encrypted data* (CED) originally addressed by Martin Abadi and Joan Feigenbaum [13], Sander and Tschudin have proposed noninteractive *computing with encrypted functions* (CEF) as a general solution to the security requirements of mobile code. The CEF problem is stated as follows:

"A has an algorithm to compute a function f. B has an input x and is willing to compute $f(x)$ for A, but A wants B to learn nothing substantial about f. Moreover, B should not need to interact with A during the computation of $f(x)$."

For letting A and B work together in the way described above, it is assumed that a function f can be encrypted to some other function $E(f)$. The encryption hides the function f and may contain the encryption of the output data. Using the term $P(f)$ to denote a program that implements the function f, A and B can use the following protocol to implement CEF:

1. A encrypts f;

2. A creates a program $P(E(f))$ which implements $E(f)$;

3. A sends $P(E(f))$ to B;

4. B executes $P(E(f))$ at x;

5. B sends $P(E(f))(x)$ to A;

6. A decrypts $P(E(f))(x)$ and obtains $f(x)$.

Obviously, the challenge is to find encryption schemes for arbitrary functions f. In a first approach, Sander and Tschudin have identified a specific class of functions — polynomials and rational functions — together with encryption schemes that lead to a first nontrivial example of cryptographically hiding a function such that it can nevertheless be executed with a noninteractive protocol. In search of an appropriate name for the new field of study, Sander and Tschudin have originally proposed the term "mobile cryptography" [10]. By varying a definition of cryptography given in [14], they have defined mobile cryptography as "the study of mathematical techniques related to aspects of information security of mobile executable code in a network."

As of this writing, CEF does not (yet) provide a general solution for the main problem of mobile code protection. Instead, it provides some evidence that the notion of blackbox security for mobile code may in fact be possible. It is possible and very likely that the field will be further explored by theoretical computer scientists and cryptographers in the future.

11.3.3   Cryptographic Traces

Both limited blackbox security and computing with encrypted functions are aimed at prevention. Contrary to that, Giovanni Vigna from the Politecnico di Milano, Italy, has developed a mechanism based on execution tracing and cryptography that allows one to detect attacks against code, state, and control flow of mobile agents [15]. More precisely, the mechanism aims at detecting any possible illegal modification of agent code, state, and execution flow. The mechanism is based on post-mortem analysis of data — called traces — that are collected during the execution of mobile code. The traces are then used as a basis for code execution verification. This way, in case of tampering, the agent's owner can prove that the claimed operations could have never been performed by the agent.

11.4   CONCLUSIONS AND OUTLOOK

In this chapter, we have elaborated on security implications of mobile code and agent-based systems. In particular, we have addressed the problems of (a) how to protect an execution environment against potentially malicious mobile code, and (b) how to protect the mobile code against potentially malicious hosts and execution environments. The intrinsic difficulty of problem (b) was first pointed out by Bennet S. Yee in [16]:

"In agent-based computing, most researchers have been concentrating on one side of the security issue: protecting the server from potentially malicious agents (...) The converse side of the agent security problem, however, is largely neglected and needs to be addressed: how do we protect agents from potentially malicious servers?"

This statement is still true. Also, a special word is due to the interdependence between solutions proposed for problems (a) and (b). If either blackbox security or CEF is used to protect mobile code against the execution environment, one obviously loses the possibility to decide whether a specific mobile code segment is malicious or not. In this case, it becomes very difficult if not impossible to make intelligent decisions with regard to the protection of the runtime environment. Consequently, some technical solutions to address problem (b) are contradictory to the possibility of finding appropriate solutions for problem (a), meaning that the solutions for problem (b) make it more difficult to find appropriate solutions for problem (a).

In addition to the language-independent technical solutions overviewed and briefly discussed in the previous sections of this chapter, one can also argue that mobile code security is primarily a language issue and that programming languages for mobile code and agent-based systems should be designed around certain security properties that hold for well-formed programs [17]. While there is some merit in this line of argument, the real world behaves differently. There generally exist some programming languages that are used for mobile code and agent-based systems. Security models and architectures are usually developed as an afterthought and the corresponding mobile code and agent-based systems are extended accordingly. For example, a security model for the IBM Aglets Workbench is described in [18]. In short, the IBM Aglets Workbench lets users create aglets, mobile agents based on the Java programming language.[7] It consists of a development kit for aglets and a platform for their execution [19]. Similarly, a security model for Safe-Tcl is described in [20]. Safe-Tcl is a mechanism for controlling the execution of programs written in the Tcl scripting language. Finally, some security-related issues related to D'Agents, a multiple-language mobile agents system (formerly knows as Agent Tcl [3]), are addressed in [21].

In summary, some research and development activity has recently addressed the issues that surround security in mobile code and agent-based systems. Unfortunately, not all issues have been properly resolved and there remain many questions to be answered before mobile agents can actually become the instrument of choice

---

[7]http://www.trl.ibm.co.jp/aglets/

for large-scale applications. For example, a group of researchers from the MITRE Corporation has used a logic of authentication in distributed systems [22] to address some issues that surround authentication for mobile agents [23]. It is assumed that further theoretical work in this area will be done, and that this kind of work will also stimulate the use and deployment of mobile code and agent-based systems in the future. In the meantime, however, strongly mobile code technologies are not expected to really take off.

REFERENCES

[1] G. Cugola, C. Ghezzi, G.P. Picco, and G. Vigna, "Analyzing Mobile Code Languages," In: J. Vitek, and C.F. Tschudin (Eds.), *Mobile Object Systems: Towards the Programmable Internet*, Springer-Verlag, Lecture Notes in Computer Science 1222, 1997, pp. 93 – 111.

[2] J.E. White, "Telescript Technology: The Foundation for the Electronic Marketplace," General Magic, Inc., Sunnyvale, CA, 1994.

[3] R.S. Gray, "Agent Tcl: A Transportable Agent System," *Proceedings of the CIKM Workshop on Intelligent Information Agents*, Baltimore, MA, 1995.

[4] J.M. Smith, K.L. Calvert, S.L. Murphy, H.K. Orman, and L.L. Peterson, "Activating Networks: A Progress Report," *IEEE Computer*, Vol. 32, No. 4, April 1999, pp. 32 – 41.

[5] D.M. Chess, "Security Issues in Mobile Code," In: G. Vigna (Ed.), *Mobile Agents and Security*, Springer-Verlag, Lecture Notes in Computer Science 1419, 1998, pp. 1 – 14.

[6] K. Thompson, "Reflections on Trusting Trust," *Communications of the ACM*, Vol. 27, No. 8, August 1984, pp. 761 – 763.

[7] S. Oaks, *Java Security*, O'Reilly & Associates, Sebastopol, CA, 1998.

[8] G.C. Necula, and P. Lee, "Safe, Untrusted Agents Using Proof-Carrying Code," In: G. Vigna (Ed.), *Mobile Agents and Security*, Springer-Verlag, Lecture Notes in Computer Science 1419, 1998, pp. 61 – 91.

[9] F. Hohl, "Time Limited Blackbox Security: Protecting Mobile Agents from Malicious Hosts," In: G. Vigna (Ed.), *Mobile Agents and Security*, Springer-Verlag, Lecture Notes in Computer Science 1419, 1998, pp. 92 – 113.

[10] T. Sander, and C. Tschudin, "Towards Mobile Cryptography," International Computer Security Institute (ICSI), TR-97-049, 1997.

[11] F. Hohl, and K. Rothermel, "A Protocol Preventing Blackbox Tests of Mobile Agents," In: R. Steinmetz (Ed.), *Kommunikation in verteilten Systemen*, Springer-Verlag, 1999, pp. 170 – 181.

[12] T. Sander, and C. Tschudin, "Protecting Mobile Agents Against Malicious Hosts," In: G. Vigna (Ed.), *Mobile Agents and Security*, Springer-Verlag, Lecture Notes in Computer Science 1419, 1998, pp. 44 – 60.

[13] M. Abadi, and J. Feigenbaum, "Secure Circuit Evaluation," *Journal of Cryptology*, Vol. 2, No. 1, 1990, pp. 1 – 12.

[14] A. Menezes, P. van Oorschot, and S. Vanstone, *Handbook of Applied Cryptography*, CRC Press, Boca Raton, FL, 1996.

[15] G. Vigna, "Cryptographic Traces for Mobile Agents," In: G. Vigna (Ed.), *Mobile Agents and Security*, Springer-Verlag, Lecture Notes in Computer Science 1419, 1998, pp. 137 – 153.

[16] B.S. Yee, "A Sanctuary for Mobile Agents," *DARPA Foundations for Secure Mobile Code Workshop*, Monterey, CA, March 1997.

[17] D. Volpano, and G. Smith, "Language Issues in Mobile Program Security," In: G. Vigna (Ed.), *Mobile Agents and Security*, Springer-Verlag, Lecture Notes in Computer Science 1419, 1998, pp. 25 – 43.

[18] G. Karjoth, D.B. Lange, and M. Oshima, "A Security Model for Aglets," In: G. Vigna (Ed.), *Mobile Agents and Security*, Springer-Verlag, Lecture Notes in Computer Science 1419, 1998, pp. 188 – 205.

[19] D. Lange, and M. Oshima, *Programming and Deploying Java Mobile Agents with Aglets*, Addison Wesley Longman, 1998.

[20] J.K. Ousterhout, J.Y. Levy, and B.B. Welch, "The Safe-Tcl Security Model," In: G. Vigna (Ed.), *Mobile Agents and Security*, Springer-Verlag, Lecture Notes in Computer Science 1419, 1998, pp. 217 – 234.

[21] R.S. Gray, D. Kotz, G. Cybenko, and D. Rus, "D'Agents: Security in a Multiple-Language Mobile-Agent System," In: G. Vigna (Ed.), *Mobile Agents and Security*, Springer-Verlag, Lecture Notes in Computer Science 1419, 1998, pp. 154 – 187.

[22] B. Lampson, M. Abadi, M. Burrows, and E. Wobber, "Authentication in Distributed Systems: Theory and Practice," *ACM Transactions on Computer Systems*, Vol. 10, 1992, pp. 265 – 310.

[23] S. Berkovits, J.D. Guttman, and V. Swarup, "Authentication for Mobile Agents," In: G. Vigna (Ed.), *Mobile Agents and Security*, Springer-Verlag, Lecture Notes in Computer Science 1419, 1998, pp. 114 – 136.

Chapter 12

Copyright Protection

In the digital world we live in today, copyright protection is becoming increasingly important. In this chapter, we overview and discuss some technologies that can be used to protect and enforce copyrights. In particular, we introduce the topic in Section 12.1, address watermarking and fingerprinting techniques in Sections 12.2 and 12.3, and draw some conclusions in Section 12.4. Note that the topic addressed in this chapter is important from a theoretical point, but that the corresponding digital copyright labeling techniques are not widely deployed in commercial products. This will probably change in the future. Also note that this chapter only briefly overviews the topic, and that further information on digital copyright labeling techniques and corresponding algorithms can be found in [1] and [2].

12.1 INTRODUCTION

The need for copyright protection has been around since the creation of technologies that allow them to make copies of specific content [3]. Three examples from the analog world illustrate this point:

- First, the invention of the printing press was followed by some serious concerns regarding the need for copyright protection. Note that the printing press provided the ability to produce multiple copies of a document at relatively low costs (as compared to the value of the document being copied). Fortunately, piracy of documents by way of printing press could easily be stopped because of the huge effort that was required, the special equipment that was needed, and the fact that the resulting copies were not exactly the same as the original documents.

- Second, the invention of various recording technologies for audio and video data was followed by concerns regarding the need for copyright protection. In the case of vinyl records, making copies also required special equipment, and copies were not as good as the original records. With the advent of magnetic tape (for both audio and video recording), however, the piracy potential increased tremendously, mainly because the copying effort was small and the equipment was ubiquitous. Fortunately (at least from the content provider's point of view), the barrier to widespread piracy of such content is the progressively degraded quality of the content with each generation of copies. A copy of a copy of a copy of an original item contains all the noise and defects introduced and amplified at each single step.

- Third, the possibility to make photostatic copies of paper documents has also caused some concerns regarding the need for copyright protection. Again, even the highest-quality copy of a document is degraded, or at least changed, because in some cases photocopiers make things more readable, increase contrast, or introduce other improvements that are nonetheless changes from the original document.

In the digital world we live in today, a multimedia document typically contains digital data that may encode text, graphics, images, audio, or video.[1] The digital representation and distribution of multimedia documents has increased the potential for misuse and theft, and has significantly intensified the problems associated with copyright protection and enforcing these rights. The problems are rooted from the intrinsic characteristics of digital data, namely that making and distributing a copy is easy, inexpensive, and fast, and that each copy is identical to the original.

Against this background, content providers and distributors of multimedia documents are generally afraid of online services, and they are looking for technical solutions to address the challenge of copyright protection and enforcing these rights.

---

[1]In this chapter, text, graphics, images, voice, or video are considered in addition to software, where the problems associated with copyright protection and enforcing these rights have been around for quite a long time.

In fact, copyright protection has found increased attention on the marketplaces for e-commerce, such as the WWW.

One of the major approaches to solve the problems associated with copyright protection and enforcing these rights is *usage control*. According to this approach, each usage of the protected material, such as viewing, playing, or printing, is controlled by some authorized rendering hardware or software. The software industry has a long tradition in deploying usage control technologies. In fact, this type of technology was recommended by the Working Group on Intellectual Property Rights for the U.S. National Information Infrastructure in 1995 [4].

Although usage control is (or may become) the predominant technology for specific applications, such as pay-TV or video-on-demand, it is unlikely that it will be the only solution in the future. There are some (legal and practical) problems related to the restrictive nature of usage control, and these problems will be prohibitive for the large-scale deployment of the technology.

Rather than attempt to restrict and control usage of protected material, another solution is to allow unlimited copying and using, but to provide evidence in the case of misbehavior. This solution uses *digital copyright labeling techniques* as further addressed in the remaining part of this chapter. In short, digital copyright labeling techniques embed digital marks into protected material to designate copyright-related information, such as origin, owner, content, or recipient. Consequently, digital copyright labels may provide evidence for copyright infringements after the event. They may also serve as a kind of deterrent to illicit copying and dissemination by making the misuse of protected material traceable and providing evidence of illegal acts accordingly. Note, however, that the use of digital copyright labeling techniques also requires a legal system that allows the copyright holders to sue illegal acts. Also note that the use of digital copyright labeling techniques is not contrary to usage control; it is rather complementary by providing another defense against misbehavior on the protected material that may have escaped from the domain of usage control.

In general, there are two types of labels for identifying and protecting copyrights as related to multimedia documents:

- A document can be marked with a label that uniquely identifies the copyright holder (*ownership labeling*);

- A document can be marked in a manner that allows its distribution to be uniquely traced (*recipient labeling*).

Unlike usage control techniques, digital copyright labeling does not limit the number of copies allowed, but may deter people from illegal copying by allowing the determination of the legitimate owner of the protected material and the corresponding copyright (in the case of ownership labeling), or by allowing an illegitimately redistributed copy to be traced back to its original recipient (in the case of recipient labeling). In the literature, ownership labels are often referred to as *watermarks*, whereas recipient labels are often referred to as *fingerprints*. These terms are also used in the remaining part of this chapter.

Although digital copyright labeling is relatively new as a means of protecting intellectual property rights, the theories and techniques behind it have been around for quite a long time. Again, refer to [2] for a comprehensive overview about the theories and techniques that can be used for digital copyright labeling. By applying multiplexing techniques as in data communications, some digital copyright labeling techniques can also be used to embed multiple labels (watermarks or fingerprints) and extract them separately. This feature will be important for identifying ownership and other intellectual property rights in works composed of many copyright assets, such as multimedia documents and presentations, as well as groupware and workflow documents.

12.2   WATERMARKING

In the physical world, the term *watermarking* refers to a technique that can be used to impress into paper a specific text or image mark (called a *watermark*). We are familiar with watermarks of varying degrees of visibility that may be added to presentation media as a guarantee of authenticity, quality, and ownership.

Similar to the physical world, a *digital watermark* is a signal added to digital data, such as a multimedia document, that can be detected or extracted later to make an assertion about the data. According to [5], a digital watermark can serve several purposes, such as ownership assertion, authentication and integrity verification, content labeling, usage control, and control protection.

The specific requirements of each watermarking technique may vary with the application, and there is no universal watermarking technique that satisfies all requirements for all applications. Consequently, each watermarking technique has to be designed within the context of the entire system in which it is being deployed. There are several parameters that are used to categorize watermarking techniques.

First, a watermark (that is produced with a watermarking technique) may be visible or invisible:[2]

- A *visible watermark* is intended to be perceptible by the user. As such, it typically contains a visual message or a company logo indicating ownership of the image;

- Contrary to that, an *invisible watermark* is intended to be imperceptible but is detected or extracted by an appropriate piece of software. Consequently, an invisibly watermarked image is similar but not identical to the original unmarked image.

While users are generally concerned with quality, convenience is also a top priority. Users prefer to have a watermarked document behave no differently and suffer no perceptible quality degradation from the original. Consequently, users generally prefer invisibly watermarked images.

Next, watermarking techniques are classified as being either fragile or robust:

- A *fragile watermark* is generally corrupted by any (image-processing) transformation. For example, watermarks for image integrity checks, in which a change must be detected or spatially localized, are necessarily fragile;

- Contrary to that, *robust watermarks* resist common (image-processing) transformations. More precisely, the watermark that is embedded in the data must be recoverable despite intentional or unintentional modifications of the image. For example, a watermark technique for images should be robust against such image-processing operations as filtering, requantization, dithering, scaling, and cropping.

Robustness is a key requirement often imposed by applications. For example, watermarks that are used for ownership assertion should be robust. Unfortunately, the requirements of truly robust watermarks are difficult to meet in practice, and the development of robust watermarking techniques is a difficult problem. In fact, a single technique satisfying all requirements imposed on robust watermarking is quite difficult to achieve and is the subject of current research and development.

More generally, digital watermarks are also classified as being either public or private:

---

[2]In the remaining parts of this section, we describe some watermarking techniques for images. Note, however, that many of these techniques are generally applicable to other forms of multimedia documents, including audio and video.

- A *public watermark* can be detected and read by anyone without having access to secret information (all the user needs is an appropriate detector software);

- Contrary to that, a *private watermark* can only be detected and read by someone who has access to an appropriate detector software and some secret information, such as a pass phrase, a pseudorandom number generator seed, or the original image.

Obviously, private watermarking technqiues are superior from a security point of view. The secret information improves security but also renders detection of the watermark difficult or impossible without the secret information. This information must be communicated and distributed to a user or third party via secure channels if the watermark detection process is not always carried out by the image owner. Thus, a private watermarking scheme cannot be used for annotation or to inform a potential user of its proprietary status; only the content owner has the secret information that is required to detect the watermark. With a private scheme, the watermark can be used only to demonstrate ownership of content once its owner discovers its illicit use. Contrary to that, public watermarking techniques are attractive for many applications. For example, if we want to detect copyright violations in an image archive or in images published on the Web, we can use mobile agents, such as Webcrawlers, to perform identity checks for as many images as we can locate. Private watermarking techniques that require the original or a reference image in the watermarking detection procedure are less suitable for such applications (they require the mobile agents to locally store images).

Depending on whether secret or public keys are used for private watermarking, secret key and public key watermarking techniques may be distinguished (similar to secret and public key cryptography):

- A *secret key watermarking technique* uses the same user key for watermark insertion and extraction or detection. Consequently, secret key watermarking schemes require secure communication channels between the image owner and the image receiver, or user, to pass the keying information.

- Contrary to that, a *public key watermarking technique* uses separate keys for watermark insertion and extraction or detection. A private key is known only by the image owner and is typically used for watermark insertion, whereas a public key is known to everybody and is typically used for watermark extraction or detection.

As illustrated in Figure 12.1, a watermarking technique or scheme must provide support for watermark insertion and watermark extraction or detection.

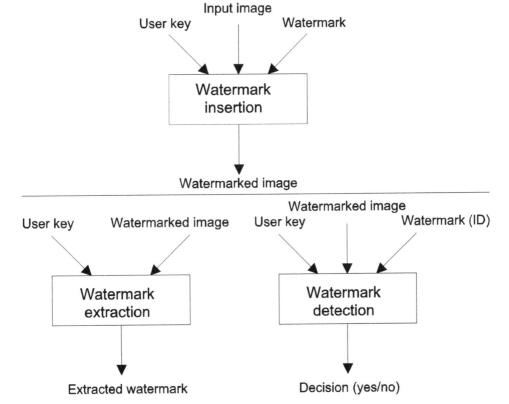

Figure 12.1 Watermark insertion, extraction, and detection.

12.2.1   Watermark Insertion

As illustrated at the top of Figure 12.1, watermark insertion takes as input a user key, an image, and a (water)mark, and produces as output a watermarked image. The specific steps involved in watermark insertion depend on the watermarking technique in use. For example, a simple watermarking scheme was proposed in [6]. It is used to illustrate the underlying principles. Let X be an image and the sequence $x_1, x_2, x_3, \ldots$ represent its pixels. To insert a watermark, we first generate a watermarking signal using a key to seed a pseudorandom generator for an m-sequence, representing a maximum-length pseudorandom sequence. The binary elements of this m-sequence are then arranged into a two-dimensional watermarking signal that actually represents a matrix. The watermarking signal is then inserted bit by bit into the least significant bit (LSB) position of the original image pixel. Since the watermarking signal is located at the LSB, it is invisible. For the same reason, however, it is also not very robust and can be removed quite easily (by replacing the LSB of each pixel with a randomly chosen bit).

12.2.2   Watermark Extraction and Detection

A digital watermark embedded in a watermarked image has to be recoverable to be of value. Depending on the way the watermark is inserted, and depending on the nature of the watermarking technique in use, the watermark can be either extracted or detected:

- In some watermarking schemes, a watermark can be extracted in its exact form, a procedure that is called watermark extraction. As illustrated on the bottom left of Figure 12.1, watermark extraction takes as input a watermarked image and a user key, and produces as output an extracted watermark.

- In other watermarking schemes, it can only be detected whether a specific watermarking signal is present in an image, a procedure that is called watermark detection. Watermark detection is particularly important for robust watermarking techniques. As illustrated on the bottom right of Figure 12.1, watermark detection takes as input a watermarked image, a user key, and a specific watermark (ID), and produces as output a binary decision whether the specific watermark is included in the image or not. Consequently, a watermark detection operation produces either "yes" or "no."

Unfortunately, watermark extraction or detection is a delicate and often complicated task. A failure is often less the result of the watermark signal than the fact that the extraction or detection algorithm is not sophisticated enough to deal with a degraded version of the signal. Thus, robustness involves engineering the watermark insertion and extraction or detection process and protocols accordingly. Again, we refer to [2] for a comprehensive overview about currently existing technologies to insert, extract, or detect watermarks in digital data.

12.2.3   Possible Attacks

The proponents of digital copyright labeling have made broad claims regarding the robustness and security of their watermarking techniques, often without specifying which attacks they are expected to survive. Many of these claims have been disproved. In fact, some recent analytical results show that for many watermarking techniques, removal is not a difficult problem [7]. Consequently, it is required that a terminology similar to the one used in cryptanalysis is developed for the analysis of watermarking techniques. According to [8], there are four classes of possible attacks against watermarking techniques:

- *Robustness attacks* aim to diminish or remove the presence of a mark in a watermarked image without harming the image beyond rendering it useless. Typical signal-processing attacks revolve around commonly used operations, such as data compression, filtering, resizing, printing, and scanning. An example is the collusion attack, in which differently watermarked versions of the same image are combined to generate a new image, thereby reducing the overall strength of the watermark.

- *Presentation attacks* are slightly different from robustness attacks in the sense that they don't necessarily remove the mark from the watermarked image. Instead, the image is manipulated so that the detector can't find the mark anymore. An exemplary presentation attack was developed at Cambridge University to foil automated Webcrawlers. The attack involves chopping a watermarked image into small parts that are then reassembled on a Web page with appropriate HTML tags. A Webcrawler sees only the individual image blocks, which are too small to contain any watermark. Obviously, this attack causes no image quality degradation, as the pixel values are preserved.

- In some watermarking schemes, the mark's detected presence can have multiple interpretations. Consequently, an attacker can engineer a situation that neutralizes the strength of any evidence of ownership presented. Against this background, *interpretation attacks* aim to forge invalid or multiple interpretations from watermark evidence. For example, an attacker can attempt to make another watermark appear in the same watermarked image with strength equal to that of the owner's watermark, thereby creating an ownership deadlock. Typically, such an attack requires in-depth analysis of the specific watermarking technique under attack.

- Finally, *legal attacks* go beyond the technical merits or scientific evidence presented by watermarking techniques. As such, they make use of existing and future legislation on copyright laws and digital information ownership, the different interpretations of the law in various jurisdictions, the credibility of the owner and of the attacker, and the ability of an attacker to cast doubt on the watermarking scheme in the courtroom.

Understanding these attacks may help propose watermarking techniques that are more robust not only in the strength of their marks but also in their ability to guard against possible attacks.

12.3   FINGERPRINTING

Contrary to digital watermarking, fingerprinting documents means introducing individual marks into each copy sold or distributed that make the copy unique. This is similar to the way fingerprints make people unique [9]. Once an illegal copy turns up, the content provider can see from the fingerprint which of the original copies was illegally redistributed. Consequently, the corresponding party can be sued for having illegitimately redistributed his or her copy.

In principle, the techniques that can be used for fingerprinting are the same that are used for watermarking. Also the attacks that can be launched against fingerprints are essentially the same. Consequently, we don't have to repeat the last section. Nevertheless, a special word is due to some recent research results in the field. Keep in mind that fingerprinting techniques and corresponding schemes are to deter people from illegal copying of documents by enabling a content provider to identify the original buyer of a copy that was redistributed illegally. Most fingerprinting schemes are symmetric in the sense that both the content provider and the buyer know the fingerprinted copy. Thus, if another copy with the same fingerprint turns up, one cannot really assign responsibility to one of them; the copy might as well have been redistributed by a dishonest employee of the content provider as by the buyer, or the content provider may want to gain money by wrongly claiming that there are illegal copies around. In other words, the content provider does not obtain means to prove in court that the buyer actually redistributed the copy. This is similar to MACs. As two people know the same secret key, non-repudiation is usually not provided by a MAC. In contrast, only one person can provide a digital signature, and thus a digitally signed message can be used to hold someone responsible in court.

Against this background, Birgit Pfitzmann and Matthias Schunter have proposed fingerprinting schemes that are asymmetric in the sense that after a sale, only the buyer knows the actual data with the fingerprint [10]. However, if the content provider later finds a copy of the data, he or she can identify its buyer (according to the fingerprint), and prove that this buyer originally bought the copy.

An obvious application of asymmetric fingerprinting is improving traitor tracing schemes for broadcast encryption. In short, broadcast encryption is intended for applications where a content provider broadcasts a lot of data in encrypted form, and only legitimate subscribers are supposed to be able to decrypt it and extract the information accordingly. A typical example is Pay-TV, where a video stream is actually transmitted over a broadcast channel in encrypted form. Traitor tracing schemes, as introduced in [11], are intended for tracing people who abuse a broadcast encryption scheme by allowing additional, illegitimate users to decrypt the data stream. Again, most traitor tracing schemes are symmetric in the sense that legitimate users of broadcast encryption share all their secrets with the information provider. Against this background, Pfitzmann has introduced the notion of an asymmetric traitor tracing scheme, where the content provider, confronted with treachery, obtains information that he could not have produced on his own [12]. Consequently, this information provides much better evidence in court. One can reasonably expect asymmetric fingerprinting techniques and asymmetric traitor tracing schemes to become important for copyright protection in the future.

12.4 CONCLUSIONS

Thanks to the proliferation of the WWW, a huge amount of multimedia documents — text, graphics, images, audio, and video — are available for browsing and downloading by millions of users worldwide over the Internet. As a result, security and copyright issues have become important. In this chapter, we briefly overviewed some techniques used for digital copyright labeling. In particular, we briefly elaborated on watermarking and fingerprinting techniques. These techniques are undoubtedly important for protecting various forms of content on the WWW.

Although digital copyright labeling as a whole is still a relatively new field of study, it has already attracted many researchers. In fact, there are several digital copyright labeling systems available today. For example, the System for Copyright Protection (SysCoP) was developed at the Frauenhofer Institute for Computer Graphics in Darmstadt, Germany [13], and is now being marketed by MediaSec

Technologies LLC.[3] More recently, many companies have been founded to develop and market digital copyright labeling systems. Examples include the Digimarc Corporation,[4] Signum Technologies,[5] ARIS Technologies, Inc.,[6] Blue Spike, Inc.,[7] and Signafy.[8]

Also, a challenging problem is how to combine technologies for data compression, copyright protection (digital watermarking and fingerprinting), as well as data encryption and authentication in an effective and yet efficient way. This problem can also be addressed in several ways. For example, the work that is being done at the IBM Almaden Research Center in San Jose, California, is directed toward the development of digital library services that protect copyright holders, owners, users, and themselves against deliberate and inadvertent misuses of content. The IBM researchers have developed and trademarked a packaging mechanism for documents that includes all necessary administrative information, such as terms and conditions of access and protected signatures to validate authenticity. The primary content is compressed and encrypted. Each package, called a *Cryptolope*, can also include information so that a user can determine not only the price of any protected piece, but also its value according to a plaintext "bill of materials" or an HTML "teaser" [14]. Upon receipt of a Cryptolope container, the browser would engage in a negotiation with a clearance center to obtain, such as for a payment, the means to open the Cryptolope. The Cryptolope will interact with and effectively control the helper application so that operations such as save, print, copy, or view can be granted separately or denied, depending on the author's intent and the kind of exchange made with the clearance center. Further information can be found on IBM's homepage for Cryptolopes.[9] Similar work is being done at Debis in Bonn, Germany [15].

Though commercial use of digital copyright labeling techniques has begun, there are still some barriers preventing the techniques from becoming effective and widespread. The major technical challenge is to develop a foolproof protection system while keeping the labels hidden. Absolute robustness is impossible, but there is much room for improvement. None of the existing systems can claim that its labels will survive all major signal-processing operations and transformations. Like

---

[3]http://www.mediasec.com
[4]http://www.digimarc.com
[5]http://www.signumtech.com
[6]http://www.musicode.com
[7]http://www.bluespike.com
[8]http://www.signafy.com
[9]http://www.software.ibm.com/security/cryptolope/

cryptography, this technology will be useful as long as it makes tampering with or removing labels a time-consuming and costly task. Just as DNA tests did in order to be accepted as legal evidence in court, digital copyright labeling techniques have to establish their status in the legal system to fulfill their mission. As of this writing, the legal status of digital watermarking and fingerprinting is still untested, and therefore unresolved. It took more than 20 years for the digital signature to establish itself as common commercial practice and inspire legislative action after the concept was first published, so there may be a long way to go. In fact, the question of how long we have to wait for digital watermarks and fingerprints to be adopted legally and socially remains to be answered [16].

REFERENCES

[1] P. Wayner, *Digital Copyright Protection*, AP Professional, 1997.

[2] F. Petitcolas, and S. Katzenbeisser, *Steganography and Watermarking*, Artech House, Norwood, MA (in press).

[3] J.M. Acken, "How Watermarking Adds Value to Digital Content," *Communications of the ACM*, Vol. 41, No. 7, July 1998, pp. 75 – 77.

[4] B.A. Lehman, and R.H. Brown, *Intellectual Property and the National Information Infrastructure*, Report of the Working Group on Intellectual Property Rights, Section C, Part II, 1995.

[5] N. Memon, and P.W. Wong, "Protecting Digital Media Content," *Communications of the ACM*, Vol. 41, No. 7, July 1998, pp. 35 – 43.

[6] R. Van Schyndel, A. Tirkel, and C. Osborne, "A Digital Watermark," *Proceedings of ICIP '94*, IEEE Press, 1994, pp. 86 – 90.

[7] S. Craver, N. Memon, B.-L. Yeo, and M. Yeung, "Resolving Rightful Ownership With Invisible Watermarking Techniques: Limitations, Attacks, and Implications," *IEEE Journal on Selected Areas in Communications*, Vol. 16, No. 4, May 1998, pp. 573 – 586.

[8] S. Craver, B.-L. Yeo, and M. Yeung, "Technical Trials and Legal Tribulations," *Communications of the ACM*, Vol. 41, No. 7, July 1998, pp. 45 – 54.

[9] N.R. Wagner, "Fingerprinting," *Proceedings of the IEEE Symposium on Security and Privacy*, 1983, pp. 18 – 22.

[10] B. Pfitzmann, and M. Schunter, "Asymmetric Fingerprinting," *Proceedings of EUROCRYPT '96*, pp. 84 – 95.

[11] B. Chor, A. Fiat, and M. Naor, "Tracing Traitors," *Proceedings of EUROCRYPT '94*, pp. 257 – 270.

[12] B. Pfitzmann, "Trials of Traced Traitors," *Proceedings of Workshop on Information Hiding*, 1996, pp. 49 – 64.

[13] J. Zhao, "A WWW Service to Embed and Prove Digital Copyright," *Proceedings of European Conference on Multimedia Applications, Services and Techniques*, 1996.

[14] J. Lotspiech, U. Kohl, and M.A. Kaplan, "Cryptographic Envelopes and Digital Library," IBM Research Report RJ 10069, 1997.

[15] E. von Faber, E. Hammelrath, and F.P. Heider, "The Secure Distribution of Digital Contents," *Proceedings of Annual Computer Security Applications Conference (ACSAC '97)*, December 1997, pp. 16 – 22.

[16] J. Zhao, E. Koch, and C. Luo, "In Business Today and Tomorrow," *Communications of the ACM*, Vol. 41, No. 7, July 1998, pp. 67 – 72.

Chapter 13

Privacy Protection and Anonymity Services

Although Web browsing feels like an anonymous activity, it is hardly that way. Web server and network administrators generally get a lot of information about users and their browsing behavior.[1] For example, the Web server logs reveal the date and time of each HTTP request, the IP address or DNS hostname of the client, the URL of the previous resource that was requested by the client, and some other information. Even more information is available to Internet service providers (ISPs) whose HTTP proxy servers may keep track of every Web site and URL visited by their subscribers.

Against this background, we address the increasingly important field of privacy protection and anonymity services for the WWW in this chapter. In particular, we introduce the topic in Section 13.1, discuss the use of cookies and their implications for the privacy of Web users in Section 13.2, address anonymous browsing and anonymous publishing in Sections 13.3 and 13.4, and draw some conclusions in Section 13.5. Note that most countries have data privacy or data protection laws to be aware of when dealing with personal data. However, we are not going to address these laws or the implications thereof in this book. If you are a lawyer or

---

[1] Refer to `http://consumer.net/anonymizer/` to learn about the information that your browser leaks when it connects to a Web server.

at least understand the language of law, refer to the references given at the end of this chapter.

13.1   INTRODUCTION

First, it is important to note that anonymity is not the same as confidentiality:

- On the one hand, confidentiality tries to protect the privacy of data being transmitted (it can be provided by appropriate cryptographic techniques, such as the ones overviewed and discussed in previous chapters of this book);

- On the other hand, anonymity tries to protect the identities of communicating parties or the relationship between them (transmitted data may be encrypted or not).

As such, anonymity services try to protect against specific forms of traffic analysis. Outside the military, the threat of traffic analysis has largely been ignored. But traffic analysis is becoming a significant threat to the privacy of Web users, and the browsing behavior of Web users is increasingly subject to observation. As Web-based e-commerce becomes more prevalent, this behavior will include the shopping habits and money spending patterns of individual users, as well as other personal data that people have traditionally considered to be private. Similarly, the Web is becoming an important source for information and intelligence gathering. In a competitive environment, a company may wish to protect its current research topics. However, monitoring HTTP data traffic may reveal the company's focus. By keeping Web browsing characteristics private, the company's interests are adequately protected, too. We saw in Chapter 7 that some electronic payment systems allow secure financial transactions over the Internet while preserving the untraceability and anonymity that normal cash allows. However, if digital cash is transmitted over a channel that identifies both the payer and the payee, the transaction may no longer stay anonymous. In this context, the use of anonymity services is mandatory.

As discussed in [1], there are three types of anonymous communication properties that can be provided individually or combined:

- Sender anonymity;

- Receiver anonymity;

- Unlinkability of sender and receiver (connection anonymity).

In short, *sender anonymity* means that the identity of the party who sent a particular message is hidden, while its receiver and the message itself might not be. Similarly, *receiver anonymity* means that the identity of the receiver is hidden, while its sender and the message itself might not be. Finally, *unlinkability of sender and receiver* (also referred to as *connection anonymity* in the remaining parts of this chapter) means that though the sender and receiver can each be identified individually as participating in some communication, they cannot be identified as communicating with each other.

A second aspect of anonymous communication is the adversary against which sender and receiver anonymity as well as unlinkability of sender and receiver must be provided and ensured. In short, the adversary might be an eavesdropper who can observe some or all messages sent or received, collaborations consisting of some senders, receivers, and other parties, as well as variations thereof. It is important to know the capabilities of a potential adversary against which one wants to protect privacy (this knowledge is sometimes made explicit in a so-called threats model).

There is some previous work in providing anonymity service for electronic mail (e-mail). For example, `anon.penet.fi` was a simple and easy-to-use anonymous e-mail forwarding service (a so-called *anonymous remailer*) that was operated by Johan Helsingius in Finland.[2] In short, the `anon.penet.fi` anonymous remailer was provided by a simple SMTP proxy server that stripped off all header information of incoming e-mail messages before forwarding them toward their destination. In addition, if not already assigned, an alias for the sender of an e-mail message was created. In the outgoing message, the real e-mail address of the sender was replaced by the alias that allowed the recipient(s) of the message to reply to the sender without knowing his or her real identity or e-mail address. Consequently, `anon.penet.fi` provided sender anonymity by simply keeping the mapping between real e-mail addresses and their aliases anonymous. The downside of this simple approach was that any user of `anon.penet.fi` had to unconditionally trust the service provider not to reveal his or her real identity or e-mail address. This level of trust may or may not be justified.[3] In either case, it is difficult for a user to judge the trustworthiness of a particular service provider. Today, there are several anonymous remailers available for public use on the Internet, and a corresponding list has been compiled by Raph Levien at the University of California at Berkeley (refer to URL

---

[2] According to a press release on February 20, 1995, over 7,000 messages were forwarded daily, and the alias database contained more than 200,000 entries.

[3] On February 8, 1995, based on a burglary report filed with the Los Angeles police, transmitted by Interpol, the Finish police presented Helsingius a warrant for search and seizure. Bound by law, he complied, thereby revealing the real e-mail address of a single user.

http://www.cs.berkeley.edu/~raph/remailer-list.html).

A more sophisticated approach to provide anonymous e-mail forwarding services was originally developed and proposed by David Chaum (the founder of the Dutch company DigiCash[4]) in the early 1980s [2]. In essence, Chaum combined cryptographic and some other privacy enhancing technologies to provide anonymity services in a *Chaum mixing network*. According to this terminology, a *Chaum mix*, or *mix* in short, refers to an anonymous remailer that is able to decrypt messages with its private key, before forwarding the decrypted messages toward their final destination. In addition to forwarding incoming e-mail messages, a Chaum mix may also try to hide the relationship between incoming and outgoing traffic. To achieve this, it typically reorders, delays, and eventually pads data traffic to disable or at least complicate traffic analysis attacks.

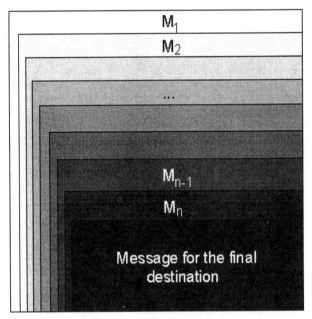

Figure 13.1   The message encapsulation scheme of a Chaum mixing network.

In a Chaum mixing network, the sender of an anonymous e-mail message first chooses a route through a series of mixes $M_1, \ldots, M_n$ to the intended destination, and wraps some extra layers of data around the message. To form the innermost

[4]http://www.digicash.com

layer, the name of the last mix M_n — the mix one hop away from the destination — is concatenated with the original message (which may be encrypted with the public key of the destination), and the result is then encrypted with the public key of the second-to-last mix M_{n-1} in the route. Consequently, the resulting bundle has one layer of routing data prepended to the original message, and it's encrypted with a key possessed only by M_{n-1}. If the bundle were to somehow arrive at M_{n-1}, it could be decrypted there, and the one layer of remaining routing data would be enough to route the message to M_n and from there to its final destination. This sort of message encapsulation can be repeated, the next time with the third-to-last mix, namely M_{n-2}. The result is a bundle that can be decrypted only by M_{n-2}. Once decrypted there, the interior can be forwarded to M_{n-1}. At the same time, however, M_{n-2} can't read the interior of the bundle, since that part is encrypted with the public key of M_{n-1} (of which the corresponding private key is known only to M_{n-1}). The result of this message encapsulation scheme is illustrated in Figure 13.1. Each layer of gray refers to one additional layer of encryption.

In short, a message for the final destination is encrypted with the public key of the last mix M_n in the route and addressed accordingly. Afterward, the result is encrypted with the public key of the second-to-last mix M_{n-1} and addressed accordingly. This continues until finally the bundle is encrypted with the public key of the first mix M_1 and addressed accordingly. One can think of this encapsulation scheme as an onion that is prepared by the sender. On the forward route to the destination, each mix peels off one layer of encryption (by decrypting the message with its private key). Later in this chapter, we see how a technology called "onion routing" employs essentially the same message encapsulation scheme on the Internet layer (refer to subsection 13.3.2).

If a Chaum mixing network were used to transmit e-mail messages only through one mix, this mix would have to be trusted not to reveal the senders' and receivers' identities (since it sees both of them). Consequently, most people forward e-mail messages through two or more mixes in an attempt to protect themselves against a single mix that may see both the sender and the receiver identities of a particular e-mail message. In other words, using two or more mixes keeps the sender anonymous to every mix but the first and the receiver anonymous to every mix but the last. Consequently, a user's identity is best hidden if he runs his own Chaum mix and directs all of his outgoing e-mail messages through it.

If you were worried about an adversary powerful enough to monitor several Chaum mixes in a network simultaneously, you would also have to worry about timing and other correlation attacks. In an extreme case, consider the situation in which a Chaum mixing network is idle until a message is sent out. Then even though an adversary can't decrypt the layered encryption, he or she can still locate the route just by watching the active parts of the network and analyzing the data traffic accordingly. Chaum mixing networks have been designed to resist such attacks using queues to batch, reorder, and process incoming messages. In fact, each mix may keep quiet — absorbing incoming messages but not retransmitting them — until its outbound buffer overflows, at which point the mix emits a randomly chosen message to its next hop. However, due to the real-time constraints of some applications, the batching, reordering, and processing of data messages in queues is not always possible. We discuss this point later in this chapter.

One question arises immediately with regard to the use of anonymous remailer services: how can the receiver of an (anonymous) e-mail message reply to the sender? The answer is that the receiver can't unless explicitly told how to do so. A simple technique is to tell the receiver to send a reply to a certain newsgroup, such as `alt.anonymous.messages`, with a specific subject field, such as `12345example`. The reply can then be grabbed by the sender from the appropriate newsgroup. This approach of replying is yet untraceable but also expensive and unreliable. A more sophisticated technique uses the knowledge of how to build an untraceable forward route from the sender to the receiver, to build an inverse untraceable backward route from the receiver to the sender. In general, the forward and backward routes are independent (they can be completely identical, partially identical, or completely disjunct). According to this technique, the sender computes a block of information that is used to anonymously return a reply from the receiver to the sender. This additional block of information is sometimes also referred to as a *return path information* (RPI) block. The RPI block is prepended to the original message and padding data that is sent from the sender to the receiver. It is then used by the receiver to build a corresponding backward route or return path.

The use of Chaum mixes to provide anonymous e-mail forwarding and RPI-based reply services was prototyped by Ceki Külcü and Gene Tsudik at the IBM Zürich Research Laboratory in Switzerland. In fact, they utilized the scripting language Perl (version 5.0) and the PGP software package (version 2.6) to actually build a system called BABEL [3].

Unfortunately, the lessons learned from anonymous remailers don't necessarily hold for WWW traffic, because the characteristics of e-mail and WWW traffic are inherently different:

- First, the WWW is an interactive medium, while e-mail is store-and-forward;

- Second, e-mail is a "push" technology, meaning that the sender of an e-mail message initiates a data transfer, possibly without the knowledge or consent of the receiver (the existence of e-mail bombing attacks illustrates this point fairly well). By contrast, the WWW is a "pull" technology, meaning that the receiver must explicitly request data being transferred from the sender.

The first difference implies that Chaum mixing networks are unacceptable (or at least difficult to use) for HTTP data traffic. Nevertheless, the second difference also offers some possibilities to improve security (in terms of anonymity). For obvious reasons, the security of an anonymity-providing system, such as a Chaum mixing network, increases as the number of available and publicly accessible cooperating nodes (Chaum mixes) increases. In the realm of e-mail, operators of anonymous remailers have often come under fire when their services were abused by people sending threatening letters or unacceptable spam (refer to `anon.penet.fi` discussed earlier in this chapter). In fact, the undesirability of handling irate users causes the number of anonymous remailers to stay considerably low, potentially impacting on the anonymity of the overall system. By contrast, a Web server can't initiate a connection with an unwilling browser and send it data when no request was made. This "consensual" nature of the Web should cause fewer potential node operators to become discouraged, and therefore lead to corresponding increases in cooperating nodes. Finally, note that Web proxy servers are also well suited to implement anonymity services mainly because of their caching capabilities (to improve network performance). The very fact that data is being cached at particular proxy servers makes it less likely that requests are forwarded all the way to the origin server. This makes traffic analysis more complicated, and harder to accomplish.

Contrary to anonymous e-mail forwarding services, there is little research going on to provide anonymity services for the Web. As a matter of fact, the consensus on WWW privacy protection is that there just isn't much and that commercial interests are unlikely to champion the cause. Nevertheless, the aim of the remaining part of this chapter is to overview and briefly discuss some technologies that are available today and that can be used to provide anonymity services for the WWW. Before we delve into the technical details, however, we want to elaborate on the use of cookies and their implications for the privacy of Web users.

13.2 COOKIES

Let's assume a WWW server that should be configured to collect information about particular users to customize subsequent user sessions.[5] In this situation, there are

---

[5] Note that the term "session" here does not refer to a persistent HTTP connection but rather to a logical session created from HTTP request and response messages that logically belong together.

two possibilities:

- The server is configured to locally store the state information on a per-user basis;

- The server is configured to download the state information to the browsers where it is stored on the server's behalf.

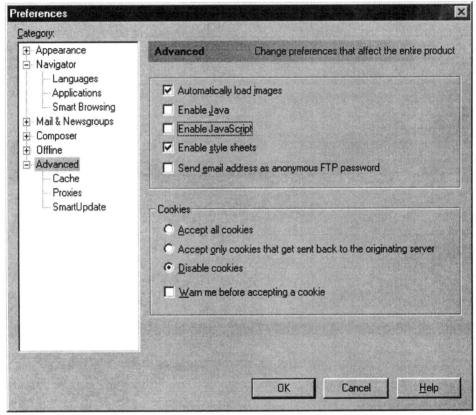

Figure 13.2   Configuring the acceptance of cookies in Netscape Navigator. © 1999 Netscape Communications Corporation.

Following the first approach, the server would have to build a huge database to store and make available state information related to particular users and user sessions. This database would tend to increase very rapidly. Contrary to that, the state information is not stored locally in the second approach. Instead, the information is downloaded to the browser where it is stored in a decentralized and fully distributed way. The next time the browser connects to the server, it simpl, retransmits the appropriate state information to the server.

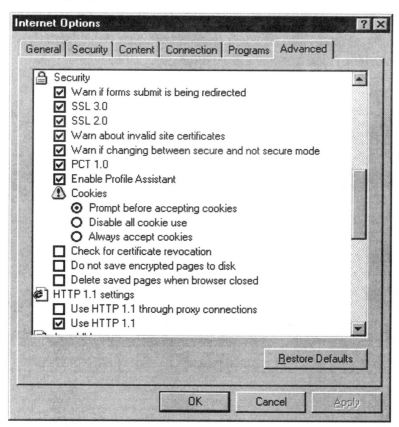

Figure 13.3 Configuring the acceptance of cookies in Microsoft Internet Explorer. © 1999 Microsoft Corporation.

The HTTP state management mechanism as specified in RFC 2109 follows the second approach [4]. It uses the term *cookie* to refer to the state information that passes between the origin server and the browser, and that gets stored by the browser. More precisely, the mechanism specifies a way to create a stateful session with HTTP request and response messages. It describes two new headers, namely the Cookie and the Set-Cookie headers, that can be used to carry state information between participating origin servers and browsers.

To initiate a session, the origin server returns an extra response header to the browser, the Set-Cookie header. The browser, in turn, returns a corresponding Cookie request header to the server once it chooses to continue a session. The origin server may ignore it or use it to determine the current state of the session. The syntax and semantics of the Set-Cookie and Cookie headers are fully specified in [4]. For example, a Set-Cookie response header may look as follows:

```
Set-Cookie: USER_NAME=Rolf; path=/; expires=Wednesday, 18-Nov-99 23:12
```

The browser stores the cookie locally.[6] If it requested a resource in path "/" on the same server (before November 18, 1999), it would send the following Cookie request header to the server:

```
Cookie: USER_NAME=Rolf
```

Now the server knows that the requesting user has been previously assigned the name "Rolf." If there are other attributes being stored in the cookie, the server may customize its behavior for this particular user.

The use of cookies raises some privacy concerns. As briefly outlined above, a server may use Set-Cookie and corresponding Cookie headers to track the path of a particular user when visiting the server. Users may object to this behavior as an intrusive accumulation of private information, even if their identities may not be evident (identities may be evident if users fill out forms that contain identifying information).

Consequently, a user should be able to enable or disable the HTTP state management mechanism, and to either reject or refuse the use of cookies accordingly. For example, in Netscape Navigator a user can either accept all cookies, accept only cookies that get sent to the originating server, or disable all cookies. The corresponding Preferences control panel (located under the Edit menu) with its three radio buttons is illustrated in Figure 13.2 (within the "Cookies" section). In this example, the entire HTTP state management mechanism is disabled (disable cookies). With the two other radio buttons a user can configure his or her browser to generate a warning before a cookie is accepted.

As illustrated in Figure 13.3, the acceptance of cookies can be configured similarly in Microsoft Internet Explorer. In this case, an Internet Options control panel

---

[6]Netscape Navigator uses a file called `cookies.txt` to store the user's cookies.

is available under the View menu. There are radio buttons to be prompted before accepting a cookie, disable all cookie use, or always accepting cookies. Although Netscape Navigator and Microsoft Internet Explorer differ in detail, the basic approach to have the user configure the browser to either accept or refuse cookies is very similar. It doesn't come as a surprise that both browsers are preconfigured to accept cookies.

If a browser does not allow a user to disable the use of cookies, it is always possible to periodically delete the file where the cookies are stored. For example, on a UNIX system, the browser can be prevented from storing and saving cookies by replacing the cookies file with a link to `/dev/null`. Similarly, on Windows and Macintosh systems, there are commercial programs that promise to sweep cookie files clear. Examples include NSClean (for Netscape Navigator) and IEClean (for Microsoft Internet Explorer).[7]

As of this writing, the HTTP state management mechanism is not cryptographically protected and must be considered to be unsecure. More recently, research has addressed possibilities to secure the HTTP state management mechanism [5]. It is left as an exercise for the reader to design and come up with cryptographic protection schemes that can be used to secure the HTTP state management mechanism. Note that a cryptographically protected cookie must be generated and verified only by the server. This simplifies key management considerably.

Finally, note that HTTP cookies as defined in [4] are designed to maintain state information between the two endpoints of an HTTP transaction, that is, the browser and the origin server. They cannot be used for storing state information between the browser and a proxy server, or between different proxies in a proxy chain. However, as was first pointed out by Ari Luotonen in [6], there is a need for something like *proxy cookies*. Note that a common way to use (or misuse) cookies is to store authentication information so that a reauthentication does not have to occur every time in future requests, but the appropriate authentication information is directly available in a corresponding cookie. To prevent spoofing attacks in this setting, it is common practice to encode, not just the username into the cookie, but also the IP address where the first request came from. Now consider the case in which the route to the server is dynamically changing in a way that a request is not guaranteed to come from the same IP address (of the proxy server) as the earlier request. In this case, the cookie may be rendered invalid. In this situation, a feature to support proxy cookies would be useful. Such a feature will hopefully emerge at some later point in time (obviously, the more secure approach is not to

---

[7]`http://www.nsclean.com`

store any static authentication information in a cache in the first place).

13.3   ANONYMOUS BROWSING

In this section, we address technologies that can be used to protect the privacy of Web users and to support anonymous browsing accordingly. In particular, we overview and discuss four technologies with increasing order of complexity and sophistication.

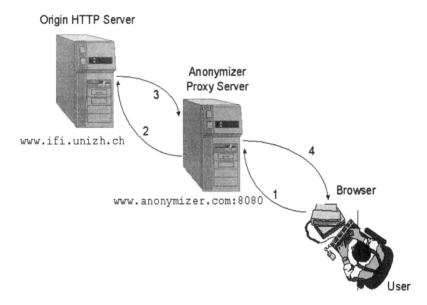

Figure 13.4   The use of the Anonymizer service.

13.3.1   The Anonymizer

The *Anonymizer*[8] is a service that allows users to browse anonymously through the WWW. As of this writing, it is probably the most heavily used anonymizing service for the Web. It is provided by an HTTP proxy server that runs on port 8080 of the server that hosts the Anonymizer homepage (located at **www.anonymizer.com**). A user can either enter the requested URL in the corresponding field of this homepage,

---

[8]Anonymizer is a trademark of Anonymizer, Inc.

or he can directly invoke the proxy server by constructing and requesting a nested URL (as explained below).

The Anonymizer service is for the Web what the `anon.penet.fi` service was for e-mail: a simple and easy-to-use anonymous forwarding service. However, contrary to `anon.penet.fi`, the Anonymizer is a commercial service for HTTP. You can either use this service for free (and pay a penalty in terms of a bonus 30 – 60 second delay per Web page and advertisements being included into the retrieved pages), or sign up for a paid account. Terms and conditions for a paid account are available from the Anonymizer homepage.

For example, if you want to use the Anonymizer service to retrieve my homepage located at URL `http://www.ifi.unizh.ch/~oppliger`, you can either type in the URL in the corresponding field of the Anonymizer homepage, or you can directly invoke the proxy server by constructing and requesting a nested URL (`http://www.anonymizer.com:8080/www.ifi.unizh.ch/~oppliger` or `http://www.anonymizer.com:8080/http://www.ifi.unizh.ch/~oppliger`). In either case, the Anonymizer's HTTP proxy server will retrieve my homepage on your behalf. This situation is illustrated in Figure 13.4. In step 1, the browser connects to `http://www.anonymizer.com:8080` and requests `www.ifi.unizh.ch/~oppliger` from the Anonymizer proxy server (the second part is not illustrated in Figure 13.4). In step 2, the proxy server contacts the Web server located at `www.ifi.unizh.ch` to retrieve the requested homepage. The homepage is returned to the proxy server in step 3, and forwarded to the browser in step 4. In doing so, the browser only leaves traces originated from `sol.infonex.com` in the log files of the corresponding Web server (`sol.infonex.com` is the DNS hostname of the machine that currently runs the Anonymizer service). Consequently, the administrator(s) of the origin Web server won't be able to reveal the IP address or DNS hostname of the system that has been used to request the above-mentioned URL using the Anonymizer service in the first place.

In summary, the Anonymizer service is well suited to hide user identities and browser IP addresses from origin HTTP servers. However, there are at least two problem areas to keep in mind and consider with care when using the service:

- First, a user must trust the service provider not to reveal his or her identity. Note that the proxy server can be set up in a way that logs all requested URLs. Consequently, the Anonymizer service provider may get a considerable amount of information about the browsing behavior of a particular user. The user, in turn, must trust the Anonymizer service provider not to reveal (or sell) this information. Also, according to the Anonymizer user agreement, the logs are kept much longer than is technically required: "Usage logs are usually kept for fifteen (15) days for maintenance purposes, monitoring spamming and monitoring abuses of netiquette. Any relevant portion(s) of such logs may be kept for as long as needed to stop the abuses." So the Anonymizer can be raided just as anon.penet.fi was a couple of years ago.

- Second, although the Anonymizer is fine at hiding user identities and browser IP addresses from origin HTTP servers, it's not so good at hiding the server identities from the network segment(s) between the browser and the Anonymizer proxy server. For example, in the HTTP session mentioned above, your network administrator (or the administrator of any proxy server between your browser and the Anonymizer service) will see that you actually request www.ifi.unizh.ch/~oppliger just by unpacking the URL that you have sent out.

Obviously, a possible solution to address the first problem is to chain several anonymous HTTP proxy servers similar to the Anonymizer, whereas a solution to address the second problem is to encrypt the target URL in a way that can be decrypted only by the appropriate proxy servers (for example, by using the public keys of these servers). This is further explored later in this chapter.

13.3.2 Onion Routing

More recently, a group of researchers at the U.S. Naval Research Laboratory (NRL) has adapted the idea of using a Chaum mixing network to provide support for anonymous connections. Anonymous connections are similar to TCP connections, but they are also resistant against passive and active attacks (including traffic analysis). Anonymous connections are bidirectional, have small latency, and can be used anywhere a TCP connection can be used. Note that a connection may be anonymous, although communication need not be (e.g., if the data stream is not encrypted). The NRL researchers have also implemented the technology in a system called *onion routing* [7 – 11].[9]

In the description that follows, the term *onion* is used to refer to a layered encrypted message (similar to the one illustrated in Figure 13.1), whereas the term *onion router* is used to refer to a Chaum mix that acts as a node in a corresponding onion routing network.

---

[9]The onion routing system is conceptually similar to the PipeNet proposal that was posted by Wei Dai to the Cypherpunks mailing list in February 1995. Contrary to the onion routing system, the PipeNet proposal has not been implemented so far.

In onion routing, instead of making TCP connections directly to a responding machine (the so-called *responder*), an initiating application (the so-called *initiator*) makes an anonymous connection through a sequence of onion routers. Contrary to normal routers, onion routers are connected by longstanding and permanent TCP connections. Although the technology is called onion routing, the routing that occurs does so at the application layer (and not at the Internet layer). More specifically, the system relies upon IP routing to route data through longstanding TCP connections. Therefore, although the series of onion routers in an anonymous connection is fixed for the lifetime of that connection, the route that data actually travels between individual onion routers is determined by the underlying IP network. Consequently, onion routing is conceptually similar to loose source routing with IP. Anonymous connections are multiplexed over longstanding connections. For any anonymous connection, the sequence of onion routers in a route is strictly defined at connection setup, and each onion router can only identify the previous and next hops along the route. Data passed along the anonymous connection appears different at each onion router, so data cannot be tracked en route and compromised onion routers cannot cooperate.

In onion routing, an application does not directly talk to a router nor to an onion router. Instead, there must be proxies that interface between the applications and the onion routing network. For example, to access a Web site through an onion routing network, one has to set the browser's HTTP proxy to an onion network entry point (a so-called "application proxy"). In fact, the initiator establishes a TCP connection to an application proxy. This proxy defines a (perhaps random) route through the onion routing network by constructing a layered data structure (an onion) and sending that onion through the network. Similar to a Chaum mixing network, each layer of the onion is encrypted with the public key of the intended onion and defines the next hop in the route. An onion's size is fixed, so each onion router adds some random padding data to replace the removed layer. The last onion router forwards data to the responder's application proxy, whose job is to pass data between the onion routing network and the responder. In addition to carrying the next hop information, each onion layer also contains seed material from which cryptographic keys will actually be derived (for encrypting or decrypting data sent forward or backward on the anonymous connection).

After sending the onion, the initiator's application proxy starts sending data through the established anonymous connection. As data moves through the anonymous connection, each onion router removes one layer of encryption, so it finally arrives as plaintext. Obviously, the layering occurs in the reverse order for data moving backward from the receiver to the initiator. Stream ciphers are used for data encryption and decryption. Similar to the original idea of a Chaum mixing network, onion routers may also randomly reorder data items they receive before forwarding them (but preserve the order of data in each anonymous connection).

As mentioned previously and contrary to the original intent of a Chaum mixing network, the batching technique is out of the question for the support of interactive applications, such as HTTP. This means that coordinated observation of the network links connecting onion routers could eventually reveal an anonymous connection's route and leak the source and destination IP addresses accordingly. Therefore, it's important to ensure that the links between the onion routers can't be simultaneously eavesdropped. The easiest way to achieve this is to put onion routers on different network segments in different buildings with different administrators — ones who would be unlikely to collude. Also note that by layering cryptographic operations in the way described above, an advantage is gained over conventional-style link layer encryption. Even though the total cryptographic overhead for passing data is the same as for link layer encryption, the protection is better. In link layer encryption, the chain is as strong as the weakest link, and one compromised node can reveal everything. In onion routing, however, the chain is as strong as its strongest link, and one honest onion router is enough to maintain the anonymity of the connection. Even if link layer encryption were used together with end-to-end encryption, compromised nodes could still cooperate to reveal route information. This is not possible in an onion routing network, since data always appears differently to each onion router.

For TCP-based application protocols that are proxy aware, such as HTTP, Telnet, and SMTP, there exist application proxies for Sun Solaris. Surprisingly, for certain application protocols that are not proxy aware, most notably rlogin, it has been possible to design interface proxies as well. In either case, the best protection results from having a connection between an application proxy and an onion router that is trusted one way or another. For example, one possibility is to place an onion router on the firewall of a corporate intranet. In this case, the onion router would serve as an interface between the machines behind the firewall and the external network (most notably the Internet).

Onion routing is a technology that deserves further study and wider deployment. In fact, to be effective, onion routing must be fairly widely deployed. Note that onion routing depends on connection-oriented transport services, such as provided by TCP, but could also be layered on top of any connection-oriented service, such as provided by the ATM adaption layer (AAL) 5. Refer to http://www.onion-router.net for current status and other useful information about onion routing.

13.3.3   Lucent Personalized Web Assistant

An increasingly large number of Web sites require users to establish an account before they can actually access the site. This approach is sometimes called "personalized Web browsing." Typically, the user is required to type in and provide at least a unique username, a password, and an e-mail address. Establishing accounts at multiple sites is generally an uncomfortable task. A user may have to invent a distinct username and a password, both unrelated to his or her true identity, for each Web site. Besides the information that the user supplies voluntarily to the Web site, additional information about the user often flows involuntarily from the browser to the Web site, due to the nature of HTTP and the use of cookies (as described in Section 13.2).

Against this background, a group of researchers at Lucent Technologies has developed a technology that makes personalized Web browsing simple, secure, and anonymous by providing convenient solutions to each of the problems mentioned above [12,13]. The technology has been implemented in a system called *Lucent Personalized Web Assistant* (LPWA).[10] In essence, LPWA is an agent that interacts with several Web sites on the user's behalf to provide support for anonymous personalized Web browsing. It automatically derives a unique pseudonym or alias for a user at each site, and transparently presents that alias to the site on request. Typically, the alias consists of a username, a password, and eventually an e-mail address. In general, different aliases are generated for each user and Web site pair, but the same alias is presented whenever the user visits a particular Web site.

Providing support for personalized Web browsing, the LPWA frees the user from the burden of inventing and memorizing distinct usernames and passwords for each Web site, and guarantees that an alias (including the e-mail address) does not reveal the real identity of the user. In addition, the LPWA also provides support for a Web site to reply to anonymous e-mail messages originated by a particular user. Finally, the LPWA is also able to filter the HTTP data traffic to preserve user privacy. As such, the developers of LPWA claim that their system "provides simultaneous user identification and user privacy, as required for anonymous personalized Web browsing [12]."

At the core of anonymous personalized Web browsing is the problem of name translation: translating from the user's e-mail address and secret to an alias that fulfills a number of properties, including anonymity, consistency, secrecy, uniqueness of an alias, and protection from creation of dossiers. To address these requirements, a collision-resistant one-way hash function is used, and this function has been named

---

[10]The LPWA was formerly known as Janus.

the Janus function. Input to the Janus function are the real LPWA username and password as well as the name of the requested Web site. Assuming the hash function to be one-way, it's computationally infeasible to produce a real username or password given only a pseudonym at a particular Web site [14].

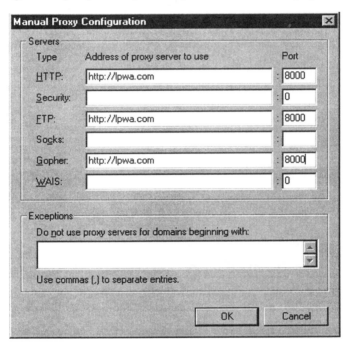

Figure 13.5   The LPWA proxy configuration for Netscape Navigator. © 1999 Netscape Communications Corporation.

In general, the LPWA can be configured as a remote proxy server (central proxy configuration), as a local proxy server (local proxy configuration), or anywhere in between (e.g., firewall proxy configuration), with different trade-offs in terms of security, trust, and convenience. The configuration of the current demonstration is a single copy of LPWA running as a proxy server at port 8000 of lpwa.com. To use this central proxy, you must first configure your browser to automatically use it. The basic idea is to set your browser's HTTP proxy to lpwa.com port 8000 as illustrated in Figure 13.5.[11]

Now consider that you want to register and access the Web site of company

---

[11]Lucent users must set their browsers' HTTP proxy to lpwa.tempo.bell-labs.com, port 8000.

X that requires the submission of a username and a password. LPWA can automatically generate this information, and even a unique e-mail address where you can receive return mail. For example, after setting your browser to use the LPWA proxy, you can go to the homepage of company X at `http://www.x.com`. LPWA will interpose a couple of pages describing the LPWA service and ask you for your real identity (or at least the one from which your pseudonyms will be derived). Then when LPWA sends you on to your original URL and the Web site asks you to register, just give the string \u as your username, \p as your password, and \@ as your e-mail address. LPWA will intercept those codes and replace them with the pseudonyms it uses for you at that particular site. Entries in the origin Web server log files will then show requests originated from `lpwa.com`.

More recently (effective July 15, 1999), Lucent Technologies shut down the LPWA demonstration site at `lpwa.com` and launched ProxyMate at URL `www.proxymate.com` instead. In short, ProxyMate is a commercial service that contains all the LPWA features. For obvious reasons, the use of the LPWA, Proxy-Mate, or similar technologies is convenient for the user, since it frees him or her from creating and inventing new aliases for various sites.

13.3.4 Crowds

Michael K. Reiter and Aviel D. Rubin from AT&T Research developed a system called *Crowds* for protecting users' anonymity on the WWW [15,16]. The system is named for the notion of "blending into a crowd." It operates by grouping users into a large and geographically diverse group (a so-called "crowd") that collectively issues requests on behalf of its members. As such, Crowds is essentially a distributed and chained Anonymizer, with encrypted links between Crowds members. HTTP traffic is forwarded to a crowd member, who flips a biased coin and, depending on the result, forwards it either to some other crowd member or to the final destination. This makes communication resistant to many passive and active attacks.

More precisely, a crowd can be thought of as a collection of users. Each user is represented in a crowd by a process that runs on his or her system. Referring to the terminology that is used in the Crowds project, this process is called a *jondo* (pronounced "John Doe" and meant to convey the image of a faceless participant). The user or a local system administrator acting on the user's behalf starts the jondo. When it is started, it contacts a server called the *blender* to request admittance to the crowd. If admitted, the blender reports to the jondo the current membership status of the crowd and information that enables the jondo to actually participate in the crowd. The user, in turn, configures the jondo to serve as proxy server by specifying its hostname and port number in his or her browser as the proxy for all services (the services that must be proxied include Gopher, HTTP, and SSL). The corresponding proxy server configuration menus of Netscape Navigator and Microsoft Internet Explorer have previously been illustrated in Figures 3.4 and 3.6.

Afterwards, any request originating from the browser is sent directly to its jondo. Upon receiving the first request from the browser, the jondo initiates the establishment of a random path of jondos to and from the origin Web server. More precisely, the jondo picks a jondo from the crowd (possibly itself) at random, and forwards the request to it. When this jondo receives the request, it flips a biased coin to determine whether or not to forward the request to another jondo. If the result is to forward, then the jondo selects a random jondo and forwards the request to it. Otherwise the jondo submits the result to the Web server for which the request was destined. Consequently, each request travels from the user's browser, through a number of jondos, and finally to the origin Web server. Subsequent requests initiated at the same jondo follow the same path (except perhaps going to a different Web server), and server response messages traverse the same path as the request messages, only in reverse.

All communications between any two jondos is encrypted using a key known only to the two jondos. Encryption keys are established as jondos join the crowd. Therefore, some group membership procedures must be defined. These procedures determine who can join the crowd and when they can join, and inform members of the crowd membership accordingly. In fact, there are many schemes and corresponding group membership protocols that can potentially be used to manage crowd memberships. While providing robust and reliable distributed solutions, many of these schemes have the disadvantage of incurring significant overhead and of providing semantics that are arguably too strong for the application at hand. In the Crowds system, a simpler and centralized solution is used. As mentioned above, membership in a crowd is controlled and reported to crowd members by the blender. To make use of the blender (and thus the crowd), the user must establish an account with the blender (i.e., an account name and password that the blender stores). When the user starts a jondo, the jondo and the blender use this shared secret (the password) to authenticate each other's communication. As a result of this communication, the blender may accept the jondo into the crowd, add the new jondo (i.e., its IP address, port number, and account name) to its list of current members, and report this list back to the jondo. In addition, the blender may also generate and report back a list of shared keys, each of which can be used to authenticate another member of the crowd. The blender then sends one key of the new jondo to each other jondo that is intended to share it (encrypted under the account password for that jondo) and informs the other jondos of the new member. At this point all members are equipped with the data they need for the new member to participate in the crowd.

Each member maintains its own list of crowd members. This list is initialized to that received from the blender when the jondo joins the crowd, and is updated when the jondo receives notices of new or deleted members from the blender. The jondo can also (autonomously) remove jondos from its list of crowd members, if it detects that the corresponding jondos have failed. This allows for each jondo's list to diverge from others' lists if different jondos have detected different failures in the crowd.

Obviously, a major disadvantage of this centralized approach to group member-ship management is that the blender is a TTP for the purposes of key distribution and membership reporting. Techniques exist for distributing trust in such a TTP among many replicas, in a way that the corruption of some fraction of the replicas can be tolerated [17]. In its present, nonreplicated form, however, the blender is best executed on a trusted computer system (e.g., with login access available only at the console). Note, however, that even though the blender is a TTP for some functions, HTTP traffic is not generally routed through the blender, and thus a passive attack on the blender does not immediately break Web transaction security. Moreover, the failure of the blender does not interfere with ongoing transactions. It is planned that in future versions of Crowds, jondos will establish mutually shared keys us-ing the Diffie-Hellman key exchange, where the blender serves only to authenticate and distribute the Diffie-Hellman public values of the Crowds members. This will eliminate the present reliance on the blender for key generation. Another possibil-ity would be the use of Kerberos or any other authentication and key distribution system [18].

In practice, firewalls present a practical problem for the deployment of Crowds. Remember from the description given above that jondos are identified by their IP addresses and port numbers. Most corporate firewalls do not allow incoming con-nections on ports other than a few well-known ones. Thus, a firewall will generally prevent a jondo outside the firewall from connecting to another jondo inside the firewall. It is conceivable that if Crowds becomes widespread, and there is demand for a special reserved port, that firewalls will open this port and allow jondos to communicate accordingly. Until then, Crowds will be most useful across academic institutions, as a service provided by ISPs, and within very large organizations.

A thorough security and performance analysis for Crowds is given in [15]. Crowds 1.0 is implemented in Perl 5.0. According to their developers, Perl was chosen for its rapid prototyping capabilities and its portability across UNIX and Microsoft platforms. While Crowds performance is already encouraging, it could be further improved by reimplementing the system in a compiled language, such as C or C^{++}. Further information on Crowds and the corresponding software can be obtained from the project's homepage that is located at URL `http://www.research.att.com/projects/crowds`. Note, however, that due to U.S. export restrictions, the software can only be obtained by U.S. and Canadian citizens.

13.4   ANONYMOUS PUBLISHING

The technologies overviewed and discussed so far address the problem of how to protect the privacy of Web users, and how to provide support for anonymous browsing. In this section, however, we want to address the problem of how to publish data anonymously on the Web. Note that the current WWW architecture provides little support for anonymous publishing. In fact, the architecture fundamentally includes identification information in the URL that is used to locate resources, and it is very hard for a Web publisher to avoid revealing this information (at least if it is required that resources published anonymously be accessible from standard Web browsers without the need of specialized client software or an anonymity tool). Also note that the browser privacy problem is orthogonal to the anonymous publishing problem, and that the two problems compose well: if full anonymity is needed, techniques for anonymous browsing will work well in tandem with an infrastructure for anonymous publishing. In fact, the second technology can be seen as a generalization of the first one.

In the subsections that follow, two basic technologies are presented that can be used to address the problem of anonymous publishing on the Web. The first technology is rather simple and straightforward, whereas the second technology is complex and more sophisticated.

13.4.1   JANUS

JANUS is a joint research project of the Forschungsinstitut für Telekommunikation (FTK) of Dortmund, Hagen, and Wuppertal in Germany.[12] One of the major results of the project was the development of an anonymous publishing service that is currently provided by the Fernuniversität Hagen. The service is freely available

---

[12]In spite of the fact that the project's name is identical to the former name of the LPWA, the two projects do not have much in common (except that they both address privacy on the Web).

to the public and accessible at the URL `http://janus.fernuni-hagen.de`. It provides anonymity services for both browsers and Web publishers (servers):

- In order to provide anonymity services for the browser, the JANUS service acts as an anonymizing HTTP proxy server. It accepts requests from arbitrary browsers, removes all data that may reveal information about the requesting user, and forwards the requests to the origin HTTP servers. Similarly, the servers' responses are relayed back to the browsers. In this way, JANUS is conceptually similar to the Anonymizer and related services for anonymous browsing.

- In order to provide anonymity services for Web publishers and to support anonymous publishing accordingly, the JANUS service is also able to encrypt and decrypt URLs on the fly in a way that these can be used as reference for a server. More precisely, if a request with an encrypted URL occurs, JANUS is able to decrypt the URL and forward it to the corresponding Web server, without enabling the user to get knowledge about the decrypted URL. Similarly, all references in the Web server's response are encrypted before the response is returned to the browser. The feature of hiding the Web server's IP address or hostname is the main advantage of using the JANUS service. In fact, it is this feature that supports anonymous publishing on the Web.

URL encryption and decryption is a suitable application for public key cryptography. Note that everybody should be able to encrypt and publish a URL, whereas only the JANUS service should be able to decrypt it. The basis of the encryption is the RSA algorithm that is used with 768-bit keys. In fact, the public key of the JANUS service consists of the following parameters (both in hexadecimal notation):

```
e = 010001
n = BC2ABB0F28DEA82BCF4CAB74C65D2CB86C0ECC9841B626C3DB0CE4EB
    2F32415DBD7C55772C33B23AA474EC7F3EE62ABBC8E6D9E631CD8469
    3D5BAD0716DD9F8FC04CBA4761D915CCD547286A1C13C6E71450E32D
    C0424E64DA54122834FCFB5D
```

For example, using JANUS to encrypt the URL `http://www.ifi.unizh.ch` would result in the following ASCII-encoded expression:

```
http://janus.fernuni-hagen.de/janus_encrypted/MTBhItbpzt39$G
X4B8FPseKRRENkacT7eBBhB1$hNqXmOYFYR+8MWrnHO2tpzc8cpN36YfwMH+
EHalQE3sapckVRhZGR7DYs2Kt0Lbxlo2PjSDxpP1N$IoTQKgP$b+EQTUw=
```

Consequently, the content provider of `www.ifi.unizh.ch` may publish this expression in order to allow users to visit his or her Web site while staying anonymous. Similarly, I could use the JANUS service to encrypt the URL of my personal homepage located at URL `http://www.ifi.unizh.ch/~oppliger`. The result of this encryption would be as follows:

```
http://janus.fernuni-hagen.de/janus_encrypted/MTAmJIaWc+bdgu
mvf7i5xnsaYsQ6MTyg+VQnJpoHW3+TDtb04ir$6gcAFlwdtEVrGhvNR8rSic
2nbsKOD6I$3mqnJmi3LCY1lfT3gRN15yEOpEserUoAgy5i4LUkVZccpWk=
```

Again, this expression could be published without revealing the fact that my homepage is actually located at `www.ifi.unizh.ch`. When you try to download this encrypted URL, JANUS decrypts the request to actually see `http://www.ifi.unizh.ch/~oppliger`. It then forwards the request and returns the result, encrypting and rewriting all of the URLs in my homepage so that your network logs show only a connection to JANUS, and even the URLs recorded in the logs do not reveal any information about the origin Web server. On the other side, the server logs at `www.ifi.unizh.ch` only reveal that the homepage was accessed by `corona.feruni-hagen.de` (or any other host that currently runs the JANUS service).

Nevertheless, there are at least three limitations and shortcomings to keep in mind when using the JANUS service:

- First, only the URLs are encrypted, so if somebody eavesdropped on the actual data streams, he or she wouldn't be fooled;

- Second, the standard cautions about single-hop forwarding services apply (meaning that coordinated and well-placed sniffers can determine the mapping for a site);

- Third, Web publishers must have the possibility to make available and somehow publish encrypted URLs.

The above-mentioned limitations and shortcomings of the JANUS service are addressed in a more sophisticated technology that is overviewed and briefly discussed next.

13.4.2   TAZ Servers and the Rewebber Network

More recently, Ian Goldberg and David Wagner from the University of California at Berkeley have developed a more comprehensive and sophisticated approach to address the anonymous publishing problem [19]. The technology they proposed can be viewed as a generalization of the JANUS service (similar to the fact that an anonymous remailer network generalizes the `anon.penet.fi` service). In fact, Goldberg and Wagner suggest the use of more (than just one) HTTP proxy servers to collectively disguise the Web server's location, and to encrypt the entire data stream between the requesting browser and the origin Web server. In addition, they also suggest the establishment of a new name space for encrypted URLs and a corresponding resolving mechanism.

More precisely, the term *rewebber* is used to refer to an HTTP proxy server that essentially implements the JANUS service's core functionality and the ability to encrypt data streams. In addition, each rewebber is also able to understand "nested" URLs (i.e., URLs of the form `http://proxy.com/http://www.realsite.com`). Most existing HTTP proxy servers already have this ability. The basic idea is then to publish a URL such as the one given above (which points to `proxy.com` instead of `www.realsite.com`), and to use public key cryptography to encrypt the real server's name (the second part of the URL) so that only the rewebber can actually decrypt and see it. Encrypted URLs are also referred to as *locators*. In the example given above, the requested URL would look something like `http://proxy.com/!RFkK4J...` (RFkK4J... being the encrypted URL or locator for `http://www.realsite.com`). The fact that the URL is encrypted is indicated by the leading ! instead of the expected `http://`. The rewebber at `proxy.com`, upon receiving the locator, would first decrypt it with its private key, and then proceed to retrieve the nested URL in the normal fashion (using HTTP to retrieve `http://www.realsite.com`). Obviously, this mechanism can be iterated to more than one rewebber, and all currently installed and operating rewebbers are collectively referred to as the *rewebber network*.

So far, the mechanism yet hides the real location of the Web server from the browser, but still has some flaws. First of all, once the browser has retrieved the resource from the rewebber, it could use one of the more powerful WWW search engines to try to find where the resource originally came from. This problem is solved by encrypting the entire resource before storing it on the server. Thus, if the resource were accessed directly (e.g., through a WWW search engine), it would look like random data. In their implementation of a rewebber network, Goldberg and Wagner have used the DESX encryption algorithm.[13] The DESX key is given to the rewebber in the encrypted part of the locator; that is, when the rewebber decrypts the locator, it finds not only a URL to retrieve, but also a DESX key with which to decrypt the resource thus retrieved. It then passes the decrypted resource back to the browser (or to the next rewebber).

The technique of encrypting a resource stored at the server has another benefit: the resource can be padded in size before being encrypted, and the rewebber will truncate the resource to its original size before passing it back to the browser. The reason for this is similar to that for encrypting the resource in the first place. If the retrieved resource is 1,234 bytes long, for example, a WWW search for encrypted resources near that size would quickly narrow down the possible choices. To thwart this, one can always add random padding to the end of encrypted resources so that their total length is one of a handful of fixed sizes (such as 10, 20, 40, 80, etc. KB).

To implement chaining, the URL in the encrypted portion of a locator is replaced with another (complete) locator, one which points to a rewebber at a different site (and preferably in a different legal jurisdiction). As mentioned above, this process can be iterated, thus making the rewebber chain listed in the locator as long as one likes. A schematic diagram of a locator containing a rewebber chain of length 3 appears in Figure 13.6. In this case, the locator uses the three rewebbers A, B, and C. Each rectangle represents an encryption with a corresponding public key. Consequently, the innermost rectangle represents an encryption with the rewebber C's public key, whereas the next two rectangles represent encryptions with the public keys of the rewebbers B and C. Similarly, Kc, Kb, and Ka represent the DESX keys that the rewebbers C, B, and A need to decrypt the appropriate locators.

Figure 13.6   A schematic diagram of a locator containing a rewebber chain of length 3 (for the rewebbers A, B, and C).

When using rewebber chaining, the resource must be encrypted multiple times before it is stored on the server. To do this, the publisher randomly selects a DESX key for each rewebber in the chain, encodes them into the locator as depicted in Figure 13.6, and iteratively encrypts the resource. In this way the publisher forms

---

[13]The DESX encryption algorithm refers to a technique intended to extend the strength of DES that was originally proposed by Ronald L. Rivest.

a locator and announces it in public (for example, by using an anonymous remailer service to post it to a newsgroup). Note that all of the security parameters, including the length of the rewebber chain, are under the full control of the publisher, so individual publishers may adjust these parameters to fit their actual anonymity requirements.

The main benefit of chaining is that only the rewebber closest to the browser ever sees the decrypted data, and only the rewebber closest to the server knows from where it is really getting data. In order to link the two, the cooperation of every rewebber in the chain would be necessary. This avoids the existence of a single point of failure, and allows the distribution of trust throughout the network. In their work, Goldberg and Wagner have also provided an analysis with regard to the number of rewebbers that should be chosen in a chain. Again, a trade-off must be made between the probability of compromise and the probability of failure. The longer the chain, the less likely it gets compromised but the more likely it fails. Contrary to that, the shorter the chain, the more likely it gets compromised but the less likely it fails.

Once a rewebber network is deployed, the stage will be set for the ability to publish anonymously on the Web. One major drawback, however, is that a locator that contains just a simple chain of rewebbers looks ugly. The following example of a locator is taken from [19]:

```
http://rewebber.com/!RjViOrawjGRT50ECKo_UBa
7Qv3FJlRbyej_Wh10g_9vpPAyeHmrYE1QL1H2ifNh2M
a4UYt3IaqeQRXXd7oxEvwR8wJ3cnrNbPF6rc1Uzr6mx
IWUtlgWOuRlLObGkAv3fX8WEcBd1JPWGT8VoYOF1jxg
PL7OvuVOxtbMPsRbQgOiY=RKLBaUYedsCnON-UQOm5J
WTE1nuoh_J5J_yg1CfkaN9jSGkdf51-gdj3RN4XHf_Y
Vyxfupgc8VPsSyFdEeROdj9kMHuPvLivE_awqAwU_3A
f8mc44QBNOfMVJjpeyHSa79KdTQ5EGlPzLK7upFXtUF
cNLSD7YLSc1gKI3X8nk15s=RXbQaqmOAx4VhKPwkLVK
_MMJaz9wchn_pI48xhTzgndt5HkO9VToLyz7EF4wGH3
XKPD7YbKVyiDZytva_sUBcdqpmPXTzApYLBnl4nDOy1
o1Pu1Rky8CxRfnC9BvQqof853n99vkuGKP9K4p3H7pl
6i8DOat-NrOIndpz5xgwZKc=/
```

Obviously, this is hard to announce in public and there is a naming problem that needs to be solved (similar to the announcement of the encrypted URLs for the JANUS service). In their work, Goldberg and Wagner have proposed to create a virtual namespace called the .taz namespace (TAZ standing for "temporary autonomous zone"), and to create new servers called *TAZ servers* to resolve this namespace. The function of a TAZ server is to offer publishers an easy way to point potential readers at their material, as well as offering readers an easy way to access it. A TAZ server consists essentially of a public database mapping virtual hostnames ending in .taz to rewebber locators. The emphasis on public is to stress that nothing in this database must be kept secret. Unlike an anonymous remailer like anon.penet.fi (which associates an alias e-mail address with a real one), TAZ servers merely associate .taz addresses with locators. Most importantly, the TAZ server administrator cannot decrypt the locators that are stored in the database.

For obvious reasons, there is the potential for a great deal of future work in the TAZ servers. Centralized solutions such as the one implemented so far may work well for a while, but in the future, decentralized solutions will be preferable, for both scalability and availability reasons. A great deal can be learned from the Internet's DNS. Anyway, more implementation and real-life deployment experience is required to better understand the engineering trade-offs. Fortunately, by separating the TAZ server from the rewebber network, and by ensuring that the TAZ database contains only public data, there is much flexibility for upgrading this part of the system.

13.5   CONCLUSIONS

In this chapter, we addressed the increasingly important field of privacy protection. More precisely, we overviewed and discussed some technologies that are used to support anonymous browsing and anonymous publishing on the Web. In addition to these technologies, there are also some voluntary privacy standards. For example, *TRUSTe* (formerly known as eTrust) is an independent, non-profit organization dedicated to establishing a trusting environment where users can feel comfortable dealing with companies on the Internet.[14] Championed by CommerceNet and the Electronic Frontier Foundation (EFF), TRUSTe's efforts focus on promoting trust through online privacy assurance, putting users in control of their personal information. Based on the principles of disclosure and informed consent, the TRUSTe Online Privacy Program utilizes a branded, online seal or trustmark to signify disclosure of a Web site's personal information privacy policy. In displaying the TRUSTe online seal or trustmark, Web sites send a clear signal to users that they have formally agreed to disclose their information gathering and dissemination practices, and that their disclosure is backed by credible third-party assurance [20]. More specifically, TRUSTe licensees agree to a number of requirements. For example,

---

[14]http://www.truste.org

a Web site must post a privacy statement linked from the homepage, which includes disclosure of the Web site's information gathering and dissemination practices. Next, the Web site must provide, at a minimum, the ability for users to opt out of having their personal information used by third parties for secondary purposes. Also, the Web site must implement reasonable mechanisms and procedures to protect personal information from loss, misuse, or unauthorized alteration. Similarly, the Web site must provide a mechanism for users to correct inaccuracies in their information. Finally, TRUSTe provides assurance to users that the site is following its stated privacy practices through initial and periodic reviews, seeding, and compliance reviews. All initial and periodic reviews are conducted at TRUSTe's facility by accessing the licensee's Web site. If TRUSTe has reason to believe a licensee is not following its stated privacy practices, an independent third party may conduct a compliance review. Compliance reviews compare the Web site's actual privacy practices with stated practices and are performed on-site at the licensee's location. Finally, TRUSTe provides a structure to resolve user complaints that cannot be adequately resolved by the TRUSTe licensee. In fact, TRUSTe's escalation process assures that complaints will be answered in a fair and timely fashion.

BBBOnLine[15] is a wholly owned subsidiary of the Council of Better Business Bureaus, and BBBOnLine's mission is to promote trust and confidence on the Internet. Similar to the TRUSTe Online Privacy Program, BBBOnLine has launched a BBBOnLine Privacy Program.[16] BBBOnLine will grant a privacy seal to companies that post privacy policies telling consumers what personal information is being collected and how it will be used. Qualifying sites commit to abide by their posted privacy policies, and agree to a comprehensive independent verification by BBBOnLine. The Privacy Program also gives consumers a mechanism for resolving disputes.

Similar to the TRUSTe Online Privacy Program and the BBBOnLine Privacy Program, the W3C project *Platform for Privacy Preferences* (P3P) seeks to provide a platform for trusted and informed online interactions [21].[17] Unlike the above-mentioned programs, however, the P3P is a specification of syntax and semantics for a negotiation protocol to be used between a user agent and a service provider. As such, P3P was designed to help users reach agreements with arbitrary services, such as provided by Web sites. As the first step toward reaching an agreement, a service sends a machine-readable proposal in which the organization responsible for the service declares its identity and privacy practices. The proposals are written in

---

[15]http://www.bbbonline.com
[16]http://www.bbbonline.com/businesses/privacy/
[17]http://www.w3.org/P3P/

XML and are automatically parsed by user agents, such as Web browsers, browser plug-ins, and proxy servers. The proposals are then compared with the privacy preferences set by the user. Consequently, users need not read the privacy policies at every Web site they visit. If a proposal matches the user's preferences, the user agent may accept it automatically. If, however, the proposal and preferences are inconsistent, the agent may prompt the user, reject the proposal, send the service an alternative proposal, or ask the service to send another proposal. As of this writing, there is a first implementation of P3P available as a Web-based service.[18]

In summary, the handling of personal information on the Web is a hotly debated topic. The need to maximize user's privacy is at odds at a fundamental level with businesses' need to minimize fraud. The first goal seeks to maximize users' anonymity, whereas the second goal requires users to be strongly and unequivocally identified and authenticated. Somehow, a compromise must be struck for this dilemma. As of this writing, this compromise has not been found yet. Also, it is not clear whether initiatives, such as the TRUSTe Online Privacy Program or the W3C P3P, will be successful on the marketplace.

Finally, it's important to note that many countries (including, for example, most countries of the European community[19]) have data privacy or data protection laws that make it a legal obligation for people storing, processing, and transmitting personal data to adequately protect the privacy of the data. Also, there are guidelines on data privacy and data protection published by international organizations, such as the OECD. Data privacy and data protection laws are important to know, but they are not covered in this book. Refer to [22] to get an overview about the current situation in the United States, or to [23] to get an international perspective on the topic.

REFERENCES

[1] A. Pfitzmann, and M. Waidner, "Networks without user observability," *Computers & Security*, Vol. 2, No. 6, pp. 158 – 166.

[2] D. Chaum, "Untraceable Electronic Mail, Return Addresses and Digital Pseudonyms," *Communications of the ACM*, Vol. 24, No. 2, February 1981, pp. 84 – 88.

[3] C. Cülcü, and G.Tsudik, "Mixing Emails with BABEL," *Proceedings of ISOC Symposium on Network and Distributed System Security*, February 1996, pp. 2 – 16.

---

[18]`http://privacy.linkexchange.com/`
[19]This is true because the European Community (EC) has published a directive on Data Protection that is now law in most countries of the EC.

[4] D. Kristol, and L. Montulli, *HTTP State Management Mechanism*, Request for Comments (RFC) 2109, February 1997.

[5] R. Sandhu, and J.S. Park, "Cooking Secure Cookies on the Web," work in progress.

[6] A. Luotonen, *Web Proxy Servers*, Prentice Hall PTR, Upper Saddle River, NJ, 1998.

[7] M.G. Reed, P.F. Syverson, and D.M. Goldschlag, "Proxies for Anonymous Routing," *Proceedings of Annual Computer Security Applications Conference (ACSAC '96)*, San Diego, CA, 1996, pp. 95 – 104.

[8] D.M Goldschlag, M.G Reed, and P.F. Syverson, "Privacy on the Internet," *Proceedings of INET '97*, June 1997.

[9] P.F. Syverson, D.M. Goldschlag, and M.G. Reed, "Anonymous Connections and Onion Routing," *Proceedings of IEEE Symposium on Security and Privacy*, 1997, pp. 44 – 54.

[10] P.F. Syverson, M.G. Reed, and D.M. Goldschlag, "Private Web Browsing," *Journal of Computer Security*, Special Issue on Web Security, Vol. 5, No. 3, 1997, pp. 237 – 248.

[11] D.M. Goldschlag, M.G. Reed, and P.F. Syverson, "Onion Routing for Anonymous and Private Internet Connections," *Communications of the ACM*, Vol. 42, No. 2, 1999, pp. 39 – 41.

[12] E. Gabber, P.B. Gibbons, Y. Matias, and A. Mayer, "How to Make Personalized Web Browsing Simple, Secure, and Anonymous," *Proceedings of Financial Cryptography*, February 1997, pp. 17 – 31.

[13] E. Gabber, P.B. Gibbons, D.M. Kristol, Y. Matias, and A. Mayer, "Consistent, Yet Anonymous Web Access with LPWA," *Communications of the ACM*, Vol. 42, No. 2, February 1999, pp. 42 – 47.

[14] D. Bleichenbacher, E. Gabber, P. Gibbons, Y. Matias, and A. Mayer, "On Secure and Pseudonymous Client-Relationships with Multiple Servers," *Proceedings of USENIX Workshop on Electronic Commerce*, August 1998, pp. 99 – 108.

[15] M.K. Reiter, and A.D. Rubin, "Crowds: Anonymity for Web Transactions," *ACM Transactions on Information and System Security*, Vol. 1, No. 1, 1998.

[16] M.K. Reiter, and A.D. Rubin, "Anonymous Web Transactions With Crowds," *Communications of the ACM*, Vol. 42, No. 2, February 1999, pp. 32 – 38.

[17] M.K. Reiter, "Distributing Trust With the Rampart Toolkit," *Communications of the ACM*, Vol. 39, No. 4, April 1996, pp. 71 - 74.

[18] R. Oppliger, *Authentication Systems for Secure Networks*, Artech House, Norwood, MA, 1996.

[19] I. Goldberg, and D. Wagner, *"TAZ Servers and the Rewebber Network: Enabling Anonymous Publishing on the World Wide Web*, CS 268 Final Report, University of California, Berkeley, CA, 1997.

[20] P. Benassi, "TRUSTe: An Online Privacy Seal Program," *Communications of the ACM*, Vol. 42, No. 2, February 1999, pp. 56 – 59.

[21] J. Reagle, and L.F. Cranor, "The Platform for Privacy Preferences," *Communications of the ACM*, Vol. 42, No. 2, February 1999, pp. 48 – 55.

[22] P. Schwartz, and J.R. Reidenberg, *Data Privacy Law: A Study of United States Data Protection*, Lexis Law Pub, 1996.

[23] C.E.H. Franklin (Ed.), *Business Guide to Privacy and Data Protection Legislation*, Kluwer Law International, 1995.

Chapter 14

Censorship on the WWW

In this chapter, we address censorship on the Internet and the WWW. In particular, we introduce the topic in Section 14.1, address two technical approaches — content blocking as well as content rating and self-determination — in Sections 14.2 and Section 14.3, and draw some conclusions in Section 14.4. By doing so, we are going to stay on the technical side and not delve into the (sometimes heated) discussions about the political and legal justification for censorship on the Internet and the WWW. These discussions are going on in almost every country that is connected (or is about to connect) to the Internet. You may refer to [1,2] for a discussion about the legal considerations and implications of censorship.

14.1 INTRODUCTION

Nowadays, the Internet in general, and the WWW in particular, is often criticized for providing an information infrastructure that can also be (mis)used for the distribution of content that is illegal or offensive, such as propagandistic material from the radical right-wing or child-pornographic images or video sequences. Most people agree that the Internet should not provide support for the distribution of such content, and several proposals have been made to prevent the Internet from being

353

(mis)used for theses purposes accordingly. The proposals fall into two categories: on the one hand, there is content blocking, and on the other hand, there is content rating and the notion of self-determination:

- The idea of *content blocking* is to make ISPs ultimatively responsible and liable for the content they provide or make available and accessible to their subscribers;

- Contrary to that, the idea of *content rating and self-determination* is to make ISP subscribers responsible for the content they actually access, and to provide support for content rating and the notion of self-determination.

In the case of content blocking, ISPs must find ways to cut off Internet and Web sites that provide or make available and accessible to their subscribers dubious content. Contrary to that, ISPs have no obligations in the case of content rating and self-determination. In this case, it is up to the content providers to have their content rated, and it is up to the Internet users and ISP subscribers to protect themselves accordingly (e.g., by configuring their browsers not to render dubious content). Consequently, the idea of content blocking is driven by the service providers, whereas the idea of content rating and self-determination is rather driven by the content providers and ISP subscribers.

If properly deployed and enforced, content rating and self-determination has some merit. All an Internet user or ISP subscriber needs in this case is a scheme that allows him or her to decide what kind of content a specific Internet or Web site actually provides. The general idea behind content rating is to classify a given document's content according to some previously defined criteria, and to control access to the document according to this classification. For some media, such as cinema movies, we are already accustomed to content rating, whereas for other media, such as television and the Web, the effectiveness and efficiency of content rating and self-determination schemes remain to be seen. In either case, it must be ensured that content rating schemes can neither be circumvented nor manipulated. For all practical purposes, this turns out to be difficult.

In the following two sections we address the technologies that are used to implement content blocking as well as content rating and self-determination.

14.2   CONTENT BLOCKING

In the recent past, several approaches have been proposed to block content identified by some parties as illegal or offensive. According to a report published by the

Australian government in 1998 [3],[1] such content can either be blocked at the packet or application level (as further explained in Chapter 3):

- In short, blocking content at the packet level requires (screening) routers to examine the source IP address of an incoming IP packet, compare it with a black list, and either forward (if the IP address isn't itemized in the black list) or drop (if the IP address is itemized in the black list) the packet;

- Blocking content at the application level requires proxy servers and application gateways that examine resources or resource information in order to decide whether the corresponding application protocol request, such as an HTTP GET method invocation, should be served or not. For example, a common approach for blocking content at the application level is to specify URLs that should not be served and place them in corresponding black lists that are distributed and installed on proxy servers. Before serving an HTTP request, a proxy server would then make sure that the requested URL is not itemized in the black list. Obviously, the granularity of such blocking decisions can be made much finer than in the case of blocking content at the packet level.

According to this brief description, packet-level blocking is sometimes also referred to as *IP address blocking*, whereas application-level blocking is also called *URL blocking*. Both technologies as well as their advantages and disadvantages are overviewed and briefly discussed next.

14.2.1 IP Address Blocking

The technologies used to implement IP address or packet-level blocking are similar to the ones discussed in Chapter 3, when we elaborated on packet filtering and stateful inspection technologies. In short, any kind of access control list (ACL) must be specified in order to distinguish packets that should be routed and packets that should be dropped. This distinction is mainly based on the information that is usually found in IP packet headers, such as source and destination IP addresses.

In general, IP address or packet-level blocking could be carried out by any ISP. In practice, however, it is more efficient to have IP address or packet-level blocking carried out by the relatively small number of Internet backbone service providers (BSPs). Since packet-level blocking involves a comparison of each IP packets source address with a supplied black list of IP addresses (the ones that are going to be

---

[1]http://203.9.218.13/reports/blocking/index.html

blocked), it can easily be implemented using ACL features of the screening routers that are operated by the BSPs. If performance is a problem, some sophisticated hashing algorithms may also be used.

As of this writing, the effectiveness of IP address or packet-level blocking is a hotly debated topic. Proponents of the technology claim that it is a possible way to effectively block illegal or offensive content on the Internet or WWW, whereas opponents of the technology refer to the following technical issues that collectively limit its effectiveness:

- First, IP address or packet-level blocking is indiscriminate in the sense that the decision to block an Internet or Web site actually means that the entire site will be blocked and made "invisible" to the Internet users and ISP subscribers. Consequently, if a site were hosted by a large company, such as an ISP or BSP, then the rest of the Web sites hosted by that company would also be blocked and made invisible to the Internet users and ISP subscribers. This poses some practical and legal problems for companies that host many (virtual) Web sites. Positively speaking, it would also be an incentive for them to remove the offensive material.

- Second, IP address or packet-level blocking may also affect other TCP/IP services than HTTP. Note that a decision to block a particular Internet or Web site because of some illegal or offensive content generally means that all other services, such as FTP, SMTP, or NNTP, will also be blocked. The reason for that is that IP address or packet-level blocking decisions are mainly based on IP addresses. Although it is possible to include port numbers (that specify particular services) in the decision rules, this is seldom done (mainly because it negatively influences the performance of the screening routers). Also, if it was done, the port numbers could also be changed, even more easily than IP addresses.

- Third, IP address or packet-level blocking devices can often be bypassed or circumvented. For example, it is possible for an Internet or Web site to regularly change its IP address, thereby bypassing the access control enforced by the black list entirely. Similarly, specific network technologies, such as IP tunneling, can be used to circumvent any IP address or packet-level blocking device.

- Fourth, IP address or packet-level blocking requires some computational power on the routing (and filtering) devices. Consequently, BSP routers may need to be upgraded to implement IP address or packet-level blocking. Note that a top-of-the-line router from Cisco Systems, appropriately configured, can carry out packet-level blocking at line speeds, whereas some older style routers may need to be replaced or upgraded to meet the requirements of contemporary internet-working performance.

In either case, support for IP address or packet-level blocking complicates the packet filtering rules that are implemented and enforced by a firewall. Finally, there are also some non-technical issues to consider. For example, not all Internet traffic passes through a BSP. Many multinational organizations have extensive IP-based networks, which may involve the use of dedicated leased lines. The employees of these organizations would not be subject to IP address or packet-level blocking as enforced by the BSPs. Also, there are increased operational costs associated with the creation, maintenance, and distribution of black lists, as well as the configuration of the corresponding screening routers' ACLs. As of this writing, there are only few statistics available to put some light on these costs.

14.2.2 URL Blocking

URL or application-level blocking requires the existence of proxy servers or application gateways that examine resources or resource information to decide whether a specific request should be served or not. Consequently, ISPs prevent their clients from accessing the Internet directly for some application protocols, such as HTTP, by forcing them to access the Internet through a proxy server, which performs blocking and may store (or rather cache) frequently accessed material. This actually requires the client to configure his browser to make use of his ISP's proxy server (as discussed in Chapter 3). The proxy server can then compare requests from clients with a supplied black list of Internet and Web sites in the case of HTTP (or newsgroups in the case of NNTP).

As of this writing, URL or application-level blocking is most commonly used in corporate intranets to control access to specific Web sites, such as `www.playboy.com` or `www.penthouse.com`. In addition, there are few countries that try to enforce URL or application-level blocking technologies for their citizens. Prominent examples include Singapore and China.

Again, the discussion about the effectiveness of URL or application-level blocking is controversial. Proponents of the technology claim that it is a possible way to effectively block illegal or offensive content on the WWW, whereas opponents of the technology refer to the following technical issues that collectively limit the effectiveness of the technology:

• First, URL or application-level blocking can be bypassed or circumvented in many ways. For example, a user can access an Internet or Web site by specifying its descriptive DNS name, or its equivalent IP address. A black list that only checks DNS names can therefore be bypassed unless it also includes the equivalent IP address(es), which double (or multiply) the size of the corresponding black list. Similarly, it is possible to regularly change the IP address or DNS name of the computer system that hosts the HTTP server, or run several HTTP servers on a specific computer system and change the port number periodically. All of these and similar changes will cause an URL or application-level blocking strategy to fail (since the URLs change). The changes can be made explicit and communicated to the users, or they can be made implicit by having corresponding URL translation services run on legitimate server machines. The latter approach is conceptually similar to the TAZ network introduced in Chapter 13 with regard to anonymous publishing on the WWW.

- Second, push technologies bypass URL or application-level blocking entirely, since content is delivered to users without specifically being requested. Note that a proxy server that implements URL or application-level blocking generally filters requests for specific content. If the content is delivered without a corresponding request, it will not be blocked by the proxy server.

- Third, the policy of forcing users to access the Internet through a single proxy server (that implements URL or application-level blocking) reduces the reliability and decreases performance of Internet connectivity, as it introduces a single point of failure. There are also some application protocols that have problems working through a proxy server at all. For example, we saw in Chapter 3 that UDP-based application protocols are not always proxy-aware.

Similar to IP address or packet-level blocking, URL or application-level blocking generally complicates the configuration of firewalls and causes additional costs. Many ISPs and Web site hosting organizations do not employ proxy servers at present, and a requirement to do so may be a financial burden for small ISPs. In addition to the hardware costs, there are the ongoing costs of maintaining and administering the proxy servers, and supporting the clients that are forced to use them. Finally, there is the enormous and expensive task of creating, updating, and distributing the black lists. Also similar to IP address or packet-level blocking, URL or application-level blocking does not apply to organizations that are directly connected to the Internet and the WWW, such as educational institutions that don't use a firewall. In addition, the following nontechnical issues must also be considered with care:

- First, ISPs may be placed in a dilemma. Note that if an ISP is asked to adopt the role of a moral arbiter, it will be placed in a difficult position by its subscribers for either going too far or not going far enough.

- Second, a blacklist is a valuable commodity in its own right and blacklists should be maintained in secure environments accordingly. Note that a blacklist is a valuable target for a hacker, and once uncovered will be published on the Internet, thereby creating a "must see" list for casual and curious users. This may have the negative side effect of publicizing the sites on blacklists more widely than if the blacklists did not exist at all.

Finally, note that blocking content and deleting content are fundamentally different operations. Blocking prevents an Internet or Web site from being accessed, whereas deletion refers to the physical removal of a resource after it has been published on the Web. The deletion of a resource (or a set of resources) can only be carried out by its (their) owner(s) or the corresponding Web site administrator(s) or law enforcement officers. Note, however, that after a resource has been deleted, it may still exist on the following locations:

- Personal computers that have originally downloaded the resource and saved it to disc;

- Proxy servers that have served the download operation and have cached the corresponding resource;

- Mirror sites that have downloaded the resource for further distribution.

In summary, both IP address or packet-level blocking and URL or application-level blocking are technically possible, but can easily be circumvented. Also as mentioned above, mandating their use may result in blacklists (either for IP addresses or URLs) becoming "hot property," with the net result and effect that the blacklisted Internet and Web sites may even become more popular than if they were not blacklisted at all. Note, however, that this is more a psychological problem than a technical one. Also note that the same argument can also be used to argue against content rating self-determination (and to promote law enforcement as being the only practical solution accordingly).

14.3   CONTENT RATING AND SELF-DETERMINATION

Rather than censoring what content is being distributed on the Internet, as the Communications Decency Act and other legislative initiatives in the United States have tried to do, the idea of *content rating and self-determination* is to enable users to judge the content of a Web site based on some objective criteria. This idea actually conforms to the general argument of human beings being ultimatively responsible for their own behaviors and activities. Unfortunately, reality often shows another picture. Referring to currently available media, such as newspapers and TV programs, one may argue that content sinks to the lowest common denominator and the floor is only reached when they hit a legal restriction on publication. This is actually a very strong argument against the usefulness of content rating and self-determination.

The *Platform for Internet Content Selection* (PICS) is an initiative created by the industry to promote content rating and self-determination [4,5]. Coordinated by the W3C, PICS aims at providing an infrastructure for associating labels with content.[2] It is "value neutral" in the sense that it does not specify the content of labels. It only specifies a label format and describes how the corresponding labels may be transmitted. As such, it is a platform on which content rating services and filtering software packages can actually be built. Computer systems can process PICS labels in the background, automatically shielding users from undesirable content or directing their attention to sites of particular interest.

Version 1.1 of the PICS specification is complete and has been adopted industry-wide. It is summarized in Appendix D of [6]. In short, the PICS specification provides the means to implement a content rating service. It consists of the following components:

- A syntax for describing a content rating service, so that computer programs can present the service and its labels to the users;

- A syntax for labels, so that computer programs can actually process them. A label describes either a single document or a group of documents (provided by an Internet or Web site). A label may include a cryptographic hash value of the associated document or may even be digitally signed;

- An embedding of labels (or lists of labels) into the RFC 822 transmission and HTML document formats. In the first case, RFC 822-style headers are used,

---

[2]http://www.w3.org/PICS/

whereas in the second case, the HTML META tag is used for embedding one or more labels in the header of an HTML document;

- An extension of HTTP, so that clients can request labels to be transmitted with a document;

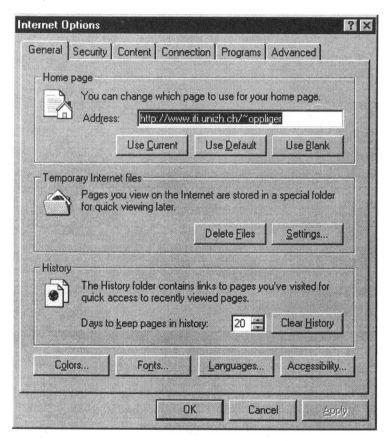

Figure 14.1   Microsoft Internet Explorer 4.0 General Internet Options menu. © 1999 Microsoft Corporation.

- A query-syntax for an online database of labels (a label bureau as discussed below).

Early in 1996, Microsoft, Netscape, SurfWatch, Microsystem Software, and some other software vendors announced their intention to ship PICS-compliant products. Some software is built directly into the Web browsers (including, for example, Microsoft Internet Explorer), whereas other software works independently from the browsers (including, for example, Microsystem Software's Cyber Patrol).

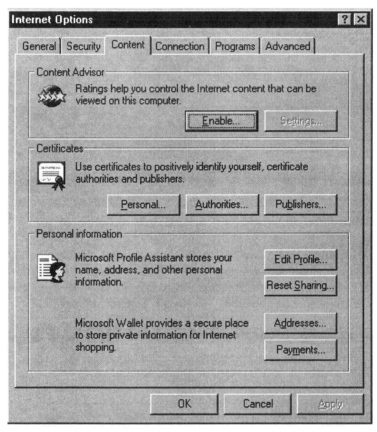

Figure 14.2   The Microsoft Internet Explorer 4.0 Content Internet Options menu. © 1999 Microsoft Corporation.

The W3C currently maintains a list of PICS-compatible filtering products and services (client software, HTTP servers, proxy servers, label bureaus, and rating services).[3] In addition, many online service providers, including America Online,

---

[3]http://www.w3.org/PICS/#Products

AT&T WorldNet, CompuServe, and Prodigy, have announced their support for PICS and the distribution of PICS-compliant software to their subscribers. In May 1996, for example, CompuServe announced that it would label all content it produces using the PICS-compliant rating service RSACi developed by the Recreational Software Advisory Council (RSAC).[4] According to the information found on its Web site, the RSAC "is an independent, nonprofit organization based in Washington, D.C, that empowers the public, especially parents, to make informed decisions about electronic media by means of an open, objective, content advisory system."

The RSACi system provides consumers with information about the level (ranging from 0 up to 4) of violence, nudity, sex, and offensive language in software games and Web sites. The corresponding RSACi levels are summarized in Table 14.1.

Table 14.1
The RSACi Levels for Violence, Nudity, Sex, and Language

Level	Violence Rating Descriptor	Nudity Rating Descriptor	Sex Rating Descriptor	Language Rating Descriptor
4	Rape or wanton, gratuitous violence	Frontal nudity (qualified as provocative display)	Explicit sexual acts or sex crimes	Crude, vulgar language or extreme hate speech
3	Aggressive violence or death to humans	Frontal nudity	Nonexplicit sexual acts	Strong language or hate speech
2	Destruction of realistic objects	Partial nudity	Clothed sexual touching	Moderate expletives or profanity
1	Injury to human being	Revealing attire	Passionate kissing	Mild expletives
0	None of the above or sports related	None of the above	None of the above or innocent kissing; romance	None of the above

In general, PICS can be used and provides support for both self-labeling (by an autonomous content provider or online publisher) and third-party labeling (by a label bureau):

- A content provider or online publisher who wants to label his or her content must first choose which rating vocabulary to use. The W3C recommends the

---

[4]http://www.rsac.org

use of a vocabulary already used by others, to make it easy for Internet users to understand the corresponding labels. Again, a list of self-rating vocabularies is available, but W3C does not endorse any particular vocabulary. Typically, the content provider or online publisher chooses a self-labeling service, connects to the corresponding Web site, and describes the resource to be published by filling out an online questionnaire. After completing the questionnaire, the service gives the content provider or online publisher a text label in a special format, which is then pasted into the corresponding HTML header (or the homepage of the corresponding Web site).

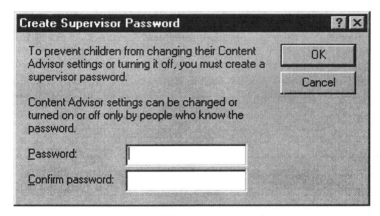

Figure 14.3   The Microsoft Internet Explorer 4.0 "Create Supervisor Password" prompt. © 1999 Microsoft Corporation.

- In addition to the self-labeling service, an independent rating agency need not get cooperation from every content provider or Web publisher whose material it labels. As with self-labeling described above, the independent labeler first needs to invent or adopt an existing vocabulary. The rater then uses a software tool to create labels that describe particular URLs. Instead of pasting those labels into documents, the independent rater distributes the labels through a separate server, which is called a *label bureau*. Filtering software will know to check at that label bureau to find the labels, much as consumers know to read particular magazines for reviews of appliances or automobiles.

Several PICS-compliant rating services are in operation today, allowing content providers and Web publishers to self-label their content. Examples include RSACi and SafeSurf. In addition, a number of companies (including EvaluWeb,

Net Shepherd, and NetView) are providing third-party labels, using their own PICS-compliant rating systems. Again, refer to the list of PICS-compatible services maintained by the W3C.[5] Unfortunately, the use and deployment of PICS and PICS-compliant rating services has not really taken off so far (and it is not likely that this situation will change in the near future).

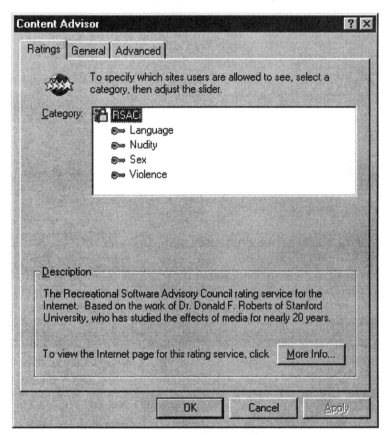

Figure 14.4 The Ratings tab of Microsoft Internet Explorer 4.0 Content Advisor. © 1999 Microsoft Corporation.

As mentioned above, Microsoft Internet Explorer provides support for PICS and RSACi. Figure 14.1 illustrates the corresponding View > Internet Options...

---

[5]http://www.w3.org/PICS/#Products

menu. Following the Content tab in this menu reveals the possibility to enable the Content Advisor as illustrated in Figure 14.2. Enabling the Content Advisor first requires the user to create a supervisor password. Figure 14.3 illustrates the corresponding "Create Supervisor Password" prompt. As illustrated in the following three figures, the Content Advisor can then be used to actually define RSACi category levels for the browser. Figure 14.4 illustrates the corresponding Ratings tab of the Content Advisor. It allows the user to view the ratings for the four RSACi categories mentioned above (language, nudity, sex, and violence).

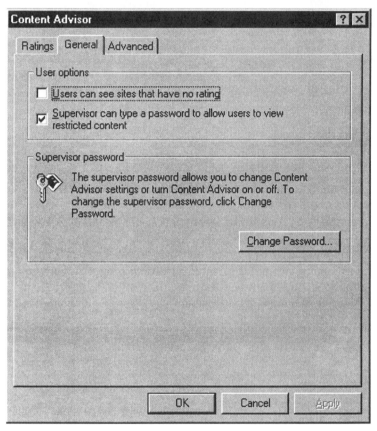

Figure 14.5   The General tab of Microsoft Internet Explorer 4.0 Content Advisor. © 1999 Microsoft Corporation.

Figure 14.5 illustrates the General tab of the Content Advisor. It allows the supervisor to specify whether users can see sites that have no rating, and to change the supervisor password. Finally, Figure 14.6 illustrates the Advanced tab of the Content Advisor. It allows the supervisor to view and modify the list of currently supported content rating systems, as well as to specify the use of an online ratings bureau. Note, however, that the use of a ratings bureau may slow down Internet access time considerably (as indicated in the corresponding menu option).

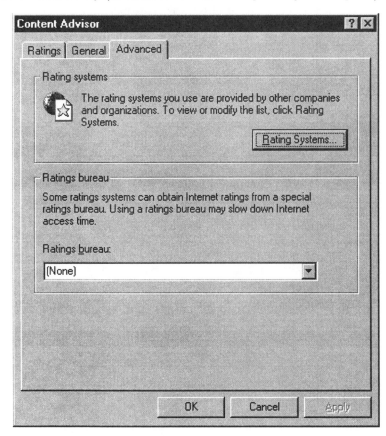

Figure 14.6   The Advanced tab of Microsoft Internet Explorer 4.0 Content Advisor. © 1999 Microsoft Corporation.

There are several points to consider with care regarding the use of content rating and self-determination technologies, such as employed by PICS and RSACi:

- First and foremost, not every label is trustworthy. For example, the creator of a computer virus can very easily distribute a misleading label claiming that the software is safe. Checking for labels merely converts the question of whether to trust a piece of software to one of trusting the label that is associated with it (and since both can be provided by the same person, it can be identical). One obvious solution is to use copyright protection labeling or cryptographic techniques to determine whether a document has been changed since its label was created and to ensure that the label is the work of its purported author.

- Second, mandatory self-labeling need not lead to censorship, so long as individuals can decide which labels to ignore. Unfortunately, people may not always have the choice. As mentioned above, Singapore and China are experimenting with national "firewalls" that are going to implement some content blocking strategies. Nevertheless, it is fair to say that improved individual controls remove one rationale for central control but do not prevent its imposition.

- Third, any content labeling system, no matter how well conceived and executed, will tend to stifle noncommercial communication. Labeling requires human time and energy; many sites of limited interest will therefore probably go unlabeled. Because of safety concerns, some people will block access to materials that are unlabeled or whose labels are untrusted. For such people, the Internet will function more like broadcasting, providing access only to sites with sufficient mass-market appeal to merit the cost of labeling.

As an added inducement to content labeling, it is worthwhile to mention that some future applications may use labels for searching as well as filtering. Thus, labeling a Web site's documents will make it easier both for some audiences to avoid the documents and for others to intentionally find them. Consequently, content labeling is a dual-use technology.

14.4   CONCLUSIONS

In general, censorship refers to the official suppression of information as published in specific media, such as newspapers, films, and books. In the past, many states have developed a highly refined system of censorship (again refer to [1,2]). Although most information is allowed to flow freely, some kinds of information are censored nationwide. In particular, we have mentioned propagandistic material from the radical right-wing and child-pornographic images or video sequences as examples.

More recently, the question has arisen whether there is need for censorship on the Internet and the WWW. If this question is answered with a "yes," the next question to ask is about technologies that can eventually be used to enforce censorship on the Internet and the WWW. This question has been addressed in this chapter. In fact, we have addressed two technologies, namely content blocking as well as content rating and self-determination.[6]

The issue of content blocking is a difficult and, at times, emotional issue. Based on a thorough analysis of content blocking technologies, the previously mentioned Australian report concludes that content blocking implemented purely by technological means will be ineffective, and neither of the two approaches (IP address or packet-level blocking and URL or application-level blocking) should be mandated [3]. Instead, the report argues that ISPs could be encouraged to offer differentiated services to their subscribers, based on access to the Internet through a proxy server. The following two services may be considered:

- A "clean" service for which the proxy server includes a list of permitted URLs. Requests for URLs found on the list should be served, whereas requests for URLs outside the list should be refused.

- A "best effort" service for which the proxy server includes a list of refused URLs. Requests for URLs found on the list should be refused, whereas requests for URLs outside the list should be served.

Obviously, the distinction between a "clean" service and a "best effort" service is similar to the distinction between the two stances of a firewall policy ("what is not explicitly allowed is refused" and "what is not explicitly refused is allowed"). In either case, ISPs may incur some costs in setting up differentiated services. These costs could either be passed on to clients in increased fees, or an ISP may see some competitive advantage in providing such an environment to clients. Alternatively, the governments may consider providing some incentives to ISPs to offer such differentiated services.

In either case, international cooperation is needed to determine jurisdiction. Locally hosted content that is either illegal or considered to be offensive is best handled

---

[6]Note that the proponents of content rating and self-determination technologies often argue that their technologies do not enforce censorship (but rather some more sophisticated access control). In either case (and whatever the claims of the corresponding proponents are), content rating and self-determination technologies are being designed for building censorship software, and as such, they represent technologies that can be used to enforce censorship.

by a direct approach to the ISP or the organization that hosts the material, requesting that the ISP or hosting organization take appropriate action. However, most content on the Internet resides on foreign servers. In fact, the content in question may be entirely legal in the jurisdiction in which it is being hosted, as a result of differences in international regulation. Consequently, the authors of [3] propose international forums to create the necessary infrastructure, so that organizations that host content could determine the jurisdiction of the client software making the request. Having determined the jurisdiction, the server could find out whether the requested content was legal in the client's jurisdiction.

Finally, at the time of this writing it is not clear whether any form of censorship on the Internet or WWW — either content blocking or content rating and self-determination — will be accepted by Internet users at all. Statistical investigations will have to clarify this point. Also, statistical investigations must be done to quantify the costs that are involved in either censorship technology. Nevertheless, it is important to note (and to remember) that law enforcement agencies in many countries mandate that ISPs keep a log of all sites accessed by their customers, and that they have access to them. Technologies, such as the ones described in Chapter 13, can be used to circumvent these logs (or to make them useless).

REFERENCES

[1] H.N. Foerstel (Ed.), *Banned in the Media: A Reference Guide to Censorship in the Press, Motion Pictures, Broadcasting, and the Internet*, Greenwood Publishing Group, Westport, CT, 1998.

[2] M.E. Price (Ed.), *The V-Chip Debate: Content Filtering From Television to the Internet*, Lawrence Erlbaum Associates, Mahwah, NJ, 1998.

[3] P. McCrea, B. Smart, and M. Andrews, "Blocking Content on the Internet: A Technical Perspective," Report prepared for the Australian National Office for the Information Economy (NOIE), June 1998.

[4] P. Resnick, "Filtering Information on the Internet," *Scientific America*, March 1997, pp. 106 – 108.

[5] P. Resnick, and J. Miller, "PICS: Internet Access Controls Without Censorship," *Communications of the ACM*, Vol. 39, No. 10, October 1996, pp. 87 – 93.

[6] S. Garfinkel, and E.H. Spafford, *Web Security & Commerce*, O'Reilly & Associates, Sebastopol, CA, 1996.

Chapter 15

Conclusions and Outlook

In this book, we addressed many technologies that are used to provide security services for the Internet and the WWW. Some of these technologies are already in use and widely deployed, whereas others have just been invented and are still being studied and improved. Keeping in mind the various security technologies, we can argue that the security problems of the Internet and the WWW will soon go away. This is the optimistic view.

Unfortunately, there is also a pessimistic view, expressed by Marcus J. Ranum, who gave a remarkable talk entitled "Security on Internet Time" at the 1997 Annual Computer Security Applications Conference (ACSAC '97) in San Diego, California. According to Ranum's talk, the situation in network security in general and Internet security in particular is bad and is going to get worse, mainly because of the accelerated development cycles within the computer and communications industries. In a world that is characterized with overcapitalization of startup companies and aggressive marketing of vaporware or concept products, it is hard to actually slow down and prolong the development cycles (that are necessary to take security more seriously into account).

Analyzing the current state, Ranum identified a number of effects that all together negatively influence security on the Internet and WWW:

- *The "everything beta" effect:* Major applications are being deployed that depend on beta-test code only. Nonbeta versions generally lack functionality that is usually required by the users.

- *The "vendor sponsored incompatibility" effect:* Due to the fact that some vendors see owning a standard as a market share lever, there are deliberate attempts to produce competing (and incompatible) standards. Examples include the various proposals for the IETF IPsec WG's key management protocol, the Java and ActiveX incompatibility, and many electronic payment systems.

- *The "wobbly code" effect:* As a result of the accelerated development cycles within the industry, most commercial products are known to be buggy and to have bugs at ship-time. The products are shipped when they only mostly work. As a consequence, beta testing has replaced quality control and assurance management for nearly all practical purposes.

- *The "security in V2.0" effect:* Many protocols are being designed without security in mind. In general, the life span of unsuccessful products is very short. So why bother about security at first place? However, if a product is successful, it will have a large installed base very rapidly, making it very difficult to add security in a later version. We discuss this point as it relates to HTTP later on.

- *The "standards rubber stamp" effect:* In practice, standardization bodies have limited power, whereas the importance of a large installed base has become paramount. Unfortunately, this is true for almost all standardization bodies (including the IETF).

- *The "additional layer" effect:* When presented with competing protocols or technologies there is a common tendency to virtualize them under layers of interfacing, instead of creating open standards that competing protocols and technologies may converge to.

Following this line of argument, the long-term effect points to a further downward spiral that may lead to a software catastrophe. Ranum also proposed a few things that one can do to prevent this catastrophe:

- The software development methodologies and techniques (including software testing and maintenance) must be improved;

- The standardization bodies must be cleaned up, meaning that commercial interests should be removed (according to the "vendor sponsored incompatibility" effect as mentioned above);

- Also, many protocols must be redesigned from scratch.

Unfortunately, these things are hard to accomplish and give little hope for improvement. In fact, it is commonly agreed that software development methodologies and techniques must be improved, and the software industry has been trying hard to do so. Similarly, it is commonly agreed that the current situation in IT standardization is not satisfactory, and that many protocols that are weak or badly designed can only be improved if they are redesigned from scratch. Consequently, Ranum concluded his talk with the insight that "we're in a lot of trouble," without providing any practical advice on how to overcome the trouble.

Although this point of view is rather pessimistic, I fully agree with it. While there are many discussions on security-related issues, the main reason for the lack of Internet and WWW security is still the enormous speed in which everything happens. HTTP is a good example to illustrate the entire problem. When Tim Berners-Lee defined the first version of HTTP, he gave little thought to security. In fact, he argued that the aim of the WWW built on top of HTTP was to publish information for the public. So why bother about security in the first place? According to this line of argument, HTTP included only a few security features that were known to be weak, such as password-based protection for files in specific branches of a directory tree. Only recently have people started to use HTTP to build intranet solutions that store and process sensitive data, and to offer e-commerce services to the general public. In these environments it has become important to strongly authenticate users, to control access to data, to protect the confidentiality and integrity of data in transmission, and to provide non-repudiation services to the parties involved. Consequently, several extensions to HTTP have been proposed, including, for example, HTTP digest authentication. In addition, some cryptographic security protocols have been proposed to either enhance HTTP, such as SSL/TLS, or to replace it entirely, such as S-HTTP. Unfortunately, the use and deployment of these secondary technologies has turned out to be slow (as compared to the primary technology which is HTTP). Had Tim Berners-Lee been security-minded when designing HTTP in the first place, Web security would not be a major issue today (and you wouldn't be reading an entire book on Web security).

The bad news is that the security problems won't go away in the near future. Applications will continue to be developed and deployed without addressing security, and users will continue to use some of these applications without caring about security. The good news, however, is that one can reasonably expect the situation to improve over time, since computer and communication security is being thought about at a steadily increasing number of universities, polytechnics, and research laboratories. Consequently, the next generation of software and communications protocol engineers have a good chance of being educated in security matters, and this education will also positively influence the security of the systems and protocols they design, implement, and eventually deploy.

Note, however, that there are many examples of security being built in by engineers who are not security experts, and these have been seriously flawed. Building a seriously secure system or protocol is indeed a hard problem. Also note that security engineering is different from any other type of engineering. Most engineering involves making things work. Contrary to that, security engineering involves figuring out how to make things not work or how to make them work differently and then preventing the corresponding failures. Consequently, security engineering involves making sure things do not fail in the presence of intelligent and malicious adversaries who force faults at precisely the wrong time and in precisely the wrong way. The fact that contemporary e-commerce applications involve multiple parties and multiple protocols further increases the complexity of the security problem. The field is wide open for further research and development.

Glossary

Access The ability of a principal to use the resources of a system or information system.

Access control The prevention of unauthorized access to resources of a system or information system, including the prevention of their use in an unauthorized manner.

Access control list A list of principals who are authorized to have access to a resource, together with their corresponding access rights.

Access control service Security service that is used to control access to a corporate network, such as an intranet.

Access right The right to access a resource.

Accountability The property that ensures that the actions of a principal may be traced uniquely to this particular principal.

Accounting The process of measuring resource usage of a principal.

Active network Network in which each data unit is replaced by an active mobile code unit that carries data and instructions telling the network how to process the data unit.

ActiveX Marketing name for a set of technologies, protocols, services, and application programming interfaces (APIs) based on Microsoft's component object model (COM). As such, ActiveX is also a system for downloading executable code over the Internet. The code is bundled into a single file called ActiveX control. In general, a file carrying an ActiveX control has the extension OCX.

Adaptive-chosen-ciphertext attack A version of the chosen-ciphertext attack where the cryptanalyst can choose ciphertexts dynamically and alter his or her choices based on the results of previous decryptions. Typically, a cryptanalyst can mount an attack of this type in a scenario in which he or she has access to a decryption device, but is unable to extract the (decryption) key from it.

Adaptive-chosen-plaintext attack A version of the chosen-plaintext attack where the cryptanalyst is able to choose plaintexts dynamically, and alter his or her choices based on the results of previous encryptions. Typically, a cryptanalyst can mount an attack of this type in a scenario in which he or she has access to an encryption device, but is unable to extract the (encryption) key from it.

Adversary Commonly used to refer to the opponent, the enemy, or any other mischievous person who desires to compromise someone else's security.

AES The advanced encryption standard (AES) is an encryption algorithm that is being evaluated to replace DES in the future.

Anonymous remailer Anonymous e-mail forwarding service (provided through an anonymizing SMTP proxy server).

Application gateway An internetworking device that interconnects one network to another for a specific application. An application gateway can either work at the application or transport layer. If the gateway works at the application layer, it is usually called an application-level gateway or proxy server. If the gateway works at the transport layer, it is usually called a circuit-level gateway.

Attack An exploitation of a vulnerability by an intruder.

Attribute authority Authority that issues (and eventually revokes) attribute certificates.

Attribute certificate Data record that provides an attribute for a principal. It is rendered unforgeable by appending a digital signature from an attribute authority.

Audit trail Evidence, in documentary or other form, that enables a review of the functioning of elements of an information system.

Authentication The process of verifying the claimed identity of a principal.

Authentication context Information conveyed during a particular instance of an authentication process.

Authentication exchange A sequence of one or more messages used and sent for authentication.

Authentication information Information used for authentication.

Authorization The process of assigning rights, which includes the granting of access based on specific access rights.

Authorization policy Part of an access control policy by which access by subjects to objects is granted or denied. An authorization policy may be defined in terms of access control lists, capabilities, or attributes assigned to subjects, objects, or both.

Availability The property that ensures a resource is available and accessible for authorized principals.

Baseline controls Control procedures that constitute minimum good practice levels of protection.

Basic authentication User authentication scheme specified for HTTP/1.0.

Bastion host A computer system that is part of a firewall configuration and hosts one (or several) application gateway(s). A bastion host must be highly secure in order to resist direct attacks from the Internet.

BETSI Secure software distribution system developed at Bellcore (Bellcore's trusted software integrity system).

Binary mail attachment Attachment to an e-mail message that contains binary data and may encode anything (from random data to executable program code).

Biometrics The science of using biological properties to identify individuals, such as fingerprints, retina scans, or voice recognition.

Birthday attack A brute force attack used to find collisions in cryptographic algorithms. The attack gets its name from the surprising result that the probability of two or more people in a group of 23 sharing the same birthday is greater than 1/2.

Bit A binary digit (either 1 or 0).

Blind signature scheme Digital signature scheme that allows one party to have a second party sign a message without revealing information about the message to the second party.

Block cipher An encryption algorithm (cipher) that encrypts a message by breaking it down into blocks and encrypting each block individually. A block is a sequence of bits of fixed length.

Block cipher based MAC A message authentication code (MAC) algorithm that is performed by using a block cipher as a keyed compression function.

Blowfish Secret key cryptosystem.

Bridge Internetworking device that operates at the data link layer in the OSI reference model.

Brute force attack Attack that requires trying all (or a large fraction of all) possible values until the right value is found (also called an exhaustive search).

CAFE European ESPRIT project Conditional Access for Europe (CAFE) that began in 1992 and lasted for three years. The aim of the project was to develop a general system to administer conditional access rights to users. The most significant outcome of the project was the development of an advanced electronic payment system.

Capability Data record that can serve as an identifier for a resource such that possession of it confers access rights for that particular resource.

Censorship The official suppression of information as published in specific media, such as newspapers, films, and books.

Certificate practice statement Written statement that specifies the policies and practices of a CA with regard to issuance and maintenance of (public key) certificates.

Certificate profile Specification of certificate contents in terms of the required syntax and semantics of each field.

Certificate revocation Process of publicly announcing that a certificate (either a public key certificate, an attribute certificate, or any other form of certificate) has been revoked and should no longer be used.

Certificate revocation list A list of certificates that have been revoked before their expiration date.

Certificate revocation tree A binary hash tree built from one (or several) certificate revocation list(s).

Certification authority Trusted third party that creates, assigns, distributes, and possibly revokes public key certificates.

Certification authority certificate Public key certificate used to hold the public key of a CA.

Certification path A sequence of public key certificates starting with a certificate issued by one principal's certification authority and ending with a certificate for another principal, where each certificate in the path contains the public key to verify the following certificate.

Channel Information transfer path.

Chosen ciphertext attack An attack where the cryptanalyst may choose the ciphertext to be decrypted.

Chosen plaintext attack An attack where the cryptanalyst may choose the plaintext to be encrypted.

Ciphertext Data produced through the use of encryption (encryption transforms plaintext into ciphertext).

Ciphertext-only attack A form of cryptanalysis where the cryptanalyst has some ciphertext but nothing else.

Claimant An entity that is or represents a principal for the purposes of authentication. A claimant includes the functions necessary for engaging in authentication exchanges on behalf of a principal.

Client A process that requests and eventually obtains a network service. A client is usually acting on a specific user's behalf.

Collision Two values x and y form a collision of a function f if $x \neq y$ but $f(x) = f(y)$.

Collision resistance Property of a hash function that makes sure that collisions are hard to find for an outsider.

Common gateway interface An interface provided by Web servers to allow their functionality to be extended in a way that is compatible between servers, regardless of their vendor.

Communication compromise Result of the subversion of a communication line within a computer network or distributed system.

Communication security Field of study that aims to protect data during its transmission in a computer network or distributed system.

Communication security service Security service that is used to protect communications within and between networks. According to the terminology of the OSI security architecture, communication security services include authentication, data confidentiality and integrity, as well as non-repudiation services.

Compression function A function that takes a fixed length input and returns a shorter output of fixed length.

Computational complexity Measures the amount of resources (space and time) that are required to solve a problem. In this context, space refers to spatial (memory) constraints involved in a certain computation, and time refers to the temporal constraints.

Computer network Interconnected collection of autonomous computer systems.

Computer security Field of study that aims to preserve computing resources against unauthorized use and abuse, as well as to protect data that encodes information from accidental or deliberate damage, disclosure, or modification.

Confidentiality The property that ensures that information is not made available or disclosed to unauthorized parties.

Connection anonymity Property that ensures that though the sender and receiver can each be identified as participating in some communication, they cannot be identified as communicating with each other.

Cookie State information that passes between the origin server and the client, and gets stored by the client.

Countermeasure A feature or function that either reduces or eliminates one (or more) system vulnerabilities or counters one (or more) threats.

Credentials Data that is needed to establish the claimed identity of a principal.

Cross-certifying CA Certification authority (CA) that is trusted to issue certificates for arbitrary principals and other CAs over which it may not have immediate jurisdiction.

Crowds A system called for protecting users' anonymity on the WWW developed at AT&T Research.

Cryptanalysis The art and science of breaking encryption or any form of cryptography. In short, it embodies the analysis of a cryptographic system and its inputs and outputs to derive confidential variables or sensitive data including the plaintext.

Cryptographic algorithm Algorithm defined by a sequence of steps precisely specifying the actions required to achieve a specific security objective.

Cryptographic protocol Distributed algorithm defined by a sequence of steps precisely specifying the actions required of two or more entities to achieve a specific security objective.

Cryptography The art and science of using mathematics to secure information. More specifically, cryptography refers to the study of mathematical techniques related to aspects of information security such as confidentiality, data integrity, entity authentication, and data origin authentication.

Cryptology Science of secure communications. As such, it also refers to the branch of mathematics concerned with cryptography and cryptanalysis.

Cryptosystem An encryption and decryption algorithm (cipher), together with all possible plaintexts, ciphertexts, and keys.

CyberCoin A micropayment system developed and marketed by CyberCash.

Daemon Program that runs in the background to perform a specific network service. Unlike other programs that execute and exit, a daemon performs its work and waits for more.

Decryption The creation of plaintext from ciphertext.

Denial-of-service attack The prevention of authorized access to a shared resource or the delaying of a time-critical operation.

DES (data encryption standard) Block cipher that was developed by IBM and the U.S. government in the 1970s as an official federal information processing standard (FIPS).

Dictionary attack A brute force attack that tries passwords and/or keys from a precompiled list of possible values (e.g., a dictionary of words). This is often done as a precomputation and offline attack.

Differential cryptanalysis A chosen plaintext attack relying on the analysis of the evolution of the differences between two plaintexts.

Diffie-Hellman key exchange A key exchange protocol allowing the participants to agree on a key over an insecure channel.

Digest Commonly used term to refer to the output of a hash function.

Digest authentication User authentication scheme based on a digest of a password (e.g., as specified for HTTP/1.1).

Digital copyright labeling techniques Techniques that secretly embed digital marks into copyrighted materials to designate copyright-related information, such as origin, owner, content, or recipient.

Digital signature Data appended to or a cryptographic transformation of a data unit that allows a recipient of the data unit to prove the source and integrity of the data unit and to protect against forgery, for example, by the recipient.

Digital timestamp A record mathematically linking a document to a time and date.

Discrete logarithm problem The problem of given a and y in a group, to find x such that $a^x = y$. For some groups, the discrete logarithm problem is a hard problem that can, for example, be used in public key cryptography.

Distributed system Multiple autonomous computer systems connected together via a network that cooperate to perform a task.

Dual-homed firewall Firewall configuration containing a dual-homed host.

Dual-homed host Host with two interfaces that interconnect to different networks. Usually, the IP routing function is disabled on a dual-homed host.

Dual signature Digital signature in which two parts of a message are dually signed by first hashing them separately, then concatenating the two hash values, and finally digitally signing the result.

eCash Electronic payment system developed by David Chaum and marketed by DigiCash.

Electronic commerce The use of an open and public network, such as the Internet, to market goods and services without having to be physically present at the point of sale. The Internet may serve several purposes, including marketing, services, and sales.

Electronic money Electronic and mathematical representation of money.

Electronic payment system System that provides support for payments using electronic means.

Elliptic curve The set of points (x, y) satisfying an equation of the form $y^2 = x^3 + ax + b$, for variables x, y and constants a, b.

Elliptic curve cryptosystem A public key cryptosystem based on the properties of elliptic curves.

Encryption The cryptographic transformation of plaintext into an apparently less readable form (called ciphertext) through a mathematical process. The ciphertext may be read by anyone who has the key that decrypts the ciphertext.

Executable content Web content that is downloaded into a browser and run on the local computer system (the term "active content" is used synonymously).

Exhaustive search Checking every possibility individually until the right value is found.

Factoring problem The problem of breaking down an integer into its (prime) factors.

Fingerprint A unique characteristic of an object. More specifically, in digital copyright labeling, a fingerprint refers to a recipient label.

Firewall A blockade between a privately owned and protected network (that is assumed to be secure and trusted) and another network, typically a public network or the Internet (that is assumed to be nonsecure and untrusted). The purpose of a firewall is to prevent unwanted and unauthorized communications into or out of the protected network.

Gateway Internetworking device that operates at any layer higher than the network layer in the OSI reference model. Typically, a gateway operates at the application layer.

Hard problem A problem that is computationally difficult to solve.

Hash function A function that takes a variable length input and returns a shorter output of fixed length. As such, it iteratively applies a compression function.

Helper application A special program that is run automatically by a Web browser when a data type other than ASCII, HTML, GIF, or JPEG is downloaded.

Hidden URL Uniform resource locator (URL) that is kept secret.

Host Addressable entity within a computer network or distributed system. The entity is typically addressed either by its name or its network address.

Host compromise The subversion of an individual host within a computer network or distributed system.

Hypertext transfer protocol A client/server protocol that works at the application layer and may be layered on top of any reliable transport service, such as provided by the transport control protocol (TCP). The hypertext transfer protocol (HTTP) is the core protocol of the World Wide Web.

IDEA (international data encryption algorithm) Secret key cryptosystem.

Information Data with meaning (concerning a particular fact or circumstance in general).

Information technology Technology that deals with information.

Initiator Principal initiating an action, such as requesting access.

Integrity The property that ensures that data is not altered undetected.

Internet Globally interconnected set of networks that use the TCP/IP communications protocol suite.

Internet Society International nonprofit membership organization formed in 1992 to promote the use of the Internet for research and scholarly communication and collaboration.

Intranet Corporate or enterprise network based on the TCP/IP communications protocol suite.

IP address blocking Content blocking technology that operates at the packet level. As such, it requires (screening) routers to examine the source IP address of an incoming IP packet, compare it with a blacklist, and either forward or drop the packet.

ISO The International Organization for Standardization (ISO) is a non-governmental, worldwide federation of national standards bodies established in 1947. The mission of the ISO is to promote the development of standardization and related activities in the world with a view to facilitating the international exchange of goods and services, and to developing cooperation in the spheres of intellectual, scientific, technological, and economic activity.

ITU The International Telecommunications Union (ITU) is a branch of the United Nations within which governments and the private sector coordinate global telecommunications networks and services. ITU activities include the coordination, development, regulation, and standardization of telecommunications (abbreviated as ITU-T).

JANUS Research project that provides support for anonymous publishing on the Web.

Java Programming language developed by Sun Microsystems. In essence, Java is an object-oriented, general-purpose programming language that has a syntax similar to C^{++}, dynamic binding, garbage collection, and a simple inheritance model.

JavaScript Scripting language developed by Netscape Communications mainly to create executable or active content.

Kerberos A symmetric encryption-based authentication and key distribution system developed at the Massachusetts Institute of Technology (MIT).

Key A sequence of symbols that controls the operations of plaintext encipherment and decipherment.

Key agreement A shared secret is derived by two (or more) parties as a function of information contributed by, or associated with, each of these, (ideally) such that no party can predetermine the resulting value.

Key establishment A process or protocol used by two or more parties to establish a shared secret key, for subsequent cryptographic use. Key establishment may be broadly subdivided into key transport and key agreement.

Key management The generation, storage, distribution, deletion, archiving, and application of keys in accordance with a specific security policy.

Key pair The full key information in a public key cryptosystem, consisting of a set of a public and private key that belong together.

Key recovery A special feature of a key management scheme that allows a secret or private key to be recovered even if the original key is lost.

Keyspace The set of all possible keys for a given cryptosystem.

Key transport One party creates or otherwise obtains a secret value, and securely transfers it to the other(s).

Known plaintext attack A form of cryptanalysis where the cryptanalyst knows both the plaintext and the ciphertext, and tries to determine the key.

Label Information associated with an object (may be security-relevant or not).

Limitation Feature that is not as general as possible.

Linear cryptanalysis A known plaintext attack that uses linear approximations to describe the behavior of a block cipher.

Link Physical connection between two hosts.

Man-in-the-middle attack Attack that includes interception, insertion, deletion, and modification of messages, reflecting messages back to the sender, replaying old messages, and redirecting messages.

Masquerade The unauthorized pretense by a principal to be a different principal.

Meet-in-the-middle attack A known plaintext attack against double encryption with two separate keys where the attacker encrypts a plaintext with a key and decrypts the original ciphertext with another key and hopes to get the same value.

Message authentication code The result of applying a function that takes a variable length input and a key to produce a fixed-length output.

Message digest The result of applying a hash function to a message.

MicroMint A micropayment scheme developed by Ron Rivest and Adi Shamir.

Millicent A micropayment system developed at Digital Equipment Corporation (DEC).

Mondex Electronic cash system based on prepaid cash cards that are issued by the company of the same name.

Multihomed host Host with multiple network interfaces. Similar to the dual-homed host, the routing function is usually disabled on a multihomed host.

NetBill An electronic payment system that was originally developed at Carnegie Mellon University and is now being marketed by CyberCash.

NetCash An electronic cash system that was developed at the Information Sciences Institute of the University of Southern California.

NetCheque An electronic check system that was developed at the Information Sciences Institute of the University of Southern California.

NetSP An authentication and key distribution system developed by IBM (Network Security Program).

Network security policy Document that describes an organization's network security concerns and specifies the way network security should be achieved in that organizational environment.

Nonce Fresh and unpredictable random number.

Non-repudiation The property that enables the receiver of a message to prove that the sender did in fact send the message even though the sender might later desire to deny ever having sent it.

Number theory A branch of mathematics that investigates the relationships and properties of numbers.

Oak Predecessor programming language for Java.

One-time pad A secret key cryptosystem in which the key is a truly random sequence of bits that is as long as the message itself, and encryption is performed by XORing the message with the key. The resulting cryptosystem is perfectly secret (unconditionally secure).

One-way function Function that is easy to compute but hard to invert, meaning that it is computationally infeasible to find the input from the output.

One-way hash function A one-way function in which the output is usually much smaller than the input.

Open system System that conforms to open system standards.

Open system standard Standard that specifies an open system, and that allows manufacturers to build corresponding component parts.

OSI reference model Preeminent model for structuring and understanding communication functions in computer networks and distributed systems. The reference model for open systems interconnection was originally proposed by the ISO/IEC JTC1 in 1978.

Packet filter A multiported internetworking device that applies a set of rules to each incoming IP packet in order to decide whether it will be forwarded or dropped. IP packets are filtered based on information that is found in packet headers.

Password Authentication information that is typically composed of a string of characters.

Password guessing The process of correctly guessing the password of a legitimate user.

Patent The sole right, granted by the government, to sell, use, and manufacture an invention or creation.

Pay-after payment system Payment system in which the payee's bank account is credited the amount of sale before the payer's account is debited.

PayNow An electronic check system that was developed and is now being marketed by CyberCash.

Pay-now payment system Payment system in which the payer's account is debited at the time of payment.

PayWord A micropayment scheme developed by Ron Rivest and Adi Shamir.

Perfect forward secrecy A protocol has perfect forward secrecy if compromise of long-term keying material does not compromise session keys that have been established in the past (assuming that the keys have been deleted after use).

Persistent connection A TCP connection that is used for one or more HTTP request and response message exchanges.

Personal certificate Public key certificate used to authenticate a particular user.

Personal proxy server A trimmed-down proxy server intended for individual use.

Plaintext The input of an encryption function or the output of a decryption function. Decryption transforms ciphertext into plaintext.

Plug-in A module that is loaded directly into the address space of a browser and is automatically run when documents of a particular data type are downloaded. Most popular helper applications, such as the Acrobat reader, the RealAudio player, and the Shockwave player, have been rewritten as plug-ins.

Precomputation attack An attack where the adversary precomputes a look-up table of values used to crack encryption or passwords.

Prepaid payment system Payment system in which a certain amount of money is taken away from the payer (for example, by debiting his or her bank account) before any purchase is made. This amount of money can afterward be used for payments.

Primality testing A test that determines, with varying degree of probability, whether or not a particular number is prime.

Principal Human or system entity that is registered in and authenticable to a computer network or distributed system.

Principal identifier Identifier used to uniquely identify a principal.

Private key Cryptographic key used in public key cryptography to sign and/or decrypt messages.

Proactive security A property of a cryptographic protocol or structure that minimizes potential security compromises by refreshing a shared key or secret.

Process Instantiation of a program running on a particular host.

Proof-carrying code Technique that can be used to protect an execution environment against potentially malicious mobile code.

Protocol Specification of the format and the relative timing of a finite sequence of messages.

Protocol stack Selection of protocols from a protocol suite to support a particular application or class of applications.

Protocol suite Set of protocols that fit a particular network model.

Proxy server Application-specific software that runs on an application-level gateway to deal with external servers on behalf of internal clients and internal servers on behalf of external clients. As such, the proxy (server) acts both as a server as well as a client: the proxy is a server to the client connecting to it, and a client to servers to which it connects.

Public key Cryptographic key used in public key cryptography to verify signatures and/or encrypt messages.

Public key certificate Data record that provides the public key of a principal, together with some other information related to the principal and the certification authority that has issued the certificate. The certificate is rendered unforgeable by appending a digital signature from a certification authority.

Public key infrastructure Infrastructure to issue and revoke public keys and public key certificates. As such, it comprises a set of agreed-upon standards, certification authorities, structures between multiple CAs, methods to discover and validate certification paths, operational and management protocols, interoperable tools, and supporting legislation.

Quantum computer A theoretical computer based on ideas from quantum theory (that is theoretically capable of operating nondeterministically).

Random number As opposed to a pseudorandom number, a truly random number is a number produced independently of its generating criteria. For cryptographic purposes, numbers based on physical measurements, such as a Geiger counter, are considered random.

RC2, RC4, RC5, and RC6 Secret key cryptosystems (Rivest ciphers).

Receiver anonymity Property that ensures that the identity of a party who received a particular message is hidden, while its sender and the message itself might not be.

Repeater Internetworking device that operates at the physical layer in the OSI reference model.

Replay attack An attack that comprises the recording and replaying of previously sent messages or parts thereof. Any constant authentication information, such as a password, a one-way hash of a password, or electronically transmitted biometric data, can be recorded and replayed.

Repudiation Denial by a principal of having participated in a communication.

Response content filtering Strategy to block executable or active content at the firewall, by having the proxy server look at the content of HTTP response messages.

Robot Automated program that crawls across the Web, downloading one document after another (also called "Web crawler" or "spider").

Root CA Certification authority that bears a self-signed certificate (the term is sometimes also used to refer to the "CA of the root of a trust" or "the most trusted CA").

Router Internetworking device that operates at the network layer in the OSI reference model and the Internet layer in the Internet model.

RSA Public key cryptosystem invented by Rivest, Shamir, and Adleman.

Salt A string of random (or pseudorandom) bits concatenated with a key or password to foil precomputation attacks.

Sandboxing Technique used to protect an execution environment against potentially malicious mobile code.

Screened subnet firewall Firewall configuration in which a subnet is located between the Internet and corporate intranet.

Screening router A router with packet filtering capabilities.

Secret key The key used in a symmetric cryptosystem that is shared between the communicating parties.

Secret sharing Splitting a secret (e.g., a private key) into many pieces such that any specified subset of n pieces may be combined to form the secret.

Secure shell (SSH) Program that is used to securely log into a remote machine, to execute commands on that machine, or to move files from one machine to another. SSH provides some strong authentication and secure communications over insecure channels.

Secure sockets layer (SSL) Intermediate layer between the transport and application layer that is used to provide security support for arbitrary TCP-based applications.

Security architecture A high-level description of the structure of a system, with security functions assigned to components within this structure.

Security association Agreement between two or more entities on the security services that will be used, and how they will be used, to communicate between themselves. A security association entity could be a host, a user, an application, or a process. A security association attribute could be a type of encryption algorithm, or the length of a key.

Security attribute A piece of security-related information that is associated to a principal in a distributed system.

Security audit An independent review and examination of system records and activities in order to test for adequacy of system controls, to ensure compliance with established policy and operational procedures, to detect breaches in security, and to recommend any indicated changes in control, policy, and procedures.

Security audit message A message generated following the occurrence of an auditable security-related event.

Security audit trail Data collected and potentially used to facilitate a security audit.

Security domain A set of machines under common administrative control, with a common security policy and security level.

Security mechanism A concrete mechanism or procedure used to actually implement one or several security services.

Security scanner A program that is able to probe a system for known security holes and configuration weaknesses.

Security service A quality of a system present to satisfy a security policy.

Security zone A group of Web sites in which a user has the same level of trust.

Self-certified public key Public key that is certified with its corresponding private key.

Sender anonymity Property that ensures that the identity of a party who sent a particular message is hidden, while its receiver and the message itself might not be.

Server Process that provides a network service.

Session hijacking Attack in which a connection is taken over after a legitimate user has authenticated himself or herself.

Session key A temporary and ephemeral secret key shared between two or more principals, with a limited lifetime.

SESAME An authentication and key distribution system developed as part of a European research and development project.

SET MasterCard and Visa developed (with some help from industry) the secure electronic transaction (SET) standard jointly to ensure secure electronic credit card transactions.

Site certificate Public key certificate used to authenticate a particular Web site.

SOCKS A circuit-level gateway that is in widespread use.

Software patent Patent applied to a computer program.

Software publisher certificate Public key certificate used to authenticate a particular software publisher (an individual programmer or a commercial software company).

SPX An authentication and key distribution system designed and prototyped by DEC.[1]

Standard A documented agreement containing technical specifications or other precise criteria to be used consistently as rules, guidelines, or definitions of characteristics to ensure that materials, products, processes, and services are fit for their purpose.

Stateful inspection Packet-filtering approach that also takes into account the context of an IP packet.

SubScrip A micropayment scheme that was developed at the University of Newcastle, Australia.

TCP/IP protocol suite Suite of data communications protocols. The suite gets its name from two of its most important protocols, namely the transmission control protocol (TCP) and the Internet protocol (IP).

TESS (the exponential security system) A toolbox set system of different but cooperating cryptographic mechanisms and functions based on the primitive of discrete exponentiation.

---

[1]The term is not an acronym. Also note that SPX also refers to a protocol used by Novell Netware.

Threat Circumstance, condition, or event with the potential to either violate the security of a system or to cause harm to system resources.

Traffic analysis The inference of information from observation of external traffic characteristics (presence, absence, amount, direction, and frequency of data traffic).

Traffic padding The generation of spurious instances of communications, spurious data units, or spurious data within data units, usually to counteract traffic analysis.

Transform Specification of the details of how to apply a specific algorithm to data.

TRUSTe An independent, non-profit organization dedicated to establishing a trusting environment where users can feel comfortable dealing with companies on the Internet.

Trusted third party A security authority or its agent, trusted by other entities with respect to security-related activities.

Tunneling Technique of encapsulating a data unit from one protocol in another, and using the facilities of the second protocol to traverse parts of the network.

URL blocking Content blocking technology that operates at the application level. As such, it requires proxy servers and application gateways that examine resources or resource information in order to decide whether the corresponding application protocol request, such as an HTTP GET method invocation, should be served.

Usage control Each usage of copyright protected material, such as viewing, playing, or printing, is controlled by some authorized rendering hardware or software.

User Principal who is accountable and ultimately responsible for his or her activities within a computer network or distributed system.

VBScript Scripting language to create executable or active content in a Microsoft environment.

Verifier A principal seeking to authenticate a claimant.

Virtual private network Network that consists of a collection of hosts that have implemented protocols to securely exchange information.

Vulnerability A weakness that could be exploited by an intruder to violate a system or the information it contains.

Watermark Ownership label.

World Wide Web A virtual network that is overlaid on the Internet. It comprises all clients and servers that communicate with one another using the hypertext transfer protocol (HTTP).

Zero knowledge proof An interactive proof where the prover proves to the verifier that he or she knows certain information, without revealing the information.

Abbreviations and Acronyms

AA	attribute authority
AAL	ATM adaption layer
AC	attribute certificate
ACL	access control list
ACT	anticlogging token
AES	advanced encryption standard
AFS	Andrew file system
AFT	authenticated firewall traversal
AH	authentication header
ANSI	American National Standards Institute
API	application programming interface
ARPA	Advanced Research Projects Agency
AS	authentication server
	applicability statement
ASCII	American Standard Code for Information Interchange
ASET	Automated Security Enhancement Tool
ASN.1	abstract syntax notation 1
ATM	asynchronous transfer mode
	automated teller machine

BAN	Burrows, Abadi, and Needham
BBN	Bolt Beranek and Newman, Inc.
BCP	best current practice
Bellcore	Bell Communications Research
BER	basic encoding rules
BETSI	Bellcore's trusted software integrity system
BIND	Berkeley Internet name daemon
BITS	Bump-in-the-stack
BITW	Bump-in-the-wire
BSP	backbone service provider
CA	certification authority
CAFE	Conditional Access for Europe
CAT	common authentication technology
CBC	cipher block chaining
CC	common criteria
CCC	Chaos Computer Club
CCI	common client interface
CCITT	Consultative Committee on International Telegraphy and Telephony (now ITU-T)
CCP	compression control protocol
CD	compact disk
	committee draft
CDP	certificate discovery protocol
CEC	Commission of the European Communities
CED	computing with encrypted data
CEF	computing with encrypted functions
CERN	European Laboratory for Particle Physics
CERT	computer emergency response team
CERT/CC	CERT coordination center
CFB	cipher feedback
CGI	common gateway interface
CHAP	challenge-response handshake authentication protocol
CKDS	conference key distribution system
CLI	command line interface
CLNP	connectionless network protocol
CMC	certificate management center
CMIP	common management information protocol

COCOM	coordinating committee for multilateral export controls
COM	component object model
COPS	computerized oracle and password system
CPS	certificate practice statement
CRC	cyclic redundancy checksum
CRL	certificate revocation list
CRMF	certificate request message format
CRS	certificate revocation system
CRT	certificate revocation tree
CSI	Computer Security Institute
CV	control value
DAC	discretionary access control
DAP	directory access protocol
DARPA	Defense Advanced Research Projects Agency
DCA	Defense Communications Agency
DCE	distributed computing environment
DCMS	distributed certificate management system
DEC	Digital Equipment Corporation
DER	distinguished encoding rules
DES	data encryption standard
DFA	differential fault analysis
DIS	draft international standard
DISA	Defense Information Systems Agency
DIT	directory information tree
DMV	Department of Motor Vehicles
DMZ	demilitarized zone
DN	distinguished name
DNS	domain name system
DNSsec	domain name system security
DoC	U.S. Department of Commerce
DoD	U.S. Department of Defense
DoS	U.S. Department of State
DOI	domain of interpretation
DOS	disk operating system
DPA	differential power analysis
DSA	digital signature algorithm
DSS	digital signature standard

E-cash	electronic cash
ECB	electronic code book
ECBS	European Committee for Banking Standards
ECC	elliptic curve cryptosystem
E-commerce	electronic commerce
ECP	encryption control protocol
EDI	electronic data interchange
EFF	Electronic Frontier Foundation
EFT	electronic funds transfer
EGP	exterior gateway protocol
EIT	Enterprise Integration Technologies
E-mail	electronic mail
ESM	encrypted session manager
ESP	encapsulating security payload
ETS	Eurpean trusted third party services
EU	European Union
FAQ	frequently asked questions
FDDI	fiber distributed data interface
FEP	front-end processor
FIPS	Federal Information Processing Standard
FIRST	Forum of Incident Response and Security Teams
FNC	Federal Networking Council
FSTC	Financial Services Technology Consortium
FSUIT	Federal Strategy Unit for Information Technology
FTK	Forschungsinstitut für Telekommunikation
FTP	file transfer protocol
FV	First Virtual
FWTK	firewall toolkit
FYI	for your information
GII	global information infrastructure
GIK	group interchange key
GISA	German Information Security Agency
GKMP	group key management protocol
GNY	Gong, Needham, and Yahalom
GOSIP	government OSI profile

GRE	generic routing encapsulation
GSS-API	generic security service API
GUI	graphical user interface
HP	Hewlett-Packard
HTML	hypertext markup language
HTTP	hypertext transfer protocol
IAB	Internet Architecture Board
IAM	Institute for Computer Science and Applied Mathematics
IANA	Internet Assigned Numbers Authority
IBM	International Business Machines Corporation
ICMP	Internet control message protocol
ICSI	International Computer Science Institute
IDEA	international data encryption algorithm
IDS	interdomain service
IEAK	Internet Explorer administration kit
IEC	International Electrotechnical Committee
IEEE	Institute of Electrical and Electronic Engineers
IESG	Internet Engineering Steering Group
IETF	Internet Engineering Task Force
IGP	interior gateway protocol
IIOP	Internet inter-ORB protocol
IKE	Internet key exchange
IKMP	Internet key management protocol
iKP	Internet keyed payments protocol
IMAP	Internet message access protocol
IP	Internet protocol
IPC	interprocess communications facility
IPKI	Internet X.509 public key infrastructure
IPng	IP next generation
IPPCP	IP payload compression protocol
IPRA	Internet policy registration authority
IPsec	IP security
IPSP	IP security protocol
IPST	IP secure tunnel protocol
IRSG	Internet Research Steering Group
IRTF	Internet Research Task Force

IS	international standard
ISAKMP	Internet security association and key management protocol
ISAPI	Internet server API
ISO	International Organization for Standardization
ISOC	Internet Society
ISODE	ISO development environment
ISP	Internet service provider
IT	information technology
ITSEC	information technology security evaluation criteria
ITU-T	International Telecommunication Union — Telecommunication Standardization Sector
IV	initialization vector
JEPI	joint electronic payment initiative
JTC1	Joint Technical Committee 1
JVM	Java virtual machine
kbps	kilobit per second
KDC	key distribution center
KDS	key distribution server
KEA	key exchange algorithm
KEK	key encryption key
KTC	key translation center
LAN	local area network
LDAP	lightweight directory access protocol
LLC	logical link control
LRA	local registration agent
	local registration authority
LSB	least significant bit
L2F	layer 2 forwarding
L2TP	layer 2 tunneling protocol
MAC	message authentication code
MAN	metropolitan area network
MBone	multicast backbone
MD	message digest
MDC	modification detection code

MHS	message handling system
MIB	management information base
MIC	message integrity check
MIME	multipurpose Internet mail extensions
MIT	Massachusetts Institute of Technology
MKMP	modular key management protocol
MLS	multilevel security
MOSS	MIME object security services
MOTO	mail order/telephone order
MPPE	Microsoft point-to-point encryption
MS-PPTP	Microsoft PPTP
MTA	message transfer agent
MTS	message transfer system
NAS	network access server
NASA	National Aeronautics and Space Agency
NAT	network address translation
NBS	National Bureau of Standards
NCP	network control protocol
NCSA	National Center for Supercomputer Application
NCSC	National Computer Security Center
NetSP	network security program
NII	national information infrastructure
NIST	National Institute of Standards and Technology
NLSP	network layer security protocol
NMS	network management station
NNTP	network news transfer protocol
NRL	U.S. Naval Research Laboratory
NSA	National Security Agency
NSAPI	Netscape server API
NSF	National Science Foundation
NSP	network security policy
NTP	network time protocol
OCSP	online certificate status protocol
OECD	Organization for Economic Cooperation and Development
OFB	output feedback
OLE	object linking and embedding

OPIE	one-time passwords in everything
ORA	organizational registration agent
ORB	object request broker
OSF	Open Software Foundation
OSI	open systems interconnection
PAC	proxy auto-config
PAP	password authentication protocol
PARC	Palo Alto Research Center
PC	personal computer
PCA	policy certification authority
PCC	proof-carrying code
PCT	private communication technology
PECAN	Perl certification authority network
PEM	privacy enhanced mail
PEP	protocol extension protocol
PFS	perfect forward secrecy
PGP	pretty good privacy
PICS	platform for Internet content selection
PIN	personal identification number
PKCS	public key cryptography standard
PKI	public key infrastructure
PKIX	public key infrastructure X.509
PKP	Public Key Partners
POP	post office protocol
	point of presence
PPP	point-to-point protocol
PPPEXT	PPP extensions
PPTP	point-to-point tunneling protocol
PSRG	Privacy and Security Research Group
PSTN	public switched telephone network
P3P	platform for privacy preferences
QoS	Quality of service
RA	registration agent
	registration authority
RACF	resource access control facility

RADIUS	remote authentication dial-in user service
RFC	Request for Comment
RIP	routing information protocol
ROM	read-only memory
RPC	remote procedure call
RPI	return path information
RSA	Rivest, Shamir, and Adleman
RSAC	Recreational Software Advisory Council
RSACi	RSAC rating service
RSVP	resource reservation protocol
SA	security association
SAID	secure association identifier
SALS	simple authentication and security layer
SATAN	security administrator tool for analyzing networks
SDK	software developer's kit
SDNS	secure data network system
SDSI	simple distributed security infrastructure
SEA	security extension architecture
SEAL	screening external access link
SECSH	Secure shell
SEMPER	Secure electronic marketplace for Europe
SEPP	secure electronic payment protocol
SESAME	secure European system for applications in a multi-vendor environment
SET	secure electronic transaction
SGC	server gated cryptography
SHA-1	secure hash algorithm 1
SHS	secure hash standard
S-HTTP	secure HTTP
SigG	Signaturgesetz (in Germany)
SigV	Signaturverordnung (in Germany)
SILS	standards for interoperable LAN/MAN security
SIP	secure Internet programming
SKAP	shared key authentication protocol
SKIP	simple key-management for Internet protocols
SLIP	serial line IP
S/MIME	Secure MIME

SMS	service management system
SMTP	simple mail transfer protocol
SNMP	simple network management protocol
SOG-IS	Senior Officials Group on Information Security
SPKAC	signed public key and challenge
SPKI	simple public key infrastructure
SP3	security protocol 3
SP4	security protocol 4
SPI	security parameters index
SPKI	simple public key infrastructure
SRA	secure RPC authentication
SRI	Stanford Research Institute
SSH	secure shell
	site security handbook
SSI	server-side include
SSL	secure sockets layer
SSO	single sign-on
SSR	secure socket relay
ST	stream protocol
STD	Internet standard
STEL	secure telnet
STS	station-to-station
STT	secure transaction technology
S/WAN	secure wide area network
SysCoP	system for copyright protection
TACACS	terminal access controller access control system
TAMU	Texas A&M University
TAN	transaction authentication number
TAZ	temporary autonomous zone
TCB	trusted computing base
Tcl	tool control language
TCP	transport control protocol
TCSEC	trusted computer system evaluation criteria
TEK	token enryption key
TESS	the exponential security system
TFTP	trivial FTP
TIS	Trusted Information Systems, Inc.

TLI	transport layer interface
TLS	transport layer security
TLSP	transport layer security protocol
TNI	trusted network interpretation
TOS	type of service
TS	technical specification
TTL	time to live
TTP	trusted third party
UC	University of California
UCB	University of California at Berkeley
UID	user identification
U.K.	United Kingdom
UPP	universal payment preamble
URI	uniform resource identifier
URL	uniform resource locator
URN	uniform resource name
U.S.	United States
UUCP	UNIX-UNIX copy protocol
VPN	virtual private network
VRML	virtual reality modeling language
VTP	virtual tunneling protocol
WAIS	wide area information services
WG	working group
WISP	working party on information security and privacy
WWW	World Wide Web
W3C	World Wide Web Consortium
XML	extensible markup language
XTACACS	extended TACACS

About the Author

Rolf Oppliger (http://www.ifi.unizh.ch/~oppliger) received M.Sc. and Ph.D. degrees in computer science from the University of Berne, Switzerland, in 1991 and 1993, respectively. After spending one year as a postdoctoral researcher at the International Computer Science Institute (ICSI) in Berkeley, California, he joined the IT Security Group of the Swiss Federal Office of Information Technology and Systems in 1995, and continued his research and teaching activities at several universities and polytechnics in Switzerland and Germany. Early in 1999, he received the Venia legendi from the Faculty of Economic Sciences at the University of Zürich, Switzerland. At the same time, he also became an Artech House series editor for computer security. In the past, he has published numerous scientific papers, articles, and books, mainly on security-related topics. He's a member of the Swiss Informaticians Society (SI) and its Working Group on Security, the Association for Computing Machinery (ACM), and the IEEE Computer Society. In addition, he serves as vice-chair of the International Federation for Information Processing (IFIP) Technical Committee 11 (TC11) Working Group 4 (WG4) on Network Security, and has been representing Switzerland within the European Senior Officials Group on Security of Information Systems (SOG-IS), and the Working Party on Information Security and Privacy (WPISP) of the Organization for Economic Cooperation and Development (OECD).

Index

abstract syntax notation one, 84
access, 375
access control, 375
access control list, 355, 375
access control service, 16, 375
access right, 375
accountability, 375
accounting, 375
acquirer, 175, 190
acquirer bank, 190
actions, 235
active network, 375
ActiveX, 263, 376
ActiveX control, 263
adaptive-chosen-ciphertext attack, 376
adaptive-chosen-plaintext attack, 376
advanced encryption standard (AES), 80, 376
adversary, 376
agent-based system, 291
Agora, 196
Anonymizer, 332
anonymous remailer, 323, 376
application gateway, 50, 376
application programming interface, 7, 278
application-level gateway, 50, 55
arbiter, 175
asymmetric cryptography, 80

attack, 376
attacker, 10
attribute authority (AA), 208, 376
attribute certificate, 208, 215, 376
audit trail, 377
authentication, 377
authentication context, 377
authentication exchange, 377
authentication header, 108
authentication information, 377
authenticator, 165
Authenticode, 258, 266
authorization, 377
authorization policy, 377
availability, 377

backbone service providers, 355
baseline controls, 377
basic authentication, 377
bastion host, 57, 377
Bellcore's trusted software integrity system (BETSI), 244, 377
binary mail attachment, 245, 377
biometrics, 377
birthday attack, 378
bit, 378
blackbox security, 299
blender, 339

411

For further information on these and other Artech House titles, including previously considered out-of-print books now available through our In-Print-Forever® (IPF®) program, contact:

Artech House
685 Canton Street
Norwood, MA 02062
Phone: 781-769-9750
Fax: 781-769-6334
e-mail: artech@artechhouse.com

Artech House
46 Gillingham Street
London SW1V 1AH UK
Phone: +44 (0)20 7596-8750
Fax: +44 (0)20 7630-0166
e-mail: artech-uk@artechhouse.com

Find us on the World Wide Web at:
www.artechhouse.com